George F. (George Frederick) Chambers, H. West (Henry West) Fovargue

The Law relating to Public Libraries & Museums and literary and scientific Institutions

George F. (George Frederick) Chambers, H. West (Henry West) Fovargue

The Law relating to Public Libraries & Museums and literary and scientific Institutions

ISBN/EAN: 9783337177478

Printed in Europe, USA, Canada, Australia, Japan

Cover: Foto ©ninafisch / pixelio.de

More available books at **www.hansebooks.com**

THE LAW

RELATING TO

PUBLIC LIBRARIES & MUSEUMS

AND

LITERARY AND SCIENTIFIC INSTITUTIONS;

WITH MUCH PRACTICAL INFORMATION USEFUL TO MANAGERS, COMMITTEES
AND OFFICERS OF ALL CLASSES OF ASSOCIATIONS AND CLUBS
CONNECTED WITH LITERATURE, SCIENCE, AND ART,

INCLUDING PRECEDENTS OF BY-LAWS AND REGULATIONS;

THE STATUTES IN FULL;

AND BRIEF NOTES OF LEADING CASES.

BY

GEORGE F. CHAMBERS, F.R.A.S.,

OF THE INNER TEMPLE, BARRISTER-AT-LAW;
LATE AN ASSISTANT BOUNDARY COMMISSIONER FOR ENGLAND AND WALES;
Author of '*A Digest of the Law relating to Public Health*' &c.

AND

H. WEST FOVARGUE;

TOWN CLERK OF EASTBOURNE AND HON. SOLICITOR OF THE LIBRARY ASSOCIATION
OF THE UNITED KINGDOM.

FOURTH EDITION.

LONDON:

KNIGHT AND CO.

4 & 4A LA BELLE SAUVAGE YARD, LUDGATE HILL
(LATE OF 90 FLEET STREET).

1899.

PREFACE

TO

THE FOURTH EDITION.

THE origin of this work is thus stated with sufficient detail in the Preface to the first edition :—

"This work owes its origin to an accidental circumstance. Some time ago I was called upon to advise on the powers possessed by Local Boards elected under the 'Local Government Act, 1858,' with respect to Public Libraries and Museums. As such Boards had, however, at the time in question no powers whatever with regard to this matter, I subsequently assisted in framing a Bill to confer powers on them, which Bill being introduced into the House of Commons in 1871 by my friend Mr. *J. G. Talbot, M.P.*, soon became the Statute 34 & 35 Vict. 71.

"It was in consequence of finding, when engaged upon Mr. *Talbot's* Bill, that there was no work in existence on the several Libraries Acts that I was led to think there might be room for such a publication as that now in the hands of the reader.

"Intended, as it is, as much for the General Public as for the Profession, it has been prepared with especial attention to clearness of arrangement and facility of reference, and will be found, it is believed, to present a complete view of the subject to which it relates, a subject which it may be hoped will, under the stimulus supplied by the Educational tendencies of the day, soon receive more attention at the hands of Ratepayers than has hitherto been the case."

In spite of its limited scope, the book became more in request than could have been anticipated; and the question soon arose whether it might not be worth while to increase its usefulness by making it a book of general reference on the Law relating to all kinds of Institutions connected with Literature, Science, and Art. This idea was carried out in the second edition, and the fourth edition is based on its predecessors, with only such alterations as the lapse of time has rendered necessary or expedient. So far as Statute and Case Law is concerned, it will, we think, be found that nothing of importance has been omitted.

One obvious reason why materials for a work like this are not very abundant, so far as regards Book II., is that such a large number of Literary and Scientific Societies derive their legal status not from Statutes at all, but from Royal Charters, or voluntary Trust Deeds, or informal agreements, which never in print come under the notice of lawyers, except in the rare cases of litigation amongst the members.

G. F. C.
H. W. F.

1 Cloisters, Temple:
   December 1898.

CONTENTS.

BOOK I.

PUBLIC LIBRARIES AND MUSEUMS.

	PAGE
INTRODUCTION	1

PART I.

DIGEST OF STATUTES.

CHAPTER I.
Interpretation of Terms used in the " Public Libraries Acts " . .   5

CHAPTER II.
How the " Public Libraries Acts " are brought into operation   .   11

CHAPTER III.
The constitution, etc., of Governing Bodies under the " Public Libraries Acts " 29

CHAPTER IV.
W at may be supplied under the " Public Libraries Acts " . . 35

CHAPTER V.
The proceedings of Governing Bodies under the " Public Libraries Acts " 39

CHAPTER VI.
Borrowing powers under the " Public Libraries Acts " . . . 43

CHAPTER VII.

The acquisition of lands, etc., for the purposes of the "Public Libraries Acts" 46

CHAPTER VIII.

Rates under the "Public Libraries Acts" 50

CHAPTER IX.

Accounts and Audit under the "Public Libraries Acts" . . 55

PART II.
OFFICIAL DOCUMENTS.

Explanatory Memorandum 57
Audit Order of the Local Government Board, November 26, 1892 . 57

PART III.
PRECEDENTS OF BY-LAWS AND REGULATIONS.

(1) Regulations for a Public Library and Museum 60
(2) Borrower's Ticket (Simplest Form) 65
(3) Borrower's Ticket (More Complete Form) 66
(4) Form of Label for Borrowed Books 67
(5) Form of General Application to Borrow Books 68
(6) Form of Application by Burgess to Borrow Books . . . 69
(7) Form of Bequest to a Public Library 69

PART IV.
STATUTES RELATING TO PUBLIC LIBRARIES AND MUSEUMS. (a)

Introduction 70
8 Vict. 16 (Companies Clauses Consolidation Act, 1845) . . . 71
*8 Vict. 18 (Lands Clauses Consolidation Act, 1845) . . . 85

(a) The titles only are given of the Statutes to which an asterisk (*) is prefixed.

CONTENTS.

	PAGE
8 Vict. 19 (Lands Clauses Consolidation (Scotland) Act, 1845)	85
10 Vict. 16 (Commissioners Clauses Act, 1847)	86
18 & 19 Vict. 40 (Public Libraries (Ireland) Act, 1855)	92
*23 & 24 Vict. 106 (Lands Clauses Amendment Act, 1860)	96
24 & 25 Vict. 97 §§ 39, 52 (Malicious Damages Act, 1861)	97
*32 & 33 Vict. 18 (Lands Clauses Amendment Act, 1869)	99
38 & 39 Vict. 55, §§ 233–39 (Public Health Act, 1875)	99
40 & 41 Vict. 15 (Public Libraries (Ireland) Amendment Act, 1877)	103
40 & 41 Vict. 54 (Public Libraries Amendment Act, 1877)	104
47 & 48 Vict. 37 (Public Libraries Act, 1884)	105
50 & 51 Vict. 42 (Public Libraries Consolidation (Scotland) Act, 1887)	107
54 & 55 Vict. 22 (Museums and Gymnasium Act, 1891)	124
55 & 56 Vict. 53 (Public Libraries Act, 1892)	130
56 Vict. 11 (Public Libraries Amendment Act, 1893)	159
56 & 57 Vict. 73 (Local Government Act, 1894)	162
57 & 58 Vict. 20 (Public Libraries (Scotland) Act, 1894)	172
57 & 58 Vict. 38 (Public Libraries (Ireland) Act, 1894)	174
61 & 62 Vict. 53 (Libraries Offences Act, 1898)	180

PART V.

DIGEST OF CASES.

Introduction	181
Digest	182
Legal Decisions in Inferior Courts	184

BOOK II.

LITERARY AND SCIENTIFIC INSTITUTIONS.

PART I.

DIGEST OF STATUTES.

Digest	189

PART II.

PRECEDENTS OF FORMAL DOCUMENTS RELATING TO THE CONSTITUTION OF LITERARY AND SCIENTIFIC INSTITUTIONS.

       PAGE
1. Official Circular of the Board of Trade 196
2. Literary or Scientific Society under the "Companies Acts, 1862, 1867, and 1877," Draft Memorandum of Association and Articles of Association 200
3. Literary or Scientific Society under the "Companies Act, 1867," § 23, Newspaper Advertisement of application having been made to the Board of Trade 215
4. Parochial Institute under the "Companies Act, 1867," § 23 . 216
5. Memorandum and Articles of Association for a Country Town Club for Gentlemen under the "Companies Acts, 1862, 1867, and 1877" 217
6. Draft Royal Charter to the North of England Institute of Mining and Mechanical Engineers 225

PART III.

PRECEDENTS OF BY-LAWS AND REGULATIONS APPLICABLE TO LITERARY AND SCIENTIFIC INSTITUTIONS.

1. Rules for a Country Town Club for Gentlemen formed under the "Companies Acts, 1862, 1867, and 1877" 231
2. Rules for a Church Institute or Reading Rooms under a Trust Deed 236
3. Rules for a Village Workmen's Club 242

PART IV.

STATUTES RELATING TO LITERARY AND SCIENTIFIC INSTITUTIONS.

7 Anne, 14 (Parochial Libraries Act, 1708) 246
39 Geo. III. 73 (Specific Legacies (Exemption from Duty) Act, 1799) 250
6 & 7 Vict. 36 (Scientific Societies (Exemption from Rates) Act, 1843) 250

CONTENTS. xi

PAGE
13 & 14 Vict. **28** (Titles of Religious Congregations Act, 1850) . . 253
16 & 17 Vict. **51**, § 16 (Succession Duty Act, 1853) . . . 257
17 & 18 Vict. **112** (Literary and Scientific Institutions Act, 1854). 257
24 & 25 Vict. **97**, § 39 (Malicious Damages Act, 1861) . . . 269
30 & 31 Vict. **131**, § 23 (Companies Amendment Act, 1867) . . 270
35 & 36 Vict. **24** (Charitable Trustees Incorporation Act, 1872) . 271
51 & 52 Vict. **42** (Mortmain and Charitable Uses Act, 1888) . . 275
54 & 55 Vict. **61** (Schools for Science and Art Act, 1891) . . . 283
54 & 55 Vict. **73** (Mortmain and Charitable Uses Act, 1891) . . 284
55 & 56 Vict. **11** (Mortmain and Charitable Uses Amendment Act, 1892) 285

PART V.

DIGEST OF CASES.

Introduction 287
Bequests 287
Clubs and Committees 294
Rating of Societies claiming exemption under 6 & 7 Vict. **36** . 300

APPENDIX TO BOOK II.

A Practical Point in Club Management. By the Very Rev. F. Pigou, Dean of Bristol 305
Forms of Bequests to Literary or Scientific Institutions . . 307
  (1) Money 307
  (2) Books and Works of Art 307

INDEXES.

GENERAL INDEX 308

INDEX OF NAMES OF CASES—
  Book I.—Public Libraries and Museums 317
  Book II.—Literary and Scientific Institutions . . . 317

INDEX OF SUBJECTS OF CASES—
  Book I.—Public Libraries and Museums 319
  Book II.—Literary and Scientific Institutions . . . 319

BOOK I.

PUBLIC LIBRARIES AND MUSEUMS.

INTRODUCTION.

ALTHOUGH the subject about to receive attention is of comparatively recent origin, the earliest Statute dating only from 1845, yet no fewer than eleven "Public Libraries Acts" were sanctioned by the Legislature between the year in question and 1871. England, Scotland, and Ireland have each been the subjects of separate legislation, and inasmuch as it will involve hardly any repetition to keep the enactments relating to the three Kingdoms entirely separate, that course will be adopted in the *Digest* which follows.

The consideration of the subject in its details will be facilitated if we first have before us an outline of the several Acts, and briefly review the circumstances relating to the passing of each.

The first Act which received the sanction of the Legislature was 8 & 9 Vict. **43**, passed in 1845. It related to Museums only, and, being very concise in its provisions, may be supposed not to have answered the purpose of its promoters, for in 1850 it was repealed by 13 & 14 Vict. **65**, which took its place.

Previously, however, to this last-named Act coming before Parliament as a Bill, a Select Committee of the House of Commons, presided over by Mr. *W. Ewart*, sat to inquire into the Public Libraries of the United Kingdom. These were found to be very few in number, and very inadequate in other respects to the growing requirements of the community, and the information collected by the Committee may be considered the cause of the passing of the Act of 1850.

The Act 13 & 14 Vict. **65** only applied to England, but by 16 & 17 Vict. **101** it was extended to Scotland and Ireland. This was in 1853.

This Extension Act only remained intact for a year; for by 17 & 18 Vict. **64,** a General Act for Scotland (1854), it was repealed as to Scotland, and by 18 & 19 Vict. **40,** a General Act for Ireland (1855), it was repealed as to Ireland.

In the same Session a new General Statute, 18 & 19 Vict. **70,** was passed to regulate the formation of Public Libraries in England. This Act repealed the former Act of 1850, except as to anything already done under it, but was itself repealed by the "Public Libraries Act, 1892" (55 & 56 Vict. **53**).

Some years now elapsed ere Parliament again turned its attention to the Law regarding Libraries and Museums, but in 1866 some alterations were made in the English Act of 1855, by 29 & 30 Vict. **114,** chiefly with reference to the adoption of the Act in Boroughs. Two important changes were also made in points of detail. The majority necessary for the adoption of the Act was no longer to be two-thirds of the persons voting at the meeting called to consider the question, but simply "more than one-half." All restrictions as to population were also removed. These two modifications applied to Scotland as well as to England. This Statute was also repealed by the "Public Libraries Act, 1892" (55 & 56 Vict. **53**).

In the Session of 1867 an Act was passed "to amend and consolidate the Public Libraries Act (Scotland)." This Statute (30 & 31 Vict. **37**), which for twenty years was the principal Act on the subject relating to Scotland, was amended in the Session of 1871 by 34 & 35 Vict. **59,** which conferred some additional powers as to management on the Public Bodies intrusted with the working of Libraries and Museums. Both Statutes were, however, repealed by the "Public Libraries (Scotland) Act, 1887" (50 & 51 Vict. **42**).

The Session of 1871 also witnessed the passing of an Act (34 & 35 Vict. **71**) conferring on Local Boards of Health constituted under the "Public Health Act, 1848," or the "Local Government Act, 1858," the same powers with respect to Libraries and Museums as those which the "Public Libraries Act, 1855," gave to Boards formed under Local Improvement Acts. This Act was repealed, but in substance re-enacted, by the "Public Libraries Act, 1892" (55 & 56 Vict. 53).

In the Session of 1877 two supplementary Acts were passed, which, though short in themselves, were of considerable practical value. By the Act 40 & 41 Vict. 15, the Statutes relating to Ireland were amended and extended; and by the Act 40 & 41 Vict. 54, important facilities for ascertaining the views of the Ratepayers by means of Voting-papers were provided, but the latter Act was repealed, so far as concerned England and Wales, in 1890, by the 53 & 54 Vict. 68.

In the Session of 1884 a short Act (47 & 48 Vict. 37) was passed to make it clear that Library Authorities might accept a Parliamentary Grant in aid of the establishment of a School of Science and Art, and also might add other Institutions to existing ones, but it was repealed, so far as concerned Scotland, in 1887, by 50 & 51 Vict. 42, and, as to England and Wales, by the "Public Libraries Act, 1892" (55 & 56 Vict. 53).

In the Session of 1887 the subject of Public Libraries was again dealt with in Parliament. The Act 50 & 51 Vict. 22 gave facilities for the establishment of Lending Libraries in Villages where the rateable value is so small that the highest Rate authorised by the "Public Libraries Acts" would be insufficient to meet the expense of building a Library, or even of renting a Room for a regular Free Library. But the provisions of the Act of 1887 were also applicable to other places than mere villages, and enabled a Town to try the experiment of a Lending Library before committing itself to any heavy permanent expenditure. The provisions of the Act relating to the Metropolis were prepared to meet the difficulty which had been felt in consequence of the small *area* of many of the Metropolitan parishes. (*a*) By another Act of the Session of 1887 (50 & 51 Vict. 42) all the previous "Public Libraries Acts" relating to Scotland were consolidated.

In 1889 a short amending Act (52 Vict. 9) was passed. It dealt with the raising of expenses and the united action of parishes by agreement. This Statute was, however, amended in 1890 by the 53 & 54 Vict. 68, and was repealed in 1892 by the 55 & 56 Vict. 53.

In 1890 the Act 53 & 54 Vict. 68 was passed. It provided for the adoption of the Acts by Voting-papers only,

(*a*) This Act, after being amended in 1890, was repealed by the Public Libraries Act, 1892" (55 & 56 Vict. 53).

and authorised the voters to fix the maximum rate at one halfpenny or three farthings or one penny. This Act also was repealed by the 55 & 56 Vict. **53**.

In the third edition of this work, published in 1889, it was urged that the law was scattered through an inconveniently large number of Statutes, and that the time had arrived for the passing of one general Statute. This was accomplished by the Consolidation Act of 1892 (55 & 56 Vict. **53**), which forms the basis of this treatise so far as regards England and Wales. But it did not long remain intact, for in the next Session (1893) an amending Act (56 Vict. **11**) was passed, modifying the method of adoption in Urban Districts and the power of Library Authorities to combine; and in 1898, by the "Libraries Offences Act, 1898" (61 & 62 Vict. **53**) power was given to provide for certain offences committed in libraries being punished.

The Consolidation Act of 1892 has been still further affected by the "Local Government (England and Wales) Act, 1894" (56 & 57 Vict. **73**). The sections of that Act which bear upon Public Libraries and Museums will be noticed in their proper places.

Attempts have more than once been made in Parliament to raise the Statutory maximum limit of $1d.$ in the £ for Public Library Rates to $2d.$,(a) and it is to be hoped that the change will come at no distant day.

In the *Digest* which follows, the Law respecting Libraries and Museums is broken up under such heads as seem calculated to facilitate reference to the subject, according to the following scheme, England, Scotland, and Ireland being each separately dealt with :—

    1. Interpretation of Terms.
    2. How the Acts are put into operation.
    3. Governing Bodies.
    4. What may be supplied under the Acts.
    5. The Proceedings of Governing Bodies.
    6. Borrowing Powers.
    7. Acquisition of Lands etc.
    8. Rates and Rating.
    9. Accounts and Audit.

(a) In isolated cases, by means of Local Acts, these attempts have been successful, but the proposal to increase the limit generally has hitherto proved abortive.

PART I.

DIGEST OF STATUTES.

CHAPTER I.

INTERPRETATION OF TERMS USED IN THE "PUBLIC LIBRARIES ACT."

ENGLAND AND WALES.

IN the construction of the "Public Libraries Act, 1892," unless the context otherwise requires— Definitions.
55 & 56 Vict. 53, 27.

"Urban District" means a municipal borough, Improvement Act district, or local government district; and "Urban Authority" means, as regards each such district, the council, improvement commissioners, or local board : (*a*)

"Financial Year" means the period of twelve months for which the accounts of a library authority are made up :

"Voter" means a person who is registered as a county elector or enrolled as a burgess in respect of the occupation of property situate in the district or parish in connection with which the voter is mentioned :

"Overseers" includes any persons authorised and required to make and levy poor rates in a parish, and acting instead of overseers :

"Common Council" means in relation to the City of London, the Mayor, Commonalty, and Citizens, acting by the Mayor, Aldermen, and Commons in common council assembled.

(2.) For the purposes of the Act, and subject to the provisions 55 & 56 Vict. 53, 1 (2).

(*a*) See now the "Local Government Act, 1894" (56 & 57 Vict. 73, 21), for some alterations in form, though not in substance, applicable to these expressions.

thereof, every urban district and every parish which is not within an urban district is a "library district."

<small>55 & 56 Vict. 53, 4.</small> (3.) "Library Authority" is defined by § 4, which provides that the Act, when adopted for any library district, is to be carried into execution, if the library district is an urban district, by the urban authority, and, if it is a parish, by the commissioners appointed under the Act. Any such authority or commissioners executing the Act are referred to as a "library authority."

<small>55 & 56 Vict. 53, 2.</small> (4.) For the purposes of the Act the vestry of a parish shall be any body of persons acting by virtue of any Act of Parliament as or instead of a vestry; and, where there is no such body, shall be the inhabitants of the parish in vestry assembled, but in the latter case the persons registered as county electors in respect of the occupation of property situate in the parish, and no other persons, shall be members of the vestry.

<small>56 & 57 Vict. 73, 75 (1-2).</small> (5.) The "Local Government Act, 1894," deals with the adoption of the "Public Libraries Act, 1892," in Parishes, and certain of the definitions of the Act of 1894 must therefore be borne in mind. For instance—

The definition of "parish" in § 100 of the "Local Government Act, 1888," does not apply to the Act of 1894, but, save as aforesaid, expressions used in the latter Act shall, unless the context otherwise requires, have the same meaning as in the former Act.

Unless the context otherwise requires—any reference to population means the population according to the census of 1891. The expression "parochial elector," when used with reference to a parish in an urban district, or in the county of London or any county borough, means any person who would be a parochial elector of the parish if it were a rural parish. "Vestry" in relation to a parish means the inhabitants of the parish whether in vestry assembled or not, and includes any select vestry either by statute or at common law. "Rateable value" means the rateable value stated in the valuation list in force, or, if there is no such list, in the last poor rate.

<small>56 & 57 Vict. 73, 21.</small> (6.) By the same Act of 1894 as from the appointed day,— (1) Urban sanitary authorities are to be called urban district councils, and their districts urban districts; but nothing in the section enacting this is to alter the style or title of the corporation or council of a borough: (2) For every rural sanitary district there is to be a rural district council

PART I.—DIGEST OF STATUTES. 7

whose district is to be called a rural district: (3) In this and every other Act of Parliament, unless the context otherwise requires, the expression "district council" includes the council of every urban district, *whether a borough or not*, and of every rural district, and "county district" includes every urban and rural district *whether a borough or not*.

(7.) In addition to the foregoing definitions, certain words and expressions used in any Act of Parliament are defined by the "Interpretation of Terms Act, 1889." It is unnecessary to give these definitions in detail, but whenever necessary they will be referred to in the text of this work. 52 & 53 Vict. 63.

Scotland.

(8.) In the construction of the "Public Libraries Consolidation Act (Scotland), 1887," the following words and expressions shall have the meanings hereby assigned if not inconsistent with the context or subject matter; Interpretation of Terms. 50 & 51 Vict. 42, 2.

"Burgh" shall include royal burgh, parliamentary burgh, burgh incorporated by Act of Parliament, burgh of regality, burgh of barony, and any populous place or police burgh administered wholly or partly under any general or local Police Act, and the boundaries of such burgh shall, for the purposes of this Act, be the boundaries to which such general or local Police Act extends:

"Parish" shall mean a parish for which a separate Poor Rate is or can be imposed, or for which a separate parochial board is or can be appointed, and shall be exclusive of the area of any burgh or part of a burgh situated therein:

"Householders" shall mean, in the case of a burgh, all persons whose names are entered on the municipal register, and in the case of a parish, all persons entitled to vote in the election of a school board in such parish, under the provisions of the "Education (Scotland) Act, 1872," and any Act amending the same: 35 & 36 Vict. 62.

"Magistrates and Councils" shall be applied collectively, and not separately, and shall include Provost, Magistrates, and Town Council, Magistrates and Commissioners of Police, and any other body of persons for the time being in office, by authority of whom the burgh general assessment is levied; and where in any burgh the Magistrates and Council form a corporate body, and there is also in the same burgh a Board of Commissioners of Police by whom the burgh general assessment is levied, the words "Magistrates and Council" shall, as regards the levying and recovering of the Library Rate, apply to such Commissioners of Police, but in every other respect it shall apply to such corporate body of Magistrates and Council:

"Chief Magistrate" shall include Provost, and shall apply to any magistrate legally acting as chief magistrate for the time being:

[8 & 9 Vict. 83.] "Board" shall mean the parochial board acting under the Act 8 & 9 Vict. **83**, and any Act amending the same:

"Committee" shall mean the committee appointed under any "Public Libraries Act" affecting Scotland for the time being, or this Act:

"Municipal Register" shall mean the register, list, or roll of persons entitled to vote in an election of Town Councillors or Commissioners of Police, in a burgh, made up according to the law in force for the time being:

"Burgh General Assessment" shall mean an assessment which, under any general or local Police Act, shall be applicable to the general purposes of such Act:

"Library Rate" shall mean the Rate or assessment authorised by this Act for the purpose of carrying the Act into execution:

"Libraries and Museums" and "Libraries or Museums" shall include schools for science, art galleries, and schools for art, and these expressions, or either of them, when used in the singular, shall include a school for science, an art gallery, and a school for art:

Words importing the masculine gender shall, when applied to householders, include female householders.

[50 & 51 Vict. 42, 3.] (**9.**) The "Public Libraries (Scotland) Acts, 1867 to 1884" (*a*) so far as the same relate to Scotland, are repealed; but such repeal does not invalidate or affect anything already done in pursuance of these Acts, and all burghs and parishes in Scotland which before the passing of the Act of 1887 adopted the recited Acts became subject to the provisions of the Act of 1887. Nothing in that Act is to [50 & 51 Vict. lxxxv.] prejudice or affect the provisions of the "Edinburgh Public Library Assessment Act, 1887."

(*a*) These Acts were 30 & 31 Vict. **37**, 34 & 35 Vict. **59**, 40 & 41 Vict. **54**, 47 & 48 Vict. **37**.

IRELAND.

(10.) In the construction of the "Public Libraries Act (Ireland), 1855" (if not inconsistent with the context or subject matter), the following terms shall have the respective meanings hereinafter assigned to them; Interpretation of Terms.
18 & 19 Vict. 40, 3.

"Town" means and includes any City, Borough, Town, or Place in which Commissioners, Trustees, or other persons have been or shall be appointed under the Act 9 Geo. IV. **82,** or the "Towns Improvement Act (Ireland), 1854," or any Local or other Act or Acts for paving, flagging, lighting, watching, cleansing, or otherwise improving any City, Borough, Town, or Place for the execution of any such Act or Acts, and in which there shall not be a Town Council or other such body elected under the Act 3 & 4 Vict. **108,** or any other Charter granted in pursuance of such Act, or any Act passed for the amendment thereof. 17 & 18 Vict. 103.

"Town Commissioners" means the Commissioners, Trustees, or other persons for the time being appointed under any such first-mentioned Acts as aforesaid.

"Town Fund" means the Town Fund, or the Rates or property vested in and under the control and direction of any Town Commissioners, and applicable to the purposes of any such Acts.

"Town Rate" means the Rate or Rates authorised to be levied by any such Town Commissioners.

"Mayor" includes Lord Mayor.

"Clerk" means, as regards an incorporated Borough, the Town Clerk of such Borough, and as regards a Town in which there shall be Town Commissioners the Clerk appointed by them.

"Householder" means a male occupier of a dwelling-house, or of any lands, tenements, or hereditaments within any Town or incorporated Borough, and entitled for the time being to vote at elections of Commissioners, Aldermen, or Councillors in such Town or Borough.

(11.) The "Public Libraries Acts Amendment Act, 1877," provides that "Ratepayer" shall mean every inhabitant who would have to pay the Free Library Assessment in the event of the Act being adopted. 40 & 41 Vict. 54, 3.

The "Public Libraries Act, 1884," which has been repealed as regards England and Scotland, also contains some definitions applicable to Ireland. (See the Act in Part IV., *post*.) 47 & 48 Vict. 37.

57 & 58 Vict. 38, 12.

(12.) By the "Public Libraries (Ireland) Act, 1894," it is provided that unless the context otherwise requires;

"Urban District" means an incorporated Borough or a Town as defined by the principal Act, that of 1855.

"Urban Authority" means, in the case of an incorporated Borough, the Council or Board of Municipal Commissioners, and in the case of a Town the Town Commissioners as defined by the principal Act.

"Voter" means a person who is registered as a parliamentary voter in respect of the ownership or occupation of property, or in respect of lodgings within the district in connection with which the voter is mentioned, and in the case of a Borough includes a freeman thereof.

"The Local Government Board" means the Local Government Board for Ireland.

"Prescribed" means prescribed by Rules made by the Local Government Board under the Act of 1894.

CHAPTER II.

HOW THE "PUBLIC LIBRARIES ACTS" ARE BROUGHT INTO OPERATION.

ENGLAND AND WALES.

I. *In Urban Districts.*

WHERE a library district is an urban district—(i.) The principal Act may, subject to the conditions contained in the second section, be adopted, and the limitation of the maximum rate to be levied for the purposes of that Act may within the limits fixed by that Act be fixed, raised, or removed, by a resolution of the urban authority. (ii.) The consent of the urban authority given by a resolution of that authority shall be substituted in an urban district for the consent of the voters in any case when the consent of the voters is required under the principal Act. § 3 of the principal Act is repealed, so far as it relates to an urban district. *[56 Vict. 11, 2. Modification as to adoption, etc. in urban districts.]*

Sub-section 3 of this third section, which provided that the Act should have effect as regards any Parish partly within partly without an urban district as if the part without the District were a separate parish, is repealed by the "Local Government Act, 1894." *[56 & 57 Vict. 73, 89]*

14. A resolution under the Act may be passed at a meeting of the urban authority, but one month at least before the meeting special notice of the meeting and of the intention to propose the resolution must be given to every member of the authority; and the notice shall be deemed to have been duly given to a member of it, if it is either (a) given in the mode in which notices to attend meetings of the authority are usually given; or (b) where there is no such mode, then signed by the clerk of the authority, and delivered to the member or left at his usual or last-known place of abode in England, or forwarded by post in a prepaid *[56 Vict. 11, 3. Provision as to a resolution of an urban authority for the adoption, etc. of the principal Act.]*

letter, addressed to the member at his usual or last-known place of abode in England. The resolution must be published by advertisement in some one or more newspapers circulating within the district of the authority, and by causing notice thereof to be affixed to the principal doors of every church and chapel in the place to which notices are usually fixed, and otherwise in such manner as the authority think sufficient for giving notice thereof to all persons interested, and shall come into operation at a time not less than one month after the first publication of the advertisement of the resolution as the Authority may by the resolution fix. A copy of the resolution is to be sent to the Local Government Board. A copy of the advertisement is to be conclusive evidence of the resolution having been passed, unless the contrary be shown; and no objection to the effect of the resolution, on the ground that notice of the intention to propose the same was not duly given, or on the ground that the resolution was not sufficiently published, may be made after three months from the date of the first advertisement.

II. *In Combinations of Neighbouring Urban Districts.*

56 Vict. 11, 4.
Power to two or more library authorities to combine.

(15.) Where the principal Act is adopted for two or more neighbouring urban districts, the library authorities of those districts may by agreement combine for any period for carrying the Act into execution; and the expenses shall be defrayed by such authorities in agreed proportions.

A joint committee may be formed, the members whereof shall be appointed by the several combining authorities in such proportions as may be agreed on, but need not be members of any of the combining authorities. Any such committee shall have such of the powers of a library authority under the principal Act, except the power of borrowing money, as the combining authorities may confer on them.

Where any of the combining authorities are Improvement Commissioners (*a*) or a Local Board (*a*) the provisions of the principal Act with respect to accounts and audit shall apply to such committee as if they were a Local Board who were a library authority under the Act.

(*a*) Now Urban District Councils under the "Local Government Act, 1894," (56 & 57 Vict. 73, 21).

PART I.—DIGEST OF STATUTES. 13

III. *In Rural Parishes.*

(16.) Under the "Local Government Act, 1894," in every *rural parish* the *parish meeting* shall, exclusively, have the power of adopting the "Public Libraries Act, 1892" (and any Act amending the same). This is one of the Acts known as "adoptive Acts" under the aforesaid Statute relating to parochial government. Transfer of powers under adoptive Acts. 56 & 57 Vict. 73, 7.

Where under any of the "adoptive" Acts a particular majority is required for the adoption or abandonment of an Act, or for any matter under such Act, the like majority of the parish meeting, or, if a poll is taken, of the parochial electors, is required; and where under any of the said Acts the opinion of the voters is to be ascertained by Voting-papers, the opinion of the parochial electors is to be ascertained by a poll taken in manner provided by the said Act of 1894.

(17.) If it should be necessary to take a poll reference must be made to the "Local Government Act, 1894," which provides [§ 48 (8)] that subject to any adaptations made by the Rules of the Local Government Board, the section which relates to the election of Councillors and applies the "Ballot Act, 1872," and other Acts, shall apply in the case of every poll consequent on a parish meeting as if it were a poll for the election of parish councillors. The poll. 56 & 57 Vict. 73, 48

The Local Government Board have issued Rules as to these details.

(18.) As this volume may be expected to come into the hands of some who are not very conversant with the interpretation of Acts of Parliament of different character which are required to be read together, it may be desirable to set out a little more in detail the steps to be taken for the adoption of the "Public Libraries Act, 1892," in Rural Parishes.

There must be a Requisition by ten or more voters, calling upon the Chairman of the Parish Meeting (or Council if there be one) to convene a Parish Meeting to consider the question.

The Parish Meeting must be held at the time and place appointed, and a resolution moved to adopt the Act.

If demanded, a Poll must be taken, by ballot, in accordance with the Local Government Board's Rules.

If the result is in favour of the adoption of the Act, then where there is a Parish Council that body will be the Library

14   BOOK I.—LIBRARIES AND MUSEUMS.

Authority; but if there be no Parish Council, then the Parish Meeting must either appoint a Committee or a special body of Commissioners to carry out the duties of a Library Authority.

55 & 56
Vict. 53, 3.
(19.) The provisions of § 3 of the "Public Libraries Act, 1892," are not expressly repealed so far as regards a Rural Parish. It is therefore desirable that as far as possible its requirements should be followed. There should therefore be a requisition by ten or more voters (*i.e.* parochial electors) to the Chairman of the Parish Meeting, or the Chairman of the Parish Council if there be one (and it would be safer to send one also to the Overseers), requesting him (or them) to call a Parish Meeting to ascertain the opinion of the voters (*ante*). The form given on p. 133 (*post*) may be used with necessary alterations.

56 & 57
Vict. 73, 45,
and Sch. I.
On receiving the requisition the Chairman of the Parish Meeting or Council, as the case may be, must convene a Parish Meeting. If he fails to do this any two Parish Councillors or six parochial electors may call it. Not less than seven clear days before the meeting public notice thereof is to be given specifying the time and place, and the business, and signed by the Convener. The public notice is to be given in the manner required for giving notice of vestry meetings (*i.e.* by notices on or near to the doors of all the churches and chapels), and by posting the notice in some conspicuous place or places within the Parish, and in such other manner as appears to the person convening the meeting desirable for giving publicity to the notice. The meeting is to begin not earlier than 6 o'clock in the evening. No form of notice is prescribed. The following form is therefore suggested:

PARISH OF   .

PARISH MEETING. "PUBLIC LIBRARIES ACT, 1892."

I, the undersigned, hereby give public notice that a Meeting of the Parochial Electors of the Parish of   will be held at   on   at the hour of   o'clock in the evening, for the purpose of considering and deciding (subject to any poll which may be legally demanded) upon the question set forth in the following requisition:

(*Here Copy the Requisition.*)

Dated the   day of   18 .
A. B., Chairman of the Parish Meeting (or Council).

If there is a Parish Council for the Parish then the Chairman of that Council, if present at the meeting, is to be

PART I.—DIGEST OF STATUTES. 15

the Chairman of the Meeting. If there is no Parish Council for the Parish, then the Chairman of the Parish Meeting will preside, but if he is absent or unwilling or unable to take the chair, the meeting may appoint a person to take the chair, and that person is to have the powers and the authority of the Chairman. 56 & 57 Vict. 73, 19 (1), and Sch. I.

Only Parochial Electors are entitled to be present, and each elector may give one vote and no more on any question. The Chairman having taken the chair, the notice calling the Meeting should be read, and then a resolution should be moved and seconded (though the seconding is not strictly necessary) to the following effect:

> That the "Public Libraries Act, 1892," be adopted for the Parish of ———
> [subject to the rate being limited to one halfpenny (or three farthings) in the pound, or *as the case may be*].

Observe that unless such is required by the Requisition the opinion of the meeting is not to be taken on any question with respect to the limitation of the rate, and even if it is then only upon the limitations specified in the Act. If no limitation is mentioned in the Requisition the penny limit will apply. 55 & 56 Vict. 53, 3 (2).

The question, having been put to the Meeting, is to be decided by the majority of those present and voting upon it. In case of an equal division of votes, the Chairman has a second or casting vote, and he is to announce his decision as to the result, and that decision is to be final unless a poll is demanded. 55 & 56 Vict. 53, 3 (4); 56 & 57 Vict. 73, 7 (2); Sch. I.

The "Public Libraries Act, 1892," provides that its adoption is to be by a mere majority of answers in favour of it.

(20.) A poll may be demanded by any one Parochial Elector, but this demand must be made before the conclusion of the meeting. The expenses of the meeting, including the expenses of any poll, are to be paid out of the poor rate and by the Parish Council, if there be one. 56 & 57 Vict. 73, Sch. I.

The poll must be taken by ballot in accordance with and subject to the provisions of § 48 of the "Local Government Act, 1894," and the Rules of the Local Government Board made thereunder.

The Rules were made by General Order of the Board on November 15, 1894, for a parish where there is no Parish Council, and on February 5, 1895, for a parish having a Parish Council. It is unnecessary to reprint these Rules here, as they are well known by this time, and may be obtained from the Queen's printers, but the following is a summary of them:

The Chairman of the Parish Meeting at which the Poll is demanded is to be the Returning Officer. But he may appoint some other person to act for him. He is to appoint an office for the purposes of the Poll, and (if there is no Parish Council) give notice thereof to the Overseers. If the Chairman does not act, he is to forward a copy of the resolution and name of proposer to the Returning Officer.

The Returning Officer is to fix the day of the Poll, not being later than the fourteenth day after it was demanded.

It is to be open during the hours last fixed for the Poll at an election of Parish Councillors, if any, or the County Council may prescribe the hours. It must be open between the hours of 6 and 8 p.m. In a parish without a Parish Council, if the County Council has made no order, it is to be open between 4 and 8 p.m.

In a parish having a Parish Council, separate Polls must be taken in each polling district or ward, if any, or the Returning Officer may divide the parish into polling districts for the Poll, so long as each district consists of an area for which separate lists of parochial electors will be available.

In a parish where there is no Parish Council there is to be one polling place and one polling station for the parish, to be determined by the Returning Officer, unless the County Council otherwise order. In any other parish the Returning Officer determines the number and situation of the polling places, unless there are not more than 500 electors, when only one polling station is to be provided, unless the County Council otherwise order. No premises licensed for the sale of intoxicating liquors may be used.

The Returning Officer is to give notice of the intended Poll 5 clear days at least before the day fixed for it. It is to be in the form prescribed in the Schedule, or to the like effect, viz.:—

NOTICE OF POLL.

PARISH of

WHEREAS at a Parish Meeting for the Parish of   (or for part of the Parish of   ), held on the   day of   189 , the following resolution was proposed by   , a parochial elector for the said Parish, viz.:—

That the Public Libraries Act, 1892, be adopted for this Parish (subject to the rate being limited to ½d. (or ¾d.) in the £," *or as the case may be*).

PART I.—DIGEST OF STATUTES. 17

AND WHEREAS a poll was demanded on the question whether the said Act should be so adopted or not,

NOTICE IS HEREBY GIVEN

1. That a Poll on the said question will be taken on the   day of 189 , between the hours of   and   .
2. That the part of the parish for which the Poll is to be taken is as follows :—   (*This paragraph to be omitted if the Poll is taken for the whole of the Parish.*)
3. (*a*) That each elector must vote in the polling district in which the property in respect of which he votes is situate, and if it is situate in more than one polling district he may vote in any one, but in one only, of such polling districts.
    (*b*) The polling districts are as follows :   (*If the parish is not divided into polling districts this paragraph should be omitted.*)
4. The Poll will be taken at one polling place situate at   . Only parochial electors will be entitled to vote. (*If there are several polling places this paragraph to be altered accordingly.*)
5. The Poll will be taken by ballot.

Dated this   day of   189 .

, Returning Officer.

(*Office for purpose of Poll.*)

If there is only one polling station the Returning Officer is to preside; if more than one, he is to appoint some person to preside at each of the other polling stations, who is to be called the Presiding Officer, and suitable persons residing in the parish are to be preferred.

The Returning Officer is to furnish each polling station with screened compartments for voting, with a sufficient number of ballot papers.

The following form of ballot paper is prescribed :—

BALLOT PAPER.

Counterfoil No.	Poll on the following question.	Answer.	
		Yes.	No.
Note.—The counterfoil is to have a number to correspond with that on the back of the ballot paper.	1. That the Public Libraries Act, 1892, be adopted for this Parish (*or as the case may be*).		

FORM OF BACK OF BALLOT PAPER.

No.
Poll consequent on Parish Meeting for   Parish [or part of   Parish]   189 .

Note.—The *number* on the ballot paper is to correspond with that on the counterfoil.

C

18 BOOK I.—LIBRARIES AND MUSEUMS.

The proposer of the resolution may in writing appoint one polling agent at each polling station, who may be paid or unpaid. Any such appointment must be delivered at the office of the Returning Officer two clear days before the Poll. The only questions authorised to be put to an elector in the polling station (and then only if required) are—

(a) Are you the person entered in the parochial register for this parish as follows (*read the whole entry from the register*)?

(b) Have you already voted at the present poll?

The votes are to be counted by the Returning Officer in the parish or in some place near thereto as soon as practicable after the close of the poll. If there is an equality of votes for or against the resolution, the Returning Officer may, if a parochial elector, give a vote in writing, but he is not otherwise to be entitled to vote at the poll.

The result must be declared in the following form, as prescribed:—

DECLARATION OF RESULT OF POLL.

PARISH of

WHEREAS a Poll of the Parochial Electors of the Parish of
(or a part of the Parish of   ) was taken on   day of
189 , on the following question, viz. :—

" That the Public Libraries Act, 1892, be adopted for the Parish of
" (*or as the case may be*),

I, the undersigned, being the Returning Officer at the said Poll, DO HEREBY GIVE NOTICE that the number of votes recorded thereat is as follows :—

In favour of the proposal	votes.
Against the proposal	votes.
Majority (in favour or against) (*as the case may be.*)	votes.

AND I DO HEREBY DECLARE that the said proposal was carried (*or lost, as the case may be*).

, Returning Officer.

35 & 36 Vict. 33; 45 & 46 Vict. 50; 47 & 48 Vict. 70.

(21.) The "Ballot Act, 1872," certain sections of the "Municipal Corporations Act, 1882," and the "Municipal Elections (Corrupt and Illegal Practices) Act, 1884," are applied and adapted. They are not set out here at length, as the Local Government Board Orders are doubtless in the possession of those who have to take Polls in parishes under them upon other matters.

Any public notice is to be given under the Order by

posting the same on or near the principal door of each church and chapel in the parish, or in some conspicuous place or places.

(22.) There are certain Sections of the "Local Government Act, 1894," which have an incidental bearing on the adoption of the "Public Libraries Acts," and which, on that account, must be noted, though it is not desirable to occupy space by setting them out in detail here.(a) These sections are:— 52, 53, 56, 57, 58, 67, Schedule II. 56 & 57 Vict. 73.

(23.) The "Public Libraries Act, 1892," extends to every library district for which it is adopted. Every urban district, and every parish in England and Wales which is not within an urban district, is a library district.

(24.) With respect to—(a) the adoption of the Act for any library district; and Extent and application of Act.

(b) the fixing, raising, and removing of any limitation on the maximum rate to be levied for the purposes of the Act; and 55 & 56 Vict. 53, 1.

(c) the ascertaining of the opinion of the voters with respect to any matter for which their consent is required under the Act; Proceedings for adoption of Act in parishes. 55 & 56 Vict. 53, 3.

the provisions which follow are to have effect.

1. Any ten or more voters in the district may address a requisition in writing to the authority hereafter in the section mentioned requiring that authority to ascertain the opinion of the voters with respect to the question stated in the requisition. Where the library district is a municipal borough the requisition may be made by the borough council:

2. On receipt of the requisition the authority is to ascertain by voting-papers the opinion of the voters with respect to the said question; but the said authority is not to ascertain the opinion of the voters on any question with respect to the limitation of the rate unless required to do so by the requisition, or with respect to any limitation of the rate other than the limitations specified in the Act:

3. The procedure for ascertaining the opinion of the voters is to be in accordance with the regulations contained in Schedule I. to the "Public Libraries Act," 1892.

4. Every question so submitted to the voters is to be decided by the majority of answers to that question recorded on the valid voting-papers, and where the majority of those answers are in favour of the adoption of the Act the same

(a) See G. F. Chambers's *Popular Summary of the Law relating to Parish Councils*, 2nd ed. (Knight & Co., 1s. 6d.)

shall forthwith, on the result of the poll being made public, be deemed to be adopted:

5. Where the opinion of the voters in any library district is ascertained upon the question as to the adoption of this Act, or upon a question as to the limitation of the rate, no further proceeding may be taken for ascertaining the opinion of the voters until one year at least from the day when the opinion of the voters was last ascertained, that is to say, the day on which the voting-papers were collected:

6. The authority to ascertain the opinion of the voters for the purposes of this section is to be in a parish the overseers.

IV. *In The City of London, London Parishes, and Metropolitan Districts.*

Application of Act to city of London. 55 & 56 Vict. 53, 21.

(25.) The city of London is a library district, and on this Act being adopted for the City, the common council will be the library authority.

The opinion of the voters in the 'city of London with respect to any question under the Act is to be ascertained by the mayor on the requisition of the common council.

The expenses incurred in the city of London in executing the Act, including all expenses in connection with ascertaining the opinion of the voters, are to be defrayed out of the consolidated rate levied by the Commissioners of Sewers, or out of a separate rate made, as the consolidated rate.

So much of the Act as limits the rate or addition to a rate to be levied in any library district for any one financial year to 1*d*. in the pound is not to extend to the city of London.(*a*)

Power for district in London to adopt Act. 55 & 56 Vict. 53, 22.

(26.) Every district mentioned in Schedule B. to the " Metropolis Management Act, 1855" (18 & 19 Vict. **120**), as amended by subsequent Acts, is to be a library district, and the Act is to apply accordingly, with modifications :—

The opinion of the voters in any such district with respect to any question under the Act is to be ascertained by the District Board on the requisition of ten or more voters :

The library authority for such district will be commissioners appointed by the District Board, and the provisions of the Act relating to commissioners appointed for a parish apply, with the substitution of " district " for " parish " and of " district board " for " vestry " :

The expenses incurred in any such district in executing

(*a*) These Commissioners were dissolved and their powers transferred to the Common Council by the 60 & 61 Vict. c. xxxiii.

the Act, including all expenses in connection with ascertaining the opinion of the voters, are to such amount as is sanctioned by the District Board to be defrayed by that board in like manner as if they had been incurred for the general purposes of the "Metropolis Management Act, 1855"; and the sums from time to time required for defraying those expenses, to the extent so sanctioned, are to be paid by the district board to any person appointed by the commissioners to receive the same; but a district board may not levy for the purposes of the Act any greater sum in any financial year than the amount produced by a rate of one penny in the pound, or any less rate specially fixed for the purpose of the Act in the district:

The enactments authorising two or more neighbouring parishes to combine in carrying the Act into execution are to have effect as if any such district were included in the term "parish," and the district board of such district in the term "vestry":

Where a parish in any such district has adopted any of the Acts repealed, or hereafter adopts the "Public Libraries Act, 1892," it is to be treated in all respects as if it were outside the district, and, in particular,—

(a) a person shall not, by reason of being a voter in the parish, be accounted a voter in the district; and
(b) a representative of the parish on the District Board shall not take part in any proceeding of the board under this section; and
(c) the parish shall not be called on to contribute to the payment of any expenses incurred in pursuance of this section; and
(d) any question of accounts arising between the parish and the other parishes in the district, or between the parish and the district, in consequence of this section, is to be decided by the Local Government Board:

After the adoption of the Act for any such district, proceedings shall not, except with the sanction of the Local Government Board, be taken for the separate adoption thereof for any parish in the District.

(27.) Numerous regulations are prescribed for ascertaining the opinion of the voters in a library district. "Presiding officer" means, in relation to any library district, the authority required under this Act to ascertain the opinion of the voters on any question, or a person appointed by that authority, and that authority is referred to as the "district authority." 55 & 56 Vict. 53, Sch. I.

BOOK I.—LIBRARIES AND MUSEUMS.

<small>55 & 56 Vict. 53, Sch. I. pt. i.</small>

(**28.**) The following is the procedure by voting-papers. The district authority, before the day appointed for the issuing of the voting-papers, is to provide the presiding officer with a copy of the burgess roll or county register, as the case may be, containing the names of the voters.

On the day appointed for issuing the voting-papers, the presiding officer is to send by post or cause to be delivered to every voter at his address a voting-paper in the form prescribed, or to the like effect.

<small>55 & 56 Vict. 53, Sch. I. pt. ii.</small>

Every voting-paper must bear the voter's registered number, and contain directions to the voter as to the day on which and the hours within which the voting-paper is to be collected or sent, and as to the place at which, if sent, it will be received.

The district authority must, before the issue of the voting-papers, appoint competent persons (who will be paid) to collect and receive the voting-papers and to assist in the scrutiny thereof. A convenient place within the district is also to be appointed at which the voting-papers are to be received, but the district authority is not to be required to collect voting-papers sent to addresses beyond the district.

Voting-papers are to be collected between 8 a.m. and 8 p.m. of the third day after that on which they were issued. Such day is the "polling-day"; and such last-mentioned hour is the "conclusion of the poll."

A voting-paper is not after collection to be delivered to any person except the presiding officer or a person appointed to receive voting-papers.

A voting-paper may be sent by prepaid post or by hand to the presiding officer at the place appointed for the receipt thereof, so that it be received by the presiding officer before the conclusion of the poll. Voting-papers, except those collected by persons appointed by the district authority, are not to be received at the appointed place after the conclusion of the poll.

Every person appointed to collect voting-papers must be appointed in writing, and must carry such writing with him, and show it to any voter on request. If any person so appointed fails to comply with this regulation, or if any unauthorised person fraudulently receives or induces any voter to part with a voting-paper, such person will be guilty of a misdemeanor, and liable to imprisonment for six months, or less; or to a fine of 20*l.*, or less; or to both imprisonment and fine.

A voting-paper which contains the answer "yes" or "no"

PART I.—DIGEST OF STATUTES.

to any question and is duly signed is to be deemed to be a valid voting-paper with respect to that question.

A voting-paper is to be deemed to be duly signed if signed by the voter with his full name or ordinary signature.

Where any voter is unable to write he may cause his voting-paper to be filled up by another person. In such case he shall attach his mark to the voting-paper, and such mark shall be attested by such other person, who shall sign his name and append his address.

FORM OF VOTING PAPER.

"*Public Libraries Act*, 1892."

BOROUGH (Parish or other Library District) of .
No. (*Here insert number of voter in burgess roll or county register, as the case may be.*)

Question 1 .	Are you in favour of the adoption of the " Public Libraries Act, 1892," for the Borough (*or parish, etc.*) of .	Answer 1. (*To be filled in* "Yes" *or* "No.")	[*To be omitted if Libraries Act already adopted.*]
Question 2 .	Are you in favour of the rate being limited to one halfpenny in the pound? (*Or to three farthings, or of the existing limitation of the rate under the "Public Libraries Act, 1892," being removed, or of the existing limitation to one halfpenny being raised to three farthings, as the case may require.*)	Answer 2. (*To be filled in* "Yes" *or* "No.")	[*To be omitted if no question stated in the requisition as to limitation of rate.*]
Question 3 .	Are you in favour of an agreement being made with (*here designate the body or bodies, according to section ten or section sixteen of this Act*) for the purpose of (*briefly state objects of proposed agreement*).	Answer 3. (*To be filled in* "Yes" *or* "No.")	[*To be omitted if no such question raised.*]

———————————{ Signature of Voter.

Note. "1. This voting-paper will be collected by an authorised collector between the hours of 8 A.M. and 8 P.M. on   day, the   18   (*insert polling day*), or may be sent by prepaid post or by hand, addressed to (*state name or designation of presiding officer, and place appointed by the district authority*). If it is sent it must be received at that address before 8 p.m. on the above-mentioned day.

"2. You may require the collector to show his authority in writing. No authority is valid unless it is (signed by *A.B.*, *or* sealed, or *as the district authority may direct*)."

Any person fabricating a voting-paper, or presenting or returning a fabricated voting-paper, knowing that the same does not bear the true answer or signature of the voter to whom it was sent or intended to be sent, will be guilty of personation, and liable to the penalties prescribed by the "Ballot Act, 1872."

35 & 36 Vict. 33.

The presiding officer, as soon as may be after the conclusion of the poll, must proceed to a scrutiny of the voting-papers, and compare the same with the roll or register, and ascertain how far the voting-papers have been duly signed.

A question put to the voters is to be deemed determined in the affirmative or negative, according as the majority of valid voting-papers contain the answer "yes" or "no."

Immediately on the conclusion of the scrutiny the presiding officer is to report to the district authority the number of voters who have voted "yes" and "no" respectively, and the number of invalid voting-papers.

The presiding officer is to seal up in separate packets the valid and the invalid voting-papers respectively, and transmit them, with his report, to the district authority.

Upon receiving the report the district authority is to cause the result of the poll to be made public.

V. *In Neighbouring Parishes.*

Power to vestries of neighbouring parishes to combine.
55 & 56 Vict. 53, 9.

(29.) Where the "Public Libraries Act, 1892," is adopted for any two or more neighbouring parishes, the vestries of those parishes may by agreement combine for any period in carrying the Act into execution; and the expenses are to be defrayed by the parishes in agreed proportions. The vestry of each parish is to appoint not more than 6 commissioners in accordance with the Act; and the commissioners so appointed will form one body, and act accordingly.

VI. *In a Parish adjoining a Library District.*

Power to annex parish to adjoining district.
55 & 56 Vict. 53, 10.

(30.) Where the voters in a parish adjoining or near a library district for which either this Act has been adopted, or the adoption thereof is contemplated, consent to such parish being annexed to the said district, such parish, with the consent of the library authority of the district, shall be annexed to that district for the purposes of the Act; the vestry of such parish shall appoint not more than 6 commissioners, and the commissioners shall during their respective terms of office be deemed members of the library authority of the said district.

(31.) The commissioners separately appointed for any two or more parishes for which the Act has been adopted may with the consent of the voters of those parishes agree to share in such proportions and for such period as may be determined by the agreement the cost of the purchase, erection, repair, and maintenance of any library building situate in one of those parishes; and also the cost of the purchase of books and newspapers, and all other expenses. This section applies, with the necessary modifications, to a museum, school for science, art gallery, or school for art. Power to library authorities to make agreements for use of library. 55 & 56 Vict. 53, 16.

(32.) Certain Acts mentioned are repealed, save so far as any of them extend beyond England and Wales; and where those Acts have been adopted for any library district, that adoption shall be deemed to have been an adoption of the Act of 1892. Repeal of Acts. Prior adoption. 55 & 56 Vict. 53, 28.

For the purpose of the section the said Acts are to be deemed adopted for any district in which they were in force immediately before the commencement of the Act of 1892.

Scotland.

(33.) In Scotland the principle of Free Libraries has taken a much deeper root than in either of the sister kingdoms, and there have been more Acts passed relating to Scotland than to either England or Ireland. The Scotch Act now in operation is the 50 & 51 Vict. 42, passed in 1887, as amended by the 57 & 58 Vict. 20 in the very important matter of adoption.

(34.) In burghs the principal Act (1887) may be adopted by a resolution of the magistrates and council of the burgh, and such resolution is substituted for a determination of the householders of the burgh in any case where such determination is required under the principal Act. Adoption of principal Act in burghs. 57 & 58 Vict. 20, 2.

(35.) A resolution under the Amending Act must be passed at a meeting of the magistrates and council, and one month at least before such meeting special notice thereof and of the intention to propose such resolution must be given to every person included in the collective expression "magistrates and council," either (a) in the mode in which notices to attend meetings of the magistrates and councils are usually Provision as to resolution of magistrates and council for adoption. 57 & 58 Vict. 20, 3.

given; or, in the option of the chief magistrate,(*b*) by forwarding a notice by post in a prepaid letter addressed to every person entitled to notice.

The resolution must, after the passing thereof, be published at least once by advertisement in a newspaper circulating in the burgh, and comes into operation at a time to be fixed in the resolution, being not less than one month after the first publication of the advertisement.

A copy of a newspaper containing the advertisement is to be conclusive evidence of the resolution having been passed unless the contrary be shown; no objection to the effect of the resolution on the ground of inadequate notice or publication can be made after three months from the first publication of the advertisement.

IRELAND.

Proceedings for adoption of Act.
57 & 58 Vict. 38, 1 (1).

(**36.**) The "Public Libraries Act (Ireland), 1855" ("the principal Act" for Ireland), may be adopted in any urban district, and the limitation of the maximum rate to be levied for the purposes thereof may, within the limits fixed, be fixed, raised, and removed by a resolution of the urban authority, or by such other means as is provided by the Act of 1894. In case the urban authority should fail to pass a resolution adopting the Act, such failure does not prejudice the right given by the Act of 1894 to voters to have their opinion ascertained in the manner provided by that Act.

Mode of passing resolution.
57 & 58 Vict. 38, 1 (1).

(**37**). Such resolution must be passed at a meeting of the authority, and one month at least before the meeting special notice of the meeting and of the intention to propose the resolution must be given to every member of the authority. The notice shall be deemed to have been duly given to a member of it if it is either—(*a*) given in the mode in which notices to attend meetings of the authority are usually given; or (*b*) where there is no such mode, then signed by the clerk, and delivered to the member, or left at or posted to his usual or last known place of abode in Ireland. The resolution must be published by advertisement in some newspaper circulating within the district, and by causing notice thereof to be posted at the place heretofore used for posting public notices outside every church and chapel, and otherwise in such manner as the authority thinks sufficient. It comes into operation at such time, not less than one month after the first publication of the advertisement, as the authority may fix. A copy of the

PART I.—DIGEST OF STATUTES. 27

resolution must be sent to the Irish Local Government Board. A copy of the advertisement is conclusive evidence of the resolution having been passed, unless the contrary be shown. No objection to the effect of the resolution, on the ground of inadequate notice or publication, can be made after three months from the first advertisement.

(38.) Any twenty or more voters in an urban district, or the urban authority, may address a requisition in writing in the prescribed form to the mayor or other chairman of the authority, requiring him to ascertain the opinion of the voters with respect to the question or questions stated in the requisition. 57 & 58 Vict. 38, 1 (2-6).

On receipt of the requisition the mayor or chairman is to proceed to ascertain by ballot the opinion of the voters with respect to the said question or questions, but he is not to ascertain the opinion of the voters with respect to the limitation of the rate unless required to do so by the requisition.

Where no register of the voters exists the urban authority must forthwith cause a register to be made.

For the purpose of ascertaining the opinion of the voters, the "Ballot Act, 1872," will, subject to alterations and adaptations (if any) as prescribed, apply as in a municipal election.

Any ballot boxes, fittings, etc., provided by any public authority for any election will, on request, and if not required for immediate use, be lent to the mayor or chairman of the urban authority, for a poll under the Act, upon such conditions as may be prescribed.

Every question so submitted is decided by the majority of answers to that question recorded on the valid ballot papers; where the majority are in favour of the adoption of the principal Act the same shall forthwith be deemed to be adopted, and must be carried into execution by the urban authority.

No further proceeding is to be taken for ascertaining the opinion of the voters until the expiration of one year at least from the day when the opinion of the voters was last ascertained, reckoned from the day of the poll. § 4 of the principal Act is repealed.(a)

(a) But § 1 of the "Public Libraries Acts Amendment Act, 1877" (40 & 41 Vict. 54), authorising, though not directing, a Local Authority to ascertain the opinions of the voters by means of voting-papers, is not repealed save by implication. (See 57 & 58 Vict. 38, 1 (3, 5).

The Section of the Act of 1877 above referred to is to the following effect:

It is competent for the prescribed Local Authority to ascertain the opinions of the majority of the ratepayers, either by the prescribed public

28   BOOK I.—LIBRARIES AND MUSEUMS.

Two or more authorities may combine.
57 & 58 Vict. 38, 3.

(**39.**) When the principal Act is adopted for two or more neighbouring districts, the authorities of those districts may by agreement combine for any period for carrying the Act into execution. The expenses of carrying the Act into execution are to be defrayed in proportions to be agreed on.

Power to urban authorities to make agreements for use of library.
57 & 58 Vict. 38, 7.

(**40.**) The urban authorities of two or more districts for which the Act has been adopted may agree to share in the cost of the purchase, erection, repair, and maintenance of any library building situate in one of the districts, and also in the cost of the purchase of books and newspapers, and all other expenses. Any urban authority may, with the consent of the Commissioners of Charitable Donations and Bequests for Ireland, or of the Commissioners of Endowed Schools in Ireland, make the like agreement with the governing body of any library established or maintained out of funds subject to the jurisdiction of either of the said Commissioners, and situate in or near the district. This section will apply, with necessary modifications, to a museum, school for science, art gallery, or school for art in like manner as to a library.

Expenses in a Borough or Town to be paid out of the Borough Fund or Town Fund.
18 & 19 Vict. 40, 5.

(**41.**) The expenses incurred in calling the meeting, whether the Act be adopted or not, and the expenses of carrying the Act into execution in a Borough, will be paid out of the Borough Fund, and in a Town out of a Town Fund; and the Council, or Board of Municipal Commissioners, or Town Commissioners, may levy as part of the Borough Rate or Town Rate, as the case may be, or by a separate Rate to be assessed and recovered in like manner as the Borough Rate or Town Rate, all moneys necessary to meet such expenses.

The Act to be incorporated with Local Acts in force.
18 & 19 Vict. 40, 16.

(**42.**) On the Act coming into operation in any Borough it shall, as regards such Borough, be incorporated with the Act 3 & 4 Vict. 108; and on the Act coming into operation in any Town it shall, as regards such Town, be incorporated with the Act or Acts in force therein relating to the Town Commissioners.

Refusal to adopt.
18 & 19 Vict. 40, 14.

(**43.**) If any meeting called to consider the adoption of the Act shall negative a proposal to that effect, no other meeting for the same purpose is to be held for at least one year.

meeting, or by the issue of a voting-paper to each ratepayer. The expenses connected with the collection and scrutiny of voting-papers are to be charged as the expenses of a public meeting would be. The decision of the majority so ascertained will be equally binding.
(*a*) This is the "Municipal Corporations (Ireland) Act, 1840," which has been materially amended by the "Local Government (Ireland) Act, 1898" (61 & 62 Vict. 37).

CHAPTER III.

THE CONSTITUTION, ETC., OF GOVERNING BODIES UNDER THE "PUBLIC LIBRARIES ACTS."

ENGLAND AND WALES.

I. *In Urban Districts.*

THE Principal Act when adopted for any library district will be carried into execution, if the library district is an urban district, by the urban authority, and, if it is a parish, by commissioners appointed under the Act; any such authority or commissioners executing the Act are designated the "library authority." {Act when adopted to be executed by library authority. 55 & 56 Vict. 53, 4.}

(**45.**) A library authority being an urban authority may appoint a committee and delegate to it all or any of their powers and duties, and the said committee will to the extent of such delegation be deemed the library authority. Persons appointed members of the committee need not be members of the urban authority. {Library Committee may be appointed. 55 & 56 Vict. 53, 15.}

(**46.**) Where there is in any urban district, or part, any authority constituted under any of the adoptive Acts,(*a*) the council of the district may resolve that the powers, duties, etc., of that authority shall be transferred to the council as from a date specified. Upon that date the same shall be transferred accordingly, and the authority shall cease to exist. After the appointed day none of the adoptive Acts can be adopted for any part of an urban district without the approval of its council. {Transfer to urban district council of powers of other authorities. 56 & 57 Vict. 73, 62.}

II. *In Rural Parishes.*

(i.) *Having a Parish Council.*

(**47.**) Where the area under any existing authority acting within a rural parish in the execution of any of the adoptive Acts is co-extensive with the parish, all powers, duties, etc., {55 & 57 Vict. 73 7 (5).}

(*a*) The "Public Libraries Acts" are amongst the Statutes included in the term "Adoptive Acts" by the "Local Government Act, 1894" (56 & 57 Vict. 73, 7 (1)).

BOOK I.—LIBRARIES AND MUSEUMS.

of that authority will, on the parish council coming into office, pass to that council.

56 & 57 Vict. 73, 7 (7).
(**48.**) When any of the adoptive Acts is adopted for the whole or part of a rural parish after the appointed day, and the parish has a parish council, such council will be the authority for executing the Act.

Committees of parish or district councils. 56 & 57 Vict. 73, 56.
(**49.**) A parish council may appoint committees, consisting either wholly or partly of members of the council, for the exercise of any powers which, in the opinion of the council, can be properly exercised by committees. A committee will not hold office beyond the next annual meeting of the council; the acts of every such committee must be submitted to the council for approval.

(ii.) *Not having a Parish Council.*

Provisions as to small parishes. 56 & 57 Vict. 73, 19.
(**50.**) In a rural parish not having a separate parish council, the following provisions will, as from the appointed day, have effect (but subject to provisions made by a grouping order, if the parish is one of a group).

56 & 57 Vict. 73, 19 (8).
(**51.**) The parish meeting may appoint a committee of their own number for any purposes which, in the opinion of the parish meeting, would be better regulated and managed by such a committee. The acts of the committee must be submitted to the parish meeting for approval.

55 & 56 Vict. 53, 5-8.
But it will probably be preferable to exercise the powers of appointing Library Commissioners for the parish contained in the " Public Libraries Act, 1892." (See pp. 32 and 39, *post.*)

56 & 57 Vict. 73, 19.
(**52.**) The Chairman of the parish meeting and the overseers of the parish will be a body corporate with perpetual succession, and may hold land for the purposes of the parish without licence in mortmain; but they must in all respects act in manner directed by the parish meeting; and any act of such body corporate must be executed under the hands, or, if an instrument under seal is required, under the hands and seals, of the chairman and overseers. The legal interest in all property which under the " Local Government Act, 1894," would, if there were a parish council, be vested in the parish council will vest in the said body corporate of the chairman and overseers of the parish, subject to all trusts and liabilities affecting the same, and all persons concerned shall make or concur in making such transfers (if any) as are requisite to give effect to this enactment. On the application of the parish meeting the county council may confer on that meeting any of the powers conferred on a parish council

PART I.—DIGEST OF STATUTES. 31

by the "Local Government Act, 1894." Any act of the parish meeting may be signified by an instrument executed at the meeting under the hands, or, if an instrument under seal is required, under the hands and seals, of the chairman presiding and two other parochial electors present.

(53.) Where any adoptive Act is in force in a part only of a rural parish, the existing authority under the Act, or the parish meeting for that part, may transfer the powers, duties, etc., of the authority to the parish council, subject to any conditions with respect to the execution thereof by means of a committee as to the authority or parish meeting may seem fit. Any such condition may be altered by a parish meeting. Supplemental provisions as to adoptive Acts. 56 & 57 Vict. 73, 53.

If the area under any authority under any adoptive Act will not after that day be comprised within one rural parish, the powers and duties of the authority shall be transferred to the parish councils of the rural parishes wholly or partly comprised in that area; or, if the area is partly comprised in an urban district, to those parish councils and the urban district council, and shall, until other provision is made, be exercised by a joint committee appointed by those councils. Where any such rural parish has not a parish council the parish meeting takes the place, for the purposes of this provision, of the parish council.

The property, debts, etc., of any authority under any adoptive Act whose powers are transferred in pursuance of the "Local Government Act, 1894," will be the property, debts, etc., of the area of that authority; and the proceeds of the property shall be credited, and the debts and liabilities, etc., incurred in respect of the said powers, duties, etc., are to be charged to the account of the rates or contributions levied in that area; and where that area is situate in more than one parish the sums credited to and paid by each parish are to be apportioned.

The county council, on the application of a parish council, may alter the boundaries of any such area if they consider that the alteration can properly be made without any undue alteration of the incidence of liability to rates and contributions, or of the right to property belonging to the area, regard being had to any corresponding advantage to persons subject to the liability or entitled to the right.

(54.) A parish or district council may concur with any other parish or district council in appointing out of their respective bodies a joint committee for any purpose in respect of which they are jointly interested, and in conferring, with or without Joint Committee. 56 & 57 Vict. 73, 57.

conditions, on any such committee any powers which the appointing council might exercise if the purpose related exclusively to their own parish or district. But a council cannot delegate to any such committee any power to borrow money or make any rate. A joint committee thus appointed will not hold office beyond the expiration of 14 days after the next annual meeting of any of the appointing councils. The costs of a joint committee are to be defrayed by the councils by whom it is appointed in such proportions as may be agreed upon, or as may be determined in case of difference by the county council.

Where a parish council can be required to appoint a committee consisting partly of members of the council and partly of other persons, that requirement may also be made in the case of a joint committee, and must be duly complied with by the parish councils concerned at the time of the appointment of such committee.

III. *In London Parishes and Metropolitan Districts.*

Constitution of commissioners for executing Act in parish.
55 & 56 Vict. 53, 5.

(55.) Where the Act is adopted for any parish the vestry must forthwith appoint not less than three nor more than nine voters in the parish to be commissioners for executing the Act. The commissioners will be a body corporate by the name of "The Commissioners for Public Libraries and Museums for the parish of   , in the county of   ," and will have perpetual succession and a common seal, with power to acquire and hold lands without licence in mortmain.

Rotation of commissioners.
55 & 56 Vict. 53, 6.

(56.) The commissioners must, as soon as conveniently may be after appointment, divide themselves by agreement, or by ballot, into three classes, one-third, or as nearly as may be one-third, of them being in each class.

The offices of the first class shall be vacated at the expiration of one year, the offices of the second class at the expiration of two years, and the offices of the third class at the expiration of three years from their appointment.

The offices of vacating commissioners shall be filled by an equal number of new commissioners appointed by the vestry from among the voters. Every newly-elected commissioner will hold office for three years from the date when the office became vacant, and no longer, unless re-elected. A person ceasing to be a commissioner may, unless disqualified, be re-elected.

PART I.—DIGEST OF STATUTES. 33

Any casual vacancy among the commissioners, whether arising by death, resignation, incapacity, or otherwise, must be filled up by the vestry as soon as may be: but the term of a commissioner appointed to fill a casual vacancy will expire at the date at which the term of the commissioner in whose place he is appointed would have expired.

(57.) It is to be noted that no qualifications of any kind are prescribed for the members of Committees of Management, to whom Councils can, if they choose, delegate their powers. It is further to be noted that Commissioners chosen by Metropolitan Vestries to carry out the Acts do not appear to be at liberty to delegate their powers at all.

<small>55 & 56 Vict. 53, 15. 56 & 57 Vict. 73, 56.</small>

SCOTLAND.

(58.) The Magistrates and Council of any Burgh, or the Board of any Parish where the Act has been adopted are, within one month after its adoption, and thereafter from year to year, in the case of a Burgh, at the first meeting after the annual election of Town Councillors or Commissioners of Police, and in the case of a Parish, at the first meeting after the annual meeting for the election of representative members of the Parochial Board, to appoint a Committee, consisting of not less than 10 nor more than 20 members, half of whom are to be chosen from amongst the Magistrates and Council, or Board, as the case may be, and the remaining half from amongst the householders of the Burgh or Parish other than the Magistrates and Council, or Board, and 3 members of such Committee are to form a quorum.

<small>General Management to be vested in a Committee appointed by Magistrates and Councils of Burghs and Boards of Parishes. 50 & 51 Vict. 42, 18.</small>

(59.) Any member of Committee has power to resign on giving at least 14 days' notice to the Clerk of the Committee of his intention; and in the event of any vacancy occurring in the Committee during its term of office by the resignation or death of any member, the Committee is forthwith to cause the same to be intimated to the Magistrates and Council, or Board, and the Magistrates and Council, or Board, as the case may be, may at a meeting thereafter elect from among themselves, or from among the householders other than themselves, according to the class in which the vacancy has arisen, a member of Committee in place of the member so resigning or dying, provided that no proceedings of the Committee will be invalid or illegal in consequence of a vacancy in the Committee.

<small>Mode of supplying casual vacancies. 50 & 51 Vict. 42, 19.</small>

D

BOOK I.—LIBRARIES AND MUSEUMS.

IRELAND.

Management to be vested in Council or Board, etc.
18 & 19 Vict. 40, 12.
(60.) The general management, regulation, and control of Libraries, Museums, or Schools of Science and Art shall be, as to any Borough, vested in the Council or Board, and as to any Town, in the Town Commissioners, or such Committee as they respectively may from time to time appoint.

Constitution of Committee.
40 & 41 Vict. 15, 4.
(61.) The Committee in which the general management, regulation, and control of such Libraries, Museums, or Schools may be vested under § 12 of the Act of 1855 may consist in part of persons not members of the Council or Board, or Commissioners.

Commissioners of Towns adopting the Act to be incorporated.
18 & 19 Vict. 40, 7.
(62.) The Town Commissioners of every Town adopting the Act shall, for the purposes thereof, be a Body Corporate, with perpetual succession, by the name of "The Commissioners for Public Libraries and Museums for the Town of   in the County of   :" by that name they may sue and be sued, and hold and dispose of lands, and use a Common Seal.

Provision for appointment of commissioners.
57 & 58 Vict. 38, 2.
(63.) If at any time after 6 months from the taking of a poll which resulted in favour of the adoption of the principal Act, the urban authority have not in the opinion of the Irish Local Government Board taken sufficient steps to carry the Act into execution, that Board may, upon the application in the prescribed manner of 10 or more voters, appoint from among the voters 5 commissioners to carry the Act into execution.

Commissioners so appointed will have all the powers and duties appertaining to the urban authority, subject to such alterations as may be prescribed. They will hold office for such time as the Local Government Board direct, and upon the expiration of their term of office the Board may either appoint successors from among the voters or may by order empower the urban authority to carry the principal Act into execution.

Any vacancy occurring among the commissioners will be filled by the Local Government Board from among the voters.

PART I.—DIGEST OF STATUTES. 35

CHAPTER IV.

WHAT MAY BE SUPPLIED UNDER THE "PUBLIC LIBRARIES ACTS."

ENGLAND AND WALES.

THE library authority of any library district for which the Act of 1892 has been adopted may provide all or any of the following institutions, namely, public libraries, public museums, schools for science, art galleries, and schools for art; and may purchase and hire land, and erect, rebuild, alter, repair, and extend buildings, and fit up, furnish, and supply the same with all requisite fittings. Where any one of the institutions mentioned has been established either before or after the passing of the Act by any library authority, that authority may establish in connection therewith any other of the said institutions without further proceedings being taken with respect to adoption. No charge is to be made for admission to a library or museum, or, in the case of a lending library, for the use thereof by the inhabitants of the district; but the library authority may grant the use of a lending library to persons not being inhabitants of the district, either gratuitously or for payment.(a) Provision of libraries museums, and schools of science and art. 55 & 56 Vict. 53, 11

(65.) The general management of every library, museum, art gallery, and school provided under the Act will be vested in the library authority; that authority may provide therein books, newspapers, maps, and specimens of art and science, and the same may be bound and repaired when necessary. Management of libraries, etc., by library authority or committee.

The authority may also appoint and dismiss salaried officers and servants, and make regulations for the safety and use of every library, etc., under their control, and for the admission of the public. 55 & 56 Vict. 53, 15

(a) The Attorney-General stated in the House of Commons, on September 13, 1887, that when books were allowed to go out of a Public Library on loan, he thought it was competent for the Library Authority to require a reasonable deposit to ensure the safe return of such books. (*Times*, September 14, 1887.)

BOOK I.—LIBRARIES AND MUSEUMS.

SCOTLAND.

(66.) The duties of those charged with the management of Libraries, etc., under the Acts are much more fully defined in the Scotch Act of 1887 than in the English Act of 1892.

Powers of Committee as regards things which they may supply.
50 & 51 Vict. 42, 21.

(67.) The Committee is to manage, regulate, and control all Libraries and Museums established under the Act, or to which the Act applies; and has power to do all things necessary for such management, including the following powers; that is to say,

To appoint Sub-committees of their own number:

To appoint, pay, and dismiss, a salaried Clerk, and Librarians, Officers, and Servants:

To purchase Books, Newspapers, Reviews, Magazines, and other Periodicals, Statuary, Pictures, Engravings, Maps, Specimens of Art and Science, and such other articles and things as may be necessary for the establishment, increase, and use of the Libraries and Museums, and to do all things necessary for keeping the same in preservation and repair:

To provide the necessary fuel, lighting, and other matters:

To sell or exchange any Books, Works of Art, or other property of which there may be duplicates, provided that the money arising from such sale, and the property received in exchange, shall be applied and held for the purposes of the Act:

To provide suitable rooms in the Libraries within which the Books, Periodicals, and Newspapers may be read.

Power to lend Books.
50 & 51 Vict. 42, 21.

(68.) The Committee may lend Books to the householders and inhabitants of the Burgh or Parish in and for which the Committee has been appointed, and at their discretion may grant the same privilege to the inmates of Industrial Schools, Training Ships, Reformatories, Barracks, and other similar institutions, established for or in the Burgh or Parish; and also to any person carrying on business within the limits of the Burgh or Parish, or to any employee engaged in employment therein, although such person or employee may not be a householder. and may not reside within such limits.

Power to issue Catalogues.
50 & 51 Vict. 42, 21.

(69.) The Committee may print Catalogues of the books, articles, and things in the Libraries or Museums under their control, and Reports of their Proceedings, and may sell the same.

Power to add to Institutions

(70.) Where any of the following Institutions, namely, a Public Library, a Public Museum, a School for Science and

PART I.—DIGEST OF STATUTES. 37

Art, a School for Science, a School for Art, or an Art Gallery has been established under any Public Library Act in force for the time being, there may at any time be established, in connection therewith, any other of the said Institutions without further proceedings being taken for the adoption of the Act of 1887. already e
tablished.
50 & 51
Vict. 42, 3

(71.) All Libraries, Museums, or Art Galleries established under the Act, or to which the Act applies, are to be open to the public free of charge, and no charge is to be made for the use of books or magazines issued for home reading. Libraries,
etc., to bc
free.
50 & 51
Vict. 42, 3

(72.) When the Magistrates and Council, or Board, accept a grant out of moneys provided by Parliament, from any Committee of the Privy Council on Education, towards the purchase of the site, or the erection, enlargement, or repair of any School for Science and Art, or School for Science, or School for Art, or of the residence of any teacher in such School, or towards the furnishing of any such School, they have power to accept such grant upon the conditions prescribed for the acceptance thereof by the Committee, and to execute such instruments as may be required for carrying into effect such conditions. On payment of the grant they and their successors will be bound by such conditions and instrument. Power to
accept
Parlia-
mentary
Grant
under con
ditions.
50 & 51
Vict. 42, 1

IRELAND.

(73.) Those charged with the management of Public Libraries may from time to time provide the necessary fuel, lighting, and other similar matters, Books, Newspapers, Maps, and Specimens of Art and Science, and cause the same to be bound or repaired, when necessary, and appoint, pay, and dismiss salaried officers and servants, and make rules and regulations for the safety and use of the Libraries and Museums, or Schools of Science and Art, and for the admission of visitors. Duties of
Library
Authori-
ties.
18 & 19
Vict. 40, 1

(74.) All Libraries and Museums established under the Act are to be open to the public free of charge. 18 & 19
Vict. 40, 1:

(75.) An urban authority may grant the use of a lending library established under the Act of 1855 to persons not being inhabitants, either gratuitously or for payment. Provision
as to use c
library.
57 & 58

(76.) The terms "Science and Art" and "Schools of Science and Art" used in the Act of 1855 include the Science and Art of Music and Schools of Music respectively; and the Council or Board of any Borough or the Town Commissioners of any Town may apply such portion as they may deem fit of Vict. 38, 4
Powers of
principal
Act ex-
tended to
schools of
music.

38 BOOK I.—LIBRARIES AND MUSEUMS.

40 & 41 Vict. 15, 3.

the Rate which they are or may be authorised to levy, under the provisions of the principal Act, towards the maintenance and support of, and payment of the salaries of teachers of a School or Schools of Music, and the purchase of musical instruments, books, and other requisites for the use of such School or Schools.

Power to establish museum.
47 & 48 Vict. 37, 3.

(77.) Where any of the following institutions, namely, a Public Museum, a Public Library, a School for Science and Art, a School for Science, a School for Art, or an Art Gallery, has been established either before or after the passing of the Act of 1884, under the "Public Libraries Acts," or any of them, there may at any time be established in connection therewith any other of the said institutions without any further proceedings for adoption being taken.

PART I.—DIGEST OF STATUTES. 39

CHAPTER V.

THE PROCEEDINGS OF GOVERNING BODIES UNDER THE "PUBLIC LIBRARIES ACTS."

ENGLAND AND WALES.

THE Acts are silent as to what are to be the business arrangements of Town Councils and Boards: it is presumed therefore that they are to work the " Libraries Acts " as they would any other Acts which they are called upon to administer. But Commissioners appointed for London parishes are not left to conduct their work wholly as they please. The Commissioners are to meet at least once in every month, and at such other times as they think fit, at some convenient place; and any one Commissioner may summon a special meeting by giving three clear days' notice in writing to each Commissioner, specifying therein the purpose for which the meeting is called. No business is to be transacted at a meeting unless a quorum of at least two are present. Meetings of Commissioners. 55 & 56 Vict. 53, 7.

(78.) Orders and proceedings of the Commissioners must be entered in books, and must be signed by at least two Commissioners; all such orders and proceedings so entered, and purporting to be so signed, are deemed to be originals, and such books may be produced as evidence of such orders and proceedings. Proceedings of commissioners to be recorded. 55 & 56 Vict. 53, 8.

(79.) The " Public Libraries Act, 1892," is one of the Acts which may be adopted by a Parish Meeting. If adopted, it will be carried into execution in accordance with the provisions of the " Local Government Act, 1894."(a) Parish Council or Meeting. 56 & 57 Vict. 73.

(80.) The " Libraries Offences Act, 1898," confers new and special powers on governing bodies in England to maintain order in Libraries and reading-rooms. The penalty for committing specified offences is £2, or less. Offences. 61 & 62 Vict. 53.

(a) As to this, see any Text Books on the "Local Government Act, 1894," such as G. F. Chambers's "Popular Summary" (Knight & Co., 1s. 6d.).

SCOTLAND.

Meetings of Committee, and appointment of Chairman.
50 & 51 Vict. 42, 20.

(81.) The Committee appointed under the Act of 1887 is, in the case of a Burgh, to meet once in every 3 months, or oftener if necessary, and in the case of a Parish, as often as may be necessary. A Chairman is to be appointed from among their own number, who is to hold office until the next election of Committee. Such Chairman is, in case of equality, to have a casting vote in addition to his own vote. In the event of a vacancy occurring in the office of Chairman, the Committee is at its first meeting thereafter to appoint a new Chairman, and in the absence of the Chairman of Committee at any meeting, the meeting is to appoint a Chairman for the time being.

Power to Committee to make by-laws.
50 & 51 Vict. 42, 22.

(82.) The Committee may make by-laws for regulating any matters connected with the control, management, protection, and use of any property under their control. The by-laws may impose penalties for breaches thereof not exceeding 5l. for each offence, and they may be repealed, altered, varied, or re-enacted. There is a proviso that such by-laws are not to be repugnant to the law of Scotland, and before being acted on they are to be signed by a quorum of the Committee, and, except in so far as they relate solely to the officers or servants of the Committee, such by-laws must be approved of by the Magistrates and Council, or the Board, as the case may be, and must be approved of and confirmed by the Sheriff of the County. Nothing is to preclude the Magistrates and Council, or Board, as the case may be, from recovering the value of articles or things damaged, or the amount of the damage sustained, against all parties liable.

By-laws to be advertised in newspaper before confirmation. Manner of stating objections.
50 & 51 Vict. 42, 23.

(83.) No by-laws or alterations requiring confirmation are to be confirmed unless notice of the intention to apply for confirmation has been given in one or more newspapers published and circulated in the district 1 month at least before the hearing of the application for confirmation. Any party aggrieved by any such by-laws or alterations, on giving notice of the nature of his objection to the Clerk to the Committee 10 days before the hearing of the application for confirmation, may, by himself or counsel, attorney, or agent, be heard thereon. Not more than one party is to be heard upon the same matter of objection.

Exhibition of by-laws

(84.) For 1 month at least before any such application for confirmation of any by-laws or alterations thereof, a copy is

PART I.—DIGEST OF STATUTES. 41

to be kept at the office of the Clerk to the Committee, and is also to be put up in some conspicuous place in each of the Libraries and Museums, and all persons may, at all reasonable times, inspect such copy without fee or reward. The Clerk is to furnish every person who shall apply for the same with a copy thereof on payment of 6d. for every 100 words copied.

<small>previous to confirmation. 50 & 51 Vict. 42, 24.</small>

(85.) The Clerk is to give a printed copy of the by-laws in force to every person applying, without charge. A copy thereof is to be painted or placed on boards in some conspicuous part of each of the Libraries and Museums, and such boards with the by-laws thereon are to be renewed from time to time as occasion shall require, and are to be open to inspection free.

<small>Printed copy of by-laws to be provided. 50 & 51 Vict. 42, 25.</small>

(86.) All by-laws or alterations duly made and confirmed are, when published and put up, to be binding upon and be observed by all parties.

<small>By-laws to be in force. 50 & 51 Vict. 42, 26.</small>

(87.) The production of a copy of the by-laws authenticated by the signature of the Sheriff who has confirmed the same, and a copy of the by-laws not requiring such confirmation, authenticated by the Common Seal of the Committee, and signed by the Chairman of the Committee at the time when the same were made, shall be evidence of such by-laws in all cases for prosecution under the same, without proof of the signatures or common seal.

<small>Evidence of by-laws. 50 & 51 Vict. 42, 27.</small>

(88.) All penalties and forfeitures exigible under the "Libraries Act," and the Acts incorporated therewith, or under any by-law, may be recovered by an ordinary small-debt action in the name of the Clerk to the Committee before either the Sheriff or Justices of the District; and the same shall be payable to the Committee and shall be applied for the purposes of the Act. In any prosecution an excerpt from the books of the Committee, certified by the Clerk or other proper officer, shall be held equivalent to the books of the Committee, and all entries in the books of the Committee bearing that any book mentioned or referred to therein has been borrowed by the person complained against shall be taken and received as evidence of the fact, and the *onus probandi* shall be thrown on the party complained against, and if decree passes against such party, he shall be found liable in costs.

<small>Penalties and forfeitures to be recovered in the name of the Clerk. 50 & 51 Vict. 42, 28.</small>

(89.) All actions at the instance of the Committee shall be brought in the name of the Clerk, and in all actions against the Committee it shall be sufficient to call the Clerk as

<small>Actions by or against Committee.</small>

BOOK I.—LIBRARIES AND MUSEUMS.

50 & 51 Vict. 42, 29.
defender, and service on him shall be sufficient. All actions brought by or against the Clerk in his official character shall be continued by or against his successors without any action of transference.

Incorporation of sections of 10 & 11 Vict. 16; 50 & 51 Vict. 42, 16.
(90.) The "Commissioners Clauses Act, 1847," shall, with respect to the liabilities of the Commissioners, and to legal proceedings by or against the Commissioners, and with respect to mortgages to be executed by the Commissioners, excepting §§ 84, 86, and 87, except where expressly varied by the Act of 1871, be incorporated with it.

IRELAND.

18 & 19 Vict. 40; 57 & 58 Vict. 38.
(91.) The Irish "Public Libraries Acts," differing from both the English and the Scotch Statutes allied to it, contain hardly any provisions for the guidance in their business arrangements of those charged with its execution. They must therefore in a certain sense strike out a course for themselves, and would do well to conform to the provisions of the English and Scotch Acts in these matters, as near as may be.

PART I.—DIGEST OF STATUTES.

CHAPTER VI.

BORROWING POWERS UNDER THE "PUBLIC LIBRARIES ACTS."

ENGLAND AND WALES.

EVERY library authority, with the sanction of the Local Government Board, and in the case of commissioners appointed for a parish, with the sanction also of the vestry, may borrow money for the purposes of the Act on the security of any fund or rate applicable for those purposes. {Borrowing by library authority. 55 & 56 Vict. 53, 19.}

§§ 233, 234, 236-39 of the "Public Health Act, 1875," relating to borrowing by a local authority will apply, with necessary modifications, to all money borrowed by any library authority, as if the library authority were an urban authority; and as if references to the "Public Libraries Act" were substituted in those sections and in the forms therein mentioned for references to the "Public Health Act, 1875."

The Public Works Loan Commissioners may in manner provided by the "Public Works Loans Act, 1875," lend money to a library authority.

(93.) Where under the "Public Libraries Acts" the consent or approval of, or other act on the part of, the vestry of a rural parish is required in relation to any expense or Rate, the parish meeting is to be substituted for the vestry; and the expression "vestry" will include any meeting of ratepayers or voters. {56 & 57 Vict. 73, 7.}

(94.) A parish council for any of the following purposes, that is to say— {Borrowing by parish council. 56 & 57 Vict. 73, 12.}

(a) for purchasing any land, or building any buildings, which the council are authorised to purchase or build; and

(b) for any purpose for which the council are authorised to borrow; and

(c) for any permanent work or other thing which the council are authorised to execute or do, and the cost of which ought, in the opinion of the county council and the Local Government Board, to be spread over a term of years;

may, with the consent of the county council and the Local Government Board, borrow money in like manner and subject to the like conditions as a local authority may borrow for defraying expenses incurred in the execution of the "Public Health Acts"; and §§ 233, 234, 236-39 of the "Public Health Act, 1875," shall apply accordingly, except that the money shall be borrowed on the security of the Poor Rate and of the whole or part of the revenues of the parish council; and except that as respects the limit of the sum to be borrowed, one-half of the assessable value is to be substituted for the assessable value for two years.

<small>38 & 39 Vict. 55.</small>

A county council may lend to a parish council, and may, if necessary, without the sanction of the Local Government Board, and irrespectively of any limit of borrowing, raise the money by loan, subject to the like conditions and in the like manner as any other loan for the execution of their duties, and subject to any further conditions which the Local Government Board may impose.

A parish council is not to borrow for the purposes of any of the adoptive Acts otherwise than in accordance with the "Local Government Act, 1894"; but the charge for the purposes of any of the adoptive Acts will ultimately be on the Rate applicable to the purposes of that Act.

SCOTLAND.

<small>Power to Council or Board to borrow on Mortgage or Bond. 50 & 51 Vict. 42, 14.</small>

(95.) For carrying the Acts into execution, the Magistrates and Council, or the Board, as the case may be, may from time to time borrow at interest on Mortgage or Bond, on the security of the rate to be levied in pursuance of the Act, a sum of money not exceeding the capital sum represented by one-fourth part of the Library Rate, authorised by the Act, capitalised at the rate of 20 years' purchase; and on repayment of such sum, or any part thereof, they may from time to time re-borrow, but so that the whole sum borrowed at any one time shall not exceed the amount of the said capital sum after deducting therefrom any sums set apart as a sinking fund as hereinafter provided.

<small>Sinking Fund. 50 & 51 Vict. 42, 15.</small>

(96.) The Magistrates and Council, or the Board, as the case may be, are required to set apart annually, as a Sinking Fund for the extinction of capital sums borrowed under the

PART I.—DIGEST OF STATUTES. 45

authority of any Library Act, a sum equal to at least one-fiftieth part of the money so borrowed, and such Sinking Fund shall be from time to time applied in repayment of the money so borrowed, and to no other purpose, and shall be lodged in a joint-stock bank of issue in Scotland, or invested in Government Securities, or lent out at interest in the name and at the discretion of the Magistrates and Council, or the Board, as the case may be, until the same be applied for the purpose before specified.

(97.) The provisions of the "Commissioners Clauses Act, 1847," with respect to the liabilities of the Commissioners, and to legal proceedings by or against the Commissioners, and with respect to mortgages by the Commissioners, excepting §§ 84, 86, and 87, shall, unless herein expressly varied, be incorporated, and the several words and expressions in that Act shall in the "Libraries Act" have the same respective meanings, unless there be something in the subject or context repugnant to such construction. The expression "the special Act" shall mean the "Libraries Act"; and the expression "the Commissioners" shall mean the Magistrates and Council or Board and the Committee under the "Libraries Act." {Parts of 10 Vict. 16 incorporated. 50 & 51 Vict. 42, 16.}

IRELAND.

(98.) The Irish "Public Libraries Act, 1855," conferred no borrowing powers on those charged with its execution, but the Act of 1877 provides that for carrying the principal Act and that Act into execution the Council, Board, or Commissioners respectively may, with the approval of the Treasury, borrow on the security of a mortgage or bond of the Borough Fund or the Town Fund, or of the rates levied in pursuance of the principal Act, such sums of money as may be required, and the Commissioners of Public Works in Ireland may from time to time advance such sums. The clauses and provisions of the "Companies Clauses Consolidation Act, 1845," with respect to the borrowing of money on mortgage or bond, and the accountability of officers, and the recovery of damages and penalties, so far as such provisions may be applicable, are incorporated. {Powers to borrow on mortgage. 18 & 19 Vict. 40. 40 & 41 Vict. 15, 5. 8 Vict. 16.}

CHAPTER VII.

THE ACQUISITION OF LANDS, ETC., FOR THE PURPOSES OF THE "PUBLIC LIBRARIES ACTS."

ENGLAND AND WALES.

Provision as to acquisition and disposal of land.
55 & 56 Vict. 53, 12.

A LIBRARY Authority may purchase land, and the "Lands Clauses Acts," with the exception of the provisions relating to the purchase of land otherwise than by agreement, are incorporated.

The library authority of any urban district may with the sanction of the Local Government Board set apart for Library, etc., purposes any land vested in that authority.

A library authority may with the sanction of the Local Government Board sell or exchange land; money arising from the sale or received by way of equality of exchange, must be applied in or towards the purchase of other land better adapted for Library, etc., purposes; or it may be applied for any purpose for which capital money may be applied, and which is approved by the Local Government Board.

A library authority may let a house or building, or any part thereof, or any land vested in them for the purposes of the "Public Libraries Acts" which is not at the time required for those purposes, but it must apply the rents and profits thereof for the purposes of the Acts.

Vestry or district board may grant land.
55 & 56 Vict. 53, 23;
18 & 19 Vict. 120.

(100.) The Vestry or District Board constituted under the "Metropolis Management Act, 1855," for any parish mentioned in Schedule A. or district mentioned in Schedule B. to that Act, as amended by any subsequent Acts, may, if the "Public Libraries Acts" are in force in such parish or district, appropriate with the sanction of the Local Government Board for the purposes of the Acts any land which is vested in such vestry or board.

Power to grant

(101.) Any person holding land for ecclesiastical, parochial, or charitable purposes may grant or convey, by way of gift,

PART I.—DIGEST OF STATUTES. 47

sale, or exchange, for any of the purposes of the "Public Libraries Acts," any quantity of such land, not exceeding in any one case one acre. But— {charity land for purposes of this Act. 55 & 56 Vict. 53, 13.}
  (a) ecclesiastical property is not to be granted without the consent of the Ecclesiastical Commissioners;
  (b) parochial property is not to be granted save by the guardians of the poor law union comprising the parish to which the property belongs, or without the consent of the Local Government Board;
  (c) other charitable property is not to be granted without the consent of the Charity Commissioners;
  (d) the land taken in exchange or the money received for such sale is to be held on the same trusts as the land exchanged or sold;
  (e) land situated in the administrative county of London, or in any urban district containing over 20,000 inhabitants, which is held on trusts to be preserved as an open space, or on trusts which prohibit building thereon, is not to be granted.

Land granted to any library authority under this section may be held without any licence in mortmain.

(102.) All land and other real and personal property, howsoever acquired for any library, museum, art gallery, or school under the Act, is vested in the library authority. {Vesting of property. 55 & 56 Vict. 53, 14}

SCOTLAND.

(103.) The Magistrates and Council or Board, as the case may be, may from time to time appropriate, for the purposes of the Act, any lands or buildings vested in them, and may, out of the Library Rate, or out of money duly borrowed, purchase, feu, or rent any land, or any suitable building. They may, upon the land so appropriated, rented, feued, or purchased, erect any building suitable for Public Libraries, Public Museums, Schools for Science, Art Galleries, and Schools for Art, and may alter or extend any buildings, and repair and improve the same, and fit up, furnish, and supply the same with all requisite furniture, fittings, and conveniences. {Lands, etc. may be appropriated, purchased, or rented. 50 & 51 Vict. 42, 10.}

(104.) The provisions of the "Lands Clauses Consolidation (Scotland) Act, 1845," with respect to the purchase of lands by agreement, and with respect to the purchase-money or compensation coming to parties having limited interests, or prevented from treating or not making a title, and with {Parts of 8 Vict. 19, incorporated. 50 & 51 Vict. 42, 11.}

respect to conveyances of land, so far as such provisions are applicable to purchases, feus, or leases authorised by the "Libraries Act," and are not expressly varied, shall be incorporated. The expression "Special Act" shall be construed to mean the "Libraries Act, 1887," and the expression "the Promoters of the Undertaking" shall be construed to mean the Magistrates and Council, or the Board, as the case may be.

Lands, etc., may be sold or exchanged.
50 & 51 Vict. 42, 12.
(105.) The Magistrates and Council, or the Board, as the case may be, may sell any lands, buildings, or other property vested in them for the purposes of the Act, or exchange the same for any lands, buildings, or other property better adapted for such purposes, and the money so arising, and the property received in exchange, shall be applied for the purposes of the "Libraries Act."

Vesting of lands, etc.,
50 & 51 Vict. 42, 13.
(106.) The lands and buildings appropriated, purchased, or rented, and all other real or personal property whatever, presented to or purchased for any Library or Museum under the Act, is in the case of a burgh vested in the Magistrates and Council, and in the case of a parish in the Board.

IRELAND.

Lands, etc., may be appropriated, purchased, or rented for the purposes of the Act.
18 & 19 Vict. 40, 9.

47 & 48 Vict. 37, 2.
(107.) Any Council, Board, or Town Commissioners may, with the approval of the Treasury, appropriate for the purposes of the Act any lands vested in them, and may also, with such approval, purchase or rent any lands or buildings. They may, upon any lands so appropriated, purchased, or rented, erect any buildings for Libraries, or Museums, or Schools of Science and Art, and may rebuild, repair, improve, and fit up the same. These words are explained by a later Statute to mean that buildings may be erected for Public Libraries, Public Museums, Schools for Science, Art Galleries, and Schools for Art, or for any one or more of those objects.

8 Vict. 18 incorporated with the Act.
18 & 19 Vict. 40, 10.
(108.) The "Lands Clauses Consolidation Act, 1845," is incorporated by the Act; but the Council, Board, or Commissioners respectively shall not purchase or take any lands otherwise than by agreement.

Lands, etc., may be sold or exchanged.
18 & 19 Vict. 40, 11.
(109.) The Council, Board, or Commissioners may, with the like approval as is required for the purchase of lands, sell, for the purposes of the Act, any lands vested in them, or exchange the same for any lands better adapted for the purposes; and the moneys to arise from such sale or exchange, or a sufficient part thereof, shall be applied towards the purchase of other lands more suitable.

PART I.—DIGEST OF STATUTES. 49

(110.) The lands and buildings acquired in the way specified in the Act, and all other real or personal property whatever, presented to or purchased for any Library, or Museum, or School of Science and Art established under the Act, shall be vested in the Mayor, Aldermen, and Burgesses, or in the Town Commissioners, as the case may be. Property vested in Council or Commissioners. 18 & 19 Vict. 40, 13.

(111.) An urban authority may let a house or building, or part thereof, or any land vested in them, for Library, etc., purposes, which is not at the time required for those purposes. The rents and profits thereof are to be applied for the purposes of the Acts. Provision as to letting of land. 57 & 58 Vict. 38, 5.

(112.) Any person holding land for public or charitable purposes may grant or convey, by way of gift, sale, or exchange, for any of the purposes of the "Public Libraries Acts," any quantity of such land, not exceeding in any one case one acre. But (i.) charitable property is not to be so granted without the consent of the Commissioners of Charitable Donations and Bequests for Ireland, and, in the case of land charged with the repayment of an advance made under the "Glebe Loan (Ireland) Acts," without the consent of the Commissioners of Public Works in Ireland; (ii.) the land taken in exchange or the money received for such sale is to be held on the same trusts as the land exchanged or sold. Power to grant certain land for purposes of Acts. 57 & 58 Vict. 38, 6.

CHAPTER VIII.

RATES UNDER THE "PUBLIC LIBRARIES ACTS."

ENGLAND AND WALES.

Expenses of library authority, how defrayed.
55 & 56 Vict. 53, 18 (1).

THE expenses incurred in a library district, including all expenses in connection with ascertaining the opinion of the voters in the district, may be defrayed—

(i.) where the library district is a municipal borough, out of the borough fund or borough rate, or a separate Rate levied as the borough rate;

(ii.) where the library district is an urban district other than a borough, out of the rate applicable to the general expenses incurred under the "Public Health Acts," or a separate Rate levied as the rate so applicable;

(iii.) where the library district is a parish, out of a Rate to be raised with and as part of the Poor Rate, subject, however, to this qualification, that every person assessed to the poor rate in respect of lands used as arable, meadow, or pasture ground only, or as woodlands or market gardens, or nursery grounds, will be entitled to an allowance of two-thirds.

Special provision as to expenses in parishes.
55 & 56 Vict. 53, 18 (2, 3).

(114.) Where the library district is a parish, and is not combined with any other parish, then—

(i.) such amount only shall be raised out of a Rate as is from time to time sanctioned by the vestry;

(ii.) the vestry to be called for sanctioning the amount must be convened in the usual manner;

(iii.) the amount proposed to be raised for the purposes of the Acts must be expressed in the notice convening the vestry, and (if sanctioned) must be paid according to the order of the vestry to such person as may be appointed by the library authority to receive it;

(iv.) in the demand note for the rate there must be stated the proportion which the amount to be raised for the purposes of the Acts bears to the total rate.

PART I.—DIGEST OF STATUTES. 51

Where a parish or a part of a parish is annexed to a library district, so much of the said expenses as is chargeable to such parish or part are to be defrayed as if such parish or part were a separate library district; but the sanction of the vestry will not be required for raising the sums due from the parish.

(115.) No rate or addition to a rate levied for the purposes of the Acts for any one financial year in any library district may exceed one penny in the pound. The Acts may be adopted for any library district subject to a condition that the maximum rate or addition to a rate levied for the purposes of the Acts in the district or in any defined portion in any one financial year is not to exceed one halfpenny or not to exceed three farthings in the pound. Such limitation if fixed at one halfpenny may be subsequently raised to three farthings, or be altogether removed; or where it is for the time being fixed at three farthings it may be removed. Limitations on expenditure for purposes of Act. 55 & 56 Vict. 53, 2

(116.) Where a library authority accepts a grant from the Department of Science and Art towards the purchase of the site, or the erection, etc., of any school for science or art, or teacher's residence, or towards the furnishing of any such school, that authority may accept the grant upon the conditions prescribed by the Department, and may execute any instruments required by that Department, and upon payment of the grant will be bound by such conditions and instruments. Power to library authority to accept parliamentary grant 55 & 56 Vict. 53, 17

(117.) Nothing in the general Acts limits or alters any rate which a library authority is authorised to levy under a local Act. Saving. 55 & 56 Vict. 53, 29.

(118.) The question of a limit to rates is further dealt with in the "Local Government Act, 1894," which refers to Rates under adoptive Acts, of which the "Public Libraries Act" is one. That Act is not to be deemed to alter the incidence of charge of any rate levied to defray expenses under any adoptive Act; and any such rate is to be made and charged as heretofore, and any property applicable to the payment of such expenses will continue to be so applicable. 56 & 57 Vict. 73, 7 (6).

(119.) A parish council must not, without the consent of a parish meeting, incur expenses which will involve a rate exceeding threepence in the pound for any local financial year, or which will involve a loan. Restrictions on expenditure. 56 & 57 Vict. 73, 11.

A parish council must not, without the approval of the county council, incur any expense which will involve a loan.

The sum raised in any local financial year by a parish

council for their expenses (other than expenses under the adoptive Acts) must not exceed a sum equal to a rate of sixpence in the pound on the rateable value. "Expenses" includes any annual charge, whether of principal or interest, in respect of any loan.

The expenses of a parish council and parish meeting are to be paid out of the poor rate; where there is a parish council that council must pay the expenses of the parish meeting; the parish council, and where there is no parish council the chairman of the parish meeting, will, for the purpose of obtaining payment of such expenses, have the same powers as a board of guardians have for obtaining contributions to their common fund.

The demand note for any rate thus to be levied must state the proportion of the rate levied for the expenses of the council or meeting, and the proportion (if any) levied for any adoptive Act, such as the "Public Libraries Act."

56 & 57 Vict. 73, 19 (7).

(120.) In a rural parish having no parish council, a rate levied for the expenses of the parish meeting, when added to expenses under any of the adoptive Acts, must not exceed sixpence in the pound in any local financial year.

(121.) Some miscellaneous provisions connected with financial matters applicable to England and Wales may here be brought together.

Charity Library.
55 & 56 Vict. 53, 16.

(122.) The library authority of any library district may, with the consent of the voters and of the Charity Commissioners, make building and maintenance agreements with the governing body of any library established or maintained out of funds subject to the jurisdiction of the Charity Commissioners, and situate in or near the library district. In case of inability, objection, or failure on the part of the governing body to enter into such an agreement, the Charity Commissioners may become party to the agreement on behalf of the governing body.

Adjustment of interests on termination of agreement.
55 & 56 Vict. 53, 24.

(123.) Any agreement between two or more vestries or library authorities, or between a library authority and any other body, may provide that on its termination an adjustment shall be made of the interests of the several parties thereto in any property, and as to the mode in which the adjustment shall be arrived at. In the event of dispute the adjustment must be made by an arbitrator appointed by the Local Government Board.

Saving for Oxford.
55 & 56 Vict. 53, 25.

(124.) Nothing in the Act is to interfere with the operation of the Act 28 & 29 Vict. 108, so far as it relates to a rate for the Oxford public library.

SCOTLAND.

(125.) The expenses of carrying the Act into execution, including all sums payable in respect of interest and sinking fund for money authorised to be borrowed, and all sums necessary for the maintenance of the Libraries and Museums, or for the purchase of the articles and things authorised to be purchased, are to be paid out of the Library Rate, which is to be levied, in the case of a Burgh, as the Burgh General Assessment; and in the case of a Parish, as the assessment leviable under the Act 8 & 9 Vict. 83.(a) — *Expenses of executing Act. 50 & 51 Vict. 42, 7.*

(126.) The Library Rate to be levied in any year is in no case to exceed 1d. in the £ of yearly rent or annual value as appearing on the valuation roll; and where, under the provisions of any General or Local Police Act, the Burgh General Assessment is or may be levied at a higher Rate upon lands or premises above a certain fixed rent than upon lower rented lands or premises, such provisions, so far as they authorise such differential Rate, are not to be applicable to the Library Rate. — *Rate not to exceed 1d. the £. 50 & 51 Vict. 42, 8.*

IRELAND.

(127.) The amount of the Rate to be levied in any Borough or Town, in any one year, for the purposes of the Act is not to exceed 1d. in the £, and in any such Borough is to levied in the same manner as the Borough Rate, and in any such Town is to be levied in the same manner as the Town Rate. — *Rate not to exceed 1d. in the £. 18 & 19 Vict. 40, 8.*

(128.) When a vote is taken as to the adoption of the "Public Libraries Act, 1855," in addition to the simple vote "Yes" or "No," such voting-paper may stipulate that its adoption shall be subject to a limitation to some lower rate of assessment than the maximum allowed by Parliament at the time. Such lower limit, if once adopted, cannot be subsequently altered except by another public vote. — *Limit of assessment. 40 & 41 Vict. 54, 2.*

(129.) Doubts having arisen as to whether authorities acting under the "Public Libraries Acts" had power to fulfil the conditions required for a Parliamentary grant in aid of the establishment of a School of Science and Art, it has been enacted that where any library authority accepts a Parliamentary grant from the Privy Council towards the purchase of the site, or the erection, etc., of any School for Science or Art, or teacher's residence, or towards the furnishing of any — *Power of library authority to accept Parliamentary grant. 47 & 48 Vict. 37, 1.*

(a) This is the "Poor Law Amendment (Scotland) Act, 1845."

BOOK· I.—LIBRARIES AND MUSEUMS.

such school, such authority shall have power to accept the grant upon the conditions prescribed by the Privy Council, and may execute such instruments as may be required, and upon payment of the grant will be bound by such conditions and instruments.

Power to urban authority to accept Parliamentary grant.
57 & 58 Vict. 38, 8.

(130.) Where an urban authority accepts a grant from the Department of Science and Art towards the purchase of the site, or the erection, etc., of any School for Science or Art, or teacher's residence, or towards the furnishing of any such school, that authority may accept the grant upon the conditions prescribed by the Department, and may execute any instruments required by that Department, and upon payment of the grant will be bound by such conditions and instruments.(*a*)

Expenses of Act.
57 & 58 Vict. 38, 9.

(131.) The expenses incurred in the execution of the Act of 1894 are to be defrayed as provided by the principal Act. Where in any urban district a limit is by law imposed upon the rating power of the urban authority, such authority may impose and levy the rate authorised by the principal Act notwithstanding such limit.

Adjustment of interests on termination of agreement.
57 & 58 Vict. 38, 10.

(132.) Any agreement under the Act of 1894, between two or more urban authorities, or between an urban authority and any other body, may provide that on the termination of the agreement an adjustment shall be made of the interests of the parties in any property to the provision of which they have contributed. In the event of any dispute the adjustment must, on the application of any of the parties, be made by an arbitrator appointed by the Local Government Board.

Power to make rules.
57 & 58 Vict. 38, 11.

(133.) The Local Government Board may make Rules for carrying into effect the objects of the Act. Those rules are to be laid before Parliament, and are to be judicially noticed and have effect as if enacted by the Act.

(*a*) This enactment, it will be noticed, is nearly a repetition of that mentioned in the previous paragraph.

PART I.—DIGEST OF STATUTES. 55

CHAPTER IX.

ACCOUNTS AND AUDIT UNDER THE "PUBLIC LIBRARIES ACTS."

ENGLAND AND WALES.

SEPARATE accounts are to be kept of the receipts and expenditure of every library authority. Those accounts are to be audited in the case of a library authority which is an urban authority, as the accounts of that authority under the "Public Health Acts." Accounts and audit. 55 & 56 Vict. 53, 20.

The accounts of a library authority being commissioners are to be audited yearly by a district auditor as if they were Poor Law accounts within the "District Auditors Act, 1879." 42 & 43 Vict 6.

The accounts of any library authority other than the council of a municipal borough are to be open at all reasonable times to the inspection, free of charge, of any ratepayer. A ratepayer may without charge make copies of those accounts. If any library authority or person having the custody of the accounts fails to allow them to be inspected, or copies to be made, such authority or person will be liable on summary conviction to a fine of 5*l*. or less.

(135.) The foregoing provisions respecting Library accounts must be taken in connection with the analogous provisions of the "Local Government Act, 1894," where it is a question of audit.

SCOTLAND.

(136.) The Magistrates and Council of a Burgh. or the Board of a Parish, are to keep books in which are to be entered true and regular accounts of their receipts, payments, and liabilities, which books are, at all reasonable times, to be open to the inspection of every person liable to be assessed for the Library Rate. The Magistrates and Council, or Board, as the case may be, are to cause such accounts to be annually audited by competent auditors, not members of the Accounts to be open to inspection, and to be audited and published annually. 50 & 51 Vict. 42, 9.

56	BOOK I.—LIBRARIES AND MUSEUMS.

Committee, after which audit the accounts are to be signed by 2 of the magistrates and Council, or 2 members of the Board, and an abstract thereof similarly signed is to be inserted in one or more newspapers circulated in the Burgh or Parish.

Estimates to be made up every April. 50 & 51 Vict. 42, 30.
(137.) The Committee every April is to cause to be made an estimate of the sums required to defray the interest of money borrowed, the payment of the sinking fund, and the expense of maintaining the Libraries or Museums for the year after Whit-Sunday then next to come, and for purchasing the books, articles, and things authorised. The Committee is to report the same to the Magistrates and Council or to the Board, and the Magistrates and Council, or the Board, are to provide the amount required out of the Library Rate to be levied by them, and to pay over to the Committee the sum necessary, according to the estimate.

IRELAND.

Accounts to be kept. 18 & 19 Vict. 40, 5.
(138.) Councils or Boards in Boroughs, and Commissioners in Towns, are to keep distinct accounts of their receipts, expenditure, and liabilities in connection with the execution of the Act.

The accounts to be audited, sent to the Lord Lieutenant, and open to inspection. 18 & 19 Vict. 40, 6.
(139.) Such accounts are to be audited in the same way as all other accounts of such Borough or Town respectively are audited, and the Council, Board, or Town Commissioners are, within one month after the accounts have been audited, to transmit to the Lord Lieutenant a correct copy of them; they are also within the time aforesaid to cause a copy of such accounts to be deposited in the office of the Clerk, which copy is to be open to the inspection of all householders of such Borough or Town respectively. Copies are also to be delivered to any householder applying for the same, upon payment of a reasonable charge, to be fixed by the Council, Board or Town Commissioners, as the case may be.

PART II.
OFFICIAL DOCUMENTS.

THERE is no one Department of State specially charged to supervise the general working of the "Public Libraries Acts," and therefore there are few materials available to be ranked under the term "Official Documents." The Local Government Board controls, in some measure, the financial arrangements of any Local Authorities which may undertake the working of the Acts, but that control is for a specific and limited purpose, and does not touch questions of general administration. When Schools of Science and Art are worked by Local Authorities, in connection with Public Libraries or Museums, the Science and Art Department at South Kensington comes to some extent in contact with such authorities, but this again is only for a limited purpose.

AUDIT ORDER OF THE LOCAL GOVERNMENT BOARD AS TO THE ACCOUNTS OF PUBLIC LIBRARIES AND MUSEUMS.

To the Commissioners for Public Libraries and Museums appointed under the "Public Libraries Act, 1855," or the "Public Libraries Act, 1892";—

To the District Auditors for the time being authorised to audit the Accounts of the said Commissioners respectively ;—

And to all others whom it may concern.

WHEREAS by Sections 3 and 5 of the "District Auditors Act, 1879," it is enacted as follows :—

"3. Where the accounts of the receipts and expenditure
"of a Local Authority are audited by a District Auditor,
"the Local Authority shall prepare and submit to the
"District Auditor at every audit (other than an extra-
"ordinary audit held in pursuance of Section 6 of
"the 'Poor Law Amendment Act, 1866'), a Financial
"Statement in duplicate in the prescribed Form and
"containing the prescribed particulars; one of such
"duplicates shall have the stamp charged under this
"Act affixed thereon, and the Auditor at the conclusion
"of the audit shall cancel that stamp, and certify on
"each duplicate, in the prescribed Form, the amount in
"words at length of the expenditure so audited and
"allowed, and further, that the regulations with respect
"to such Statement have been duly complied with, and
"that he has ascertained by the audit the correctness
"of the Statement."

"5. Where any accounts of the receipts and expenditure
"of a Local Authority are subject by law to be audited
"by a District Auditor, the Local Government Board
"may from time to time by Order make, and when
"made revoke and vary, such regulations as seem to
"the Board necessary or proper respecting the audit of
"such accounts, including the form of keeping the
"accounts of the Local Authority and their officers, the
"day or days to which the accounts are to be made up,
"the time within which they are to be examined by the
"Local Authority, the mode in which, if it is so pre-
"scribed, they are to be certified by the Local Authority
"or any officer of that Authority, the mode of publishing
"the time and place of holding the audit, the persons
"by whom such accounts are to be produced for audit,
"and the mode of conducting the audit, and an Order
"under this section shall be deemed to be an Order
"within the meaning of section ninety-eight of the
"'Poor Law Amendment Act, 1834.'"

And whereas the Commissioners for Public Libraries and
Museums, being Local Authorities, the Accounts of whose
receipts and expenditure are audited as mentioned in the
said Section 3, We, the Local Government Board, by an
Order dated the 25th day of September, 1886, prescribed
the Form of the Financial Statement to be prepared and
submitted to the District Auditor by such Commissioners;

PART II.—OFFICIAL DOCUMENTS.

And whereas it is expedient that the said Order should be rescinded, that a fresh Form of Financial Statement should be prescribed, and that Regulations should be prescribed as hereinafter mentioned :

NOW THEREFORE, We hereby rescind the above cited Order, and We hereby Order and Prescribe as follows :—

ARTICLE I.—The regulations contained in this Order shall be observed with respect to the Financial Statement and the Accounts of the Commissioners for Public Libraries and Museums, as such Local Authorities as aforesaid, except in so far as We may from time to time assent to any departure from such regulations.

ARTICLE II.—The Financial Statement to be prepared and submitted to the District Auditor in duplicate by the said Commissioners, in accordance with the provisions of the Section first above recited, shall be in the Form in the Schedule to this Order, and shall contain the particulars therein specified ; and the Certificate of the District Auditor to be appended to each such duplicate shall be in the Form set forth at the foot of the said Statement.

ARTICLE III.—The Accounts of the said Commissioners and of their officers shall be made up and balanced to the Twenty-fifth day of March in each year.

[Appended to this Order there are a number of elaborate blank columns of Tabular Matter which it has not been deemed necessary to reproduce in this volume. Copies of the whole document in its complete form may be purchased of the Queen's Printers.]

> Given under the seal of office of the Local Government Board this 26th day of November, 1892.
>
> H. H. FOWLER, *President.*
> S. B. PROVIS, *Assistant Secretary.*

60   BOOK I.—LIBRARIES AND MUSEUMS.

PART III.

PRECEDENTS OF FORMS, ETC.

I.

REGULATIONS FOR A PUBLIC LIBRARY AND MUSEUM.(a)

55 & 56 Vict. 53, 15 (2).
Duties of Librarian.

1. The Chief Librarian shall have the general superintendence of the Library and Museum, and shall be responsible for the safe keeping of the books, newspapers, specimens, and other property belonging thereto. He shall keep such books of account and registers as the Library Committee shall require, and shall comply with all the lawful directions of the Committee applicable to his office.

Committee not to divide property.

2. The Library Committee shall not give or divide any money or property to or between any of its members.

Days and hours of opening.

3. The Library, Reading-Room, and Museum shall be open to the public from 10 A.M. to 9 P.M. every day except Sunday, Christmas Day, and Good Friday, and except such other days as the Committee may from time to time deem necessary for the execution of repairs or for cleaning the premises.

Admission.

4. No charge for admission shall be made, but the Librarian and attendants are authorised to exclude persons who appear intoxicated, or in an uncleanly condition, or who are under [14] years of age.

Prohibitions.

5. No audible conversation is permitted in the Library or in the Reading-Room; nor is smoking, gaming, betting, or profane or indecent language allowed in any part of the

(a) In Scotland these may be "By-Laws" with the legal attributes thereof. (See 50 & 51 Vict. 42, 22).

PART III.—PRECEDENTS OF FORMS, ETC. 61

building. Refreshments are only to be served or taken in the rooms (if any) which are prescribed for the purpose.

6. No visitor shall be allowed to pass within the railing which separates the tables from the book-cases, nor to remove any book from a shelf except by permission of an attendant. *Visitors not to remove books.*

7. Every person on entering the building shall write, or cause to be written, his name, residence, and occupation, in a book to be provided for that purpose; and such signature shall be deemed to imply that the writer is prepared to admit that these By-Laws are binding on him. Without such signature as aforesaid, no person shall be permitted to use either the Library, the Reading-Room, or the Museum. Wilfully giving a false name or a false address shall subject the offender to a penalty as hereinafter prescribed. *Visitors to enter their names.*

8. Every reader shall apply for the books he wants by entering their names on tickets provided for the purpose. He shall sign each ticket, and such signature shall operate as a receipt for the book named on such ticket; and he shall, before quitting the Library, return each book into the hands of an attendant, and claim the re-delivery of the corresponding receipt, with the view of its being cancelled; otherwise he will be held responsible for the book to which it refers. *Application for books.*

9. Every reader who shall leave the Library or Reading-Room without returning to the Librarian, or to an attendant, any book lent to him, or who shall soil, write in, or otherwise damage any book, may be called upon to pay the full value of the said book, or to replace the said book within [one] week with a new copy of the said book of equal value; but in any such case he shall be entitled to receive the damaged copy. *Return of books.*

10. The Librarian shall exclude any person who shall neglect or decline to comply with any of these By-laws; and he shall not permit any person to remain on the premises who shall wilfully offend against any By-Law, or be guilty of any disorderly or improper conduct. He may also for sufficient reasons withhold any book from any person desirous of borrowing the same. Any person who may consider himself aggrieved by any act of the Librarian may appeal to the Library Committee. *Powers of Librarian.*

11. Catalogues shall be kept on the tables for the use of visitors. *Catalogues.*

12. Readers desirous of recommending books for addition *Suggestion book.*

to the Library, or of making any suggestions as to its management, may do so in the "Suggestion Book" provided for that purpose. Such book shall be laid before the Library Committee at stated intervals. Readers making entries in that book must append their names and addresses.

Illustrated works.
13. Certain costly illustrated works are only issued after a written application to the Library Committee. Illustrations of all kinds may be copied, but not traced, it having been found that the practice of tracing often leads to serious damage being done to illustrations.

Damage to books.
14. Readers are particularly requested to take care not to soil any books lent to them, nor to turn down the leaves. They are also requested to report to the Librarian any accidental injury which may happen to a book whilst in their possession, or which they may discover to have occurred previously.

Loan of books.
15. Under certain regulations hereafter set forth, certain classes of books may be borrowed for removal from the premises; but, except in accordance with those special regulations, no book, map, manuscript, or newspaper shall be removed by any visitor from the Library or the Reading-Room on any pretence whatever.

Regulations as to borrowing.
16. No person shall be allowed to borrow a book from the Library for perusal elsewhere without first filling up and signing a paper in the form marked A. (see *post*); nor without also (if required by the Librarian) obtaining a Ratepayer to become a surety for him, and such Ratepayer will be required to sign a voucher in the form marked B. (see *post*). This engagement will remain in force until notice in writing of his desire to withdraw from it be given to the Librarian by the person making it; the Librarian will give a release on ascertaining that no liability has been incurred, or if incurred, upon ascertaining that the liability has ceased. This voucher must be [signed in the presence of and] delivered to the Librarian, who may, if he thinks proper, delay for a reasonable time, not exceeding [3] days, the grant of books to the person recommended, in order to permit of inquiry respecting him or the Ratepayer signing the voucher. When the name of a person desiring to be enrolled as a borrower is duly entered in the book kept for that purpose, the borrower will receive a ticket, the production of which from time to time will entitle him (subject to these By-Laws) to borrow books for the term of one year from the date of issue of the said ticket, but no borrower shall be per-

PART III.—PRECEDENTS OF FORMS, ETC. 63

mitted to have more than [3] books in his possession at the same time.

17. The same Ratepayer shall not at one and the same time be surety for more than [3] different borrowers without the special sanction of the Library Committee. *Restriction on sureties.*

18. All books borrowed must be returned to the Library within the time specified on the respective covers. For every book not duly returned, a fine of [1d.] shall be paid for the whole or any portion of the first week, and a fine of [1d.] for [every week] or portion of a week afterwards. At the end of the [8th week] after the expiration of the period for which the book may be kept, application will be made to the borrower or to the borrower's surety for the return of the book, or payment of its value. *Books to be returned within specified times.*

19. If in any case [6 months] shall have elapsed between the due return of a book lent, and an application for another, a new voucher must be produced, as on a first application. *Renewal of vouchers.*

20. The Librarian shall carefully examine, or cause to be examined, each book on its return, and if the same be found to have sustained any disfigurement, or injury, he shall require the borrower or his surety to pay the amount of the injury done, or otherwise to procure a new copy of the book of equal value to the one injured; in the latter case the person who replaces the book shall be entitled to the damaged copy at the time when he deposits the new one. Books thus ceasing to be the property of the Library shall in all cases be stamped as follows:—"   Public Library: removed by authority as damaged." Books lost or stolen shall continue the property of the Library, although replaced or paid for. *Books to be examined.*

21. No borrower shall wilfully alter or erase any figure on the label of a book whilst the same is in his custody. All books borrowed from the Library must be returned, irrespective of the time allowed for reading, on or before [June 22] in each year, when the Library will be closed until [July 1]. And all books borrowed must also be returned at such other times as may be appointed by the Committee, of which [14 days'] previous notice will be posted in the Library. Borrowers offending against this By-Law will incur a penalty of [1s.], and will risk the forfeiture of their privilege of borrowing books unless they can prove ignorance of the notice. *Labels not to be tampered with.*

22. Every borrower who is about to leave the neighbourhood, or who intends to cease using the Library, is requested to return his ticket to the Librarian to have it cancelled; *Borrowers leaving the place.*

otherwise he and his surety will be held responsible for any books that may be issued in his name.

Addresses. 23. Every borrower when he changes his residence is required to hand his ticket to the Librarian and notify his new address, otherwise he will risk the forfeiture of his privilege of borrowing books.

Tickets to be produced. 24. Every borrower must on demand produce his ticket each time that he makes application for a book; and borrowers are cautioned against losing their tickets, as they will be held responsible for any books that may be issued in their names. Tickets that are lost can only be replaced at the expiration of [one week's] written notice to the Librarian and on the payment of [6d.]. In the interim the issue of books to the borrower shall be suspended.

Books not to be lent by borrowers. 25. No borrower shall part with the possession of a book entrusted to him, or lend it to any person other than to a member of his own family resident under the same roof as himself.

Re-borrowing. 26. No book can be renewed if another person has applied to borrow it. Books cannot be exchanged more than once in the same day.

Delivery of borrowed books. 27. No borrower on returning a book shall leave it on the counter, or give it to another borrower, but he shall deliver it to the Librarian or to an assistant. Every borrower is held responsible for any book not duly delivered as aforesaid.

Recovery of fines. 28. If a borrower shall not bring back to the Library within due time any book lent to him, or shall refuse or neglect to pay on demand any fine, or the amount of any injury for which he is responsible under these By-Laws, or to procure another copy of a book as before provided, then such fine, the amount of such injury, or the value of such book, shall be a debt due from such borrower and recoverable either from him or his surety, or from both of them jointly, at the discretion of the Library Committee, by process of Law.

Damage to property. 29. The preceding By-Laws shall be applicable, so far as may be, to all cases where damage or injury is done to any property in the Library or Museum, whether books or not.

Applications for books. 30. Every person who desires to borrow a book for removal from the Library is advised to present a list of at least [6] books likely to be useful to him and in the order of his preference, so that in case one book may be out another may be offered in its stead. Applications for single books, and also verbal applications, have been found to cause great

PART III.—PRECEDENTS OF FORMS, ETC. 65

inconvenience, and cannot be permitted. Every list drawn up in accordance with the foregoing requirement must contain the "Class Letter," "Catalogue Number," and "Title," accurately set out for the guidance of the Librarian in looking for the books. He must also sign a receipt for each book that is issued to him, and each such receipt will be re-delivered to him when the book to which it relates is duly returned to the Librarian in proper condition.

31. Every person who shall offend against any of the foregoing By-Laws to which no penalty is affixed shall pay for every such offence a penalty of £2, to be recovered according to the provisions of the "Summary Jurisdiction Acts." Provided, nevertheless, that the Justices or Court before whom any complaint shall be made for a breach of any of these By-Laws may, if they see fit, reduce this or any penalty herein prescribed.(a) Penalties.

II.

BORROWER'S TICKET (SIMPLEST FORM).

MANCHESTER PUBLIC FREE LIBRARIES.

Title and No. of Book requested ...
....
Signature...
Address..
Occupation........................ Date ....

Books must not be taken from the Reading-Room, and must be handed to the attendants when done with.

(a) Let it be noted that there is no power to insert this penalty clause in Regulations made for Libraries established in England and Wales or Ireland'; it is only a Scotch power at present.

F

III.

Borrower's Ticket (More Complete Form).

BRIGHTON PUBLIC LIBRARY.—REFERENCE LIBRARY.

READER'S TICKET.

Author.	Title of Work.	Case.	Shelf.	No.

1.—Readers must not order more than one work on the same Ticket.

2.—Every Book must be returned into the Assistant's hands by the Reader, who will be held responsible for it until the Receipt-Ticket has been given him by the Assistant.

3.—Readers are requested to report any damage or imperfection which they may discover in the books they receive.

4.—Tracing is forbidden. In copying, the paper must not be laid upon the pages of the book.

5.—It is expressly forbidden to *take out of the Reading-Rooms* any book or other article belonging to the Library.

6.—Applications for books *to read at home* must be made at the Window in the Lobby between 10 A.M. and 9 P.M.

F. W. MADDEN, M.R.A.S., *Librarian.*

Reader's Signature ....

Reader's Address ....

Date .... 18.........

IV.

FORM OF LABEL FOR BORROWED BOOKS.

EASTBOURNE FREE PUBLIC LIBRARY.

LENDING DEPARTMENT.

Borrowers are requested not to leave the Books on the Counter, nor to give them into the hands of other Borrowers, but to deliver them to the Library Assistants.

Borrowers' Cards are not transferable.

Books lost or injured while in charge of Borrowers must be replaced, or the amount chargeable for their loss or injury must be paid by the Borrowers or their Guarantors.

Borrowers detaining Books beyond the time allowed for reading will be fined one penny per week or any portion of a week. When books are kept more than 4 weeks, printed notices shall be sent to the Borrowers, who will be required to defray expenses.

If the figures on the label of any Book be altered or erased while the Book is in charge of a Borrower, his card shall be forthwith suspended.

The Library is open for the delivery and return of Books from TEN o'clock in the Forenoon until NINE o'clock in the Evening, except on Friday, when the Library closes at Two o'clock in the afternoon.

BORROWERS REQUIRED TO GIVE NOTICE OF CHANGE OF RESIDENCE.

SPECIAL NOTICE.

☞ All Books borrowed from the Library must be returned annually, irrespective of the time allowed for reading, on or before June 30, when the Library will be closed for such period as the Committee shall appoint. Borrowers neglecting to comply with this regulation will be fined the sum of threepence for each day in default, and be liable to the loss of their privileges.

Class .... No. ....

☞ Time allowed for reading this Work, 14 days, including the day of issue.

N.B.—Works in Classes F and J will not be renewed; all others may be renewed once.

⁎ The Committee confidently rely on the good feeling of those who may use the Library for the conscientious and careful protection of every Book from injury, and for the punctual observance of the conditions.

By Order,

THE COMMITTEE.

F 2

V.

FORM OF GENERAL APPLICATION TO BORROW BOOKS.

No. ....

EASTBOURNE FREE PUBLIC LIBRARY.

To the Mayor, Aldermen, and Burgesses of the Borough of Eastbourne.

NAME.

I _____

| ADDRESS. | OCCUPATION. |

of No.

being over 14 years of age, apply for a Ticket entitling me to the privilege of Borrowing Books from the Free Public Library, according to the Rules adopted by the Committee; and

NAME.

I _____

ADDRESS.

of No.

being a Burgess of the said Borough, beg to recommend the applicant as a fit and proper person to be entitled to such privilege, and hereby undertake to replace or pay the value (not exceeding Twenty Shillings (a)) of any Book belonging to the Corporation of the Borough of Eastbourne, which shall be lost or materially injured by the said Borrower.

Dated this .... day of ...., 189 ......

Signature of Guarantor ....

Witness ....

Address ....

This Voucher must be signed in ink and be left at the Library for examination, and on the following day, on being found correct, the Applicant will, on application, receive a ticket (for which one penny will be charged), entitling him or her to borrow books.

When the person who has signed this engagement shall desire to withdraw from the responsibility, he must give notice in writing to the Librarian, who will release him as soon as he shall have ascertained that no liability has been incurred.

J. H. HARDCASTLE, *Librarian.*

N.B.—This Voucher must be signed by a responsible Guarantor, whose name is on the Burgess List for the time being of the Borough of Eastbourne, and it must be renewed every two years.

☞ Borrowers are required to give immediate notice of any change of Residence.

It is necessary that Borrowers should be Ratepayers of the Municipal Borough, or be Residents therein of more than 14 years of age.

(a) If this amount is unlimited or is over 5l. the guarantee should be stamped.

PART III.—PRECEDENTS OF FORMS, ETC. 69

VI.

FORM OF APPLICATION BY BURGESS TO BORROW BOOKS.

No..............

EASTBOURNE FREE PUBLIC LIBRARY.

To the *Mayor, Aldermen, and Burgesses of the Borough of Eastbourne.*

I, the undersigned, being a Burgess of the Borough of Eastbourne, apply for a Ticket entitling me to the privilege of Borrowing Books from the Free Public Library, and I hereby undertake to replace or pay the value (not exceeding Twenty Shillings) of any Book belonging to the Library which shall be lost, injured, or not duly returned by me. I also further undertake to pay the fines, and all expenses incurred in recovering the same, in accordance with the Rules and Regulations of the Committee, to which in all respects I bind myself.

Signed ....

ADDRESS. Change of Address to be immediately notified.	OCCUPATION. For Statistical Purposes only.	AGE.
Of No.		

Dated this .... day of ...., 189....

This Voucher must be signed in ink and be left at the Library for examination, and on the following day, on being found correct, the Applicant will, on application, receive a Ticket (for which one penny will be charged), entitling the owner to borrow books. Tickets must be applied for personally and renewed every two years.

Persons whose names do not appear on the current Burgess List should produce their last Rate or Rent Receipt, if desiring to borrow upon their own responsibility. A Burgess List may be seen at the Library.

Books can be taken out of the Library by persons resident in, or ratepayers of the Borough of Eastbourne, but no books can be had by any person under 14 years of age.

J. H. HARDCASTLE, *Librarian.*

VII.

FORM OF BEQUEST TO A PUBLIC LIBRARY.

I BEQUEATH the sum of   to the [Mayor, Aldermen, and Burgesses acting by the Council of the Borough of   , *or* to the District Council, *or* the Free Library Commissioners of   , *or as the case may be*] to be applied by such [Council *or* Commissioners] for the purposes of the Free Library and Museum, or either of them, and I direct that such sum shall be paid, free of legacy duty, out of such part of my personal estate as may be legally applied for such purposes, and I declare that such sum may be paid to the Treasurer for the time being of the said [Council or Board or Commissioners], whose receipts shall be a valid discharge of the same. (*a*)

(*a*) See the " Mortmain and Charitable Uses Act, 1888 " (51 & 52 Vict., 42) as regards bequests.

PART IV.

STATUTES RELATING TO PUBLIC LIBRARIES AND MUSEUMS.

THE Statutes here printed are given in their chronological order, without any attempt at classification.

It is believed that for purposes of reference the inconvenience of having to examine several sets of Statutes to find any required one, is greater, on the whole, than the inconvenience of having kindred Statutes separated from one another by others, because those others happen to be of intermediate date.

Repealed provisions are either omitted altogether, or where for any reason entire omission would have been undesirable, such provisions are printed in italic.

The Marginal Notes have been in many cases simplified and shortened, so as to make them more convenient.

The Foot-notes are designed to prevent a person who consults only the Statutes being misled for want of sufficient cross references to earlier and later Statutes.

Having regard to the limited constituency (so to speak) to which this work appeals, it has not been deemed expedient to increase its bulk by reprinting here all the various Clauses Acts, which, in whole or in part, as the case may be, are incorporated by the "Public Libraries Acts."

The text of the *Revised Statutes*, up to date, has been made use of as far as possible; and omissions by reason of repeals, etc., are therefore not particularised in citations from that edition of the Statutes. But where the citations are from the *Law Reports Statutes*, exclusively, reasons are given to explain omissions. Formal words ("Be it enacted, etc." . . . . .) are uniformly struck out everywhere that they occur in the original text at the commencement of sections.

[8 Vict.] *Companies Clauses Consolidation* [c 16]

8 VICT. 16.

An Act for consolidating in one Act certain Provisions usually inserted in Acts with respect to the Constitution of Companies incorporated for carrying on Undertakings of a Public Nature. (a) [8th May, 1845.]

Revised Statutes, 2nd ed., vol. vii. pp. 444, 459, and 465.

And with respect to the borrowing of money by the Company on mortgage or bond, be it enacted as follows: — *Power to Borrow Money.*

38. If the Company be authorised by the special Act to borrow money on mortgage or bond, it shall be lawful for them, subject to the restrictions contained in the special Act, to borrow on mortgage or bond such sums of money as shall, from time to time, by an order of a general meeting of the Company, be authorised to be borrowed, not exceeding in the whole the sum prescribed by the special Act, and for securing the repayment of the money so borrowed, with interest, to mortgage the undertaking, and the future calls on the shareholders, or to give bonds in manner hereinafter mentioned. *Company may borrow such sums as shall be authorised by a general meeting.*

(a) The sections and schedules here given are incorporated by the Irish Libraries Act of 1877. They were incorporated by the repealed Act of 1855 as to England and Wales, but the incorporation of the provisions with respect to the borrowing of money was repealed by the Act of 1887, and *none* of the provisions are incorporated by the English Act of 1892. Nor are they incorporated by the Scotch Act.

39. If, after having borrowed any part of the money so authorised to be borrowed on mortgage or bond, the Company pay off the same, it shall be lawful for them again to borrow the amount so paid off, and so from time to time; *If borrowed money be repaid, Company may again borrow.*

But such power of re-borrowing shall not be exercised without the authority of a general meeting of the Company, unless the money be so re-borrowed in order to pay off any existing mortgage or bond.

40. Where by the special Act the Company shall be restricted from borrowing any money on mortgage or bond until a definite portion of their capital shall be subscribed or paid up, or where by this or the special Act the authority of *Evidence of authority for borrowing.*

72 BOOK I.—LIBRARIES AND MUSEUMS.

Certificate of justice. Order of general meeting.
a general meeting is required for such borrowing, the certificate of a justice that such definite portion of the capital has been subscribed or paid up, and a copy of the order of a general meeting of the Company authorising the borrowing of any money, certified by one of the directors or by the secretary to be a true copy, shall be sufficient evidence of the fact of the capital required to be subscribed or paid up having been so subscribed or paid up, and of the order for borrowing money having been made;

And upon production to any justice of the books of the Company, and of such other evidence as he shall think sufficient, such justice shall grant the certificate aforesaid.

Mortgages and bonds to be by deed— Form.
41. Every mortgage and bond for securing money borrowed by the Company shall be by deed under the common seal of the Company, duly stamped, and wherein the consideration shall be truly stated;

And every such mortgage deed or bond may be according to the form in the Schedule (C) or (D) to this Act annexed, or to the like effect.

Borrowing of money on mortgages.
42. The respective mortgagees shall be entitled one with another to their respective proportions of the tolls, sums, and premises comprised in such mortgages, and of the future calls payable by the shareholders, if comprised therein, according to the respective sums in such mortgages mentioned to be advanced by such mortgagees respectively, and to be repaid the sums so advanced, with interest, without any preference one above another by reason of priority of the date of any such mortgage, or of the meeting at which the same was authorised.

Mortgages entitled to proportions of tolls, etc., without preference.

Mortgage not to preclude receipt of calls.
43. No such mortgage (although it should comprise future calls on the shareholders) shall, unless expressly so provided, preclude the Company from receiving and applying to the purposes of the Company any calls to be made by the Company.

Obligees in bonds entitled to proportion of tolls, etc. without preference.
44. The respective obligees in such bonds shall, proportionally according to the amount of the moneys secured thereby, be entitled to be paid, out of the tolls or other property or effects of the Company, the respective sums in such bonds mentioned, and thereby intended to be secured, without any preference one above another by reason of priority of date of any such bond, or of the meeting at which the same was authorised, or otherwise howsoever.

Register of mortgages
45. A register of mortgages and bonds shall be kept by the secretary, and within fourteen days after the date of any

such mortgage or bond an entry or memorial, specifying the number and date of such mortgage or bond, and the sums secured thereby, and the names of the parties thereto, with their proper additions, shall be made in such register;

And such register may be perused at all reasonable times by any of the shareholders, or by any mortgagee or bond creditor of the Company, or by any person interested in any such mortgage or bond, without fee or reward.

and bonds to be kept— Inspection.

46. Any party entitled to any such mortgage or bond may from time to time transfer his right and interest therein to any other person; and every such transfer shall be by deed duly stamped, wherein the consideration shall be truly stated; And every such transfer may be according to the form in the Schedule (E) to this Act annexed, or to the like effect.

Transfers of mortgages and bonds to be by deed— Form.

47. Within thirty days after the date of every such transfer, if executed within the United Kingdom, or otherwise within thirty days after the arrival thereof in the United Kingdom, it shall be produced to the secretary, and thereupon the secretary shall cause an entry or memorial thereof to be made in the same manner as in the case of the original mortgage;

And after such entry every such transfer shall entitle the transferee to the full benefit of the original mortgage or bond in all respects;

And no party, having made such transfer, shall have power to make void, release, or discharge the mortgage or bond so transferred, or any money thereby secured;

And for such entry the Company may demand a sum not exceeding the prescribed sum, or, where no sum shall be prescribed, the sum of two shillings and sixpence;

And until such entry the Company shall not be in any manner responsible to the transferee in respect of such mortgage.

Transfers of mortgages and bonds to be registered —Fee.

48. The interest of the money borrowed upon any such mortgage or bond shall be paid at the periods appointed in such mortgage or bond, and if no period be appointed, half-yearly, to the several parties entitled thereto, and in preference to any dividends payable to the shareholders of the Company.

Payment of interest on moneys borrowed.

49. The interest on any such mortgage or bond shall not be transferable, except by deed duly stamped.

Transfers of interest.

50. The Company may, if they think proper, fix a period for the repayment of the principal money so borrowed with the interest thereof, and in such case the Company shall cause such period to be inserted in the mortgage deed or bond;

Money borrowed to be repaid at time fixed. Place of payment.

And upon the expiration of such period the principal sum, together with the arrears of interest thereon, shall, on demand, be paid to the party entitled to such mortgage or bond;

And if no other place of payment be inserted in such mortgage deed or bond, such principal and interest shall be payable at the principal office or place of business of the Company.

If no time fixed, money borrowed to be repaid at six months' notice. Notice by company. Notice to company.

51. If no time be fixed in the mortgage deed or bond for the repayment of the money so borrowed, the party entitled to the mortgage or bond may, at the expiration or at any time after the expiration of twelve months from the date of such mortgage or bond, demand payment of the principal money thereby secured, with all arrears of interest, upon giving six months' previous notice for that purpose;

And in the like case the Company may at any time pay off the money borrowed, on giving the like notice;

And every such notice shall be in writing or print, or both, and if given by a mortgagee or bond creditor shall be delivered to the secretary or left at the principal office of the Company, and if given by the Company shall be given either personally to such mortgagee or bond creditor or left at his residence, or if such mortgagee or bond creditor be unknown to the directors, or cannot be found after diligent inquiry, such notice shall be given by advertisement in the "London" or "Dublin Gazette," according as the principal office of the Company shall be in England or Ireland, and in some newspaper as after mentioned.

Interest to cease on expiration of notice to pay off mortgage or bond.

52. If the Company shall have given notice of their intention to pay off any such mortgage or bond at a time when the same may lawfully be paid off by them, then at the expiration of such notice all further interest shall cease to be payable on such mortgage or bond, unless, on demand of payment made pursuant to such notice, or at any time thereafter, the Company shall fail to pay the principal and interest due at the expiration of such notice on such mortgage or bond.

Arrears of interest. When to be enforced by appointment of a receiver. Arrears of principal and interest. Joint mortgages.

53. Where by the special Act the mortgagees of the Company shall be empowered to enforce the payment of the arrears of interest, or the arrears of principal and interest, due on such mortgages, by the appointment of a receiver, then, if within thirty days after the interest accruing upon any such mortgage has become payable, and, after demand thereof in writing, the same be not paid, the mortgagee may, without prejudice to his right to sue for the interest so in

arrear in any of the superior courts of law or equity, require the appointment of a receiver, by an application to be made as hereinafter provided;

And if within six months after the principal money owing upon any such mortgage has become payable, and, after demand thereof in writing, the same be not paid, the mortgagee without prejudice to his right to sue for such principal money, together with all arrears of interest, in any of the superior courts of law or equity, may, if his debt amount to the prescribed sum alone, or if his debt does not amount to the prescribed sum, he may, in conjunction with other mortgagees whose debts, being so in arrear, after demand as aforesaid, shall, together with his, amount to the prescribed sum, require the appointment of a receiver, by an application to be made as hereinafter provided.

54. Every application for a receiver in the cases aforesaid shall be made to two justices, and on any such application it shall be lawful for such justices, by order in writing, after hearing the parties, to appoint some person to receive the whole or a competent part of the tolls or sums liable to the payment of such interest, or such principal and interest, as the case may be, until such interest, or until such principal and interest, as the case may be, together with all costs, including the charges of receiving the tolls or sums aforesaid, be fully paid; *Receiver to be appointed by two justices. Tolls, etc., to be paid to receiver. When power of receiver to cease.*

And upon such appointment being made, all such tolls and sums of money as aforesaid shall be paid to and received by the person so to be appointed;

And the money so to be received shall be so much money received by or to the use of the party to whom such interest, or such principal and interest, as the case may be, shall be then due, and on whose behalf such receiver shall have been appointed;

And after such interest and costs, or such principal, interest, and costs, have been so received, the power of such receiver shall cease.

55. At all seasonable times the books of account of the Company shall be open to the inspection of the respective mortgagees and bond creditors thereof, with liberty to take extracts therefrom without fee or reward. *Access to books by mortgagees.*

And with respect to the Accountability of the Officers of the Company, be it enacted as follows: *Accountability of officers.*

109. Before any person intrusted with the custody or

BOOK I.—LIBRARIES AND MUSEUMS.

Security from officers intrusted with money.

control of moneys, whether treasurer, collector, or other officer of the Company, shall enter upon his office, the Directors shall take sufficient security from him for the faithful execution of his office.

Officers to account, on demand.

110. Every officer employed by the Company shall from time to time, when required by the Directors, make out and deliver to them, or to any person appointed by them for that purpose, a true and perfect account in writing under his hand of all moneys received by him on behalf of the Company;

And such account shall state how, and to whom, and for what purpose such moneys shall have been disposed of;

And, together with such account, such officer shall deliver the vouchers and receipts for such payments;

And every such officer shall pay to the Directors, or to any person appointed by them to receive the same, all moneys which shall appear to be owing from him upon the balance of such accounts.

Summary remedy against parties failing to account.

111. If any such officer fail to render such account, or to produce and deliver up all the vouchers and receipts relating to the same in his possession or power, or to pay the balance thereof, when thereunto required, or if for 3 days after being thereunto required he fail to deliver up to the Directors, or to any person appointed by them to receive the same, all papers and writings, property, effects, matters, and things, in his possession or power, relating to the execution of this or the Special Act, or any Act incorporated therewith, or belonging to the Company, then, on complaint thereof being made to a Justice, such Justice shall summon such officer to appear before two or more justices at a time and place to be set forth in such summons, to answer such charge;

And upon the appearance of such officer, or in his absence upon proof that such summons was personally served upon him, or left at his last known place of abode, such Justices may hear and determine the matter in a summary way, and may adjust and declare the balance owing by such officer;

And if it appear, either upon confession of such officer, or upon evidence, or upon inspection of the account, that any moneys of the Company are in the hands of such officer, or owing by him to the Company, such Justices may order such officer to pay the same;

And if he fail to pay the amount it shall be lawful for such Justices to grant a warrant to levy the same by distress, or, in default thereof, to commit the offender to gaol, there to remain without bail for a period not exceeding 3 months, unless the same be sooner paid.

112. If any such officer refuse to make out such account in writing, or to produce and deliver to the Justices the several vouchers and receipts relating thereto, or to deliver up any books, papers, or writings, property, effects, matters, or things, in his possession or power, belonging to the Company, such Justices may lawfully commit such offender to gaol, there to remain until he shall have delivered up all the vouchers and receipts, if any, in his possession or power, relating to such accounts, and have delivered up all books, papers, writings, property, effects, matters, and things, if any, in his possession or power, belonging to the Company. *Officers refusing to deliver up documents, etc., to be imprisoned.*

113. Provided always, that if any Director or other person acting on behalf of the Company shall make oath that he has good reason to believe, upon grounds to be stated in his deposition, and does believe, that it is the intention of any such officer as aforesaid to abscond, it shall be lawful for the Justice before whom the complaint is made, instead of issuing his summons, to issue his warrant for the bringing such officer before such two Justices as aforesaid; *Where officer about to abscond, a warrant may be issued in the first instance.*

But no person executing such warrant shall keep such officer in custody longer than 24 hours without bringing him before some Justice;

And it shall be lawful for the Justice before whom such officer may be brought either to discharge such officer, if he think there is no sufficient ground for his detention, or to order such officer to be detained in custody, so as to be brought before two Justices, at a time and place to be named in such order, unless such officer give bail to the satisfaction of such Justice for his appearance before such Justices to answer the complaint of the Company.

114. No such proceeding against or dealing with any such officer as aforesaid shall deprive the Company of any remedy which they might otherwise have against such officer, or any surety of such officer. *Sureties not to be discharged.*

And with respect to the Recovery of Damages not specially provided for, and Penalties, be it enacted as follows: *Damages, etc.*

142. In all cases where any damages, costs, or expenses are by this or the Special Act, or any Act incorporated therewith, directed to be paid, and the method of ascertaining the amount or enforcing the payment thereof is not provided for, *Provision for damages not otherwise provided for.*

78 BOOK I.—LIBRARIES AND MUSEUMS.

such amount, in case of dispute, shall be ascertained and determined by two Justices;

And if the amount so ascertained be not paid by the Company or other party liable to pay the same within 7 days after demand, the amount may be recovered by distress of the goods of the Company or other party liable as aforesaid;

And the Justices by whom the same shall have been ordered to be paid, or either of them, on application, shall issue their or his warrant accordingly.

Distress against the treasurer. **143.** If sufficient goods of the Company cannot be found whereon to levy any such damages, costs, or expenses payable by the Company, the same may, if the amount thereof do not exceed 20*l*., be recovered by distress of the goods of the Treasurer of the Company;

And the Justices aforesaid, or either of them, on application, shall issue their or his warrant accordingly;

But no such distress shall issue against the goods of such Treasurer unless 7 days' previous notice in writing, stating the amount so due, and demanding paying thereof, have been given to such Treasurer or left at his residence;

And if such Treasurer pay any money under such distress as aforesaid, he may retain the amount so paid by him, and all costs and expenses occasioned thereby, out of any money belonging to the Company coming into his custody or control, or he may sue the Company for the same.

Method of proceeding before justices in questions of damages, etc. **144.** Where in this or the Special Act, or any Act incorporated therewith, any question of compensation, expenses, charges, or damages is referred to the determination of any one Justice, or more, it shall be lawful for any Justice, upon the application of either party, to summon the other party to appear before one Justice, or before two Justices, as the case may require, at a time and place to be named in such summons;

And upon the appearance of such parties, or in the absence of any of them, upon proof of due service of the summons, it shall be lawful for such one Justice or such two Justices, as the case may be, to hear and determine such question, and for that purpose to examine such parties or any of them, and their witnesses, on oath;

And the costs of every such inquiry shall be in the discretion of such Justices, and they shall determine the amount thereof.

145. The Company shall publish the short particulars of

the several offences for which any penalty is imposed by this or the Special Act, or any Act incorporated therewith, or by any By-Law of the Company affecting other persons than the shareholders, officers, or servants of the Company, and of the amount of every such penalty, and shall cause such particulars to be painted on a board, or printed upon paper and pasted thereon, and shall cause such board to be hung up or affixed on some conspicuous part of the principal place of business of the Company, and where any such penalties are of local application shall cause such boards to be affixed in some conspicuous place in the immediate neighbourhood to which such penalties are applicable or have reference; *Publication of penalties.*

And such particulars shall be renewed as often as the same or any part thereof is obliterated or destroyed;

And no such penalty shall be recoverable unless it shall have been published and kept published in the manner hereinbefore required.

146. If any person pull down or injure any board put up or affixed as required by this or the Special Act, or any Act incorporated therewith, for the purpose of publishing any By-Law or penalty, or shall obliterate any of the letters or figures thereon, he shall forfeit for every such offence a sum not exceeding 5*l.*, and shall defray the expenses attending the restoration of such board. *Penalty for defacing boards used for such publication.*

147. Every penalty or forfeiture imposed by this or the Special Act, or any Act incorporated therewith, or by any By-Law made in pursuance thereof, the recovery of which is not otherwise provided for, may be recovered by summary proceeding before two Justices; *Penalties to be summarily recovered before two justices.*

And on complaint being made to any Justice he shall issue a summons, requiring the party complained against to appear before two Justices at a time and place to be named in such summons;

And every such summons shall be served on the party offending, either in person or by leaving the same with some inmate at his usual place of abode;

And upon the appearance of the party complained against, or in his absence, after proof of the due service of such summons, it shall be lawful for two Justices to proceed to the hearing of the complaint, and that although no information in writing or in print shall have been exhibited before them;

And upon proof of the offence, either by the confession of the party complained against or upon the oath of one credible witness or more, it shall be lawful for such Justices to convict the offender, and upon such conviction to adjudge the offender to pay the penalty or forfeiture incurred, as well as such costs attending the conviction as such Justices shall think fit.(*a*)

(*a*) This section is repealed in whole or in part by the " Summary Jurisdiction Act, 1884," 47 & 48 Vict. 43, Sched.

Penalties may be levied by distress.

148. If forthwith upon any such adjudication as aforesaid the amount of the penalty or forfeiture, and of such costs as aforesaid, be not paid, the amount of such penalty and costs shall be levied by distress, and such Justices, or either of them, shall issue their or his warrant of distress accordingly.(*a*)

(*a*) See note to § 147.

Imprisonment in default of distress.

149. It shall be lawful for any such Justice to order any offender so convicted as aforesaid to be detained and kept in safe custody until return can be conveniently made to the warrant of distress to be issued for levying such penalty or forfeiture, and costs, unless the offender give sufficient security, by way of recognisance or otherwise, to the satisfaction of the Justice, for his appearance before him on the day appointed for such return, such day not being more than 8 days from the time of taking such security;

But if before issuing such warrant of distress it shall appear to the Justice, by the admission of the offender or otherwise, that no sufficient distress can be had within the jurisdiction of such Justice whereon to levy such penalty or forfeiture, and costs, he may, if he thinks fit, refrain from issuing such warrant of distress;

And in such case, or if such warrant shall have been issued, and upon the return thereof such insufficiency as aforesaid shall be made to appear to the Justice, then such Justice shall, by warrant, cause such offender to be committed to gaol, there to remain without bail for any term not exceeding 3 months, unless such penalty or forfeiture, and costs, be sooner paid and satisfied.(*a*)

(*a*) See note to § 147.

Distress— how to be levied.

150. Where in this or the Special Act, or any Act incorporated therewith, any sum of money, whether in the nature of penalty or otherwise, is directed to be levied by distress, such sum of money shall be levied by distress and sale of the goods and chattels of the party liable to pay the same, and the overplus arising from the sale of such goods and chattels, after satisfying such sum of money, and the expenses of the distress

and sale, shall be returned, on demand, to the party whose goods shall have been distrained.

151. No distress levied by virtue of this or the Special Act, or any Act incorporated therewith, shall be deemed unlawful, nor shall any party making the same be deemed a trespasser, on account of any defect or want of form in the summons, conviction, warrant of distress, or other proceeding relating thereto, nor shall such party be deemed a trespasser *ab initio* on account of any irregularity afterwards committed by him, but all persons aggrieved by such defect or irregularity may recover full satisfaction for the special damage in an action *upon the case*. Distress not unlawful for want of form.

152. The Justices by whom any such penalty or forfeiture shall be imposed may, where the application thereof is not otherwise provided for, award not more than one-half thereof to the informer, and shall award the remainder to the Overseers of the Poor of the parish in which the offence shall have been committed, for the benefit of the poor of such parish; Application of penalties.

Or if the place wherein the offence shall have been committed shall be extra-parochial, then such Justices shall direct such remainder to be applied for the benefit of the poor of such extra-parochial place, or of any adjoining parish or district, and shall order the same to be paid over to the proper officer for that purpose.

153. No person shall be liable to the payment of any penalty or forfeiture imposed by virtue of this or the Special Act, or any Act incorporated therewith, for any offence made cognizable before a Justice, unless the complaint respecting such offence shall have been made before such Justice within 6 months next after the commission of such offence.(*a*) Penalties to be sued for within six months.

(*a*) See note to §147.

154. If, through any act, neglect, or default on account whereof any person shall have incurred any penalty imposed by this or the Special Act, or any Act incorporated therewith, any damage to the property of the Company shall have been committed by such person, he shall be liable to make good such damage as well as to pay such penalty; Damage to be made good in addition to penalty.

And the amount of such damages shall, in case of dispute, be determined by the Justices by whom the party incurring such penalty shall have been convicted, and on non-payment of such damages, on demand, the same shall be levied by distress, and such Justices, or one of them, shall issue their or his warrant accordingly.

BOOK I.—LIBRARIES AND MUSEUMS.

Penalty on witnesses making default.

155. It shall be lawful for any Justice to summon any person to appear before him as a witness in any matter in which such Justice shall have jurisdiction, under the provisions of this or the Special Act, or any Act incorporated therewith, at a time and place mentioned in such summons, and to administer to him an oath to testify the truth in such matter;

And if any person so summoned shall, without reasonable excuse, refuse or neglect to appear at the time and place appointed for that purpose, having been paid or tendered a reasonable sum for his expenses, or if any person appearing shall refuse to be examined upon oath or to give evidence before such Justice, every such person shall forfeit a sum not exceeding £5 for every such offence.(*a*)

(*a*) See note to § 147.

Transient offenders.

156. It shall be lawful for any officer or agent of the Company, and all persons called by him to his assistance, to seize and detain any person who shall have committed any offence against the provisions of this or the Special Act, or any Act incorporated therewith, and whose name and residence shall be unknown to such officer or agent, and convey him, with all convenient despatch, before some Justice without any warrant or other authority than this or the Special Act;

And such Justice shall proceed with all convenient despatch to the hearing and determining of the complaint against such offender.

Form of conviction.

157. The Justices before whom any person shall be convicted of any offence against this or the Special Act, or any Act incorporated therewith, may cause the conviction to be drawn up according to the Form *in the Schedule (G) to this Act annexed.*(*a*)

(*a*) See note to § 147.

Proceedings not to be quashed for want of form.

158. No proceeding in pursuance of this or the Special Act, or any Act incorporated therewith, shall be quashed or vacated for want of form, nor shall the same be removed by *certiorari* or otherwise into any of the Superior Courts.

Parties allowed to appeal to Quarter Sessions, on giving security.

159. If any party shall feel aggrieved by any determination or adjudication of any Justice with respect to any penalty or forfeiture under the provisions of this or the Special Act, or any Act incorporated therewith, such party may appeal to the General Quarter Sessions for the county or place in which the cause of appeal shall have arisen;

PART IV.—STATUTES.—8 VICT. c. 16. 83

But no such appeal shall be entertained unless it be made within 4 months next after the making of such determination or adjudication, nor unless 10 days' notice in writing of such appeal, stating the nature and grounds thereof, be given to the party against whom the appeal shall be brought, nor unless the appellant forthwith after such notice enter into recognisances, with 2 sufficient sureties, before a Justice conditioned duly to prosecute such appeal, and to abide the order of the Court thereon.(a)

(a) See note to § 147.

160. At the Quarter Sessions for which such notice shall be given the Court shall proceed to hear and determine the appeal in a summary way, or they may, if they think fit, adjourn it to the following Sessions; Court to make such order as they think reasonable.

And upon the hearing of such appeal the Court may, if they think fit, mitigate any penalty or forfeiture, or they may confirm or quash the adjudication, and order any money paid by the appellant, or levied by distress upon his goods, to be returned to him, and may also order such further satisfaction to be made to the party injured as they may judge reasonable;

And they may make such order concerning the costs, both of the adjudication and of the appeal, as they may think reasonable.

SCHEDULES referred to by the foregoing Act.

SCHEDULE (C).

Form of Mortgage Deed.

" The   Company."

Mortgage, Number   £

By virtue of [*here name the Special Act*], we, " The Company," in consideration of the sum of   pounds paid to us by A. B., of   do assign unto the said A. B., his executors, administrators, and assigns, the said undertaking [and (*in case such loan shall be in anticipation of the Capital authorised to be raised*) all future calls on shareholders], and all the tolls and sums of money arising by virtue of the said Act, and all the estate, right, title, and interest of the company in the same, to hold unto the said A. B., his executors, administrators, and assigns, until the said sum of   pounds, together with interest for the same at the rate of

G 2

for every one hundred pounds by the year, be satisfied [the principal sum to be repaid at the end of   years from the date hereof (*in case any period be agreed upon for that purpose*)], [*at   or any place of payment other than the principal office of the company*]. Given under our Common Seal, this   day of   in the year of our Lord   .

SCHEDULE (D).

Form of Bond.

" The   Company."

Bond, Number   £

By virtue of [*here name the Special Act*], we, "The Company," in consideration of the sum of   pounds to us in hand paid by A. B., of   do bind ourselves and our successors unto the said A. B., his executors, administrators, and assigns, in the penal sum of   pounds.

The condition of the above obligation is such, that if the said company shall pay to the said A. B., his executors, administrators, or assigns, [at   (*in case any other place of payment than the principal office of the company be intended*),] on the   day of   which will be in the year One thousand eight hundred and   the principal sum of   pounds, together with interest for the same at the rate of   pounds per centum per annum, payable half-yearly on the   day of   and   day of   then the above-written obligation is to become void, otherwise to remain in full force. Given under our Common Seal, this   day of   One thousand eight hundred and   .

SCHEDULE (E).

Form of Transfer of Mortgage or Bond.

I A. B. of   in consideration of the sum of   paid to me by G. H. of   do hereby transfer to the said G. H., his executors, administrators, and assigns, a certain bond [or mortgage] number   made by " The   Company " to   bearing date the   day of   for securing the sum of   and   interest [*or if such transfer be by endorsement*, the within security], and all my right, estate,

PART IV.—STATUTES.—8 VICT. c. 16.   85

and interest in and to the money thereby secured [*and if the transfer be of a mortgage*, and in and to the tolls, money, and property thereby assigned]. In witness whereof I have hereunto set my hand and seal, this   day of   One thousand eight hundred and   .

[8 Vict.]   *Lands Clauses Consolidation.*   [c. 18]   1845.

8 VICT. **18**.

An Act for consolidating in one Act certain Provisions usually inserted in Acts authorising the taking of Lands for Undertakings of a Public Nature.   [8th May, 1845.

Revised Statutes, 2nd ed. vol. vii. p. 508.

[The above Act is incorporated by the "Public Libraries and Museums (Ireland) Act, 1855" (18 & 19 Vict. **40**, 10), the "Technical and Industrial Institutions Act, 1892" (55 & 56 Vict. **29**, 4), "Public Libraries Act, 1892 (55 & 56 Vict. **53**, 12), except the compulsory powers. It is amended and extended in various ways by the "Lands Clauses Amendments Acts, 1860, 1869, and 1883" (23 & 24 Vict. **106**; 32 & 33 Vict. **18**; 46 Vict. **15**.)]

[8 Vict.] *Lands Clauses Consolidation (Scotland).* [c. 19] 1845

8 VICT. **19**.

An Act for consolidating in one Act certain Provisions usually inserted in Acts authorising the taking of Lands for Undertakings of a Public Nature in Scotland.
[8th May, 1845.

Revised Statutes, 2nd ed. vol. vii. p. 554.

* * * * * *

Purchase of Lands by Agreement   . . §§ 6— 16
Purchase Money or Compensation coming to
 parties of limited interests   . . . . §§ 67—79
Conveyances of Lands . . . . §§ 80—82

[All the above enactments are incorporated by the "Public Libraries Consolidation (Scotland) Act, 1887" (50 & 51 Vict. **42**, 11).]

1847. [10 Vict.] *Commissioners Clauses.* [c. 16]

10 VICT. 16.

Revised Statutes, 2nd ed. vol. viii. p. 88.

An Act for consolidating in one Act certain Provisions usually contained in Acts with respect to the Constitution and Regulation of Bodies of Commissioners appointed for carrying on Undertakings of a Public Nature.(a)

[23rd April, 1847.

(a) The sections here given are incorporated by the " Public Libraries Consolidation (Scotland) Act, 1887 " (50 & 51 Vict. 42, 16).

Interpretations in this and the special Act.

3. The following words and expressions, both in this and the special Act, and any Act incorporated therewith, shall have the several meanings hereby assigned to them, unless there be something in the subject or the context repugnant to such construction ; (that is to say)

Words importing the singular number only, shall include the plural number, and words importing the plural number only, shall include the singular number:

Words importing the masculine gender only, shall include females :

The word "person" shall include a Corporation, whether aggregate or sole :

The word "lands" shall extend to messuages, lands, tenements, and hereditaments or heritages of any tenure :

The word "month" shall mean calendar month :

The expression "superior courts," where the matter submitted to the cognisance of the Court arises in England or Ireland, shall mean Her Majesty's superior courts of record at Westminster or Dublin, as the case may require, and shall include the Court of Common Pleas of the County Palatine of Lancaster, and the Court of Pleas of the County of Durham; and where such matter arises in Scotland it shall mean the Court of Session :

The word "oath" shall include affirmation in the case of Quakers, and any declaration lawfully substituted for an oath in the case of any other persons allowed by law to make a declaration instead of taking an oath :

PART IV.—STATUTES.—10 VICT. c. 16. 87

The word "County" shall include riding or other division of a County having a separate commission of the peace, and in Scotland Stewartry, and any ward or other division of a County or Stewartry having a separate sheriff, and it shall also include County of a City or County of a Town:

The word "justice" shall mean justice of the peace acting for the place where the matter requiring the cognisance of any such justice arises; and where any matter is authorised or required to be done by two justices, the expression "two justices" shall be understood to mean two or more justices met and acting together:

The word "sheriff" shall mean the sheriff depute of the County or ward of a County in Scotland and the steward depute of the Stewartry in Scotland in which any matter submitted to the cognisance of the sheriff arises, and shall include the substitutes of such sheriff depute and steward depute respectively:

The expression "quarter sessions" shall mean quarter sessions as defined in the special Act; and if such expression be not there defined, it shall mean the general or quarter sessions of the peace which shall be held at the place nearest to the undertaking for the County or place in which the undertaking, or the principal office thereof, is situate, or for some division of such County having a separate commission of the peace:

The expression "the clerk" shall mean the clerk of the Commissioners, and shall include the word "secretary":

The expression "the Town" shall mean the Town or District named in the special Act which within the powers of the Commissioners are to be exercised.

And with respect to the liabilities of the Commissioners and to legal proceedings by or against the Commissioners, be it enacted as follows: {*Legal Proceedings.*}

60. No Commissioner, by being party to or executing in his capacity of Commissioner any contract or other instrument on behalf of the Commissioners, or otherwise lawfully executing any of the powers given to the Commissioners, shall be subject to be sued or prosecuted, either individually or collectively, by any person whomsoever;

And the bodies or goods or lands of the several Commis- {*Commissioners not to be personally liable for acts done in the capacity of a commissioner*}

88   BOOK I.—LIBRARIES AND MUSEUMS.

Commissioners to be indemnified for acts done in the execution of their office.

sioners shall not be liable to execution of any legal process by reason of any contract or other instrument so entered into, signed, or executed by them, or by reason of any other lawful act done by them in the execution of any of their powers as Commissioners;

And the Commissioners respectively, their heirs, executors, and administrators, shall be indemnified out of the rates and other moneys coming to the hands of the Commissioners by virtue of this and the special Act for all payments made or liability incurred in respect of any acts done by them, and for all losses, costs, and damages which they may incur in the execution of the powers granted to them.

Actions or suits to be brought in the name of any two commissioners or their clerk.

61. In all actions and suits in respect of any matter or thing relating to the execution of this or the special Act, to be brought by or against the Commissioners, it shall be sufficient, where such Commissioners are not a body corporate, to state the names of any two of the Commissioners, or the name of their clerk, as the party, plaintiff or defendant, representing the Commissioners in any such action or suit, and no such action or suit shall abate or be discontinued, or require to be transferred, by reason of the death of any such Commissioner, or by his ceasing to be a Commissioner, or by the death, suspension, or removal of such clerk.

Executions to be levied on the goods belonging to commissioners by virtue of their office only.

62. Execution upon every judgment or decree against the Commissioners in any such action or suit shall be levied on the goods, chattels, or personal effects belonging to the Commissioners by virtue of their office, and shall not in any manner extend to charge or make liable the persons, or private lands or goods of any of the Commissioners, or the heirs, executors, or administrators of any of them.

Commissioners and clerk to be reimbursed all damages, etc.

63. Every Commissioner or clerk in whose name any such legal proceedings shall be carried on, either as plaintiff or defendant, on behalf of the Commissioners, shall be reimbursed, out of the moneys which shall come into the hands of the treasurer of the Commissioners by virtue of his office, all damages, costs, charges, and expenses to which any such Commissioner or clerk may be put, or with which he may become chargeable, by reason of being so made plaintiff or defendant.

How indictments to be preferred.

64. The Commissioners may prefer a bill of indictment against any person who shall steal or wilfully injure any property or thing belonging to the Commissioners, or under their management, or institute any other proceeding which may appear to them necessary for the protection of such property,

and in every such case it shall be sufficient to state generally the property or thing in respect of which such proceeding shall have been taken to be the property of the Commissioners, as they shall be described in the special Act, without naming the individual Commissioners.

And with respect to the mortgages to be executed by the Commissioners, be it enacted as follows:— *Mortgages.*

75. Every mortgage or assignment in security of rates or other property authorised to be made under the provisions of this or the special Act shall be by deed duly stamped, in which the consideration shall be truly stated; *Form of mortgage.*

And every such deed shall be under the common seal of the Commissioners if they be a body corporate, or if they be not a body corporate shall be executed by the Commissioners, or any five of them, and may be according to the form in the Schedule (B) to this Act annexed or to the like effect;

And the respective mortgagees or assignees in security shall be entitled one with another to their respective proportions of the rates and assessments or other property comprised in such mortgages or assignations respectively, according to the respective sums in such mortgages or assignations mentioned to be advanced by such mortgagees or assignees respectively, and to be repaid the sums so advanced, with interest, without any preference one above another by reason of the priority of advancing such moneys, or of the dates of any such mortgages or assignations respectively.

76. A register of mortgages or assignations in security shall be kept by the clerk to the Commissioners, and where by the special Act the Commissioners are authorised or required to raise separate sums on separate rates or other property, a separate register shall be kept for each class of mortgages or assignations in security, and within fourteen days after the date of any mortgage or assignation in security an entry or memorial of the number and date thereof, and of the names of the parties thereto, with their proper additions, shall be made in the proper register, and every such register may be perused at all reasonable times by any person interested in any such mortgage or assignation in security without fee or reward. *Register of mortgages to be kept and to be open to inspection.*

77. Any person entitled to any such mortgage or assignation may transfer his right and interest therein to any other *Transfers of mortgages.*

person, and every such transfer shall be by deed duly stamped, wherein the consideration shall be truly stated, and every such transfer may be according to the form in the Schedule (C) to this Act annexed, or to the like effect.

Register of transfers to be kept. 78. Within thirty days after the date of every such transfer, if executed within the United Kingdom, or otherwise within thirty days after the arrival thereof in the United Kingdom, it shall be produced to the clerk to the Commissioners, and thereupon such clerk shall cause an entry or memorial thereof to be made, in the same manner as in the case of the original mortgage or assignation in security, and for such entry the clerk may demand a sum not exceeding five shillings, and after such entry every such transfer shall entitle the transferee, his executors, administrators, or assigns, to the full benefit of the original mortgage or assignation in security, and the principal and interest thereby secured, and such transferee may in like manner assign or transfer the same again *toties quoties*, and it shall not be in the power of any person, except the person to whom the same shall have been last transferred, his executors, administrators, or assigns, to make void, release, or discharge the mortgage or assignation so transferred, or any money thereby secured.

Interest on mortgages to be paid half-yearly. 79. Unless otherwise provided by any mortgage or assignation in security, the interest of the money borrowed thereupon shall be paid half-yearly to the several parties entitled thereto.

Power to borrow money at lower rate of interest to pay off securities at a higher rate. 80. If the Commissioners can at any time borrow or take up any sum of money at a lower rate of interest than any securities given by them and then be [*sic*] in force shall bear, they may borrow such sum at such lower rate as aforesaid, in order to pay off and discharge the securities bearing such higher rate of interest, and may charge the rates and other property which they may be authorised to mortgage or assign in security under this or the special Act, or any part thereof, with payment of such sum and such lower rate of interest, in such manner and subject to such regulations as are herein contained with respect to other moneys borrowed on mortgage or assignation in security.

Repayment of money borrowed at a time and place agreed upon. 81. The Commissioners may, if they think proper, fix a period for the repayment of all principal moneys borrowed under the provisions of this or the special Act, with the interest thereof, and in such case the Commissioners shall cause such period to be inserted in the mortgage deed or assignation in security;

And upon the expiration of such period the principal sum, together with the arrears of interest thereon, shall, on demand be paid to the party entitled to receive such principal money and interest, and if no other place of payment be inserted in such deed, such principal and interest shall be payable at the office of the Commissioners.

82. If no time be fixed in the mortgage deed or assignation in security for the repayment of the money so borrowed, the party entitled to receive such money may, at the expiration or at any time after the expiration of twelve months from the date of such deed, demand payment of the principal money thereby secured, with all arrears of interest, upon giving six months' previous notice for that purpose, and in the like case the Commissioners may at any time pay off the money borrowed, on giving the like notice; and every such notice shall be in writing or print, or both, and if given by a mortgagee or creditor shall be delivered to the clerk or left at the office of the Commissioners, and if given by the Commissioners shall be given either personally to such mortgagee or creditor, or left at his residence, or if such mortgagee or creditor be unknown to the Commissioners, or cannot be found after diligent inquiry, such notice shall be given by advertisement in the "London Gazette" if the office of the Commissioners is in England, the "Edinburgh Gazette" if it is in Scotland, or in the "Dublin Gazette" if it is in Ireland. *Repayment of money borrowed when no time or place has been agreed upon.*

83. If the Commissioners shall have given notice of their intention to pay off any such mortgage or assignation in security at a time when the same may lawfully be paid off by them, then at the expiration of such notice all further interest shall cease to be payable thereon, unless, on demand of payment made pursuant to such notice, or at any time thereafter, the Commissioners fail to pay the principal and interest due at the expiration of such notice on such mortgage or assignation in security. *Interest to cease on expiration of notice to pay off a mortgage debt.*

85. Whenever the Commissioners shall be enabled to pay off one or more of the mortgages or assignations in security which shall be then payable, and shall not be able to pay off the whole of the same class, they shall decide the order in which they shall be paid off by lot among the class to which such one or more of the mortgages or assignations in security belong, and shall cause a notice, signed by their clerk, to be given to the persons entitled to the money to be paid off, pursuant to such lot, and such notice shall express the *Mode of paying off mortgages.*

92   BOOK I—LIBRARIES AND MUSEUMS.

principal sum proposed to be paid off, and that the same will be paid, together with the interest due thereon, at a place to be specified, at the expiration of six months from the date of giving such notice.

Account books to be open to the inspection of mortgagees.
88. The books of account of the Commissioners shall be open at all seasonable times to the inspection of the respective mortgagees or assignees in security of the Commissioners, with liberty to take extracts therefrom without fee or reward.

[18 & 19 Vict.]   *Public Libraries Ireland.*   [c. 40]

Revised Statutes, 2nd ed. vol. ix. p. 508.

18 & 19 VICT. 40.

An Act for further promoting the establishment of free Public Libraries and Museums in Ireland.   [26th June, 1855.

16 & 17 Vict. 101, and § 99 of 17 & 18 Vict. 103, repealed.
All Public Libraries and Museums established in Ireland under either of those Acts shall be considered as having been established under this Act.

Short title.
2. In citing this Act for any purpose whatever it shall be sufficient to use the expression the "Public Libraries Act (Ireland), 1855."

Interpretation of terms.
3. In the construction and for the purposes of this Act (if not inconsistent with the context or subject-matter) the following terms shall have the respective meanings hereinafter assigned to them: that is to say,

"Town" shall mean and include any City, Borough, Town, or place in which Commissioners, Trustees, or other persons have been or shall be elected or appointed under the Act of the 9th year of King George IV., chapter 82, or the "Towns Improvement Act (Ireland), 1854," or any Local or other Act or Acts for paving, flagging, lighting, watching, cleansing, or otherwise improving any City, Borough, Town, or place for the execution of any such Act or Acts, or superintending the execution thereof, and in which there shall not be a Town Council or other such body elected under the Act of the 3rd and 4th years of her present Majesty, chapter 108,

PART IV.—STATUTES.—18 & 19 VICT. c. 40.   93

or any other Charter granted in pursuance of such Act, or any Act passed for the amendment thereof;

"Town Commissioners" shall mean the Commissioners, Trustees, or other persons for the time being elected or appointed under any such first-mentioned Acts as aforesaid;

"Town Fund" shall mean the Town Fund, or the Rates or property vested in and under the control and direction of any Town Commissioners, and applicable to the purposes of any such Acts;

"Town Rate" shall mean the Rate or Rates authorised to be levied by any such Town Commissioners;

"Mayor" shall include Lord Mayor;

"Clerk" shall mean, as regards an incorporated Borough, the Town Clerk of such Borough, and as regards a Town in which there shall be Town Commissioners, the Clerk appointed by the Town Commissioners;

"Householder" shall mean a male occupier of a dwellinghouse, or of any lands, tenements, or hereditaments within any town or incorporated Borough, and entitled for the time being to vote at elections of Commissioners, Aldermen, or Councillors in such Town or Borough.(a)

(a) See 40 & 41 Vict. 54, 3, for definition of "Ratepayer."

4. [§ 4 is repealed by 57 & 58 Vict. 38, 1 (9).] <small>Expenses of carryin</small>
5. The expenses incurred in calling and holding the meet- <small>Act into</small> ing, whether this Act shall be adopted or not (a), and the <small>execution</small> expenses of carrying this Act into execution in such Borough, shall be paid out of the Borough Fund, and in such Town out of the Town Fund;

And the Council, or Board of Municipal Commissioners, or Town Commissioners, may levy as part of the Borough Rate or Town Rate, as the case may be, or by a separate Rate to be assessed and recovered in like manner as the Borough Rate or Town Rate, all moneys from time to time necessary for defraying such expenses;

And distinct accounts shall be kept of the receipts, payments, and liabilities of the Council with reference to the execution of this Act.

(a) As to the adoption of the Act, see 40 & 41 Vict. 54, 1; and 57 & 58 Vict. 38, 1.

6. Such accounts shall be audited in the same way as all <small>Accounts</small> other accounts of such Borough or Town respectively are <small>to be audited</small>

94 BOOK I.—LIBRARIES AND MUSEUMS.

and deposited for inspection. audited, and the said Council or Board or Town Commissioners shall, within one month after the same shall have been audited, transmit to the Lord Lieutenant or other Chief Governor or Governors of Ireland for the time being a true and correct copy of such accounts;

And shall also within the time aforesaid cause a copy of such accounts to be deposited in the office of the Clerk;

And the said accounts shall be open to the inspection of all householders of such Borough or Town respectively, and copies thereof shall be delivered to any such householder applying for the same, upon payment of a reasonable charge for the same, to be fixed by the Council or Board or Town Commissioners, as the case may be.

Commissioners to be incorporated. 7. The Town Commissioners of every Town adopting this Act shall for the purposes thereof be a Body Corporate, with perpetual succession, by the name of "The Commissioners for Public Libraries and Museums for the Town of   in the County of   ," and by that name may sue and be sued, and hold and dispose of lands, and use a Common Seal.

Rate not to exceed 1d. in the £. 8. The amount of the Rate to be levied in any Borough or Town in any one year for the purposes of this Act shall not exceed the sum of 1d. in the £, and in any such Borough shall be assessed, raised, collected, and levied in the same manner as the Borough Rate, and in any such Town shall be assessed, raised, collected, and levied in the same manner as the Town Rate.(*a*)

(*a*) As to the fixing of a lower rate, see 40 & 41 Vict. 54, 2.

Lands, etc., may be appropriated, purchased, or rented for the purposes of the Act 9. The Council or Board of any Borough, and the Town Commissioners of any Town respectively, may from time to time, with the approval of Her Majesty's Treasury, appropriate for the purposes of this Act any lands vested, as the case may be, in a Borough in the Mayor, Aldermen, and Burgesses, and in a Town in the Town Commissioners, and may also, with such approval, purchase or rent any lands or any suitable buildings, and the Council or Board and Town Commissioners respectively may, upon any lands so appropriated, purchased, or rented respectively, erect any buildings suitable for Public Libraries or Museums or Schools of Science and Art, or both, and may apply, take down, alter, and extend any buildings for such purposes, and rebuild, repair, and improve the same respectively, and fit up, furnish, and

PART IV.—STATUTES.—18 & 19 VICT. c. 40.

supply the same respectively with all requisite furniture, fittings, and conveniences.(*a*)

(*a*) This section is thus explained by the "Public Libraries Act, 1884":— "Buildings may, under the said section, be erected for Public Libraries, Public Museums, Schools for Science, Art Galleries, and Schools for Art, or for any one or more of these objects." (47 & 48 Vict. 37, 2). *Sed quære*: —Does it extend to Schools of Music (see 40 & 41 Vict. 15, 3)?

10. The "Lands Clauses Consolidation Act, 1845," shall be incorporated with this Act; But the Council or Board, and Commissioners respectively shall not purchase or take any lands otherwise than by agreement. *8 Vict. 18, incorporated.*

11. The Council or Board and Commissioners aforesaid respectively may, with the like approval as is required for the purchase of lands, sell any lands vested in the Mayor, Aldermen, and Burgesses, or Board, or Town Commissioners respectively, for the purposes of this Act, or exchange the same for any lands better adapted for the purposes; *Lands, etc., may be sold or exchanged.*

And the moneys to arise from such sale, or to be received for equality of exchange, or a sufficient part thereof, shall be applied in or towards the purchase of other lands better adapted for such purposes.

12. The general management, regulation, and control of such Libraries and Museums or Schools of Science and Art shall be, as to any Borough, vested in and exercised by the Council or Board, and as to any Town, in and by the Town Commissioners, or such Committee (*a*) as they respectively may from time to time appoint, who may from time to time purchase and provide the necessary fuel, lighting, and other similar matters, books, newspapers, maps, and specimens of art and science, for the use of the Library or Museum, and cause the same to be bound or repaired, when necessary, and appoint salaried officers and servants, and dismiss the same, and make Rules and Regulations for the safety and use of the Libraries and Museums or Schools of Science and Art, and for the admission of visitors.(*b*) *General management to be vested in Council or Board, or Town Commissioners.*

(*a*) The Committee may consist in part of persons not members of the Board, etc. (40 & 41 Vict. 18, 4).
(*b*) The Act 40 & 41 Vict. 15, 3, authorises the appropriation of part of the Rate to Schools of Music.

13. The lands and buildings so to be appropriated, purchased, or rented as aforesaid, and all other real and personal property whatever presented to or purchased for any Library *Property vested in Council, Board and*

BOOK I.—LIBRARIES AND MUSEUMS.

Commissioners respectively. or Museum or School of Science and Art established under this Act shall be vested, in the case of a Borough, in the Mayor, Aldermen, and Burgesses, and in the case of a Town, in the Town Commissioners.(*a*)

(*a*) As to Schools of Music see 40 & 41 Vict. 15, 3.

If a Meeting negatives adoption, no other Meeting for a year. 14. If any meeting called as hereinbefore provided to consider as to the adoption of this Act for any Borough or Town shall determine against such adoption, no meeting for a similar purpose shall be held for the space of one year at least from the time of holding the previous meeting.

Admission to be free. 15. The admission to all Libraries and Museums established under this Act shall be opened to the public free of all charge.

Act to be incorporated with Local Acts in force in Borough or Town. 16. Upon the coming into operation of this Act in any Borough it shall, as regards such Borough, be incorporated with the said Act of the 3rd and 4th Victoria, chapter 108, and upon the coming into operation of this Act in any Town it shall, as regards such Town, be incorporated with the Act or Acts in force therein relating to the powers and duties of the Town Commissioners.

1860. [23 & 24 Vict.] *Lands Clauses Amendment.* [c. 106]

23 & 24 VICT. 106.

Revised Statutes, 2nd ed vol. x. p. 369. An Act to amend the *"Lands Clauses Consolidation Act,* 1845," *in regard to sales and compensation for land by way of a Rent-charge, annual Feu-duty, or Ground-annual, and to enable Her Majesty's Principal Secretary of State for the War Department to avail himself of the powers and provisions contained in the same Acts.* (*a*)

[20th August, 1860.

(*a*) See § 8, and the Memorandum appended to the "Lands Clauses Consolidation Act, 1845," (*ante*).

[24 & 25 VICT.] *Malicious Damage.* [c. 97] 1861.

24 & 25 VICT. 97.

An Act to consolidate and amend the Statute Law of England and Ireland relating to Malicious Injuries to Property. [6th August, 1861.

Revised Statutes, 2nd ed. vol. x. pp. 711, 714.

39. Whoever shall unlawfully and maliciously destroy or damage any book, manuscript, picture, print, statue, bust or vase, or any other article or thing kept for the purpose of Art, Science, or Literature, or as an object of curiosity, in any Museum, Gallery, Cabinet, Library, or other repository which is either at all times or from time to time open for the admission of the public, or of any considerable number of persons, to view the same, either by the permission of the proprietor thereof or by the payment of money before entering the same, or any picture, statue, monument, or other memorial of the dead, painted glass, or other ornament or work of art, in any Church, Chapel, Meeting House, or other place of divine worship, or in any building belonging to the Queen, or to any County, Riding, Division, City, Borough, Poor-Law Union, Parish, or place, or to any University, or College, or hall of any University, or to any Inn of Court, or to any Street, Square, Churchyard, Burial Ground, Public Garden or Ground, or any statue or monument exposed to public view, or any ornament, railing, or fence surrounding such statue or monument, shall be guilty of a misdemeanour, and being convicted thereof, shall be liable to be imprisoned for any term not exceeding six months, with or without hard labour, and, if a male under the age of sixteen years, with or without whipping; provided that nothing herein contained shall be deemed to affect the right of any person to recover, by action at law, damages for the injury so committed. (*a*)

Destroying or damaging works of art in museums, libraries, or other places.

(*a*) A copy of this Section should be placed in conspicuous positions in the various rooms, and the offer of a reward may assist in detecting offenders. In connection with the Battersea Public Libraries proceedings were taken in the County Court against the guarantor for damage to a book which the borrower failed to make good; he was ordered to pay the amount claimed and costs, after examination of the form of guarantee. The Chelsea Public Libraries Authority have also been successful in obtaining the conviction of

H

a reader for tearing a leaf from a magazine; he was fined £2 and costs, together with the value of the magazine. Similar proceedings have been taken in Manchester, Wolverhampton, Chester, Liverpool, and other places.

52. Whosoever shall wilfully or maliciously commit any damage, injury, or spoil to or upon any real or personal property whatsoever, either of a public or private nature, for which no punishment is hereinbefore provided, shall on conviction thereof before a justice of the peace, at the discretion of the justice, either be committed to the common gaol or house of correction, there to be imprisoned only, or to be imprisoned and kept to hard labour, for any term not exceeding two months, or else shall forfeit and pay such sum of money, not exceeding five pounds, as to the justice shall seem meet, and also such further sum of money as shall appear to the justice to be a reasonable compensation for the damage, injury, or spoil so committed, not exceeding the sum of five pounds; which last-mentioned sum of money shall, in the case of private property, be paid to the party aggrieved, and in the case of property of a public nature, or wherein any public right is concerned, the money shall be applied in the same manner as every penalty imposed by a justice of the peace under this Act; and if such sums of money, together with costs (if ordered), shall not be paid either immediately after the conviction, or within such period as the justice shall at the time of the conviction appoint, the justice may commit the offender to the common gaol or house of correction, there to be imprisoned only, or to be imprisoned and kept to hard labour, as the justice shall think fit, for any term not exceeding two months, unless such sums and costs be sooner paid. Provided, that nothing herein contained shall extend to any case where the party acted under a fair and reasonable supposition that he had a right to do the act complained of, nor to any trespass, not being wilful and malicious, committed in hunting, fishing, or in the pursuit of game, but that every such trespass shall be punishable in the same manner as if this Act had not passed. (*a*)

(*a*) The distinction between §§ 39 and 52 is that the former section can only be made use of by way of Indictment, whilst the latter section is available for summary proceedings before Magistrates; and the greater simplicity of the latter procedure is considered by many Library Authorities to outweigh the value of the more comprehensive language of § 39.

{32 & 33 Vict.] *Lands Clauses Amendment.* [c. 18] 1869.

32 & 33 VICT. 18.

An Act to amend the "*Lands Clauses Consolidation Act.*" (a)   Revised
[24th June, 1869.   Statutes 2nd ed.

(a) See § 4, and the Memorandum appended to the "Lands Clauses Consolidation Act, 1845," *ante*.   vol. xii. p. 452

[38 & 39 Vict.]   *Public Health.*   [c. 55] 1875.

38 & 39 VICT. 55.

An Act for consolidating and amending the Acts relating to   Revised
Public Health in England. (a)   [11th August, 1875.   Statute 2nd ed.

(a) The Sections here given are, as regards England and Wales, incorporated by the "Public Libraries Act, 1892" (55 & 56 Vict. 53, 19).   vol. xiii. pp. 790, 865.

BORROWING POWERS.

233. Any Local Authority may with the sanction of the Local Government Board, for the purpose of defraying any costs, charges, and expenses incurred or to be incurred by them in the execution of the "Sanitary Acts," or of this Act, or for the purpose of discharging any loans contracted under the "Sanitary Acts," or this Act, borrow or re-borrow, and take up at interest any sums of money necessary for defraying any such costs, charges and expenses, or for discharging any such loans as aforesaid.

Power to borrow on credit of Rates.

An Urban Authority may borrow or re-borrow any such sums on the credit of any fund or all or any Rates or Rate out of which they are authorised to defray expenses incurred by them in the execution of this Act, and for the purpose of securing the repayment of any sums so borrowed, with interest thereon, they may mortgage to the persons by or on behalf of whom such sums are advanced any such fund or Rates or Rate.

*   *   *   *   *   *

BOOK I.—LIBRARIES AND MUSEUMS.

Regulations as to exercise of borrowing powers

234. The exercise of the powers of borrowing conferred by this Act shall be subject to the following regulations; viz.,

(1.) Money shall not be borrowed except for permanent works (including under this expression any works of which the cost ought in the opinion of the Local Government Board to be spread over a term of years):

(2.) The sum borrowed shall not at any time exceed, with the balances of all the outstanding loans contracted by the Local Authority under the "Sanitary Acts" and this Act, in the whole the assessable value for 2 years of the premises assessable within the District in respect of which such money may be borrowed :

(3.) Where the sum proposed to be borrowed with such balances (if any) would exceed the assessable value for one year of such premises, the Local Government Board shall not give their sanction to such loan until one of their Inspectors has held a Local Inquiry and reported to the said Board:

(4.) The money may be borrowed for such time, not exceeding 60 years, as the Local Authority, with the sanction of the Local Government Board, determine in each case ;

And, subject as aforesaid, the Local Authority shall either pay off the money so borrowed by equal annual instalments of principal or of principal and interest, or they shall in every year set apart as a sinking fund, and accumulate in the way of compound interest by investing the same in the purchase of Exchequer bills or other Government securities, such sum as will with accumulations in the way of compound interest be sufficient, after payment of all expenses, to pay off the moneys so borrowed within the period sanctioned:

(5.) A Local Authority may at any time apply the whole or any part of a sinking fund set apart under this Act in or towards the discharge of the moneys for the repayment of which the fund has been established ;

Provided that they pay into the fund in each year, and accumulate until the whole of the moneys borrowed are discharged, a sum equivalent to the interest which would have been produced by the sinking fund or the part of the sinking fund so applied :

(6.) Where money is borrowed for the purpose of discharging a previous loan, the time for repayment of the money so borrowed shall not extend beyond the unexpired portion of the period for which the original loan was sanctioned, unless with the sanction of the Local Government Board, and shall in no case be extended beyond the period of 60 years from the date of the original loan.

Where any Urban Authority borrow any money for the purpose of defraying private improvement expenses, or expenses in respect of which they have determined a part only of the District to be liable, it shall be the duty of such Authority, as between the Ratepayers of the District, to make good, so far as they can, the money so borrowed, as occasion requires, either out of Private Improvement Rates, or out of a Rate levied in such part of the District as aforesaid.

* * * * * *

236. Every Mortgage authorised to be made under this Act shall be by deed, truly stating the date, consideration, and the time and place of payment, and shall be sealed with the common seal of the Local Authority, and may be made according to the form contained in Schedule IV. to this Act, or to the like effect. *Form of mortgage.*

237. There shall be kept at the Office of the Local Authority a Register of the Mortgages on each Rate, and within 14 days after the date of any Mortgage an entry shall be made in the Register of the number and date thereof, and of the names and description of the parties thereto, as stated in the deed. *Register of mortgages.*

Every such Register shall be open to public inspection during office hours at the said Office, without fee or reward;

And any Clerk or other person having the custody of the same, refusing to allow such inspection, shall be liable to a penalty not exceeding £5.

238. Any mortgagee or other person entitled to any Mortgage under this Act may transfer his estate and interest therein to any other person by deed duly stamped, truly stating its date and the consideration for the transfer; *Transfer of mortgages.*

And such transfers may be according to the form contained in Schedule IV. to this Act, or to the like effect.

There shall be kept at the Office of the Local Authority a Register of the transfers of Mortgage charged on each Rate, and within 30 days after the date of such deed of transfer, if executed within the United Kingdom, or within 30 days after its arrival in the United Kingdom, if executed elsewhere, the same shall be produced to the Clerk of the Local

Authority, who shall, on payment of a sum not exceeding 5s., cause an entry to be made in such Register of its date, and of the names and description of the parties thereto, as stated in the transfer;

And until such entry is made the Local Authority shall not be in any manner responsible to the transferee.

On the registration of any transfer the transferee, his executors, or administrators shall be entitled to the full benefit of the original mortgage, and the principal and interest secured thereby;

And any transferee may in like manner transfer his estate and interest in any such Mortgage;

And no person except the last transferee, his executors, or administrators shall be entitled to release or discharge any such mortgage or any money secured thereby.

If the Clerk of the Local Authority wilfully neglects or refuses to make in the Register any entry by this section required to be made, he shall be liable to a penalty not exceeding £20.

Receiver may be appointed in certain cases.
239. If at the expiration of six months from the time when any principal money or interest has become due on any Mortgage of Rates made under this Act, and after demand in writing, the same is not paid, the mortgagee or other person entitled thereto may, without prejudice to any other mode of recovery, apply for the appointment of a Receiver to a Court of Summary Jurisdiction;

And such Court may, after hearing the parties, appoint in writing under their hands and seals some person to collect and receive the whole or a competent part of the Rates liable to the payment of the principal or interest in respect of which the application is made, until such principal or interest, or both, as the case may be, together with the costs of the application and of collection, are fully paid.

On such appointment being made, all such Rates, or such competent part thereof as aforesaid, shall be paid to the person appointed, and when so paid shall be so much money received by or to the use of the mortgagee or mortgagees of such Rates, and shall be rateably apportioned between them:

Provided that no such application shall be entertained unless the sum or sums due and owing to the applicant amount to £1,000, or unless a joint application is made by two or more mortgagees or other persons to whom there may be due, after such lapse of time and demand as last aforesaid, moneys collectively amounting to that sum.

[40 & 41 Vict.] *Public Libraries Act (Ireland)* [C. 15] 1877.
Amendment.

40 & 41 VICT. 15.

An Act to amend the Public Libraries Act *(Ireland)*, 1855.   Law
[28th June, 1877.] Reports Statutes,
WHEREAS, etc.:   vol. xii.
1. In citing this Act for any purpose whatever it shall be p. 124
sufficient to use the expression "The Public Libraries (Ireland) Short title.
Amendment Act, 1877."
2. The term "principal Act" shall mean the Public Interpretation.
Libraries Act (Ireland), 1855.
3. The terms "science and art" and "schools of science Powers of
and art" used in the said principal Act shall be deemed to principal
include the science and art of music and schools of music tended to
respectively; and the council or board of any borough or the schools of
town commissioners of any town shall be at liberty to apply music.
such portion as they may deem fit of the rate which they are
or may be authorised to levy, under the provisions of the
principal Act, towards the maintenance and support of, and
payment of the salaries of teachers of a school or schools of
music, and the purchase of musical instruments, books, and
other requisites for the use of such school or schools.
4. The committee in which the general management, Constitution of the
regulation, and control of such libraries, museums, or schools committee
may be vested under the provisions of the 12th section of the of management.
principal Act, may consist in part of persons not members of
the council or board, or commissioners.
5. For carrying the principal Act and this Act into Powers to
execution the council, board, or commissioners respectively borrow on
may, with the approval of the Commissioners of Her Majesty's mortgage.
Treasury, from time to time borrow, at interest, on the
security of a mortgage or bond of the borough fund or the
town fund, or of the rates levied in pursuance of the principal
Act, such sums of money as may be by them respectively
required, and the Commissioners of Public Works in Ireland
may from time to time advance and lend any such sums of
money. The clauses and provisions of the "Companies
Clauses Consolidation Act, 1845," with respect to the borrowing of money on mortgage or bond, and the accountability
of officers, and the recovery of damages and penalties, so far

as such provisions may respectively be applicable to the purposes of the principal Act and of this Act, shall be respectively incorporated therewith.

Acts to be construed as one. 6. The said principal Act and this Act shall be read and construed together as one Act.

1877. [40 & 41 Vict.] *Public Libraries Acts Amendment.* [c. 54]

40 & 41 VICT. 54.

Law Reports Statutes, vol. xii. p. 306. An Act to amend the Public Libraries Acts. (a)

[14th August, 1877.

(a) This Act is repealed so far as concerns England and Wales by 53 & 54 Vict. 68, which was itself repealed by 55 & 56 Vict. 53, the provisions of which Act are now operative in that part of the United Kingdom. Though not specifically repealed so far as regards Scotland, the provisions of the Scotch Act, 50 & 51 Vict. 42, must be taken to be substituted for those in this Act.

WHEREAS by the Public Libraries Acts, 18 & 19 Vict. 40, for Ireland; 29 & 30 Vict. 114, for England; and 30 & 31 Vict. 37, for Scotland, the mode by which the Act is to be adopted is prescribed to be by public meeting, and it has been found that in many cases a public meeting is a most incorrect and unsatisfactory mode, and fails to indicate the general opinion of the ratepayers, and it is desirable to ascertain these opinions more correctly:

Be it enacted, etc.:

Ratepayers' opinions may be ascertained by voting-papers. 1. It shall be competent for the prescribed local authority in any place or community which has the power to adopt one of the above recited Acts, to ascertain the opinions of the majority of the ratepayers either by the prescribed public meeting or by the issue of a voting-paper to each ratepayer, and the subsequent collection and scrutiny thereof, and any expense in connection with such voting-papers shall be borne in the same way as the expense of a public meeting would be borne, and the decision of the majority so ascertained shall be equally binding.

Ratepayers may stipulate for modified 2. In addition to the simple vote "Yes" or "No" to the adoption of the Act, such voting-paper may stipulate that its adoption shall be subject to a limitation to some lower

PART IV.—STATUTES.—47 & 48 VICT. c. 37.

rate of assessment than the maximum allowed by Act of Parliament in force at the time, and such lower limit, if once adopted, shall not be subsequently altered except by public vote similarly taken. {.sc Assessment.}

3. "Ratepayer" shall mean every inhabitant who would have to pay the Free Library assessment in event of the Act being adopted. {.sc Definition.}

4. This Act may be cited as the Public Libraries Amendment Act, 1877. {.sc Short title.}

[47 & 48 Vict.] *Public Libraries Act*, 1884.   [c. 37] 1884.

47 & 48 VICT. 37.

An Act to amend the Public Libraries Acts.

[28th July, 1884.

Law Reports Statutes, vol. xx. p. 64.

BE it enacted, etc.:

1. Whereas doubts have arisen as to whether authorities acting under the Public Libraries Acts have power to fulfil the conditions required for a parliamentary grant in aid of the establishment of a school of science and art, and it is expedient to remove such doubts: It is therefore hereby declared and enacted that— {.sc Power of council, board, etc., to accept parliamentary grant.}

Where any authority acting under the Public Libraries Acts accepts a grant out of moneys provided by Parliament from any Committee of the Privy Council on Education towards the purchase of the site, or the erection, enlargement, or repair, of any school for science and art, or school for science, or school for art, or of the residence of any teacher in such school, or towards the furnishing of any such school, such authority shall have power to accept such grant upon the conditions prescribed for the acceptance thereof by the said Committee, and to execute such instruments as may be required by the said Committee for carrying into effect such conditions, and upon payment of the grant shall, together with their successors, be bound by such conditions and instrument, and have power and be bound to fulfil and observe the same.

2. Whereas § 18 of the "Public Libraries Act, 1855," as regards England, (*a*) and § 9 of the "Public Libraries Act (Ireland), 1855," as regards Ireland, provide for the erection {.sc Explanation of 18 & 19 Vict. 70, 18;}

106   BOOK I.—LIBRARIES AND MUSEUMS.

18 & 19 Vict. 70, 9, and
30 & 31 Vict. 37, 10.

of buildings "suitable for public libraries, or museums, or both, or for schools for science or art":

And whereas § 10 of the "Public Libraries Act (Scotland), 1867," (a) provides for the erection of buildings "suitable for public libraries, art galleries, or museums, or each respectively," and doubts are entertained as to the meaning of those provisions: Now, therefore, it is hereby declared and enacted that—

Buildings may under the said sections be erected for public libraries, public museums, schools for science, art galleries, and schools for art, or for any one or more of those objects.

(a) Repealed, and other provisions substituted.

Power to establish library, museum, or school for science or art in connection with any of the others of them.

3.—(1.) Where any of the following institutions, namely, a public museum, a public library, a school for science and art, a school for science, a school for art, or an art gallery has been established either before or after the passing of this Act under the Public Libraries Acts, or any of them, there may at any time be established in connection therewith any other of the said institutions without any further proceedings being taken under the said Acts.

(2.) Section 10 of the "Public Libraries Amendment Act (England and Scotland), 1866," and section 17 of the "Public Libraries Act (Scotland), 1867," are hereby repealed, without prejudice to anything done under those sections. (a)

(a) Both these Acts have since been wholly repealed.

4. In this Act,—

Definitions.

The expression "Public Libraries Acts" means as respects England, Scotland, and Ireland respectively, the Acts mentioned in the first, second, and third parts respectively of the schedule to this Act.

The expression "authority acting under the Public Libraries Acts" means the council, board, magistrates, or commissioners, acting in execution of the said "Public Libraries Act."

Short titles.

5. This Act may be cited as the "Public Libraries Act, 1884."

*   *   *   *   *   *

The Acts mentioned in the third part of the schedule to this Act may be cited together with this Act as the Public Libraries (Ireland) Acts, 1855 to 1884.

SCHEDULE. (a)

PART III.

Public Libraries (Ireland) Acts.

Session and Chapter	Title
18 & 19 Vict. 40	The Public Libraries Act (Ireland), 1855.
40 & 41 Vict. 15	The Public Libraries (Ireland) Amendment Act, 1877.
40 & 41 Vict. 54	The Public Libraries Amendment Act, 1877.

(a) Repealed as to Scotland by 50 & 51 Vict. 42, and as to England and Wales by 55 & 56 Vict. 53.

[50 & 51 Vict.] *Public Libraries Consolidation* [C. 42] 1887.
(Scotland).

50 & 51 VICT. 42.

An Act to amend and consolidate the Public Libraries (Scot-   Law
land) Acts.   [16th September, 1887.   Reports
  Statutes,
  vol. xxiv.
WHEREAS, etc.:   p. 166.

1. This Act may be cited as the "Public Libraries Conso- Short title.
lidation (Scotland) Act, 1887," and shall apply to Scotland
only.

2. The following words and expressions in this Act shall Defini-
have the meanings hereby assigned to them, unless there be tions.
something in the subject or context repugnant to such construction; that is to say,

"Burgh" shall include Royal Burgh, Parliamentary
Burgh, Burgh incorporated by Act of Parliament, Burgh
of Regality, Burgh of Barony, and any populous place
or Police Burgh administered wholly or partly under
any general or local Police Act, and the boundaries of
such Burgh shall, for the purpose of this Act, be the
boundaries to which such general or local Police Act
extends:

"Parish" shall mean a Parish for which a separate Poor
Rate is or can be imposed, or for which a separate
parochial board is or can be appointed, and shall be

108 BOOK I.—LIBRARIES AND MUSEUMS.

exclusive of the area of any Burgh or part of a Burgh situated therein :

" Householders " shall mean, in the case of a Burgh, all persons whose names are entered on the Municipal Register, and in the case of a Parish, all persons entitled to vote in the election of a School Board in such Parish, under the provisions of the " Education (Scotland) Act, 1872," and any Act amending the same :

35 & 36 Vict. 62.

" Magistrates and Council " shall be applied collectively, and not separately, and shall include Provost, Magistrates, and Town Council, Magistrates and Commissioners of Police, and any other body of persons for the time being in office, by authority of whom the Burgh General Assessment is levied; and where in any Burgh the Magistrates and Council form a Corporate Body, and there is also in the same Burgh a Board of Commissioners of Police by whom the Burgh General Assessment is levied, the words " Magistrates and Council " shall, as regards the levying and recovering of the Library Rate, apply to such Commissioners of Police, but in every other respect it shall apply to such Corporate Body of Magistrates and Council :

" Chief Magistrate " shall include Provost, and shall apply to any Magistrate legally acting as Chief Magistrate for the time being :

" Board " shall mean the Parochial Board acting under the Act 8 & 9 Vict. 83, and any Act amending the same :

8 & 9 Vict. 83.

" Committee " shall mean the Committee appointed under any Public Libraries Act affecting Scotland for the time being, or this Act :

" Municipal Register " shall mean the Register, List, or Roll of persons entitled to vote in an election of Town Councillors or Commissioners of Police, in a Burgh, made up according to the law in force for the time being :

" Burgh General Assessment " shall mean an Assessment which, under any general or local Police Act, shall be applicable to the general purposes of such Act :

" Library Rate " shall mean the Rate or Assessment authorised by this Act for the purpose of carrying the Act into execution :

" Libraries and Museums " and " Libraries or Museums " shall include Schools for Science, Art Galleries, and Schools for Art, and these expressions, or either of

PART IV.—STATUTES.—50 & 51 VICT. c. 42. 109

them, when used in the singular, shall include a School
for Science, an Art Gallery, and a School for Art:
Words importing the masculine gender shall, when applied
to householders, include female householders.

3. " The Public Libraries (Scotland) Acts, 1867 to 1884," Repeal.
so far as the same relate to Scotland, are hereby repealed; 30 & 31
but such repeal shall not invalidate or affect anything already 34 & 35
done in pursuance of these Acts, or any of them, and all Vict. 59;
Burghs and Parishes in Scotland which before the passing of Vict. 54;
this Act have adopted the recited Acts shall thereafter be 47 & 48
subject to the provisions of this Act:
Provided always, that nothing in this Act contained shall 50 & 51
prejudice or affect the provisions of the "Edinburgh Public Vict. 85.
Library Assessment Act, 1887."

4 (a). Upon the requisition in writing of the Magistrates and Adoption
Council of any Burgh, or of ten or more householders in any of Act.
Burgh or Parish, the Chief Magistrate of such Burgh, or, in
the case of a Parish, the Sheriff of the County in which such
Parish or the greater part of the area thereof is situated,
shall ascertain the opinions of the householders in such Burgh
or Parish as to the adoption of this Act in the manner set
forth in Schedules (A) or (B) hereto annexed, which
schedules shall be construed and have effect as part of this Act.

Provided that where in any Burgh the number of householders exceeds 3,000, the Chief Magistrate shall adopt the
procedure, by way of voting-paper, set forth in Schedule
(A), but in any other case it shall be optional to the Chief
Magistrate or to the Sheriff, as the case may be, to adopt
such procedure by way of voting-paper, or the procedure by
way of Public Meeting, set forth in Schedule (B).

(a) Repealed so far as relates to burghs by 57 & 58 Vict. 20, 2.

5 (a). In the event of the householders determining by a If not
majority of votes that this Act shall be adopted in any Burgh adopted, no
or Parish, the same shall from thenceforth come into operation procedure
therein;   for 2 years.
But if by a majority of votes they shall determine against the
adoption, the like procedure shall not take place for the space
of at least 2 years from the date of such determination.

(a) Repealed so far as relates to burghs by 57 & 58 Vict. 20, 2.

6 (a). The expenses of the procedure for determining as to Expenses
the adoption of this Act shall, if the Act be not adopted, be of deter-
paid, in the case of a Burgh, out of the Burgh General Assess- to adop-
ment, and in the case of a Parish, out of the assessment for tion.

BOOK I.—LIBRARIES AND MUSEUMS.

the relief of the poor in such Parish, or where there is no such assessment, by a Rate which the Board are hereby empowered to levy and recover for this purpose, in the same manner and subject to the same conditions as are applicable to the Library Rate;

But if the Act shall have been adopted the expenses of the procedure under which it has been adopted shall be payable out of the Library Rate, and it shall be in the power of the Chief Magistrate or of the Sheriff, as the case may be, immediately upon the adoption of the Act to borrow such sum or sums as may be necessary to defray such expenses on the security of the Library Rate to be afterwards levied (a).

(a) Repealed so far as relates to burghs by 57 & 58 Vict. 20, 2.

Expenses of carrying Act into execution.
7. The expenses of carrying this Act into execution, when adopted, including all sums payable in respect of interest and sinking fund for money authorised to be borrowed, and all sums necessary for the maintenance and management of the Libraries and Museums established under this Act, or to which this Act applies, or for the purchase of the articles and things authorised by this Act to be purchased, shall be paid out of the Library Rate, which shall be levied and recovered, in the case of a Burgh (a), by the Magistrates and Council, from the same description of persons and property, and with and under the like powers, provisions, and exceptions as the Burgh General Assessment, and in the case of a Parish by the Board, from the same description of persons and property, and with and under the like powers, provisions, and exceptions as the assessment leviable under the Act 8 & 9 Vict. 83.

(a) As to Edinburgh, see 50 & 51 Vict. c. lxxxv.

Rate not to exceed 1d. per £.
8. The amount of the Library Rate to be levied in any year shall in no case exceed the sum of 1d. in the £ of yearly rent or annual value as appearing on the valuation roll.

And where, under the provisions of any general or local Police Act, the Burgh General Assessment is or may be levied at a higher rate upon lands or premises above a certain fixed rent than upon lower rented lands or premises, such provisions, so far as they authorise such differential rate, shall not be applicable to or affect the Library Rate.

Accounts to be open to inspection, and to be audited
9. The Magistrates and Council of a Burgh, or the Board of a Parish, as the case may be, shall provide and keep books in which shall be entered true and regular accounts of their receipts, payments, and liabilities with reference to the

execution of this Act, which books shall, at all reasonable times, be open, without fee or reward, to the inspection of every person liable to be assessed for the Library Rate ; *and published annually.*

And the Magistrates and Council or Board, as the case may be, shall cause such accounts to be annually audited by one or more competent Auditors, not being members of the Committee, after which audit the accounts shall be signed by two of the Magistrates and Council, or two members of the Board, as the case may be, and an abstract thereof similarly signed shall be printed and shall be inserted in one or more newspapers published or circulated in the Burgh or Parish.

10. The Magistrates and Council or Board, as the case may be, may from time to time appropriate, for the purposes of this Act, any lands or buildings vested in them, and may, out of the Library Rate, or out of money borrowed as herein provided, purchase, feu, or rent any land, or any suitable building ; *Lands, etc., may be appropriated, purchased, or rented.*

And may, upon the land so appropriated, rented, feued, or purchased, erect any building suitable for Public Libraries, Public Museums, Schools for Science, Art Galleries, and Schools for Art, or for any one or more of those objects, and may alter or extend any buildings for such purposes, and repair and improve the same respectively, and fit up, furnish, and supply the same respectively with all requisite furniture, fittings, and conveniences.

11. The clauses and provisions of the "Lands Clauses Consolidation (Scotland) Act, 1845," with respect to the purchase of lands by agreement, and with respect to the purchase-money or compensation coming to parties having limited interests, or prevented from treating or not making title, and with respect to conveyances of lands, so far as such clauses and provisions are applicable to purchases, feus, or leases authorised by this Act, and are not herein expressly varied, shall be incorporated with this Act ; *Parts of 8 & 9 Vict. 19, incorporated.*

And the expression "the special Act" used in such clauses and provisions shall be construed to mean this Act ;

And the expression "the promoters of the undertaking" used in such clauses and provisions shall be construed to mean the Magistrates and Council, or the Board, as the case may be.

12. The Magistrates and Council, or the Board, as the case may be, may sell any lands, buildings, or other property vested in them for the purposes of this Act, or exchange the same for any lands, buildings, or other property better adapted for such purposes, and the money arising from such *Lands, etc., may be sold or exchanged.*

sale, and the property received in exchange, shall be applied and held for the purposes of this Act.

Lands, etc., vested in Magistrates, etc., and Boards.

13. The lands and buildings so to be appropriated, purchased, or rented, and all other real or personal property whatever, presented to or purchased for any Library or Museum established under this Act or to which this Act applies, shall in the case of a Burgh be vested in the Magistrates and Council, and in the case of a Parish in the Board.

Powers of borrowing.

14. The Magistrates and Council, or the Board, as the case may be, may from time to time borrow at interest on mortgage or bond on the security of the Rate to be levied in pursuance of this Act, for the purposes thereof, a sum or sums of money not exceeding the capital sum represented by one-fourth part of the Library Rate, authorised by this Act, capitalised at the rate of 20 years' purchase of such sum ;

And on repayment of such sum or sums, or any part thereof, they may from time to time re-borrow in manner and for the purposes aforesaid, but so that the whole sum borrowed at any one time shall not exceed the amount of the said capital sum after deducting therefrom any sums set apart as a sinking fund as hereinafter provided.(*a*)

(*a*) As to Edinburgh, see 50 & 51 Vict. c. lxxxv., *post*.

Sinking fund.

15. The Magistrates and Council, or the Board, as the case may be, are hereby required to set apart annually, as a sinking fund for the extinction of capital sums, borrowed under the authority of any Library Act in force for the time being, or of this Act, a sum equal to at least one-fiftieth part of the money so borrowed, and such sinking fund shall be from time to time applied in repayment of the money so borrowed, and to no other purpose whatever, and shall be lodged in a Joint Stock Bank of issue in Scotland, or invested in Government securities, or lent out at interest in the name and at the discretion of the Magistrates and Council, or the Board, as the case may be, until the same be applied for the purpose before specified.

Parts of 10 Vict. 16, incorporated.

16. The clauses and provisions (*a*) of the "Commissioners Clauses Act, 1847," with respect to the liabilities of the Commissioners, and to legal proceedings by or against the Commissioners, and with respect to mortgages to be executed by the Commissioners, excepting §§ 84, 86, and 87, shall, unless herein expressly varied, be incorporated with this Act, and the several words and expressions. to which by the last recited Act meanings are assigned, shall in this Act

PART IV.—STATUTES.—50 & 51 VICT. c. 42. 113

have the same respective meanings, unless there be something in the subject or context repugnant to such construction;

And the expression "the special Act" used in such clauses and provisions herewith incorporated shall mean this Act;

And the expression "the Commissioners" shall mean the Magistrates and Council, or Board, and the Committee in the discharge of their respective duties under this Act.

(a) These provisions will be found at p. 87 et seq., ante.

17. When the Magistrates and Council, or Board, as the case may be, accept a grant out of moneys provided by Parliament, from any Committee of the Privy Council on Education, towards the purchase of the site, or the erection, enlargement, or repair of any School for Science and Art, or School for Science, or School for Art, or of the residence of any teacher in such School, or towards the furnishing of any such School, they shall have power to accept such grant upon the conditions prescribed for the acceptance thereof by the said Committee, and to execute such instruments as may be required by the said Committee for carrying into effect such conditions, and upon payment of the grant shall, together with their successors, be bound by such conditions and instrument, and have power and be bound to fulfil and observe the same. {.sidenote}Power to accept parliamentary grant under conditions.

18. The Magistrates and Council of any Burgh, or the Board of any Parish where this Act has been adopted, shall, within 1 month after its adoption, and thereafter from year to year, in the case of a Burgh, at the first Meeting after the annual election of Town Councillors or Commissioners of Police, and in the case of a Parish, at the first Meeting after the annual Meeting for the election of representative Members of the Parochial Board, appoint a Committee, consisting of not less than 10 nor more than 20 Members, half of whom shall be chosen from amongst the Magistrates and Council, or Board, as the case may be, and the remaining half from amongst the householders of the Burgh or Parish other than the Magistrates and Council, or Board, and three Members of such Committee shall form a quorum. {.sidenote}Committee to be appointed.

19. Any Member of Committee shall have power to resign office upon giving at least fourteen days' previous notice to the Clerk of the Committee of his intention so to resign; {.sidenote}Appointments to vacancies in Committee.

And in the event of any vacancy occurring in the Committee during their term of office by the resignation or death of any Member, the Committee shall forthwith cause the same

I

114   BOOK I.—LIBRARIES AND MUSEUMS.

to be intimated to the Magistrates and Council, or Board, and the Magistrates and Council, or Board, as the case may be, may at a meeting thereafter elect from among themselves, or from among the householders other than themselves, according to the class in which the vacancy has arisen, a Member of Committee in place of the Member so resigning or dying, provided that no proceedings of the Committee shall be invalidated or be illegal in consequence of a vacancy or vacancies in the number of the Committee.

Meetings of Committee, and appointment of Chairman.

20. The Committee appointed as aforesaid shall, in the case of a Burgh, meet once in every three months, or oftener if necessary, and in the case of a Parish, as often as may be necessary, to determine as to any business falling to be transacted by them, and shall appoint a Chairman from among their own number, who shall hold office until next election of Committee;

And such Chairman shall, in case of equality, have a casting vote in addition to his vote as an individual;

Provided that, in the event of a vacancy occurring in the office of Chairman, the Committee shall at their first meeting thereafter appoint a new Chairman, and in the absence of the Chairman of Committee at any meeting, the meeting shall appoint a Chairman for the time being, who at that meeting shall exercise the privileges of the Chairman of Committee.

Powers of Committee.

21. The Committee shall manage, regulate, and control all Libraries and Museums established under this Act, or to which this Act applies: and shall have power to do all things necessary for such management, including the following powers; that is to say,

To appoint Sub-Committees of their own number:

To appoint a salaried clerk, and salaried librarians, officers, and servants to act during the pleasure of the Committee, and to pay and dismiss them:

To purchase books, newspapers, reviews, magazines, and other periodicals, statuary, pictures, engravings, maps, specimens of Art and Science, and such other articles and things as may be necessary for the establishment, increase, and use of the Libraries and Museums under their control, and to do all things necessary for keeping the same in a proper state of preservation and repair:

To provide from time to time the necessary fuel, lighting, and other matters:

To sell or exchange any books, works of art, or other

PART IV.—STATUTES.—50 & 51 VICT. c. 42.

property of which there may be duplicates, provided that the money arising from such sale, and the property received in exchange shall be applied and held for the purposes of this Act :

To provide suitable rooms in the Libraries within which the books, periodicals, and newspapers may be read :

To lend out, for the purpose of being read by the householders and inhabitants of the Burgh or Parish in and for which the Committee has been appointed, the books of any Library under their control, or such of them as they may consider proper; and at their discretion to grant the same privilege to the inmates of Industrial Schools, Training Ships, Reformatories, Barracks, and other similar Institutions, established for or in the Burgh or Parish; and also to any person carrying on business within the limits of the Burgh or Parish, or to any employee engaged in employment therein, although such person or employee may not be a householder, and may not reside within such limits :

To compile and print catalogues of all or any books, articles, and things in the Libraries or Museums under their control, and reports of their proceedings, and to sell the same, the proceeds to be applied for the purposes of this Act.

22. It shall be lawful for the Committee to make by-laws for regulating all or any matters and things whatsoever connected with the control, management, protection, and use of any property, articles, or things under their control for the purposes of this Act, and to impose such penalties for breaches of such by-laws, not exceeding £5 for each offence, as may be considered expedient;

And from time to time, as they shall think fit, to repeal, alter, vary, or re-enact any such by-laws, provided always that such by-laws and alterations thereof shall not be repugnant to the law of Scotland, and before being acted on shall be signed by a quorum of the Committee, and, except in so far as they relate solely to the officers or servants of the Committee, such by-laws shall be approved of by the Magistrates and Council, or the Board, as the case may be, and shall be approved of and confirmed by the Sheriff of the County in which the Burgh or Parish, or the greater part of the area thereof, is situated ;

Provided also, that nothing herein contained shall preclude the Magistrates and Council, or Board, as the case may be,

Power to Committee to make by-laws.

from recovering the value of articles or things damaged, or the amount of the damage sustained, against all parties liable for the same. (*a*)

(*a*) It is the practice in some towns to charge for a borrowers' ticket. This could only be justified by a By-law duly made under this section, and it might be held to be contrary to § 32 *post*).

Newspaper publication of by-laws before confirmation, and time and manner of stating objections.

23. No by-laws or alterations thereof requiring confirmation shall be confirmed, as before mentioned, unless notice of the intention to apply for confirmation of the same shall have been given in one or more newspapers published and circulated in the district one month at least before the hearing of the application for confirmation, and any party aggrieved by any such by-laws or alterations thereof, on giving notice of the nature of his objection to the Clerk to the Committee 10 days before the hearing of the application for confirmation, may, by himself or his counsel, attorney, or agent, be heard thereon, but not so as to allow more than one party to be heard upon the same matter of objection.

Exhibition of by-laws previous to confirmation.

24. For one month at least before any such application for confirmation of any by-laws or alterations thereof, a copy of such proposed by-laws or alterations shall be kept at the office of the Clerk to the Committee, and shall also be put up in some conspicuous place in each of the Libraries and Museums of the Committee, and all persons may, at all reasonable times, inspect such copy without fee or reward;

And the Clerk to the Committee shall furnish every person who shall apply for the same with a copy thereof, or of any part thereof, on payment of sixpence for every one hundred words so to be copied.

Printed copy of by-laws to be provided.

25. The Clerk to the Committee shall give a printed copy of the confirmed by-laws, for the time being in force, to every person applying for the same, without charge;

And a copy thereof shall be painted or placed on boards, and put up in some conspicuous part of each of the Libraries and Museums of the Committee, and such boards with the by-laws thereon shall be renewed from time to time as occasion shall require, and shall be open to inspection without fee or reward.

By-laws when confirmed and published to be in force.

26. All by-laws or alterations thereof, made and confirmed according to the provisions of this Act, when so published and put up, shall be binding upon and be observed by all parties, and shall be a sufficient warrant for all persons acting under the same.

Evidence of by-laws.

27. The production of a written or printed copy of the

by-laws requiring confirmation as aforesaid, authenticated by the signature of the sheriff who shall have confirmed the same, and a written or printed copy of the by-laws not requiring such confirmation, authenticated by the Common Seal of the Committee, and signed by the Chairman of the Committee at the time when the same were made, shall be evidence of the existence and making of such by-laws in all cases for prosecution under the same, without proof of the signature of such sheriff, or the Common Seal of the Committee, or the signature of their Chairman;

And with respect to the proof of the publication of such by-laws it shall be sufficient to prove that a board containing a copy thereof was put up and continued in manner by this Act directed.

28. All penalties and forfeitures exigible under this Act, and the Acts incorporated wholly or partially herewith, or under any by-law made in pursuance thereof, may be recovered by an ordinary small-debt action in the name of the Clerk to the Committee for the time being before either the sheriff or justices of the district; *Recovery of penalties and forfeitures.*

And the same shall be payable to the Committee, and shall, when recovered, be applied by them for the purposes of this Act;

And in any prosecution under this Act an excerpt from the books of the Committee, certified by the Clerk or other proper officer, shall be held equivalent to the books of the Committee, and all entries in the books of the Committee bearing that any book or books mentioned or referred to therein has or have been borrowed by the person complained against shall be taken and received as evidence of the fact, and the *onus probandi* shall be thrown on the party complained against, and if decree passes against such party, he shall be found liable in costs.

29. All actions at the instance of the Committee shall be brought in name of the Clerk to the Committee, and in all actions against the Committee, it shall be sufficient to call the Clerk to the Committee for the time being as defender, and service on him shall be sufficient service; *Actions by or against. Committee.*

And all actions brought by or against the Clerk to the Committee in his official character shall be continued by or against his successors in office without any action of transference.

30. The Committee shall in the month of April in every year make up, or cause to be made up, an estimate of the *Estimates to be made up.*

sums required in order to defray the interest of any money borrowed, the payment of the sinking fund, and the expense of maintaining and managing all Libraries or Museums under their control for the year after Whit-Sunday then next to come, and for the purpose of purchasing the books, articles, and things authorised by this Act to be purchased for such Libraries or Museums, and shall report the same to the Magistrates and Council in the case of a Burgh, or to the Board in the case of a Parish, and the Magistrates and Council or the Board, as the case may be, shall provide the amount required out of the Library Rate to be levied by them, and shall pay over to the Committee the sum necessary for the annual expenditure by them in terms of their estimate.

Power to add to institutions established.

31. Where any of the following institutions, namely, a Public Library, a Public Museum, a School for Science and Art, a School for Science, a School for Art, or an Art Gallery has been established under any Public Library Act in force for the time being, or under this Act, there may at any time be established, in connection therewith, any other of the said institutions without further proceedings being taken for the adoption of this Act.

Libraries, etc., to be free.

32. All Libraries, Museums, or Art Galleries established under this Act, or to which this Act applies, shall be open to the public free of charge, and no charge shall be made for the use of books or magazines issued for home reading.

SCHEDULES.

§ 4.

SCHEDULE (A).

PROCEDURE FOR DETERMINING BY VOTING PAPER AS TO THE ADOPTION OF THE ACT.

(1.) Upon receipt of the requisition specified in the Act,(*a*) the Chief Magistrate or the Sheriff, as the case may be, shall, without unnecessary delay, cause to be printed, and to be delivered or sent by post to each householder, an intimation and a voting paper, in the respective forms appended hereto, and the intimation may be prefixed to the voting paper and on the same paper therewith, or may be printed separately,

(*a*) As to the adoption of the Act in a Burgh see 57 & 58 Vict. 20 (*post*).

provided it be delivered or posted simultaneously with the voting paper.

(2.) In the case of a Burgh, the voting paper shall bear the number of the householder on the Municipal Register, and where the Burgh is divided into Wards, the number of the Ward; and in the case of a Parish the voting paper shall bear a number relative to the entry of the householder in a copy of the Valuation Roll applicable to such Parish, or in a list of the householders in such Parish, which copy or list, distinguishing the amount of rental at which each person is assessed, the assessor, under the Acts in force for the valuation of lands and heritages in Scotland, is hereby required to make, certify, and furnish to the Sheriff, within 14 days of an application by him to that effect, on payment of a fee of not more than 1s. for each 100 names; and such copy or list, certified as aforesaid, shall be sufficient proof of the qualification of the householders named therein.

(3.) The intimation aforesaid shall specify the place at which the voting paper is to be collected, and shall also specify a day for collection, hereinafter called the day of the poll, being not less than 3 lawful days, nor more than 10 lawful days from the last date of the delivery or of the posting of the voting papers to the householders.

(4.) The Chief Magistrate or the Sheriff, as the case may be, shall, before the issue of such voting papers, appoint a competent person as collector thereof, on such terms and for such remuneration as may be reasonable; and he shall also, by himself or through the collector aforesaid, at any time before or during the collection or scrutiny of the voting papers, appoint such number of assistant collectors as may be necessary for carrying out the procedure herein specified.

(5.) The Chief Magistrate or the Sheriff, as the case may be, shall, at least 3 days previous to the day of the poll, intimate such day and the place or places and hours fixed for collecting such votes by advertisement in 1 or more newspapers published or circulating in the Burgh or Parish; and the said advertisement shall also specify the name of the collector appointed as aforesaid, and an address where voting papers may be received from such collector, in terms of the immediately succeeding article.

(6.) The collector, or an assistant collector, shall attend at the address specified in such advertisement for at least three specified hours of each of the two lawful days immediately preceding the day of the poll, and shall, on the application of any householder, and on being satisfied that such householder has not already received a voting paper, supply a voting paper to such applicant; and the collector, or any assistant collector, shall, at any time after the issue of the voting papers, and before seven o'clock afternoon of the day of the poll, on being satisfied that a voting paper has been inadvertently lost, destroyed, or rendered useless, have power to supply a duplicate voting paper, which shall be marked "duplicate" before being issued.

(7.) Voting papers duly filled up and subscribed by the householders, to whom the same are respectively applicable, may be transmitted by post to the collector, at the address specified in the aforesaid advertisement, provided that such voting papers reach the collector before eight o'clock of the afternoon of the day of the poll, and that the householders so transmitting prepay the postage thereof, otherwise the same shall not be received.

(8.) On the day of the poll the Chief Magistrate, or the Sheriff, as the case may be, shall cause the place or places specified in the intimation accompanying the voting paper to be kept open from eight o'clock morning till eight o'clock afternoon, and such place, or each of such places, if more than one, shall be under the charge of the collector, or of an assistant collector, who shall give his personal attendance during the hours specified for the purpose of receiving all voting papers which may be handed to him.

(9.) In the case of a Burgh divided into Wards, there shall be at least one place for the collection of voting papers in each Ward, and in any Burgh or Parish where more than one place for collection shall have been appointed, the collection in all of such places shall take place on the same day, and the intimation accompanying the voting paper shall specify the particular place where such voting paper is to be collected. The collector, or assistant collector, in charge of any such place for collection shall not be bound to receive a voting paper which shall have been directed to be lodged at some other such place.

(10.) Where any householder is unable to write, he may attach his mark to the voting paper, provided that such voting paper be signed by a witness, whose address shall be appended to his signature.

(11.) Any person fabricating a voting paper, or presenting or returning a fabricated voting paper, or any voting paper, knowing that the same does not bear the true signature of

PART IV.—STATUTES.—50 & 51 VICT. c. 42.   121

the householder to whom such voting paper is intended to apply, shall be guilty of personation, and shall be liable to the penalties of that offence as set forth in the Ballot Act, 1872.

(12.) No voting paper shall be received after eight o'clock afternoon of the day of the poll; and in the event of there being more than one place for collection, each assistant collector shall immediately after the close of the poll transmit the voting papers received by him to the collector, and the whole voting papers shall thereafter be under the charge of the collector, subject to the directions of the Chief Magistrate, or of the Sheriff, as the case may be.

(13.) The collector, subject as aforesaid, shall, as soon as may be after the conclusion of the poll, proceed to a scrutiny of the voting papers, and shall, with such assistance as may be necessary, compare the same with the municipal register, or with the copy roll, or list of householders, as the case may be, and shall ascertain how far the voting papers have been filled up in terms of the directions thereon, and have been duly signed by the householders to whom such voting papers were respectively issued; and immediately on the conclusion of such scrutiny he shall report to the Chief Magistrate, or to the Sheriff, as the case may be, the number of householders who have voted for the adoption of the Act, and the number who have voted against its adoption. He shall also report the total number of voting papers received, and the number, if any, which have been rejected by him, and the cause of such rejection.

(14.) Upon receiving the report of the collector, the Chief Magistrate, or the Sheriff, as the case may be, shall, if satisfied of the accuracy of such report, cause the result of the poll to be made public in such manner as he shall think most expedient.

FORM OF INTIMATION.

Public Libraries Consolidation (Scotland) Act, 1887.

Burgh [*or* Parish] of

No. [*insert number of householder on register, roll, or list*].

[*Insert place and date of issue*].

To [*insert name of householder*].

In terms of the "Public Libraries Consolidation (Scotland) Act, 1887," I have to intimate that a requisition having been presented to me by the prescribed number of householders of the Burgh [*or* Parish] of   to take the opinion of the householders as to whether the Act should be adopted in said Burgh [*or* Parish], I have caused the subjoined [*or* accompanying] voting paper to be issued to you as a householder of said Burgh [or Parish], which voting paper, duly filled up and subscribed by you, will be received within [*name of place*] on   the   day of   next, between the hours of eight o'clock morning and eight o'clock afternoon.

The voting paper may be delivered personally or by a messenger, provided it bear your signature.

In lieu of delivery of the voting paper in manner above mentioned, it is competent to any householder to post it addressed to [*name and address of collector*], provided the postage be prepaid, and that the voting paper reach the collector before eight o'clock afternoon of the said [*insert day of poll*]. The risk of delivery before the hour specified rests with the householder adopting this method of return.

(Signed)   A.B., Chief Magistrate,
[or Sheriff].

FORM OF VOTING PAPER.

Public Libraries Consolidation (Scotland) Act, 1887.

Burgh [or Parish] of   .

No. [*insert number of Householder on register, roll, or list*].

VOTING PAPER.

To be delivered on the   day of   , 18   [*insert day of poll*], between the hours of eight o'clock morning and eight o'clock afternoon at [*insert place of collection*].

In reply to the question whether the Public Libraries Consolidation (Scotland) Act, 1887, should be adopted by the Burgh [or Parish] of   , I vote *

[*Signature of householder.*]

* Fill in 'Yes' or 'No,' according as the voter does, or does not, desire the adoption of the Act.

NOTE.—Any person fabricating a voting paper, or presenting or returning a fabricated voting paper, or any voting paper, knowing that the same does not bear the true signature of the householder to whom such voting paper is intended to apply, is guilty of personation, and is liable to the penalties of that offence as set forth in the Ballot Act, 1872.

§ 4.

SCHEDULE (B).

PROCEDURE FOR DETERMINING BY PUBLIC MEETING AS TO THE ADOPTION OF THE ACT.

(1.) Upon receipt of the Requisition specified in the Act, the Chief Magistrate, or the Sheriff, as the case may be, shall convene a Meeting of the householders in some convenient place within the Burgh or the Parish, as the case may be, for the purpose of determining whether the Act shall be adopted within such Burgh or Parish.

(2.) Such Meeting shall be held on a day not less than 14

days or more than 30 days after the receipt of the Requisition, and notice of the Meeting shall be given not less than 7 days preceding its date by posting within the Burgh or Parish, as the case may be, handbills in the form annexed hereto, and also by advertisement, in the said form, inserted at least once in every daily newspaper published within the Burgh or Parish, as the case may be, and in the event of there being no daily newspaper so published, then at least once in one or more newspapers published or circulating within the Burgh or Parish.

(3.) The Chief Magistrate, in the case of a Burgh, shall provide himself with a copy of the Municipal Register, and the Sheriff, in the case of a Parish, shall provide himself with a copy of the Valuation Roll applicable to such Parish, or a list of the householders therein, which copy or list shall be made, certified, and furnished to the Sheriff on his application in the manner directed in Schedule (A).

(4.) At the Meeting called as aforesaid all householders on the Municipal Register, in the case of a Burgh, or on the copy or list furnished and certified as aforesaid, in the case of a Parish, shall be entitled to vote, and no other person or persons whatever shall be so entitled, and the Chief Magistrate, or the Sheriff, as the case may be, shall take such measures as may be necessary for the exclusion of non-qualified persons from the Meeting, or for preventing such persons from voting, and for securing that the votes of such persons, if given, shall not be counted; and, if necessary for this purpose, he may require that every householder intending to be present at the Meeting, or present thereat, shall enter his name and address on a card to be furnished to him, and that all such cards shall be delivered up before entering the Meeting, or before the votes are recorded; and every person knowingly and falsely representing himself to be a householder in such Burgh or Parish, and as such entitled to vote, shall be guilty of personation, and shall be liable to the penalties of that offence as set forth in the Ballot Act, 1872.

(5.) The Chief Magistrate, or the Sheriff, as the case may be, shall attend and shall preside at the Meeting, and shall appoint a clerk who shall make regular minutes of the proceedings thereof, and the Chief Magistrate, or Sheriff, as the case may be, shall in case of equality have a casting vote.

(6.) The result of the vote, whether for or against the adoption of the Act, shall be announced by the Chief Magistrate, or Sheriff, as the case may be, at the Meeting itself, or in any other way he may think most expedient, provided such announcement be made without unnecessary delay.

FORM OF NOTICE OF PUBLIC MEETING.

Burgh [or Parish] of .

Notice is hereby given, that under and in virtue of the powers contained in the Public Libraries Consolidation (Scotland) Act, 1887, the householders of the Burgh [or Parish] of   are required to meet upon   , the   day of   next, at   o'clock, within   , when a vote will be taken as to whether the Act shall be adopted by the said Burgh [or Parish].

[*In the case of a Burgh add*] By the Act "householders" are defined to mean "all persons entered on the Municipal Register," and "Municipal Register" is defined to mean "the Register, List, or Roll of persons entitled to vote in an election of Town Councillors or Commissioners of Police in a Burgh, made up according to the law in force for the time being."

[*In the case of a Parish add*] By the Act "householders" are defined to mean "all persons entitled to vote in the election of a School Board in a Parish under the provisions of the Education (Scotland) Act, 1872, and any Act amending the same."

[The Chief Magistrate, or the Sheriff, as the case may be, may append any regulations he may think expedient for securing order, and for effecting the purpose of the Meeting.]

Dated at   , the   day of   , 18   .
                    (Signed)   A.B., Chief Magistrate,
                                        [or Sheriff].

1891 [54 & 55 Vict.] *Museums and Gymnasiums*, 1891. [c. 22]

54 & 55 VICT. 22.

An Act to enable Urban Authorities to provide and maintain Museums and Gymnasiums. [3rd July, 1891.

Law Reports Statutes, vol. xxviii. p. 52.

BE it enacted, etc.

1. This Act may be cited as the "Museums and Gymnasiums Act, 1891."

2.—(1.) This Act shall extend to any district where the same is adopted as hereinafter provided, but only so far as the adoption extends.

(2.) This Act shall not extend to Scotland or the administrative county of London.

3.—(1.) This Act may be adopted by any urban authority for their district either wholly or so far as it relates to museums only or to gymnasiums only.

(2.) The adoption shall be by a resolution passed at a meeting of the urban authority, and one month at least before such meeting special notice of the meeting and of the intention to propose such resolution shall be given to every member of the authority, and the notice shall be deemed to have been duly given to a member of it, if it is either—

(*a.*) Given in the mode in which notices to attend meetings of the authority are usually given; or

(*b.*) Where there is no such mode, then signed by the clerk of the authority, and delivered to the member or left at his usual or last known place of abode in England, or forwarded by post in a prepaid letter, addressed to the member at his usual or last known place of abode in England.

(3.) Such resolution shall be published by advertisement in some one or more newspapers circulating within the district of the authority, and by causing notice thereof to be affixed to the principal doors of every church and chapel in the place to which notices are usually fixed, and otherwise in such manner as the authority think sufficient for giving notice thereof to all persons interested, and shall come into operation at a time not less than one month after the first publication of the advertisement of the resolution as the authority may by the resolution fix, and upon its coming into operation the Act shall extend to that district.

(4.) A copy of the resolution shall be sent to the Local Government Board.

(5.) A copy of the advertisement shall be conclusive evidence of the resolution having been passed, unless the contrary be shown; and no objection to the effect of the resolution, on the ground that notice of the intention to propose the same was not duly given, or on the ground that the resolution was not sufficiently published, shall be made after three months from the date of the first advertisement.

4. An urban authority may provide and maintain museums for the reception of local antiquities or other objects of interest, and gymnasiums with all the apparatus ordinarily used therewith, and may erect any buildings, and generally do all things necessary for the provision and maintenance of such museums and gymnasiums. (*a*) Power to provide museum and gymnasium.

(*a*) Probably outsiders cannot be appointed Members of a Committee to Manage a Museum under this Act.

5. A museum provided under this Act shall be open to the public not less than three days in every week free of charge, but subject thereto an urban authority may admit any person or class of persons thereto as they think fit, and Admission to museum.

126   BOOK I.—LIBRARIES AND MUSEUMS.

may charge fees for such admission, or may grant the use of the same or of any room therein, either gratuitously or for payment, to any person for any lecture or exhibition, or for any purpose of education or instruction, and the admission to the museum or room the use of which is so granted may be either with or without payment as directed by the urban authority, or with the consent of the urban authority by the person to whom the use of the museum or room is granted.

Admission to gymnasium.

6.—(1.) A gymnasium provided under this Act shall be open to the public free of charge for not less than two hours a day during five days in every week.

(2.) Subject thereto the urban authority—

(*a.*) may regulate the admission of the public to such gymnasium, either by classes or otherwise, as they think fit, and may charge fees for such admission; and

(*b.*) may, for not more than two hours in each day, grant the exclusive use thereof to any person or body of persons for the purpose of gymnastic exercises, for such payment and on such terms and conditions as they think fit.

(3.) An urban authority may (for not more than 24 days in one year nor more than 6 consecutive days) close the gymnasium for use as a gymnasium, and grant the use of the same gratuitously or for payment to any person for the purpose of any lecture, exhibition, public meeting, entertainment, or other public purpose, and the admission on such days shall be either with or without payment as directed by the urban authority, or with the consent of the urban authority by the person to whom the use of the same is granted.

Regulations and by-laws.

7.—(1.) An urban authority may make regulations for all or any of the following matters, namely:—

(*a.*) For fixing the days of the week or hours of the day, as the case may be, during which the museum or gymnasium is to be open to the public free of charge:

(*b.*) For giving special facilities to students for the use of the museum:

(*c.*) For fixing the fees to be paid for the admission of persons to the museum and for the use thereof either by students or in any other special manner:

(*d.*) For regulating the use of the gymnasium either by classes or otherwise, and fixing the scale of fees to be paid for such use:

PART IV.—STATUTES.—54 & 55 VICT. c. 22. 127

(e.) For prescribing conditions on which the exclusive use of the museum, or any room therein, or of the gymnasium is granted in any case:

(f.) For determining the duties of the instructor, officers, and servants of the urban authority in connection with a museum or gymnasium:

(g.) Generally for regulating and managing the museum or gymnasium.

(2.) The urban authority may make by-laws for regulating the conduct of persons admitted to the museum or gymnasium, and may by any such by-law provide for the removal from the museum or gymnasium of any person infringing any such by-law by any officer of the urban authority or by any constable.

All the provisions with respect to by-laws contained in sections 182 to 186 of the "Public Health Act, 1875," and any enactment amending or extending those sections, shall apply to all by-laws from time to time made by an urban authority under the powers of this Act. *38 & 39 Vict. 55.*

8. An urban authority may at such time as they think fit close a museum or gymnasium provided by them for repairs, and shall give a fortnight's notice of their intention to close the same by affixing a notice to that effect on the door of the museum or gymnasium, as the case may be, or otherwise as they think fit. *Closing of museum or gymnasium for repairs.*

9. An urban authority may appoint and pay such officers and servants as they think fit for the purpose of a museum or gymnasium provided under this Act, and may employ and pay instructors in connection with a gymnasium. *Appointment of officers and servants.*

10.—(1.) The fees and other money received by an urban authority under this Act shall be applied in defraying the expenses of the museum or gymnasium in respect of which they are received. *Expenses and borrowing.*

(2.) So far as such expenses are not so defrayed, they shall be defrayed as part of the general expenses of the execution by the urban authority of the "Public Health Acts."

(3.) An urban authority may borrow for the purposes of this Act in like manner and subject to the like conditions as for the purpose of defraying the said general expenses, and for that purpose sections 233, 234, and 236 to 239, both inclusive, of the "Public Health Act, 1875" (relating to borrowing), and sections 242 and 243 of the same Act (relating to loans by the Public Works Loan Commissioners), *38 & 39 Vict. 55.*

as amended by § 2 of the "Public Works Loans Act, 1879," shall apply.

(4.) Separate accounts shall be kept of the receipts and expenditure of an urban authority in connection with any museum or gymnasium established under this Act, and such accounts shall be audited in like manner and with the like power to the officer auditing the same, and with the like incidents and consequences, as the accounts of the urban authority are for the time being required to be audited by law.

(5.) The amount expended by an urban authority under this Act shall not in any year exceed the amount produced by a rate of a halfpenny in the pound for a museum, and the like amount for a gymnasium established under this Act.

11.—(1.) Land for the purposes of this Act may be acquired by an urban authority in like manner as if those purposes were purposes of the "Public Health Act, 1875," and §§ 175 to 178, both inclusive, of that Act (relating to the purchase of land) shall apply accordingly, but no land shall be so acquired otherwise than by agreement.

(2.) An urban authority may, with the consent of the Local Government Board, appropriate, for the purposes of this Act, any land which may be for the time being vested in them, or at their disposal. (*a*)

(*a*) As regards bequests of land by will for purposes of museums it must be remembered that by the "Mortmain Act, 1888" (51 & 52 Vict. 42, 6 (3)) Testators are restricted to the amount of 2 acres. That Act contains a definition of the term "public museum" which may be useful for certain other purposes besides its immediate purpose.

12.—(1.) Where it appears to an urban authority that a museum or gymnasium which has been established under this Act for seven years or upwards is unnecessary or too expensive, they may, with the consent of the Local Government Board, sell the same for the best price that can reasonably be obtained for the same, and shall convey the same accordingly.

(2.) Any moneys arising from such sale shall be applied toward the repayment of any money borrowed for the purpose of the museum or gymnasium sold, and, so far as not required for that purpose, shall be applied to any purpose to which capital moneys are properly applicable, and which may be approved by the Local Government Board.

13. All powers given to an urban authority under this Act shall be deemed to be in addition to and not in derogation of any other powers conferred by Act of Parliament, law, or custom, and such other powers may be exercised in the same manner as if this Act had not been passed.

14. In this Act the expression "urban authority" means an urban sanitary authority under the "Public Health Acts," and the expression "district" means an urban sanitary district under those Acts. *Interpretation.*

15. In the application of this Act to Ireland the following provisions shall have effect :— *Application of Act to Ireland.*

(1.) The expression "Public Health Acts" shall include the "Public Health (Ireland) Act, 1878," and the Acts amending the same ; 41 & 42 Vict. 52.

(2.) The "Public Health (Ireland) Act, 1878," shall be substituted for the "Public Health Act, 1875," and in particular a reference to sections 175 to 178 of the "Public Health Act, 1875," shall be taken to be a reference to sections 202 to 204 of the "Public Health (Ireland) Act, 1878," and a reference to sections 182 to 186 of the "Public Health Act, 1875," shall be taken to be a reference to sections 219 to 223 of the "Public Health (Ireland) Act, 1878," and a reference to sections 233, 234, and 236 to 239, both inclusive, of the "Public Health Act, 1875," shall be taken to be a reference to sections 237, 238, and 240 to 243, both inclusive, respectively, of the "Public Health (Ireland) Act, 1878," and a reference to sections 242 and 243 of the "Public Health Act, 1875," shall be taken to be a reference to section 246 of the "Public Health (Ireland) Act, 1878 " ;

(3.) The Local Government Board for Ireland shall be substituted for the Local Government Board ;

(4.) A reference to a place of abode in England shall be construed to be a reference to a place of abode in Ireland.

[55 & 56 Vict.] *Public Libraries Act*, 1892. [c. 53]

55 & 56 VICT. 53.

An Act to consolidate and amend the Law relating to Public Libraries. [27th June, 1892.

BE it enacted, etc.

Adoption of Act and Constitution of Library Authority

1.—(1.) This Act shall extend to every library district for which it is adopted. (*a*)

(2.) For the purposes of this Act and subject to the provisions thereof every urban district (*b*) and every parish in England and Wales which is not within an urban district shall be a library district. (*c*)

[Sub-section 3 was repealed by 56 & 57 Vict. **73.**]

(*a*) See § 3 as to method of adoption.
(*b*) See definition in § 27.
(*c*) As to the City of London see § 21, and as to the Metropolitan Districts see § 22.

2.—(1.) A rate *or addition to a rate* (*a*) shall not be levied for the purposes of this Act for any one financial year (*b*) in any library district (*c*) (*e*) to an amount exceeding one penny in the pound. (*d*)

(2.) This Act may be adopted for any library district (*e*) subject to a condition that the maximum rate (*f*) or addition to a rate to be levied for the purposes of this Act in the district or in any defined portion of the district (*g*) in any one financial year (*h*) shall not exceed one halfpenny or shall not exceed three farthings in the pound, but such limitation if fixed at one halfpenny may be subsequently raised to three farthings, or altogether removed, or where it is for the time being fixed at three farthings may be removed. (*h*)

(*a*) The words in italics appear to be mere surplusage. They are intended to meet the case where a lower limit than a penny rate is originally fixed and is subsequently increased.
(*b*) See § 27 for definition.
(*c*) Except the City of London (§ 21) and any District where the limit, if any, is prescribed in a Local Act (§ 29).
(*d*) This Sub-section does not absolutely set at rest the difficulty as to whether or not the amount realised by the rate must be expended in the year for which it is levied. Probably the maximum rate may be levied *in addition* to any surplus remaining from the previous years, for there is

PART IV.—STATUTES.—55 & 56 VICT. c. 53.   131

no provision in the Act corresponding with § 2 of the repealed Act of 1866 (limiting the amount to be *paid* in Boroughs in the year) or § 3 of the repealed Act of 1871 (limiting the amount to be *expended* in Local Board Districts). And it is conceived that proceedings could only be taken against an Authority for an infringement of this Sub-section when it *levied* more in one year than the amount prescribed. The side-note, however, refers to limitations on "expenditure," but it may be reasonably argued that this does not affect the clause itself. The Local Government Board, on appeal, has determined that credit balances may be carried forward (58 J. P., 207).
It would appear that the amount to be levied is not to exceed the amount which a penny in the pound would realise after allowing for empty property, deductions, and allowances, *i.e.* the amount which the rate actually yields. In *Brown ex parte Liverpool Corporation In Re*, where the rate, *under a local Act*, was limited, the Justices having refused to issue a distress warrant against the Overseers, it was held that the Justices were right, and that a penny rate means a penny rate on the nominal rateable value, although part of it is unproductive, and that a deficiency thus arising cannot be supplied out of the productive part.—(31 L. J., M. C., 108 [*Reg.* v. *Liverpool JJ.*] 6 L. T., 241.)
Whether the cost of collecting the rate is (except in Parishes) to be deducted is very doubtful, and especially where a separate rate is levied. At Chelsea the Commissioners were charged by the Rating Authority (in that case the Board of Guardians) for collecting the Library Rate, when the Metropolitan District Auditor surcharged the amount, being evidently of opinion that the charge for collecting the rate was not properly payable by the Commissioners, but *quære* whether it should not be deducted in ascertaining the actual yield of the rate where the maximum is levied. The matter was dealt with by the "Public Libraries Amendment Act, 1889," which provided that in a Parish the expenses should be paid out of a rate "to be raised with and as part of the Poor Rate." This provision is now incorporated in § 18 (1 c); but the phrase "with and as part of the Poor Rate" does not make it clear that the cost of collecting the Poor Rate is not to be deducted so as to ascertain the actual yield of the rate.
The Local Government Board have stated that they were advised that in a Parish the Library Commissioners were not themselves to make the rate, but were to call upon the Overseers to make it under § 13 of the Act of 1855. The present Act, following the Act of 1889, expressly provides that the rate is to be raised "with and as part of the Poor Rate."
(c) See definition, § 1 (2).
(f) Not the *actual* rate to be used, but the *maximum* rate to be levied.
(g) *Quære* whether it might be held to be legal to take the vote in one part for the full rate and at the same time for a reduced rate in another. The voting-paper does not appear to provide for this—unless separate voting-papers may be used in each part.
(h) As to alteration of any maximum prescribed by the voters, see § 3 (b). Other provisions as to rating will be found as follows:—As to mode of collection and deductions, § 18; as to exemptions by Local Acts, §§ 25 and 29. Observe that by § 18 (2) in a Parish the Vestry must sanction the amount to be expended.

3. With respect to— {Proceedings for adoption of Act.(a)}
(*a*) the adoption of this Act for any library district (*a*); and
(*b*) the fixing, raising, and removing of any limitation on the maximum rate to be levied for the purposes of this Act; (*b*) and
(*c*) the ascertaining of the opinion of the voters (*c*) with

k 2

respect to any matter for which their consent is required under this Act; (*d*)

the following provisions shall have effect; that is to say,

(1.) Any ten or more voters (*c*) in the library district (*a*) may address a requisition (*l*) in writing to the authority hereafter in this section mentioned requiring that authority to ascertain the opinion of the voters (*c*) in the district with respect to the question or questions stated in the requisition: Provided that where the library district is a municipal borough the requisition may be made by the council of the borough:

(2.) On receipt of the requisition the said authority shall (*e*) proceed to ascertain by means of voting papers (*f*) the opinion of the voters with respect to the said question or questions; but the said authority shall not ascertain the opinion of the voters on any question with respect to the limitation of the rate unless required to do so by the requisition, or with respect to any limitation of the rate other than the limitations specified in this Act:

(3.) The procedure for ascertaining the opinion of the voters shall be in accordance with the regulations contained in the First Schedule to this Act; and those regulations shall have effect as if they were enacted in the body of this Act: (*g*)

(4.) Every question so submitted to the voters (*c*) shall be decided by the majority (*h*) of answers to that question recorded on the valid (*i*) voting papers, and where the majority of those answers is in favour of the adoption of this Act, the same shall forthwith, on the result of the poll being made public, be deemed to be adopted: (*j*)

(5.) Where the opinion of the voters in any library district (*a*) is ascertained upon the question as to the adoption of this Act, or upon a question as to the limitation of the rate, no further proceeding shall be taken for ascertaining the opinion of the voters until the expiration of one year at least from the day when the opinion of the voters was last ascertained, that is to say, the day on which the voting papers were collected:

(6.) The authority to ascertain the opinion of the voters for the purposes of this section shall be in a municipal borough the mayor, and in any other urban district the chairman of the urban authority, and in a parish the overseers. (*a*) (*k*)

PART IV.—STATUTES.—55 & 56 VICT. c. 53.   133

(a) This Section now applies only to the City of London and the Metropolis. As regards Urban Districts, it was repealed by 56 Vict. 11, 2 (2) *post*, which Act now regulates the adoption in such districts. In rural parishes the adoption is regulated by 56 & 57 Vict. 73, 7, *post*.

(b) See § 2 as to what maximum may be fixed. The "authority" may not take the opinion of the voters on this point unless required to do so by the requisition. See Sub-section (2) *post* and observe note (a).

(c) *I.e.*, County Electors. See § 27. In the City of London the Common Council, and not the voters, must make the requisition (§ 21).

(d) Such as agreements under §§ 9 and 10 for the combination of neighbouring Parishes or the annexation of a Parish adjoining or near a Library District for the purposes of the Act, or agreements by Library Authorities for joint use of Library (§ 16). See also question 3 in the Form of voting-paper, p. 158, *post*.

(e) In the event of neglect or refusal, the only remedy would be by *Mandamus*. No time is fixed for taking the poll.

(f) See Schedule I. Part II. for form of voting-paper.

(g) This is an important provision, necessitating strict compliance with the Regulations, which will be judicially noticed if necessary.

(h) See Rule 14 in the Regulations.

(i) See Rules 10 and 11.

(j) A form for announcing the result of the poll is set out on p. 157, *post*.

(k) See *Reg.* v. *Morris* (*Times*, June 13, 1888).

(l) No form of Requisition is prescribed, but the following form may be used:—

TO THE OVERSEERS OF THE POOR FOR THE PARISH OF   .

We, the undersigned, being ten or more voters in the Parish aforesaid, being a Library District within the meaning of the Public Libraries Act, 1892, do hereby require you (as the authority mentioned in Section 3 of the said Act) to ascertain the opinion of the voters in the said Parish as to the adoption of the said Act for the said Parish [and whether they are in favour of the rate being limited to *one halfpenny* in the pound].*

Dated this   day of   , 18 .
Name   .   Address   .   No. on Register of County Electors,   .

* *Omit the words in brackets if not required. See* § 3 (2).

4. This Act when adopted for any library district (a) shall be carried into execution, if the library district is an urban district, (b) by the urban authority, (c) and, if it is a parish, by the commissioners appointed under this Act; (d) and any such authority or commissioners executing this Act are hereinafter referred to as a "Library Authority." {.Act when adopted to be executed by library authority.}

(a) See definition, § 1 (2).

(b) This includes a Borough.

(c) *I.e.* in a Borough, the Town Council, (see § 27); in an Urban District the District Council (56 & 57 Vict. 73, 21), but though in a Borough the Act is to be carried into execution by the Town Council as being the Urban Authority under the "Public Health Act, 1875," the expenses are not payable out of the rates levied under that Act.

(d) See the next Section; but where there is a Parish Council, that Council will be the Authority—56 & 57 Vict. 73, 7 (5, 7). For Metropolitan provisions, see §§ 21 and 22.

134   BOOK I.—LIBRARIES AND MUSEUMS.

Constitution of commissioners for executing Act in parish.

5.—(1.) Where this Act is adopted for any parish (*a*) the vestry (*b*) shall forthwith appoint not less than three nor more than nine voters (*c*) in the parish to be commissioners (*d*) for carrying this Act into execution.

(2.) The commissioners shall be a body corporate by the name of "The Commissioners for Public Libraries and Museums for the parish of   , in the county of   ," and shall have perpetual succession and a common seal, with power to acquire and hold lands for the purposes of this Act, without any licence in mortmain (*e*).

(*a*) Or Metropolitan District (§ 22); but see 56 & 57 Vict. 73, 7 and 19.
(*b*) Or District Board in the Metropolis (see § 22). As to the constitution of the Vestry, see § 26, but the provisions of the "Local Government Act, 1894" (56 & 57 Vict. 73, 7, 19, and 33), will supersede the provisions of this section, so that in Parishes where a Parish Council is elected they will execute the Act in lieu of Commissioners (§ 7), and in other Rural Parishes a Committee may be appointed by the Parish Meeting (§ 19). And possibly in Metropolitan Districts the Local Government Board may transfer the Commissioners' powers to the District Council (§ 33).
(*c*) *I.e.* County Electors or Burgesses (§ 27).
(*d*) There appears to be no provision which would disqualify a Commissioner once appointed who ceases to be a voter during the term of his office.
(*e*) There is no limit to the area of lands which the Commissioners may acquire and hold, as in the case of Municipal Corporations, but they must be acquired and held " for the purposes of this Act; " and see § 12 as to the acquisition and disposal of land.
The Local Government Board advised under the repealed Acts that in a Parish the Library Commissioners were not themselves to make a Rate, but were to call upon the Overseers to make it. This is now so provided in § 18 (1*c*). The Commissioners' expenses are subject to approval by the Vestry—see § 18 (2); but this provision may be held to be superseded by the provisions of the "Local Government Act, 1894," already referred to.

Rotation of commissioners.

6.—(1.) The commissioners (*a*) shall, as soon as conveniently may be after their appointment, divide themselves by agreement, or in default of agreement by ballot, into three classes, one-third or as nearly as may be one-third of them being in each class.

(2.) The offices of the first class shall be vacated at the expiration of one year, the offices of the second class at the expiration of two years, and the offices of the third class at the expiration of three years from the time of their appointment.

(3.) The offices of vacating commissioners shall be filled by an equal number of new commissioners to be appointed by the vestry (*b*) from among the voters (*c*) in the parish; and every newly elected commissioner shall hold his office for

PART IV.—STATUTES.—55 & 56 VICT. c. 53.   135

the term of three years from the date when the office became vacant, and no longer, unless re-elected; but a person, on ceasing to be a commissioner, shall, unless disqualified, (*d*) be re-eligible.

(4.) Any casual vacancy among the commissioners, whether arising by death, resignation, incapacity, or otherwise, (*d*) shall as soon as may be after the occurrence thereof be filled up by the vestry; (*a*) but the term of office of a commissioner appointed to fill up a casual vacancy shall expire at the date at which the term of office of the commissioner in whose place he is appointed would have expired.

(*a*) This Section is much more explicit than the Section in the Act of 1855 which it replaces; but it is of practically no importance, except in the Metropolis, in view of the provisions of the " Local Government Act, 1894," referred to under § 5, *ante*. The retirement of Commissioners was settled under the repealed Acts by the Vestry by ballot. Under this Section the Commissioners themselves are to decide their rotation either by " agreement " or " ballot."

(*b*) Or District Board in the Metropolis (§ 22). See the notes to § 5, *ante*.

(*c*) See § 27 for definition; but doubtless where a Parish Council is elected the qualifications for election as a parish councillor (56 & 57 Vict. 73, 3), will apply, so that residence within 3 miles will be sufficient, and no person is to be disqualified by sex or marriage.

(*d*) A Commissioner ceasing to be a voter during his term of office does not appear to be disqualified.

7. The commissioners shall meet at least once in every month, and at such other times as they think fit, at some convenient place; and any one commissioner may summon a special meeting by giving three clear days' notice in writing to each commissioner, specifying therein the purpose for which the meeting is called. Business shall not be transacted at any meeting of the commissioners unless at least two of them are present. (*a*)

Meetings of commissioners.

(*a*) Parish Councils and Committees appointed by the Parish Meeting in Rural Parishes will probably be governed by the Regulations in the " Local Government Act, 1894." (See the notes to § 5, *ante*.) Where Commissioners are still appointed (*e.g.* in Metropolitan Parishes) they have no power to appoint a Committee, as they are not included in § 15 (3) of the " Public Libraries Act, 1892."

8. All orders and proceedings of the commissioners shall be entered in books to be kept for that purpose, and shall be signed by the commissioners or any two of them; and all such orders and proceedings so entered, and purporting to be so signed, shall be deemed to be original orders and proceedings, and such books may be produced and read as

Proceedings of commissioners to be recorded

136   BOOK I.—LIBRARIES AND MUSEUMS.

evidence of all such orders and proceedings upon any judicial proceeding.

Power to vestries of neighbouring parishes to combine.
9.—(1.) Where this Act is adopted for any two or more neighbouring (*a*) (*b*) parishes, (*c*) the vestries (*d*) of those parishes may by agreement combine for any period in carrying this Act into execution, and the expenses of carrying this Act into execution shall be defrayed by the parishes in such proportions as may be agreed on by the vestries. (*e*)

(2.) The vestry of each of the said parishes shall appoint not more than six (*f*) commissioners in accordance with the provisions of this Act, and the commissioners so appointed for the several parishes shall form one body of commissioners, and shall act accordingly in the execution of this Act. (*g*)

(*a*) As to combination of neighbouring Urban Districts see § 4 of the Act of 1893. There is no provision for the *combination* of a rural parish and an Urban District. It may be annexed under § 10. Possibly a joint Committee may be appointed (see 56 & 57 Vict. 73, 57).
(*b*) Not necessarily *adjoining*.
(*c*) *I.e.* Parishes which are not within any Urban District, § 1 (2).
(*d*) See § 26 for definition of Vestry, and particularly the notes to § 5 as to the effect of the "Local Government Act, 1894."
(*e*) § 14 of the Act of 1855 provided that the Vestries might agree as to the erection of a Public Library or Museum, or both, in any one of the Parishes. This is omitted here, because the Joint Commissioners have all the powers of a Library Authority.
(*f*) § 14 of the Act of 1855, now repealed, provided for the appointment of not more than *three* Commissioners by each Vestry. The change to *six* should be noted.
(*g*) This Section provides for the combination of *Parishes* which are not in any Urban District. § 16, *post*, should be read in connection with it. § 10, *post*, authorises annexation by any "Library District" of a Parish, if near or adjoining, but there was no provision for a combination of two Urban Districts, until the Act of 1893 (p. 162), nor have the Library Authorities in such Districts power to enter into agreements for the use of one Library under § 16 (1). As to Metropolitan Districts, see § 22 (4).

Power to annex parish to adjoining district.
10. Where the voters (*a*) in a parish (*b*) adjoining or near (*c*) any library district (*d*) for which either this Act has been adopted, or the adoption thereof is contemplated, consent to such parish being annexed (*e*) to the said district, such parish, subject to the consent of the library authority (*f*) of the said district being also given, shall be annexed to and form part of that district for the purposes of this Act; the vestry (*g*) of such parish shall appoint not more than six commissioners in accordance with the provisions of this Act, and the commissioners so from time to time appointed shall during their respective terms of office be deemed for all the purposes of this Act to be members of the library authority of the said district. (*h*)

PART IV.—STATUTES.—55 & 55 VICT. c. 53.   137

(a) *I.e.*, Burgesses or County Electors (§ 27). A majority of answers on valid voting-papers decides the question (see § 3 (c), and form of voting-paper, question 3). The provisions of the "Local Government Act, 1894," probably supersede these provisions (see §§ 7 and 19 of that Act, and the notes to § 5, *ante*).
(b) *I.e.*, a Parish not within any Urban District (§ 1 (2)).
(c) The words "or near" are new. Previous to the Act of 1892 only Parishes whose boundaries adjoined any Borough, etc., could be "annexed;" by the addition of the words "or near," a Parish some distance apart may for the purposes of this Section be "annexed" to any Borough, Urban District, or Parish in which the Act has been adopted.
(d) See definition, § 1 (2)..
(e) Observe that § 9 relates to the "combination" of Parishes, and this Section to the "annexation" of a Parish to an adjoining District.
(f) See definition, § 4.   (g) See § 26.
(h) It is doubtful whether this section applies to Metropolitan Districts. (See the notes to § 22 (4).)

11.—(1.) The library authority (a) of any library district (b) for which this Act has been adopted may, subject to the provisions of this Act, (c) provide all or any of the following institutions, namely, public libraries, public museums, schools for science, art galleries, and schools for art, (d) and for that purpose may purchase and hire land (e) and erect, take down, rebuild, alter, repair, and extend buildings, and fit up, furnish, and supply the same with all requisite furniture, fittings, and conveniences. (f)

Provision of libraries, museums, and schools of science and art.

(2.) Where any of the institutions mentioned in this section has been established either before or after the passing of this Act by any library authority (a) under this Act or the Acts hereby repealed, that authority may establish in connection therewith any other of the said institutions without further proceedings being taken with respect to the adoption of this Act. (f)

(3.) No charge shall be made for admission (g) to a library or museum (h) provided under this Act (i) for any library district, or, in the case of a lending library, (j) for the use thereof by the inhabitants of the district; but the library authority, if they think fit, may grant the use of a lending library to persons not being inhabitants of the district, either gratuitously or for payment. (k)

(a) See § 4. As to the City of London, see § 21, and the Metropolis, § 22.
(b) See § 1 (2).
(c) See § 12, as to the acquisition and disposal of land, and § 19, as to borrowing. In rural parishes the question may arise whether the provisions of the "Local Government Act, 1894," as to these matters apply instead of or in addition to the provisions of this Act.
(d) See the "Schools for Science and Art Act, 1891," 54 & 55 Vict. 61.
(e) The sanction of the Local Government Board was required by the

138   BOOK I.—LIBRARIES AND MUSEUMS.

repealed Acts on the purchase or hire of any land or buildings (§ 18 of the Act of 1855 as amended), but this requirement is not repeated in the present Act ; and though it does not say specifically that "buildings" may be hired, the Authority may "provide" Libraries, etc., and, having the power to hire "land," it has the power to hire "buildings," since the expression "land" includes (unless a contrary intention appears) messuages, tenements, and hereditaments, and houses and buildings of any tenure, by virtue of § 3 of the "Interpretation Act, 1889" (52 & 53 Vict. 63.)   See § 12, as to the purchase of land, and § 19 (p. 156, *post*), as to borrowing.

(*f*) Always subject to the limit on the rate to be levied. And the repayment of principal and interest, being for "the purposes of this Act," must be provided out of the rate.

(*g*) Probably, so long as free access to the Library or Museum is provided, a charge for admission to some other part of the building might be made, *e.g.* to a Lecture.   (See § 12 (4).)

(*h*) This does not include an Art Gallery or School for Science or Art. As to gifts of land for the erection of Art Galleries, etc., see the "Mortmain and Charitable Uses Amendment Act, 1892" (55 Vict. 11).

(*i*) The repealed Act provided that there should be no charge for admission to Libraries and Museums established under it.

(*j*) This is the first reference to "Lending Libraries." Probably they are included in the term "Libraries," but it was deemed necessary to amend the Act of 1885 by § 5 of the "Public Libraries Amendment Act, 1887," so as to authorise the establishment of branch Lending Libraries—a provision which does not appear to be repeated.

(*k*) The proviso is new and should be carefully noted ; it would appear to meet the case of persons employed but not residing in the district. At Chesterfield, under the repealed Acts, the Town Council decided that non-residents of the Borough should be allowed to use the Library subject to conditions.

Provision as to acquisition and disposal of land.

12.—(1.) For the purpose of the purchase of land under this Act by a library authority the " Lands Clauses Acts," with the exception of the provisions relating to the purchase of land otherwise than by agreement, shall be incorporated with this Act.

(2.) The library authority (*a*) of any library district which is an urban district (*b*) may, with the sanction of the Local Government Board, appropriate for the purposes of this Act any land (*c*) which is vested in that authority (*d*).

(3.) A library authority (*a*) may, with the sanction of the Local Government Board, sell any land (*c*) vested in them for the purposes of this Act, or exchange any such land for other land better adapted for those purposes, and the money arising from the sale or received by way of equality of exchange, shall be applied in or towards the purchase of other land better adapted for the said purposes [or may be applied for any purpose for which capital money may be applied, and which is approved by the Local Government Board.] (*e*)

(4.) A library authority may let a house or building, or any part thereof, or any land vested in them for the purposes

PART IV.—STATUTES.—55 & 56 VICT. c. 53. 139

of the Act, which is not at the time of such letting required
for those purposes, and shall apply the rents and profits
thereof for the purposes of this Act. (*f*)

(*a*) § 4.
(*b*) § 27. The expression includes Metropolitan Districts (§ 23).
(*c*) Or buildings. (See note (*e*) to § 11).
(*d*) If the Authority, with the consent of the Local Government Board, appropriates lands for the purposes of the Acts they are not required to charge the penny rate with any rent or purchase money.
See the case of *A. G.* v. *Sunderland Corporation* (45 L. J., Ch. 839; L. R., 2 Ch., D. 634; 34 L. T., 921; 40 J. P., 364) as to the powers of a Municipal Corporation with respect to land vested in it.

RATING OF FREE LIBRARIES AND MUSEUMS.—The institutions in the following towns are *totally exempted* from local rates, viz.: Aston, Birkenhead, Birmingham, Blackburn, Brierley Hill, Cambridge, Canterbury, Cardiff, Carlton, Clitheroe, Coventry, Darlington, Derby, Doncaster, Exeter, Folkestone, Gateshead, Hanley, Harrogate, Kidderminster, Leek, Leicester, Loughborough, Macclesfield, Manchester, Newport, Northampton, Norwich, Plymouth, Richmond, Rochdale, Sheffield, Southampton, Southport, Truro, Warwick, Watford, Wednesbury, Whitehaven, Wigan, Winsford, Yarmouth, Aberdeen, Hawick, Thurso, Wick, Dundalk, Clerkenwell, Fulham, Lambeth, St. Giles, Stoke Newington, Westminster. The following are *partially exempt*: Blackpool, Bolton, Bootle, Bristol, Fleetwood, Newcastle-on-Tyne, South Shields, Worcester. The Act 6 & 7 Vict. 36, 1, provides that any society instituted for purposes of Science, Literature, or the Fine Arts exclusively, and occupying for the transaction of its business any lands, houses, or buildings, may obtain exemption from rates on certain conditions. As to the effect of this Act reference should be made to the cases cited at p. 287, *post*. If free Libraries and Museums do not come within the terms of the Section quoted, and therefore have no *legal* right to claim exemption, yet they certainly have an *equitable* right to be exempted, for they ought to be placed in no worse position than private institutions, since their objects are identical and their usefulness more general. Moreover, the sum at the disposal of the Authority (which must cover rent or repayment of principal and interest) is already felt to be unnecessarily limited. And this *equitable* view has been entertained in many towns very favourably, where the Assessment Committees have fixed a nominal sum as the amount at which the buildings are to be rated. (See the list of Towns where the Library buildings are partially exempt.)

In the case of *Andrews* v. *Bristol, Mayor*, it was, however, held that Libraries were liable to the property tax, but this case has been over-ruled by the House of Lords in the case of *Manchester* v. *MacAdam*, where it was decided that the Public Library of Manchester was a literary or scientific institution within the meaning of Rule 6 of § 61, and Schedule A of 5 & 6 Vict. 35, and was therefore not liable to be rated.

(*e*) The words in brackets [ ] are new. There is no provision as to any purpose for which "capital money" may be applied. It is probably intended to mean for the erection of buildings, purchase of land, or reduction of loans.

(*f*) This sub-section is new. It might enable an Authority to erect a building with shops under or over the Library, etc., so as to let the same at a profit. The rents and profits may probably be used *in addition* to the rate.

13.—(1.) Any person holding land for ecclesiastical, paro- Power to chial, or charitable purposes may, subject as hereinafter grant charity.

provided, grant, or convey, by way of gift, sale, or exchange, for any of the purposes of this Act any quantity of such land, not exceeding in any one case one acre, in any manner vested in such person.

(2.) Provided that—

(a) ecclesiastical property shall not be granted or conveyed for those purposes without the consent of the Ecclesiastical Commissioners; and

(b) parochial property shall not be so granted or conveyed save by the board of guardians of the poor law union comprising the parish to which the property belongs, or without the consent of the Local Government Board; and

(c) other charitable property shall not be so granted or conveyed without the consent of the Charity Commissioners; and

(d) the land taken in exchange or the money received for such sale shall be held on the same trusts as the land exchanged or sold; and

(e) land situated in the administrative county of London, or in any urban district containing according to the last published census for the time being over twenty thousand inhabitants, which is held on trusts to be preserved as an open space, or on trusts which prohibit building thereon, shall not be granted or conveyed for the purposes of this Act.

(3.) Any land granted or conveyed to any library authority under this section may be held by that authority without any licence in mortmain. (a)

(a) This is a reproduction of § 8 of the "Public Libraries Amendment Act, 1890." As to London see §§ 21 and 22.

14. All land appropriated, purchased, or rented, and all other real and personal property presented to or purchased or acquired for any library, museum, art gallery, or school under this Act shall be vested in the library authority. (a)

(a) § 4. And as to London see §§ 21 and 22.

15.—(1.) The general management, regulation, and control of every library, museum, art gallery, and school provided under this Act shall be vested in and exercised by the library authority, (a) and that authority may provide therein books, newspapers, maps, and specimens of art and science, and cause the same to be bound and repaired when necessary. (b)

PART IV.—STATUTES.—55 & 56 VICT. c. 53. 141

(2.) The library authority (*a*) may also appoint salaried officers and servants, and dismiss them, and make regulations (*c*) for the safety and use of every library, museum, gallery, and school under their control, and for the admission of the public thereto. (*d*)

(3.) Provided that a library authority (*a*) being an urban authority (*e*) may if they think fit appoint a committee and delegate to it all or any of their powers and duties under this section, (*f*) and the said committee shall to the extent of such delegation be deemed to be the library authority. Persons appointed to be members of the committee need not be members of the urban authority. (*g*)

(*a*) See § 4. As to the City of London, see § 21, and as to the Metropolis, § 22.

(*b*) § 21 of the Act of 1855, from which the whole of this Section is taken, enacted that the Authority might provide "the necessary fuel, lighting, and other similar matters." These words are omitted, probably as being unnecessary, since § 11 authorises the provision of the various institutions, and § 18 provides for the payment of all expenses in and incidental to the execution of the Act.

(*c*) The regulations may impose *fines for the detention of books*. As to this, see *Nottingham Corporation* v. *Abbott*; also *Holborn District* v. *Bull* (99 L. T. Newsp., 295). Under the "Stamp Act, 1891," the guarantees or acknowledgments ought to be stamped unless the liability is expressly limited to a sum under 5*l*. (54 & 55 Vict. 39, Sched. Agreement, Exemption 1).

The following is a copy of an information for non-return of a book in a case at Richmond with which the librarian has favoured the editors, viz.: "Did unlawfully and without just cause detain a certain book, to wit, . . . of the value of . . . to the possession of which the said [librarian's name] claims to be entitled after due notice of his claim to the same." This information was laid under a Metropolitan Act (2 & 3 Vict. 71, 40).

(*d*) The regulations cannot impose any charge for the admission of inhabitants of the District to a Library or Museum, or for the use of a Lending Library, but may fix a payment to be made by persons not inhabitants (§ 11, 3).

(*e*) See § 27. Commissioners appointed for a Parish under § 5 are not included; but in Rural Parishes and Urban Districts (not being Boroughs) probably the Parish or the District Council may appoint a Committee under § 56 of the "Local Government Act, 1894." In Rural Parishes where there is no Parish Council, § 19 of that Act may apply. As to joint Committees, see § 57 of "Local Government Act, 1894;" also § 53 (2).

(*f*) This is more explicit than the repealed Section. A Library Authority acting by a Committee must define the duties and powers delegated. If so provided, its proceedings (within its delegation) need not to be subject to the approval of the Authority. This is doubtless the intention of the Act, especially in view of the provision that co-optative members may be appointed members of "the Committee," and their appointment might be rendered practically nugatory if the Authority retained the power to exercise control over the Committee's proceedings.

The question whether the Committee appointed under § 21 of the Act of 1855 had power to act without obtaining the approval of the body appointing was one upon which opinion and practice were divided. It is to

142 BOOK I.—LIBRARIES AND MUSEUMS.

be observed that the powers and duties of the Committee when appointed are limited to the matters named in the Section, so that it will have no power to levy a rate, and there is nothing in the Act to prevent the Council or Board retaining the right to exercise control over the Committee's proceedings.

(*g*) Co-opted members have the same powers as members of the Authority when acting on the Committee.

Power to library authorities to make agreements for use of library.

16.—(1.) The commissioners separately appointed for any two or more parishes for which this Act has been adopted (*a*) may with the consent of the voters (*b*) in each of those parishes agree to share in such proportions and for such period as may be determined by the agreement the cost of the purchase, erection, repair, and maintenance of any library building (*c*) situate in one of those parishes, and also the cost of the purchase of books and newspapers for such library, and all other expenses connected with the same. (*d*)

(2.) The library authority of any library district (*e*) may with the consent of the voters (*b*) in the district and of the Charity Commissioners make the like agreement with the governing body of any library established or maintained out of funds subject to the jurisdiction of the Charity Commissioners, and situate in or near the library district;

And, in case of inability, objection, or failure on the part of the governing body to enter into such agreement, the Charity Commissioners may, if they think fit, become party to the agreement on behalf of the governing body. (*f*)

(3.) This section shall apply, with the necessary modifications, to a museum, school for science, art gallery, or school for art in like manner as to a library. (*g*)

(*a*) These powers will apply to Parish Councils which supersede Commissioners. The provisions of the "Local Government Act, 1894," should be consulted. The Section does not apply to Urban Districts or the City of London; but see now the "Public Libraries Amendment Act, 1893 (56 Vict. 11, 4). It is doubtful whether it applies to Metropolitan Districts or not. See particularly § 22 (4). The requirement of the repealed Section, that the Parishes should be "adjoining," is omitted.

(*b*) See § 3 (*c*).

(*c*) The repealed § 3 of the Act of 1889 was limited to Libraries. Sub-section 3 of this Section is, therefore, of great importance, and should be noted.

(*d*) Section 9 authorises "Vestries" of *neighbouring* Parishes to combine. This Section authorises "Commissioners" to amalgamate. It is not stipulated that the Parishes should be even "neighbouring," nor is any limit fixed here upon the number of Commissioners to be appointed from each Parish as in § 9. The side note is misleading, as only Library Authorities in Parishes may exercise the power under Sub-section 1. (But see note (*a*).)

It is to be observed that § 18 (3) provides that in a Parish annexed to a Library District (*i.e.* under § 10) the expenses do not require the sanction

PART IV.—STATUTES.—55 & 56 VICT. c. 53. 143

of the Vestry. And this applies to a combination of Parishes under § 9.
(See § 18 (2).) Expenses under agreements within this Sub-section would
appear to require the sanction of the Vestry as well as the voters (§ 18 (2)) ;
but probably compliance with the "Local Government Act, 1894," at the
Parish Meeting will obviate any difficulty.

(e) This Sub-section is taken from § 7 of the repealed Act of 1890. It
is not limited, like the preceding Sub-section, to Parishes.

(f) The words in brackets are an important addition to the Act of 1890.
As to the adjustment of interests on the termination of an agreement, see
§ 24.

(g) Sub-section 3 is new. It is conceivable that it may have a considerable
effect in broadening the work of existing Library Authorities, especially
where aid is sought from public funds applicable to technical education.

17. Where a library authority (a) accepts a grant out of money provided by Parliament from the Department of Science and Art (b) towards the purchase of the site, or the erection, enlargement, or repair of any school for science and art, or school for science, or school for art, or of the residence of a teacher in any such school, or towards the furnishing of any such school, that authority may accept the grant upon the conditions prescribed by the Department of Science and Art, and may execute any instruments required by that Department for carrying into effect those conditions, and upon payment of the grant shall be bound by such conditions and instruments, and have power and be bound to fulfil and observe the same. (c) {.sidenote: Power to library authority to accept parliamentary grant}

(a) See § 4. As to the City of London, § 21, and the Metropolis, § 22.
(b) In § 1 of the Act of 1884, on which this Section is based, the Education Department was named instead of the Department of Science and Art. The effect, however, is the same.
(c) For the conditions on which grants are made, see the *Directory* of the Science and Art Department, published annually, price Sixpence (Eyre & Spottiswoode).

Financial Provisions.

18.—(1.) The expenses incurred in a library district (a) in and incidental to the execution of this Act, including all expenses in connection with ascertaining the opinion of the voters in the district, (b) may be defrayed : {.sidenote: Expenses of library authority —how defrayed.}

(a) Where the library district is a municipal borough out of the borough fund or borough rate, or a separate rate to be made, assessed, and levied in like manner as the borough rate ; (c) and

(b) Where the library district is an urban district other than a borough, (d) out of the rate applicable to the general expenses incurred in the execution of the Public Health

Acts, (e) or a separate rate to be made, assessed, and levied in like manner as the rate so applicable; (c) and
(c) Where the library district is a parish, out of a rate to be raised with and as part of the poor rate, (c) subject, however, to this qualification, that every person assessed to the poor rate in the said parish in respect of lands used as arable, meadow, or pasture ground only, or as woodlands or market gardens, or nursery grounds, shall be entitled to an allowance of two-thirds of the sum assessed upon him in respect of those lands for the purposes of this Act.(f)

(2.) Where the library district is a parish, and is not combined with any other parish (g) for the execution of this Act, then—

(i.) Such amount only shall be raised out of a rate for the purposes of this Act as is from time to time sanctioned by the vestry (h) of the parish; (i) and

(ii.) The vestry to be called for the purpose of sanctioning the amount shall be convened in the manner usual in the parish; and

(iii.) The amount for the time being proposed to be raised for the purposes of this Act shall be expressed in the notice convening the vestry, and (if sanctioned) shall be paid according to the order of the vestry to such person as may be appointed by the library authority to receive it; and

(iv.) In the notices requiring the payment of the rate there shall be stated the proportion which the amount to be thereby raised for the purposes of this Act bears to the total amount of the rate.

(3.) Where a parish or a part of a parish is annexed in pursuance of this Act to any library district, (j) so much of the said expenses as is chargeable to such parish or part shall be defrayed in like manner as if such parish or part were a separate library district, but the sanction of the vestry shall not be required for raising the sums from time to time due from the parish for meeting those expenses. (k)

(a) See § 1 (2) for definition. The expenses are subject to the limitations in that Section. As to expenses in the City of London, see § 21 (3), and in a Metropolitan District, § 22 (3).
(b) And this whether the Act is adopted or not.
(c) See note to § 2, as to the cost of collecting the rate. Parish Councils and Commissioners in a Parish will be subject to the provisions of the "Local Government Act, 1894."

PART IV.—STATUTES.—55 & 56 VICT. c. 53. 145

(d) *I.e.*, what was a Local Board or Improvement Act District until the passing of the "Local Government Act, 1894."
(e) *I.e.*, the General District Rate.
(f) *Reg.* v. *Blenkinsop* (92 L. T. Newspaper, 9 : 56 J. P., 246). A Public Library rate being imposed under 18 & 19 Vict. 70, 13, the Overseers, by mistake, considered that a railway company were liable to pay one-third only in respect of their nett annual value. This reduced rate only was demanded and paid for five years, when the next Overseers discovered the mistake and then sought under 17 Geo. II. 38, 11, to recover the unpaid differences for the five years as arrears. *Held* that the Overseers were authorised by the latter Act so to treat the unpaid balance as arrears.
(g) *I.e.*, under § 9. As to Parishes "annexed" to a Library District see Sub-section (3). Parishes amalgamated by agreement under Section 16 do not appear to be exempt from the conditions of this Sub-section.
(h) For constitution of Vestry, see § 26. The repealed Act of 1890 provided that all references to Vestries should mean the voters. But the "Parish Meeting" now takes the place of the Vestry (56 & 57 Vict. 73, 7 (3)).
(i) This follows § 1 of the "Public Libraries Amendment Act, 1889" [repealed]. It is difficult to conceive the reason for the resuscitation of the Vestry's veto on the expenses in a Parish not annexed to a Library District (see Sub-section 3 and § 10), for the consent of the voters having once been obtained to a certain limit of expenditure the Vestry or Parish Meeting ought to have no power to impose, as it might, any further restriction. And what would the result be if the Parish Meeting refused to sanction certain expenditure? Again it is to be observed that Commissioners of Parishes who have entered into agreements under § 16 are not exempted from the provisions of Sub-section 2, and such agreements might be rendered nugatory if the Vestry or Parish Meeting in any year refused to sanction the expenses.
(j) *I.e.*, under § 10. See Sub-section 2 of this Section, and § 9, as to Parishes combined with other Parishes, and the preceding note.
(k) It is to be noted that the provisions in the corresponding Sections of the repealed Acts which limited the amounts to be "paid" or "expended" to one penny in the pound are not repeated, and attention is directed to the notes on § 2.

19.—(1.) Every library authority, (*a*) with the sanction of the Local Government Board, and in the case of a library authority being commissioners appointed for a parish, with the sanction also of the vestry of such parish, may borrow money for the purposes of this Act on the security of any fund or rate applicable for those purposes. (*b*)

Borrowing by library authority.

(2.) §§ 233, 234, and 236 to 239, both inclusive, of the "Public Health Act, 1875," relating to borrowing by a local authority shall apply, with the necessary modifications, to all money borrowed by any library authority for the purposes of this Act, as if the library authority were an urban authority, and as if references to this Act were substituted in those sections and in the forms therein mentioned for references to the "Public Health Act, 1875." (*c*)

(3.) The Public Works Loan Commissioners may in manner provided by the "Public Works Loans Act, 1875," lend any

L

money which may be borrowed by a library authority for the purposes of this Act.

(a) See § 4 for definition. As to the City of London, see § 21, and the Metropolis, § 22.
(b) This applies to every Parish, whether combined with another or not. See note (i) to § 18. But where there is a Parish Council the provisions of the "Local Government Act, 1894" (56 & 57 Vict. 73, 12) regulate their borrowing. § 12 of that Act provides that a Parish Council shall not borrow for the purpose of the "Public Libraries Act" otherwise than in accordance with the "Local Government Act, 1894." Probably the sanction of the Parish Meeting is not now required.
(c) These provisions of the "Public Health Act, 1875," are set out *post*. It does not appear that a mortgage of the Library or other buildings may be made.

Accounts and audit.

20.—(1.) Separate accounts shall be kept of the receipts and expenditure under this Act of every library authority and their officers, and those accounts shall be audited in like manner and with the like incidents and consequences, in the case of a library authority being an urban authority, and of their officers, as the accounts of the receipts and expenditure of that authority and their officers under the "Public Health Acts." (a)

(2.) The accounts of the receipts and expenditure of a library authority being commissioners appointed under this Act, and of their officers, shall be audited yearly by a district auditor in like manner and with the like incidents and consequences as in the case of an audit under the Acts relating to the relief of the poor, and those commissioners shall be a local authority within the meaning of the "District Auditors Act, 1879." (b)

42 & 43 Vict. 6.

(3.) The accounts of the receipts and expenditure under this Act of any library authority other than the council of a municipal borough (c) shall be open at all reasonable times to the inspection, free of charge, of any ratepayer (d) in the library district, and any such ratepayer may without charge make copies of and extracts from those accounts; and if any library authority or any person being a member thereof or employed by them and having the custody of the accounts fails to allow the accounts to be inspected, or copies or extracts to be made, as required by this section, such authority or person shall for each offence be liable on summary conviction in manner provided by the "Summary Jurisdiction Acts" to a fine not exceeding five pounds.

(a) There is no regulation as to the *form* in which accounts are to be kept in a Borough or other Urban District, but the form specified for Commissioners may usefully be followed. In Boroughs the Elective Auditors

PART IV.—STATUTES.—55 & 55 VICT. c. 53. 147

and Mayor's Auditor will audit the accounts unless the Borough has been combined with an Urban District other than a Borough, in which case the District Auditor will audit them ("Public Libraries Amendment Act, 1893," § 4). In Urban Districts other than Boroughs the District Auditor will audit the accounts. In Parishes where the Parish Council acts as the Library Authority, the provisions of the "Local Government Act, 1894," § 58, will apply, and where Commissioners are appointed the provisions of Sub-section (2) of this Section will apply.

(b) This also applies to a Metropolitan District (§ 22 (2)). The Local Government Board has issued an Order on this subject which is printed at p. 57, *ante*.

(c) The accounts in a Borough may be inspected under the provisions of the "Municipal Corporations Act, 1882" (45 & 46 Vict. 50, 233).

(d) Not necessarily a voter.

Provisions affecting London only.

21.—(1.) The city of London shall be a library district, (a) and on this Act being adopted for the city, the Common Council (b) shall be the library authority. (c)

Application of Act to city of London.

(2.) The opinion of the voters in the city of London with respect to any question under this Act (d) shall be ascertained by the mayor on the requisition of the Common Council. (e)

(3.) The expenses incurred in the city of London in and incidental to the execution of this Act, including all expenses in connection with ascertaining the opinion of the voters, shall be defrayed out of the consolidated rate levied by the Commissioners of Sewers, or a separate rate to be made, assessed, and levied by those commissioners in like manner as the consolidated rate. (f)

(4.) So much of this Act as limits the rate or addition to a rate to be levied in any library district for any one financial year to one penny in the pound shall not extend to the city of London. (g)

(a) See § 1 (2).
(b) See definition in § 27.
(c) See § 4. And as such Library Authority the Common Council will have the powers and be subject to the duties specified with regard to Library Authorities generally (subject to the provisions of this Section), but not to such as relate to Parishes.
(d) See § 3.
(e) Note that voters cannot requisition the chairman of the Authority to take a poll, as in other Library Districts, the power being limited to the Common Council itself.
(f) See § 18 as to expenses in other Districts.
(g) The adoption of the Act may, therefore, be without any rating limit, and, unless the Common Council in the requisition desires the opinion of the voters to be taken on any suggested limitation, the Lord Mayor has no power to put any question with respect thereto (§ 3 (2)); but there is nothing to prevent the Common Council from suggesting any limit it thinks desirable.

148   BOOK I.—LIBRARIES AND MUSEUMS.

Power for district in London to adopt Act.
18 & 19 Vict. 120

22. Every district mentioned in Schedule (B) to the "Metropolis Management Act, 1855," as amended by any subsequent Acts, (*a*) shall be a library district, (*b*) and the provisions of this Act shall apply accordingly with the following modifications:—

(1.) The opinion of the voters in any such district with respect to any question under this Act (*c*) shall be ascertained by the district board on the requisition in writing of any ten or more of such voters:

(2.) The library authority for such district shall be commissioners appointed by the district board, (*d*) and the provisions of this Act relating to commissioners appointed for a parish shall apply with the substitution of "district" for "parish" and of "district board" for "vestry": (*e*)

(3.) The expenses incurred in any such district in and incidental to the execution of this Act, including all expenses in connection with ascertaining the opinion of the voters, shall to such amount as is sanctioned by the district board (*f*) be defrayed by that board in like manner as if they had been incurred for the general purposes of the "Metropolis Management Act, 1855," and the sums from time to time required for defraying those expenses, to the extent so sanctioned, shall be paid by the district board to any person appointed by the commissioners to receive the same; but nothing in this enactment shall enable a district board to levy (*g*) for the purposes of this Act any greater sum in any financial year than the amount produced by a rate of one penny in the pound, or any less rate specially fixed for the purpose of this Act in the district: (*h*)

(4.) The enactments authorising two or more neighbouring parishes to combine in carrying this Act into execution shall have effect as if any such district were included in the term "parish" and the district board of such district in the term "vestry": (*h*)

(5.) Where a parish in any such district has adopted the Acts hereby repealed or any of them, or hereafter adopts this Act, (*i*) it shall be treated in all respects for the purposes of this Act as if it were outside the district, and, in particular,—

(*a*) a person shall not, by reason of being a voter in the parish, be accounted for the purposes of this section as a voter in the district; and

PART IV.—STATUTES.—55 & 56 VICT c. 53.   149

(b) a representative of the parish on the district board shall not take part in any proceeding on the board under this section; and
(c) the parish shall not be called on to contribute to the payment of any expenses incurred in pursuance of this section; and
(d) any question of accounts arising between the parish and the other parishes in the district, or between the parish and the district, in consequence of this section, shall be decided finally by the Local Government Board:

(6.) After the adoption of this Act for any such district, proceedings shall not, except with the sanction of the Local Government Board, be taken for the separate adoption thereof for any parish in the district. (i)

(a) The following is the list of Districts mentioned in Schedule (B):—

Parishes united into Districts for the purposes of the Act.

Whitechapel District: St. Mary, Whitechapel; Christchurch, Spitalfields; St. Botolph, without Aldgate, in the County of Middlesex; Holy Trinity, Minories; St. Katherine, precinct of; Mile End, New Town, Hamlet of; Liberty of Norton Folgate; Old Artillery Ground; Tower, District of.
Westminster District: St. Margaret; St. John the Evangelist.
Greenwich District: St. Paul, Deptford, including Hatcham; Hatcham; St. Nicholas, Deptford; Greenwich.
Wandsworth District: Clapham; Tooting Graveney; Streatham; St. Mary, Battersea, excluding Penge; Wandsworth; Putney, including Roehampton.
Hackney District: Hackney; St. Mary, Stoke Newington.
St. Giles District: St. Giles-in-the-Fields; St. George, Bloomsbury.
Holborn District: St. Andrew, Holborn above Bars; St. George the Martyr; St. Sepulchre, in the County of Middlesex; Saffron Hill, Hatton Garden; Ely Rents and Ely Place; The Liberty of Glasshouse Yard.
Strand District: St. Anne, Soho; St. Paul, Covent Garden; St. John the Baptist, Savoy, or precinct of the Savoy; St. Mary-le-Strand; St. Clement Danes; Liberty of the Rolls.
Fulham District: St. Peter and St. Paul, Hammersmith; Fulham.
Limehouse District: St. Anne, Limehouse; St. John, Wapping; St. Paul, Shadwell; Ratcliffe, Hamlet of.
Poplar District: All Saints, Poplar; St. Mary, Stratford-le-Bow; St. Leonard, Bromley.
St. Saviour's District: Christ Church; St. Saviour (including the Liberty of the Clink).
Plumstead District: Charlton, next Woolwich; Plumstead; Eltham; Lee; Kidbrooke.
Lewisham District: Lewisham, including Sydenham; Chapelry; Hamlet of Penge.
St. Olave District: St. Olave; St. Thomas, Southwark; St. John, Horsleydown.

150 BOOK I.—LIBRARIES AND MUSEUMS.

(*b*) See § 1. The limitations on expenditure provided in § 2 will apply; and see Sub-section 3 of this Section.

(*c*) See § 3. The District Board will in a Metropolitan District be the Authority referred to in that Section.

(*d*) Not the Vestry. And as such Library Authority the Commissioners will have all the powers applicable to Library Authorities generally (see §§ 4, 11, as to the provision of Libraries, etc.; § 15, as to management; § 18, as to expenses; § 19, as to borrowing; and § 20, as to accounts). § 23 *post* will apply in lieu of § 12 as to the appropriation of land.

(*e*) See § 5 as to the constitution of Commissioners; § 6, as to rotation; § 7, as to meetings; § 8, as to proceedings; § 16, as to agreements for the joint use of a Library. § 10 (power to annex Parish to adjoining District), does not appear to apply to a Metropolitan District, as the provisions made applicable by this Sub-section are limited to those which relate to "Commissioners" (see note *h*). § 9 (combination of Parishes), applies (see Sub-section 4 of this Section).

(*f*) This corresponds with the provisions as to a Parish (see § 18). If the District is "combined" with another under Sub-section 4 and § 9, the District Board's veto will still apply. But it is very doubtful whether the power to annex a District to another Library District (under § 10) applies (see note *h*). If it does not, the saving in § 18 (3) does not apply to such a Metropolitan District (see the notes to § 18).

(*g*) The words "or expend" are omitted.

(*h*) See §§ 9 and 18, and particularly 18 (2). There is no direct incorporation of § 10 (power to annex Parish to adjoining District), and, as before pointed out, it is very doubtful whether this power extends to Metropolitan Districts. The only provision which appears to warrant the conclusion that § 10 is incorporated is that in Sub-section 2, which enacts that the provisions of this Act *relating to Commissioners* shall apply. It is submitted that § 10 is not a provision "relating to Commissioners" within this Section, like §§ 5 to 8. Certainly it authorises the Vestry to appoint Commissioners, but so does Section 9; and if this submission be inaccurate, there was no necessity for the Sub-section 4 now under comment, as § 9 would be one "relating to Commissioners," and would be incorporated by Sub-section 2.

(*i*) The Act may be adopted for a Parish in the Metropolis unless the District in which the Parish is situated has adopted it (see Sub-section 6). The legislation on this subject has been very confusing. § 11 of the Act of 1887 corresponded in effect with Sub-section 6, but it was repealed by the Act of 1890 (Schedule II.).

Power to vestry or district board in London to appropriate land for library, etc.

23. The vestry (*a*) or district board constituted under the "Metropolis Management Act, 1855," for any parish mentioned in Schedule (A) (*b*) or district mentioned in Schedule (B) (*c*) to that Act, as amended by any subsequent Acts, may, if this Act is in force in such parish or district, appropriate with the sanction of the Local Government Board for the purposes of this Act any land (*d*) which is vested in such vestry or board. (*e*)

(*a*) See § 26 as to constitution of Vestry.
(*b*) The following is the list of Parishes in Schedule (A):—

St. Marylebone; St. Pancras; Lambeth; St. George, Hanover Square; St. Mary, Islington; St. Leonard, Shoreditch; Paddington; St. Matthew,

PART IV.—STATUTES.—55 & 56 VICT. c. 53. 151

Bethnal Green; St. Mary, Newington, Surrey; Camberwell; St. James, Westminster; Chelsea; St. James and St. John, Clerkenwell, to be considered as one Parish; Kensington, St. Mary Abbott; St. Luke, Middlesex; St. George the Martyr, Southwark; Bermondsey; St. George-in-the-East; St. Martin-in-the-Fields; Hamlet of Mile End, Old Town; Woolwich; Rotherhithe; St. John, Hampstead.

(c) See § 22, note (a), for the list.
(d) Land includes buildings (see § 11, note d).
(e) See § 12 (2) as to appropriation of sites in Urban Districts.

Supplemental Provisions.

24. Any agreement under this Act between two or more vestries (a) or library authorities, (b) or between a library authority and any other body, (c) may provide that on the termination of the agreement an adjustment shall be made of the interests of the several parties thereto in any property to the provision of which they have contributed, and as to the mode in which the adjustment shall be arrived at, (d) and in the event of any dispute the adjustment shall on the application of any of the parties be made by an arbitrator appointed by the Local Government Board. Adjustment of interests on termination of agreement.

(a) See § 26 as to the constitution of Vestries.
(b) See §§ 9, 10, and 16 respectively.
(c) The words " or between a Library Authority and any other body " are new. *Quære*, Do they cover agreements between Library Authorities and individuals? Probably they apply to agreements under § 13.
(d) This provision follows that in § 3 of the Act of 1889 [repealed]. The words which follow are new.

25. Nothing in this Act shall interfere with the operation of the Act of the session of the 28th and 29th years of the reign of Her present Majesty, chapter 108, so far as it relates to the collection of a rate for a public library in Oxford. Saving for Oxford.

26. For the purposes of this Act the vestry of a parish shall be any body of persons acting by virtue of any Act of Parliament as or instead of a vestry, and, where there is no such body, shall be the inhabitants of the parish in vestry assembled, but in the latter case the persons registered as county electors in respect of the occupation of property situate in the parish, and no other persons, shall be members of the vestry. (a) Constitution and proceedings of vestry for purposes of Act.

(a) The Act of 1890 provided that all references to " Vestries " should be construed as references to the voters. This Section must now be read (at any rate so far as regards Rural Parishes) subject to the provisions of the " Local Government Act, 1894." (See particularly § 7 (3).)

BOOK I.—LIBRARIES AND MUSEUMS.

Definitions.

27. In this Act, unless the context otherwise requires,—

The expression "urban district" means a municipal borough, Improvement Act district, or local government district; and "urban authority" means, as regards each such district, the council, improvement commissioners, or local board:

The expression "financial year" means the period of twelve months for which the accounts of a library authority are made up:

The expression "voter" means a person who is registered as a county elector or enrolled as a burgess in respect of the occupation of property situate in the district or parish in connection with which the voter is mentioned:

The expression "overseers" includes any persons authorised and required to make and levy poor rates in a parish, and acting instead of overseers:

The expression "common council" means in relation to the city of London the mayor, commonalty, and citizens, acting by the mayor, aldermen, and commons in common council assembled. (*a*)

(*a*) For definition of "Library District," see § 1 (2); of "Library Authority," § 4; and "Vestry," § 26.

Repeal.

28.—(1.) The Acts mentioned in the Second Schedule to this Act shall be repealed as from the commencement of this Act, save so far as any of them extend beyond England and Wales; and where those Acts have been adopted for any library district, that adoption shall be deemed to have been an adoption of this Act, and this Act shall apply accordingly.

(2.) For the purpose of this section the said Acts shall be deemed to have been adopted for any district in which they were in force immediately before the commencement of this Act.

Saving as to local Acts.

29. Nothing in this Act shall be deemed to limit, or to reduce or alter the limit of any rate which any library authority is authorised to levy under or by virtue of any local Act.

Commencement.

30. This Act shall come into operation on the first day of October next after the passing thereof.

Short title.

31 This Act may be cited as the "Public Libraries Act, 1892."

PART IV.—STATUTES.—55 & 56 VICT. c. 53. 153

SCHEDULES.

FIRST SCHEDULE. (a)

Regulations for Ascertaining the Opinion of the Voters in a Library District.

(a) These regulations now apply only to Metropolitan Districts and Parishes. They were repealed as regards Urban Districts by the "Public Libraries Act, 1893" (56 Vict. 11, 2 (2)); and as regards Rural Parishes by the "Local Government Act, 1894" (56 & 57 Vict. 73, 7 (1)).

In these regulations the expression "presiding officer" means, in relation to any Library District, the Authority required under this Act to ascertain the opinion of the voters in that District on any question, (a) or a person appointed by that Authority, (b) and that Authority is referred to in these regulations as the "District Authority."

PART I. PROCEDURE BY VOTING PAPERS.

1. The District Authority (a) shall, before the day appointed for the issuing of the voting papers, provide the presiding officer (c) with a copy of the [*burgess roll, or*] county register [*as the case may be*], or of the part or parts thereof containing the names of all the voters (d) in the Library District.

2. On the day appointed for issuing the voting papers the presiding officer shall send by post, or cause to be delivered to every voter, at his address appearing in the roll, or register, a voting paper in the form contained in Part II. of this Schedule, or to the like effect.

3. Every voting paper shall bear the number of the voter on the roll, or register, as the case may be, and shall contain directions to the voter, in accordance with these regulations, as to the day on which, and the hours within which, the voting paper is to be collected or sent, and as to the place at which, if sent, it will be received.

4. The District Authority shall, before the issue of the voting papers, appoint such a number of competent persons as may be necessary to collect and receive the voting papers, and to assist in the scrutiny thereof, on such terms and for such remuneration as may be reasonable, and shall also

appoint a convenient place within the District at which the voting papers are to be received; but the District Authority shall not be required to collect any voting papers which have been sent by them to addresses beyond the limits of the District. (*e*)

5. Voting papers shall be collected between 8 A.M. and 8 P.M. of the third day after that on which they were issued. (*f*) Such day is hereinafter in these regulations referred to as the polling day, and such last-mentioned hour is hereinafter referred to as the "conclusion of the poll."

6. A voting paper shall not, after collection, be delivered up to any person except the presiding officer, or a person appointed to receive voting papers.

7. The persons appointed to collect the voting papers shall, either before or as soon as may be after the conclusion of the poll, deliver the voting papers collected by them to the presiding officer or to a person appointed to receive the same.

8. A voting paper may be sent by prepaid post or by hand to the presiding officer at the place appointed by the District Authority for the receipt thereof, so that it be received by the presiding officer at such appointed place before the conclusion of the poll. Voting papers, except those collected by persons appointed by the District Authority, shall not be received at the appointed place after the conclusion of the poll.

9. Every person appointed to collect voting papers shall be appointed in writing (*g*) by the District Authority, and shall carry such writing with him while employed in the collection, and shall show it to any voter who may require him to do so. If any person so appointed fails to comply with this regulation, or if any unauthorised person fraudulently receives or induces any voter to part with a voting paper, such person shall be guilty of a misdemeanour, and liable, on conviction, to imprisonment for a term not exceeding six months, or to a fine not exceeding twenty pounds, or to both imprisonment and fine.

10. A voting paper which contains the answer "yes" or "no" to any question put to the voters, and is duly signed, shall be deemed to be a valid voting paper with respect to that question. (*h*)

A voting paper shall be deemed to be duly signed if signed by the voter with his full name or ordinary signature.

11. Where any voter is unable to write he may cause his

PART IV.—STATUTES.—55 & 56 VICT. c. 53.   155

voting paper to be filled up by another person. In such case he shall attach his mark to the voting paper, and such mark shall be attested by such other person, who shall sign his name and append his address thereto. A voting paper to which such mark is attached, and which is duly attested, shall be deemed to be duly signed.

12. Any person fabricating a voting paper, or presenting or returning a fabricated voting paper, knowing that the same does not bear the true answer or signature of the voter to whom it was sent or intended to be sent, shall be guilty of personation, and liable to the penalties of that offence, as provided by the Ballot Act, 1872 (35 & 36 Vict. 33).

13. The presiding officer shall, as soon as may be after the conclusion of the poll, proceed to a scrutiny of the voting papers, and shall compare the same with his copy of the roll, or register, and ascertain how far the voting papers have been duly signed by the voters. (*d*)

14. A question put to the voters (*d*) shall be deemed to be answered and determined in the affirmative or negative, according as the majority of valid voting papers returned contain the answer " yes " or " no " to that question.

15. Immediately on the conclusion of the scrutiny the presiding officer shall report to the District Authority the number of voters who have voted " yes " or " no " respectively to each question put to them, and the number of voting papers which are invalid. (*i*)

16. The presiding officer shall seal up in separate packets the valid and the invalid voting papers respectively, and shall transmit them, together with his report, to the District Authority. (*a*)

17. Upon receiving the report of the presiding officer the District Authority shall cause the result of the poll to be made public in such manner as they think fit. (*j*)

(*a*) *I.e.*, in London the Lord Mayor (§ 21 (2)); in Metropolitan Districts the District Board (§ 22 (1)); in a Parish the Overseers (§ 3 (6)).

(*b*) Note that the " District Authority " has power to delegate his or their duties to another person subject to the regulations. (See particularly Rules 4 and 6.)

(*c*) *I.e.*, if the " Authority " appoints a deputy who comes also within the definition of " presiding officer."

(*d*) *I.e.*, County electors.

(*e*) The expenses, whether the Act is adopted or not, are payable out of the rates (§ 18 ; § 21 (3) as to the City of London ; and § 22 (3) as to Metropolitan Districts).

(*f*) Note that this requirement is imperative. No alternative is left to the presiding officer.

BOOK I.—LIBRARIES AND MUSEUMS.

(g) The following form (though not prescribed) may be used:—

FORM OF APPOINTMENT OF COLLECTOR OF VOTING PAPERS.

Parish of
We, the undersigned, being the Overseers of the Parish of   and
the District Authority within the meaning of the Public Libraries Act, 1892, and the regulations made thereby for ascertaining the opinion of the voters in the Parish, do hereby appoint Mr.   of   to (deliver and) collect the voting papers for ascertaining the opinion of the voters in the said Parish pursuant to the provisions of the said Act and Regulations.

     Dated this   day of   189 .

   Signed   , Overseer (or *as the case may be*).

(h) If it contains more than this (except as in Rule 11), it appears that it cannot be deemed valid. And this would appear to apply if any method other than that specified is adopted to signify either assent or dissent. Reference should be made to the case of *Reg.* v. *Morris* (*Times*, June 13, 1888).

(i) The form of report given on p. 157 is suggested with the necessary modifications applicable to the particular Districts.

(j) The following form for announcing the result of the Poll may be useful:—

FORM FOR ANNOUNCING THE RESULT OF POLL.

Parish of (Metropolitan District *or* City of London as the case may be).

PUBLIC LIBRARIES ACT, 1892.

We, the undersigned, being the Overseers of the Poor (*or as the case may be*), and the Authority to ascertain the opinion of the voters under the Public Libraries Act, 1892, do hereby publish the result of the Poll: that is to say,

Number of valid voting papers in favour of the adoption
of the Act . . . .
Number of valid voting papers against the adoption of
the Act . . . .
(Or the questions and result may be set out if preferred in
the Form given on p. 157.)

   Majority *in favour* . . . . . .
   Number of invalid papers . . . . .

The majority of the answers recorded on the valid voting papers being *in favour* of the adoption of the Act, the same is by Section 3 of the said Act deemed to be forthwith adopted for the said Parish.

  Dated this   day of   , 18 .

     , Overseers (or Lord Mayor or Chairman of
       District Board).

PART IV.—STATUTES.—55 & 56 VICT. c. 53.   157

FORM OF REPORT OF RESULT OF POLL.
Parish of
Public Libraries Act, 1892.

To the Overseers of the said Parish, being the District Authority within the meaning of the Public Libraries Act, 1892, and the Regulations made thereby for ascertaining the opinion of the voters in the said Parish.

I have to report that I have scrutinised the voting papers in the poll of the voters in the Parish on the following questions, and do certify and report the result to be as follows :—

		Number of Voting Papers			MAJORITY (In favour or against)
		containing the answer YES	containing the answer No	Invalid	
Question 1	Are you in favour of the adoption of the Public Libraries Act, 1892, for the Parish of ?				
Question 2	Are you in favour of the rate being limited to one halfpenny in the pound (or to three farthings, or of the existing limitation of the rate under the Public Libraries Act, 1892, being removed, or of the existing limitation to one halfpenny being raised to three farthings, as the case may require) ?				
Question 3	Are you in favour of an agreement being made with (here designate the body or bodies, according to Section 10 or Section 16 of this Act) for the purpose of (briefly state objects of proposed agreement) ?				

* The total number of voting papers issued was   .   .   .
* ,,   ,,   ,,   ,,   ,,   delivered was   .   .   .
* ,,   ,,   ,,   ,,   ,,   collected was   .   .   .

Dated this   day of   , 18 .
                                            , Presiding Officer.

* This information is not required by the regulations, but instead of vitiating the report it would improve it.

PART II. FORM OF VOTING PAPER. (a)

Public Libraries Act, 1892

Borough (Parish or other Library District) of   No.   (Here insert number of voter in burgess roll or county register, as the case may be.)

Question 1 .	Are you in favour of the adoption of the Public Libraries Act, 1892, for the Borough (*or* Parish, etc.) of ?	Answer 1. (*To be filled in* " Yes " *or* " No.")
Question 2 .	Are you in favour of the rate being limited to one halfpenny in the pound (*or* to three farthings, *or* of the existing limitation of the rate under the Public Libraries Act, 1892, being removed, *or* of the existing limitation to one halfpenny being raised to three farthings, *as the case may require*) ?	Answer 2. (*To be filled in* " Yes " *or* " No.")
Question 3 .	Are you in favour of an agreement being made with (*here designate the body, or bodies, according to Section* 10 *or Section* 16 *of this Act*) for the purpose of (*briefly state objects of proposed agreement*) ?	Answer 3. (*To be filled in* " Yes " *or* " No.")

Question 1.—To be omitted if Libraries Act already adopted. Question 2.—To be omitted if no question stated in the requisition as to limitation of rate. Question 3.—To be omitted if no such question raised.

..................................Signature of Voter.

1. This voting paper will be collected by an authorised collector between the hours of 8 A.M. and 8 P.M. on   day, the   , 18   (*insert polling day*), or may be sent by prepaid post or by hand, addressed to (*state name or designation of presiding officer, and place appointed by the District Authority*). If it is sent it must be received at that address before 8 P.M. on the above-mentioned day.

2. You may require the collector to show his authority in writing. No authority is valid unless it is (signed by *A. B.*, *or* sealed, or *as the District Authority may direct*).

(a) The matter on this page forms part of the 1st Schedule of the Statute and its use is therefore obligatory, but it is printed here (out of place) to avoid the necessity of breaking the page.

SECOND SCHEDULE.

Acts Repealed.

Session and Chapter	Short Title
18 & 19 Vict. 70	The Public Libraries Act, 1855.
29 & 30 Vict. 114	The Public Libraries Amendment Act (England and Scotland), 1866.
34 & 35 Vict. 71	The Public Libraries Act, 1855, Amendment Act, 1871.
47 & 48 Vict. 37	The Public Libraries Act, 1884.
50 & 51 Vict. 22	The Public Libraries Acts Amendment Act, 1887.
52 & 53 Vict. 9	The Public Libraries Acts Amendment Act, 1889.
53 & 54 Vict. 68	The Public Libraries Acts Amendment Act, 1890.

[56 Vict.] *Public Libraries (Amendment) Act*, 1893. [c. 11] 1893.

56 VICT. 11.

An Act to amend the Public Libraries Act, 1892.

[9th June, 1893.]

BE it enacted, etc.

1. This Act may be cited as the "Public Libraries (Amendment) Act, 1893," and shall be construed as one with the "Public Libraries Act, 1892" (in this Act referred to as the principal Act), and these two Acts may be together cited as the "Public Libraries Acts, 1892 and 1893."

2.—(1.) Where a library district is an urban district—
(i.) The principal Act may, subject to the conditions contained in the second section of that Act, (*a*) be adopted, and the limitation of the maximum rate to be levied for the purposes of that Act may within the limits fixed by that Act be fixed, raised, or removed, by a resolution of the urban authority under this Act: (*b*)
(ii.) The consent of the urban authority (*c*) given by a resolution of that authority under this Act shall be substituted in an urban district for the consent of the voters in any case when the consent of the voters is required under the principal Act.

(2.) Section 3 of the principal Act is hereby repealed, so far as it relates to an urban district.

Law Reports Statutes, vol. xxx. p. 25. Short title. 55 & 56 Vict. 53. Modification as to adoption, etc., in urban districts.

(*a*) These conditions relate to the limitations on expenditure for the purposes of the Act, namely, a rate of 1*d*., ¾*d*., or ½*d*.

(b) No form of resolution is prescribed, but the following is sufficient:—

FORM OF RESOLUTION.

That the "Public Libraries Act, 1892," be adopted for the Urban District of   (subject to the rate not exceeding ½d. or ¾d. in the £, or *as the case may be*), and that the same do come into operation in the said district on the   day of   , 189   .

FORM OF RESOLUTION ALTERING THE LIMITATION OF THE RATE.

That the "Public Libraries Act, 1892," having been adopted for the Urban District of   (subject to the rate not exceeding ½d. in the £, or *as the case may be*), this Council do hereby resolve that the said limitation be removed from and after the   day of   , 189   .

(c) The Urban Authority in a borough is the Town Council. In any other urban district, the Urban District Council

Provision as to a resolution of an urban authority for the adoption, etc., of the principal Act.

3.—(1.) A resolution under this Act shall be passed at a meeting of the urban authority, and one month at least before the meeting special notice of the meeting (*a*) and of the intention to propose the resolution shall be given to every member of the authority, and the notice shall be deemed to have been duly given to a member of it, if it is either—

(*a*.) given in the mode in which notices to attend meetings of the authority are usually given; or

(*b*.) where there is no such mode, then signed by the clerk of the authority, and delivered to the member or left at his usual or last known place of abode in England, or forwarded by post in a prepaid letter addressed to the member at his usual or last known place of abode in England.

(2.) The resolution shall be published by advertisement (*b*) in some one or more newspapers circulating within the district of the authority, and by causing notice thereof to be affixed to the principal doors of every church and chapel in the place to which notices are usually fixed, and otherwise in such manner as the authority think sufficient for giving notice thereof to all persons interested, and shall come into operation at a time not less than one month after the first publication of the advertisement of the resolution as the authority may by the resolution fix.

(3.) A copy of the resolution shall be sent to the Local Government Board.

(4.) A copy of the advertisement shall be conclusive evidence of the resolution having been passed, unless the contrary be shown; and no objection to the effect of the resolution, on the ground that notice of the intention to

PART IV.—STATUTES.—56 VICT. c. 11.

propose the same was not duly given, or on the ground that the resolution was not sufficiently published, shall be made after three months from the date of the first advertisement.

(a) SUGGESTED FORM OF NOTICE TO MEMBERS OF THE URBAN AUTHORITY.

Urban District of

To   being a member of the Urban Authority for the district of

I HEREBY GIVE YOU SPECIAL NOTICE that a meeting of the Urban District Council for the District of will be held at in the said District, on the day of 189 , at the hour of to take into consideration and determine upon the following motion, which Mr. a member of the Urban Authority, intends to propose, namely:

(Here copy the resolution; see note (b), page 160.)

This special notice is sent to you one month at least before the meeting, as required by the provisions of the "Public Libraries (Amendment) Act, 1893."

      I am, Sir,
           Your obedient Servant,
                  Town Clerk (or Clerk).

(b) SUGGESTED ADVERTISEMENT ON THE PASSING OF THE RESOLUTION.

Urban District of

PUBLIC LIBRARIES ACT, 1892:

PUBLIC LIBRARIES (AMENDMENT) ACT, 1893.

NOTICE IS HEREBY GIVEN, that at a meeting of the Urban District Council (being the Urban Authority within the meaning of the "Public Libraries (Amendment) Act, 1893," for the district of held on the day of 189 , in pursuance of notice duly given in accordance with the statutory requirements in that behalf, the following resolution was passed, namely:—

(Here copy the resolution; see note (b), page 160).

                  Town Clerk (or Clerk).

4.—(1.) Where the principal Act is adopted for two or more neighbouring urban districts, the library authorities of those districts may by agreement combine for any period for carrying the Act into execution; and the expenses of carrying the Act into execution shall be defrayed by such authorities in such proportions as may be agreed on by them.(a)

(2.) For the purposes of the Act a joint committee may be formed, the members whereof shall be appointed by the several combining authorities in such proportions as may be agreed on, but need not be members of any of the combining

Power to two or more library authorities to combine

authorities. Any such committee shall have such of the powers of a library authority under the principal Act, except the power of borrowing money, as the combining authorities may agree to confer upon them.(*b*)

(3.) Where any of the combining authorities are improvement commissioners or a local board the provisions of the principal Act with respect to accounts and audit shall apply to such committee as if they were a local board who were a library authority under the Act.(*c*)

(*a*) § 9 of the Act of 1892 (55 & 56 Vict. 53) empowers Vestries of neighbouring Parishes to combine, and § 10 of that Act gives power to annex a Parish to an adjoining Library District.

(*b*) Subject to the power being such as may be exercised by a Library Authority.

(*c*) See § 20 of the Act of 1892.

1894. [56 & 57 Vict.] *Local Government Act*, 1894. [c. 73]

56 & 57 VICT. 73.

Law Reports Statutes, vol. xxx. p. 375.

An Act to make further provision for Local Government in England and Wales.(*a*) [5th March, 1894.

Transfer of power under adoptive Acts.

7.—(1.) As from the appointed day, in every rural parish the parish meeting shall, exclusively, have the power of adopting any of the following Acts, inclusive of any Acts amending the same (all which Acts are in this Act referred to as "the adoptive Acts"); namely,—
(*a*) The "Lighting and Watching Act, 1833";
(*b*) The "Baths and Washhouses Acts, 1846 to 1882";
(*c*) The "Burial Acts, 1852 to 1885";
(*d*) The "Public Improvements Act, 1860";
(*e*) The "Public Libraries Act, 1892."

(2.) Where under any of the said Acts a particular majority is required for the adoption or abandonment of the Act, or for any matter under such Act, the like majority of the parish meeting, or, if a poll is taken, of the parochial electors, shall be required, and where under any of the said Acts the opinion of the voters is to be ascertained by voting papers, the opinion of the parochial electors shall be ascertained by a poll taken in manner provided by this Act.(*b*)

PART IV.—STATUTES.—56 & 57 VICT. c. 73. 163

(3.) Where under any of the said Acts the consent or approval of, or other act on the part of, the vestry of a rural parish is required in relation to any expense or rate, the parish meeting shall be substituted for the vestry, and for this purpose the expression "vestry" shall include any meeting of ratepayers or voters.(b)

(4.) Where there is power to adopt any of the adoptive Acts for a part only of a rural parish, the Act may be adopted by a parish meeting held for that part.(c)

(5.) Where the area under any existing authority acting within a rural parish in the execution of any of the adoptive Acts is co-extensive with the parish, all powers, duties, and liabilities of that authority shall, on the parish council coming into office, be transferred to that council.(d)

(6.) This Act shall not alter the incidence of charge of any rate levied to defray expenses incurred under any of the adoptive Acts, and any such rate shall be made and charged as heretofore, and any property applicable to the payment of such expenses shall continue to be so applicable.

(7.) When any of the adoptive Acts is adopted for the whole or part of a rural parish after the appointed day, and the parish has a parish council, the parish council shall be the authority for the execution of the Act.(d)

(a) Only the sections of the "Local Government Act, 1894," which affect the provisions of the "Public Libraries Acts" are given in this volume. For the complete provisions of that Act see Chambers's *Popular Summary of the Law relating to Parish Councils* (Knight & Co., 1s. 6d.).
(b) The procedure to be followed for the adoption of the "Public Libraries Act" in a Rural Parish is fully set out at pp. 13–19 (*ante*).
(c) § 1 (3) of the "Public Libraries Act, 1892," provided for the adoption of the Act in a parish partly within and partly without an urban district, but that provision was repealed by the "Local Government Act, 1894." Under that Act such parts of parishes as are outside urban districts may be constituted separate parishes either by the Local Government Board or County Council.
(d) Thus Public Library Commissioners will not in future be appointed in Parishes having a Parish Council (see § 53).

9.—(1.) For the purpose of the acquisition of land by a parish council the "Lands Clauses Acts" shall be incorporated with this Act, except the provisions of those Acts with respect to the purchase and taking of land otherwise than by agreement, and § 178 of the "Public Health Act, 1875," shall apply as if the parish council were referred to therein.(a)

(2.) If a parish council are unable to acquire by agreement and on reasonable terms suitable land for any purpose for which they are authorised to acquire it, they may represent

Powers for acquisition of land.

M 2

164   BOOK I.—LIBRARIES AND MUSEUMS.

the case to the county council, and the county council shall inquire into the representation.(*b*)

(*a*) See § 12 of the "Public Libraries Act, 1892."
(*b*) This sub-section would probably apply to the acquisition of land by a Parish Council for a Public Library.

Restrictions on expenditure.   **11.**—(1.) A parish council shall not, without the consent of a parish meeting, incur expenses or liabilities which will involve a rate exceeding threepence in the pound for any local financial year, or which will involve a loan.(*a*)

(2.) A parish council shall not, without the approval of the county council, incur any expense or liability which will involve a loan.(*b*)

(3.) The sum raised in any local financial year by a parish council for their expenses (other than expenses under the adoptive Acts) shall not exceed a sum equal to a rate of sixpence in the pound on the rateable value of the parish at the commencement of the year, and for the purpose of this enactment the expression "expenses" includes any annual charge, whether of principal or interest, in respect of any loan.

(4.) Subject to the provisions of this Act, the expenses of a parish council and of a parish meeting, including the expenses of any poll,(*c*) shall be paid out of the poor rate; and where there is a parish council that council shall pay the said expenses of the parish meeting of the parish ; and the parish council, and where there is no parish council the chairman of the parish meeting, shall, for the purpose of obtaining payment of such expenses, have the same powers as a board of guardians have for the purpose of obtaining contributions to their common fund.

(5.) The demand note for any rate levied for defraying the expenses of a parish council or a parish meeting, together with other expenses, shall state in the prescribed form the proportion of the rate levied for the expenses of the council or meeting, and the proportion (if any) levied for the purpose of any of the adoptive Acts.

(*a*) But the rate for Library purposes must not exceed the limit fixed on the adoption of the Act, and in any case not more than a penny in the pound (55 & 56 Vict. 53, 2).
(*b*) This provision would seem to apply to loans for Library purposes, but see § 19 of the "Public Libraries Act, 1892."
(*c*) See § 18 of the "Public Libraries Act, 1892."

Borrowing by Parish Council.   **12.**—(1.) A parish council for any of the following purposes, that is to say—

PART IV.—STATUTES.—56 & 57 VICT. c. 73. 165

(a) for purchasing any land, or building any buildings, which the council are authorised to purchase or build; and

(b) for any purpose for which the council are authorised to borrow under any of the adoptive Acts; (a) and

(c) for any permanent work or other thing which the council are authorised to execute or do, and the cost of which ought, in the opinion of the county council and the Local Government Board, to be spread over a term of years;

may, with the consent of the county council and the Local Government Board, borrow money in like manner and subject to the like conditions as a local authority may borrow for defraying expenses incurred in the execution of the "Public Health Acts," and §§ 233, 234, and 236 to 239 of the "Public Health Act, 1875," shall apply accordingly, except that the money shall be borrowed on the security of the poor rate and of the whole or part of the revenues of the parish council, and except that, as respects the limit of the sum to be borrowed, one half of the assessable value shall be substituted for the assessable value for two years.

(2.) A county council may lend to a parish council any money which the parish council are authorised to borrow, and may, if necessary, without the sanction of the Local Government Board, and irrespectively of any limit of borrowing, raise the money by loan, subject to the like conditions and in the like manner as any other loan for the execution of their duties, and subject to any further conditions which the Local Government Board may by general or special order impose.

(3.) A parish council shall not borrow for the purposes of any of the adoptive Acts otherwise than in accordance with this Act, but the charge for the purpose of any of the adoptive Acts shall ultimately be on the rate applicable to the purposes of that Act.

(a) See § 19 of the "Public Libraries Act, 1892."

19. In a rural parish not having a separate parish council, the following provisions shall, as from the appointed day, but subject to provisions made by a grouping order, if the parish is grouped with some other parish or parishes, have effect:— *Provision as to small parishes*

(3.) The parish meeting may appoint a committee of their own number for any purposes (a) which, in the opinion of the parish meeting, would be better regulated and managed by means of such a committee, and all the acts of the committee shall be submitted to the parish meeting for their approval;

(4.) All powers, duties, and liabilities of the vestry shall, except so far as they relate to the affairs of the Church or to ecclesiastical charities, or are transferred by this Act to any other authority, be transferred to the parish meeting; (b)

(6.) The chairman of the parish meeting and the overseers of the parish shall be a body corporate by the name of the chairman and overseers of the parish, and shall have perpetual succession, and may hold land for the purposes of the parish without licence in mortmain; but shall in all respects act in manner directed by the parish meeting, and any act of such body corporate shall be executed under the hands, or if an instrument under seal is required under the hands and seals, of the said chairman and overseers;

(7.) The legal interest in all property which under this Act would, if there were a parish council, be vested on the appointed day in the parish council shall vest in the said body corporate of the chairman and overseers of the parish, subject to all trusts and liabilities affecting the same, and all persons concerned shall make or concur in making such transfers (if any) as are requisite to give effect to this enactment; (c)

(9.) A rate levied for defraying the expenses of the parish meeting (when added to expenses under any of the adoptive Acts) shall not exceed sixpence in the pound in any local financial year.(d)

(a) This may include the management of the Public Library after the adoption of the Act, but the requirement that the Committee's proceedings shall be approved by the Parish Meeting might be a hindrance, and the appointment of Commissioners under § 5 of the "Public Libraries Act, 1892," seems to be the preferable course to follow in small Rural Parishes.
(b) See § 5 of "Public Libraries Act, 1892."
(c) Does this extend to a Public Library already established in a Rural Parish?
(d) The Library rate must not exceed the limit fixed by the Parish Meeting, and in any case not more than a penny in the pound.

Power to apply certain provisions of Act to

33 —(1.) The Local Government Board may, on the application of the council of any municipal borough, including a county borough, or of any other urban district, make an order conferring on that council or some other representative body

within the borough or district, all or any of the following matters, namely, the appointment of overseers and assistant overseers, the revocation of appointment of assistant overseers, any powers, duties, or liabilities of overseers, and any powers, duties, or liabilities of a parish council, and applying with the necessary modifications the provisions of this Act with reference thereto. *urban districts and London.*

(3.) Any order under this section may provide for its operation extending either to the whole or to specified parts of the area of the borough or urban district, and may make such provisions as seem necessary for carrying the order into effect.

(4.) The order shall not alter the incidence of any rate, and shall make such provisions as may seem necessary and just for the preservation of the existing interests of paid officers.

(5.) An order under this section may also be made on the application of any representative body within a borough or district.

(6.) The provisions of this section respecting councils of urban districts shall apply to the administrative county of London in like manner as if the district of each sanitary authority in that county were an urban district, and the sanitary authority were the council of that district.(*a*)

(*a*) This sub-section empowers the Local Government Board to vest the Management of Public Libraries in Metropolitan Vestries, who would then be under no necessity to appoint Library Commissioners, since the control of the Public Library is part of the "powers, duties, or liabilities of a Parish Council" (56 & 57 Vict. 73, 7 (5, 7).)

48.—(3.) At every election regulated by rules framed under this Act, the poll shall be taken by ballot, and the "Ballot Act, 1872," and the "Municipal Elections (Corrupt and Illegal Practices) Act, 1884," and sections 74 and 75 and Part IV. of the "Municipal Corporations Act, 1882," as amended by the last-mentioned Act (including the penal provisions of those Acts) shall, subject to adaptations, alterations, and exceptions made by such rules, apply in like manner as in the case of a municipal election. Provided that— *Supplemental provisions as to elections, polls, and tenure of office.*

(*a*) § 6 of the "Ballot Act, 1872," shall apply in the case of such elections, and the returning officer may, in addition to using the schools and public rooms therein referred to free of charge, for taking the poll, use the

168   BOOK I.—LIBRARIES AND MUSEUMS.

same, free of charge, for hearing objections to nomination papers and for counting votes; and

(b) § 37 of the "Municipal Elections (Corrupt and Illegal Practices) Act, 1884," shall apply as if the election were an election mentioned in the First Schedule to that Act.

(6.) Any ballot boxes, fittings, and compartments provided by or belonging to any public authority for any election (whether parliamentary, county council, municipal, school board, or other), shall, on request, and if not required for immediate use by the said authority, be lent to the returning officer for an election under this Act, upon such conditions and either free of charge or, except in the prescribed cases, for such reasonable charge as may be prescribed.

(7.) The expenses of any election under this Act shall not exceed the scale fixed by the county council, and if at the beginning of one month before the first election under this Act a county council have not framed any such scale for their county, the Local Government Board may frame a scale for the county, and the scale so framed shall apply to the first election, and shall have effect as if it had been made by the county council, but shall not be alterable until after the first election.

(8.) This section shall, subject to any adaptations made by the said rules, apply in the case of every poll, consequent on a parish meeting, as if it were a poll for the election of parish councillors.(a)

(a) § 7 (2) provides for the adoption of the "Public Libraries Act, 1892," by a poll, and this matter has been dealt with on a previous page.

Supplemental provisions as to transfer of powers.

52.—(1.) Any power which may be exercised, and any consent which may be given by the owners and ratepayers of a parish or by the majority of them under any of the Acts relating to the relief of the poor or under the School Sites Acts or the Literary and Scientific Institutions Act, 1854, so far as respects the dealing with parish property or the spending of money or raising of a rate may, in the case of a rural parish, be exercised or given by the parish meeting of the parish.

Supplemental provisions as to adoptive Acts.

53.—(1.) Where on the appointed day any of the adoptive Acts is in force in a part only of a rural parish, the existing authority under the Act, or the parish meeting for that part, may transfer the powers, duties, and liabilities of the authority to the parish council, subject to any conditions with respect

PART IV.—STATUTES.—56 & 57 VICT. c. 73.   169

to the execution thereof by means of a committee as to the authority or parish meeting may seem fit, and any such conditions may be altered by any such parish meeting.

(2.) If the area on the appointed day under any authority under any of the adoptive Acts will not after that day be comprised within one rural parish, the powers and duties of the authority shall be transferred to the parish councils of the rural parishes wholly or partly comprised in that area, or, if the area is partly comprised in an urban district, to those parish councils and the district council of the urban district, and shall, until other provision is made in pursuance of this Act, be exercised by a joint committee appointed by those councils. Where any such rural parish has not a parish council the parish meeting shall, for the purposes of this provision, be substituted for the parish council.

(3.) The property, debts, and liabilities of any authority under any of the adoptive Acts whose powers are transferred in pursuance of this Act shall continue to be the property, debts, and liabilities of the area of that authority, and the proceeds of the property shall be credited, and the debts and liabilities and the expenses incurred in respect of the said powers, duties, and liabilities, shall be charged to the account of the rates or contributions levied in that area, and where that area is situate in more than one parish the sums credited to and paid by each parish shall be apportioned in such manner as to give effect to this enactment.

(4.) The county council on the application of a parish council may, by order, alter the boundaries of any such area if they consider that the alteration can properly be made without any undue alteration of the incidence of liability to rates and contributions or of the right to property belonging to the area, regard being had to any corresponding advantage to persons subject to the liability or entitled to the right.

56.—(1.) A parish or district council may appoint committees (a) consisting either wholly or partly of members of the council, for the exercise of any powers which, in the opinion of the council, can be properly exercised by committees, but a committee shall not hold office beyond the next annual meeting of the council, and the acts of every such committee shall be submitted to the council for their approval. Committees of parish or district councils.

Provided that where a committee is appointed by any district council for any of the purposes of the Public Health Acts or Highway Acts, the council may authorise the committee to institute any proceeding or do any act which the council might have instituted or done for that purpose other than the raising of any loan or the making of any rate or contract.

(2.) Where a parish council have any powers and duties which are to be exercised in a part only of the parish, or in relation to a recreation ground, building, or property held for the benefit of a part of a parish, and the part has a defined boundary, the parish council shall, if required by a parish meeting held for that part, appoint annually to exercise such powers and duties a committee consisting partly of members of the council and partly of other persons representing the said part of the parish.

(3.) With respect to committees of parish and district councils the provisions in the First Schedule to this Act shall have effect.(*a*)

(4.) This section shall not apply to the council of a borough.(*b*)

(*a*) § 15 (3) of the "Public Libraries Act, 1892," authorises the appointment of a Library Committee in a Borough or other Urban District. (See p. 141, *ante*.)

(*b*) For the full text of the Act see Chambers's *Popular Summary*, already mentioned.

Joint committees.

57.—(1.) A parish or district council may concur with any other parish or district council or councils in appointing out of their respective bodies a joint committee for any purpose in respect of which they are jointly interested, and in conferring, with or without conditions or restrictions, on any such committee any powers which the appointing council might exercise if the purpose related exclusively to their own parish or district.

(2.) Provided that a council shall not delegate to any such committee any power to borrow money or make any rate.

(3.) A joint committee appointed under this section shall not hold office beyond the expiration of fourteen days after the next annual meeting of any of the councils who appointed it.

(4.) The costs of a joint committee under this section shall be defrayed by the councils by whom it is appointed in such proportions as they may agree upon, or as may be determined in case of difference by the county council.

(5.) Where a parish council can under this Act be required to appoint a committee consisting partly of members of the

PART IV.—STATUTES.—56 & 57 VICT. c. 73. 171

council and partly of other persons, that requirement may also be made in the case of a joint committee, and shall be duly complied with by the parish councils concerned at the time of the appointment of such committee.(a)

(a) The power contained in this section is supplemental to the powers of the Public Libraries Acts for the "combination" of Library Districts or the "annexation" of one district to another, and may be useful. (See §§ 9 and 10 of 55 & 56 Vict. 53, p. 136, *ante*).

58.—(1.) The accounts of the receipts and payments of parish and district councils, and of parish meetings for parishes not having parish councils, and their committees and officers, shall be made up yearly to the thirty-first day of March, or in the case of accounts which are required to be audited half-yearly, then half-yearly to the thirtieth day of September and the thirty-first day of March in each year, and in such form as the Local Government Board prescribe.(a) Audit of accounts of district and parish councils and inspection.

(2.) The said accounts shall, except in the case of accounts audited by the auditors of a borough (but inclusive of the accounts of a joint committee appointed by a borough council with another council not being a borough council), be audited by a district auditor, and the enactments relating to audit by district auditors of accounts of urban sanitary authorities and their officers, and to all matters incidental thereto and consequential thereon, shall apply accordingly, except that in the case of the accounts of rural district councils, their committees and officers, the audit shall be half-yearly instead of yearly.

(3.) The Local Government Board may, with respect to any audit to which this section applies, make rules modifying the enactments as to publication of notice of the audit and of the abstract of accounts and the report of the auditor.

(4.) Every parochial elector of a rural parish may, at all reasonable times, without payment, inspect and take copies of and extracts from all books, accounts, and documents belonging to or under the control of the parish council of the parish or parish meeting.(b)

(5.) Every parochial elector of a parish in a rural district may, at all reasonable times, without payment, inspect and take copies of and extracts from all books, accounts, and documents belonging to or under the control of the district council of the district.(b)

172 BOOK I.—LIBRARIES AND MUSEUMS.

(a) See § 20 of 55 & 56 Vict. 53, p. 146, *ante*.
(b) And see § 20 (3) of 55 & 56 Vict. 53, p. 146, *ante*.

Transfer of property and debts and liabilities.

67. Where any powers and duties are transferred by this Act from one authority to another authority—

(1.) All property held by the first authority for the purpose or by virtue of such powers and duties shall pass to and vest in the other authority, subject to all debts and liabilities affecting the same; and

(2.) The latter authority shall hold the same for the estate, interest, and purposes, and subject to the covenants, conditions, and restrictions for and subject to which the property would have been held if this Act had not passed, so far as the same are not modified by or in pursuance of this Act; and

(3.) All debts and liabilities of the first authority incurred by virtue of such powers and duties shall become debts and liabilities of the latter authority, and be defrayed out of the like property and funds out of which they would have been defrayed if this Act had not passed.(a)

(a) See § 7 (5, 7), p. 163. § 19, p. 165. § 33 (6), p. 167.

SECOND SCHEDULE.—ENACTMENTS REPEALED.

"The Public Libraries Act, 1892" (55 and 56 Vict. **53**); Sub-section three of section one; the First Schedule so far as it applies to rural parishes.

1894. [57 & 58 Vict.] *Public Libraries (Scotland) Act*, 1894. [c. 20]

57 & 58 VICT. 20.

Law Reports Statutes, vol. xxxi. p. 34.

An Act to amend the Public Libraries Consolidation (Scotland) Act, 1887.(a) [20th July, 1894.

(a) This Act corresponds with the English Act of 1892, and reference may usefully be made to that Act for forms of Notice, Resolutions, Advertisement, etc. These forms with a few consequential alterations will do for use in Scotland.

BE it enacted, etc.:

Short title and construction. **1.** This Act may be cited as the "Public Libraries (Scotland) Act, 1894," and shall be construed as one with the "Public Libraries Consolidation (Scotland) Act, 1887" (in this Act referred to as the principal Act), and these two Acts may be together cited as the "Public Libraries (Scotland) Acts, 1887 and 1894."   50 & 51 Vict. 42.

2.—(1.) In burghs the principal Act may be adopted by a resolution of the magistrates and council of the burgh, and such resolution shall be substituted for a determination of the householders of the burgh in any case where such determination is required under the principal Act.   Modification as to adoption of principal Act in burghs.

(2.) §§ 4, 5, and 6 of the principal Act are hereby repealed, so far as they relate to burghs.

3.—(1.) A resolution under this Act shall be passed at a meeting of the magistrates and council, and one month at least before such meeting special notice thereof and of the intention to propose such resolution shall be given to every person included in the collective expression "magistrates and council," either—   Provision as to resolution of magistrates and council of burgh for adoption.

(a) in the mode in which notices to attend meetings of the magistrates and council are usually given; or, in the option of the chief magistrate,

(b) by forwarding a notice by post in a prepaid letter addressed to the usual or last known place of abode of every person entitled to notice under this section.

(2.) The resolution shall, after the passing thereof, be published at least once by advertisement in one or more newspapers circulating in the burgh, and shall come into operation at a time to be fixed in the resolution itself, being not less than one month after the publication or first publication of the advertisement thereof hereinbefore provided.

(3.) A copy of the newspaper or newspapers containing the advertisement shall be conclusive evidence of the resolution having been passed unless the contrary be shown; and no objection to the effect of the resolution on the ground that notice of the intention to propose the same was not duly given, or on the ground that the resolution was not sufficiently published, shall be made after three months from the publication or first publication of the advertisement.

174 BOOK I.—LIBRARIES AND MUSEUMS.

1894.   [57 & 58 Vict.] *Public Libraries (Ireland) Act*, 1894. [c. 38]

57 & 58 VICT. 38.

Law Reports Statutes, vol. xxxi. p. 90.

An Act to amend the Public Libraries (Ireland) Acts.

[17th August, 1894.

BE it enacted, etc.

Adoption of Act and Constitution of Library Authority.

Proceedings for adoption of Act.

1.—(1.) The "Public Libraries Act (Ireland), 1855" (in this Act referred to as the principal Act), may be adopted in any urban district, and the limitation of the maximum rate to be levied for the purposes thereof may, within the limits fixed thereby, be fixed, raised, and removed by a resolution of the urban authority, or by such other means as is provided by this Act. Provided, however, that in case the urban authority should fail to pass a resolution adopting the said Act, such failure shall not prejudice the right by this Act given to voters to have their opinion ascertained in the manner by this Act provided. (*a*)

(i.) Such resolution shall be passed at a meeting of the authority, and one month at least before the meeting special notice of the meeting and of the intention to propose the resolution shall be given to every member of the authority, and the notice shall be deemed to have been duly given to a member of it if it is either—

(*a*) Given in the mode in which notices to attend meetings of the authority are usually given ; or

(*b*) Where there is no such mode, then signed by the clerk of the authority, and delivered to the member, or left at his usual or last known place of abode in Ireland, or forwarded by post in a prepaid letter, addressed to the member at his usual or last known place of abode in Ireland.

(ii.) The resolution shall be published by advertisement in some one or more newspapers circulating within the district of the authority, and by causing notice thereof to be posted at the place heretofore used for posting public notices outside every church and chapel within the district, and otherwise in such manner as the authority think sufficient for giving notice thereof to all persons interested, and shall come into operation at such time, not less than one month after the first publication of the advertisement of the resolution, as the authority may by the resolution fix.

(iii.) A copy of the resolution shall be sent to the Local Government Board.

(iv.) A copy of the advertisement shall be conclusive evidence of the resolution having been passed, unless the contrary be shown; and no objection to the effect of the resolution, on the ground that notice of the intention to propose the same was not duly given, or on the ground that the resolution was not sufficiently published, shall be made after three months from the date of the first advertisement.

(2.) Any 20 or more voters in an urban district, or the urban authority of the district, may address a requisition in writing in the prescribed form to the mayor or other chairman of the authority, requiring him to ascertain the opinion of the voters in the district with respect to the question or questions stated in the requisition.

(3.) On receipt of the requisition the mayor or chairman shall proceed to ascertain by ballot the opinion of the voters with respect to the said question or questions, but shall not ascertain the opinion of the voters on any question with respect to the limitation of the rate unless required to do so by the requisition.

(4.) Where no register of the voters exists the urban authority shall forthwith cause such register to be made for the purposes aforesaid.

(5.) For the purpose of ascertaining the opinion of the voters, the "Ballot Act, 1872" (including the penal provisions of that Act), shall, subject to such alterations and adaptations (if any) as may be prescribed, apply in like manner as in the case of a municipal election.

(6.) Any ballot boxes, fittings, and compartments provided by or belonging to any public authority for any election (whether parliamentary, municipal, or other) shall, on request, and if not required for immediate use by the said authority, be lent to the mayor or chairman of the urban authority, for a poll under this Act, upon such conditions, and either free of charge or, except in the prescribed cases, for such reasonable charge as may be prescribed.

(7.) Every question so submitted to the voters shall be decided by the majority of answers to that question recorded on the valid ballot papers, and where the majority of those answers are in favour of the adoption of the principal Act the same shall forthwith, on the result of the poll being made public, be deemed to be adopted, and shall be carried into execution by the urban authority.

(8.) Where the opinion of the voters in any district is ascertained upon the question as to the adoption of the principal Act, or upon a question as to the limitation of the rate, no further proceeding shall be taken for ascertaining the opinion of the voters until the expiration of one year at least from the day when the opinion of the voters was last ascertained, that is to say, the day on which the poll was taken.

(9.) § 4 of the principal Act is hereby repealed.(*b*)

(*a*) This is not given in the English or Scotch Acts of 1893 and 1894.
(*b*) The forms given on p. 160 may usefully be followed, making the consequential alterations.

Provision for appointment of commissioners.

2.—(1.) If at any time after the expiration of six months from the taking of a poll in manner provided by this Act, where the majority of the answers were in favour of the adoption of the principal Act, the urban authority have not in the opinion of the Local Government Board taken proper or sufficient steps to carry the Act into execution, that Board may, if they think fit, upon the application in the prescribed manner of ten or more voters, appoint from among the voters five commissioners to carry the principal Act into execution.

(2.) The commissioners so appointed shall have all the powers and perform all the duties conferred and imposed on the urban authority by the principal Act and the Acts amending the same, including this Act, subject to such alterations and adaptations as may be prescribed. They shall hold office for such time as the Local Government Board direct, and upon the expiration of their term of office the Board may either appoint their successors from among the voters or may by order empower the urban authority to carry the principal Act into execution.

(3.) Any vacancy occurring among the said commissioners shall be filled by the Local Government Board from among the voters.

Power to two or more authorities to combine.

3.—(1.) When the principal Act is adopted for two or more neighbouring districts, the authorities of those districts may by agreement combine for any period for carrying the

Act into execution, and the expenses of carrying the Act into execution shall be defrayed by such authorities in such proportions as may be agreed on by them.

(2.) For the purposes of this section, a joint committee may be formed, the members whereof shall be appointed by the several combining authorities in such proportions as may be agreed on, but need not be members of any of the combining authorities. Any such committee shall have such of the powers of an urban authority under the principal Act, except the power of borrowing money, as the combining authorities may agree to confer upon them.

(3.) In the event of the combining authorities failing to agree as to the proportions in which the expenses of carrying the Act into execution are to be defrayed, or as to the proportions in which the members of a joint committee under this section are to be appointed, those proportions shall, on the application of any such authority, be determined by the Local Government Board.

4. An urban authority may, if they think fit, grant the use of a lending library established under the principal Act to persons not being inhabitants of their district, either gratuitously or for payment. *Provision as to use of library.*

5. An urban authority may let a house or building, or any part thereof, or any land vested in them for the purposes of the principal Act, or the Acts amending the same, including this Act, which is not at the time of such letting required for those purposes, and shall apply the rents and profits thereof for the purposes of those Acts. *Provision as to letting of land.*

6.—(1.) Any person holding land for public or charitable purposes may, subject as hereinafter provided, grant or convey, by way of gift, sale, or exchange, for any of the purposes of the principal Act, or the Acts amending the same, including this Act, any quantity of such land, not exceeding in any one case one acre, in any manner vested in such person. *Power to grant certain land for purposes of Acts.*

(2.) Provided that—

(a) charitable property shall not be so granted or conveyed without the consent of the Commissioners of Charitable Donations and Bequests for Ireland, and, in the case of land charged with the repayment of an advance made under the "Glebe Loan (Ireland) Acts," without the consent of the Commissioners of Public Works in Ireland; and

(b) the land taken in exchange or the money received for

178   BOOK I.—LIBRARIES AND MUSEUMS.

such sale shall be held on the same trusts as the land exchanged or sold.

Power to urban authorities to make agreements for use of library.

7.—(1.) The urban authorities of any two or more districts for which this Act has been adopted may agree to share in such proportions and for such period as may be determined by the agreement the cost of the purchase, erection, repair, and maintenance of any library building situate in one of those districts, and also the cost of the purchase of books and newspapers for such library, and all other expenses connected with the same.

(2.) The urban authority of any district may, with the consent of the Commissioners of Charitable Donations and Bequests for Ireland, or of the Commissioners of Endowed Schools in Ireland, as the case may be, make the like agreement with the governing body of any library established or maintained out of funds subject to the jurisdiction of either of the said Commissioners, and situate in or near the district.

(3.) This section shall apply, with the necessary modifications, to a museum, school for science, art gallery, or school for art in like manner as to a library.

Power to urban authority to accept parliamentary grant.

8. Where an urban authority accepts a grant out of money provided by Parliament from the Department of Science and Art towards the purchase of the site, or the erection, enlargement, or repair, of any school for science and art, or school for science, or school for art, or of the residence of a teacher in any such school, or towards the furnishing of any such school, that authority may accept the grant upon the conditions prescribed by the Department of Science and Art, and may execute any instruments required by that Department for carrying into effect those conditions, and upon payment of the grant shall be bound by such conditions and instruments, and have power and be bound to fulfil and observe the same.

Financial Provisions.

Expenses of Act.

9.—(1.) The expenses incurred in and incidental to the execution of this Act shall be defrayed in manner provided by the principal Act with regard to the expenses of carrying that Act into execution.

(2.) Where in any urban district a limit is by law imposed upon the rating power of the urban authority, it shall be lawful for such authority to impose and levy the rate authorised by the principal Act notwithstanding such limit.

Supplemental Provisions.

10. Any agreement under this Act between two or more urban authorities, or between an urban authority and any other body, may provide that on the termination of the agreement an adjustment shall be made of the interests of the several parties thereto in any property to the provision of which they have contributed, and as to the mode in which the adjustment shall be arrived at, and in the event of any dispute the adjustment shall, on the application of any of the parties, be made by an arbitrator appointed by the Local Government Board. *Adjustment of interests on termination of agreement.*

11. The Local Government Board may make rules for carrying into effect the objects of this Act, and those rules shall be laid before both Houses of Parliament as soon as may be after they are made, and shall be judicially noticed and have effect as if enacted by this Act. *Power to make rules.*

12. In this Act, unless the context otherwise requires,— *Definitions.*

The expression "urban district" means an incorporated borough or a town as defined by the principal Act:

The expression "urban authority" means, in the case of an incorporated borough, the council or board of municipal commissioners, and in the case of a town the town commissioners as defined by the principal Act:

The expression "voter" means a person who is registered as a parliamentary voter in respect of the ownership or occupation of property, or in respect of lodgings within the district in connection with which the voter is mentioned, and in the case of a borough includes a freeman thereof:

The expression "the Local Government Board" means the Local Government Board for Ireland:

The expression "prescribed" means prescribed by rules made by the Local Government Board under this Act.

13. This Act may be cited as the "Public Libraries (Ireland) Act, 1894." *Short title.*

180   BOOK I.—LIBRARIES AND MUSEUMS.

1898.   61 & 62 Vict.]   *Libraries Offences Act*, 1898.   [c. 53]

61 & 62 VICT. 53.

Law Reports Statutes, vol. xxxv. p. 266.

Short title.

Penalty for offences.

An Act to provide for the Punishment of Offences in Libraries.   [August 12, 1898.

BE it enacted, &c.

1. This Act may be cited as the "Libraries Offences Act, 1898."

2. Any person who, in any library or reading-room to which this Act applies, to the annoyance or disturbance of any person using the same :—
   (1) behaves in a disorderly manner;
   (2) uses violent, abusive, or obscene language;
   (3) bets or gambles;
   (4) or who, after proper warning, persists in remaining therein beyond the hours fixed for the closing of such library or reading-room,
shall be liable on summary conviction to a penalty not exceeding forty shillings.

Application of Act.

3. This Act shall apply—
   (a) to any library under the "Public Libraries Act, 1892;" and

56 & 57 Vict. 39.
59 & 60 Vict. 25.

   (b) to any library or reading-room maintained by a Society registered under the "Industrial and Provident Societies Act, 1894," or under the "Friendly Societies Act, 1896," or by any registered Trade Union.

Extent of Act.

4. This Act shall not apply to Scotland or Ireland.

ADDITIONAL POWERS OBTAINED BY LOCAL ACTS.

Certain towns in Great Britain have obtained by means of Local Acts various additional powers with respect to Libraries and Museums, and it is not unlikely that, as time goes on, some of these powers will be embodied in general Acts. It has therefore been thought useful to give the titles and dates of these local Acts :—

"Manchester Improvement Act, 1871" (34 & 35 Vict. c. lxv.).

"Edinburgh Public Library Assessment Act, 1887" (50 & 51 Vict. c. lxxxv.).

"Sheffield Corporation Act, 1890" (53 & 54 Vict. c. ccxxv.).

181

PART V.
DIGEST OF CASES.

THE following explanations as to the objects aimed at in this Digest may conveniently be given as a guide to the reader consulting it.

Where a decision was appealed against, references to Reports of the Case in its earlier stages are usually omitted unless some special reasons for not doing so were found to exist.

Much confusion often arises in citing references to periodicals running over a long term of years, where there exists an "Old" and a "New" Series of each. Having considered this matter in connection with the *Law Journal* and *Law Times*, and bearing in mind that the "New Series" of each of these periodicals has now been going on for many years, and that references to the "Old Series" are not only few, but cannot increase, it has been decided on reflection to suppress the letters "N. S." usually appended to references to the above-named periodicals, and to do the converse thing, that is, append the letters "O. S." to such references as apply to the "Old Series" of each respectively. This arrangement, it is to be understood, is limited to the *Law Journal* and *Law Times*, and does not extend to any other works, so that the *Common Bench Reports*, for instance, are cited in the usual way, "*Common Bench*" and "*Common Bench, New Series*," and so on in other instances.

The ample Index appended, coupled with a little ingenuity on the part of the reader in always turning to more heads than one, will, it is hoped, render reference to the Cases a task free from serious difficulty.

Though the *Weekly Reporter* is not as a rule cited, many of the Cases will be found therein. The dates appended will facilitate search. The *Weekly Reporter* and the *Jurist* are usually only cited in instances where no other Report was to be had, but this has not been from any distrust of the *Weekly Reporter* at any rate, because we have often found it to be a very trustworthy and useful publication. It was necessary, however, to draw the line somewhere, or there would have been a superfluity of references in many places.

Cases which are obsolete by reason of subsequent legislation, or because they have been overruled, are usually suppressed altogether. If in a few instances the titles of such Cases have been given with an asterisk prefixed, this has been done because it was judged convenient for some reason or other that arguments or *Dicta* mentioned in the Reports of these Cases should not be entirely lost from record.

The reader who concerns himself with such details will find that great pains have been taken to exhibit the references not only correctly but methodically. Every reference has been specially verified and very carefully read at press. It should be stated, however, that this remark does not apply to the *Justice of the Peace*, for the Library of the Inner Temple only contains a file of that periodical for recent years. The earlier *J. P.* references are therefore mostly second-hand.

Care has been taken in the Index to distinguish Cases of the same name from one another, and we hope that in no instance has the same Case been printed by mistake under two or more names, though the fact that certain Reporters are very careless in their system of naming the Cases which they report has made the task of collation one of considerable trouble and difficulty.

1892. [1]
Andrews v. *Bristol, Mayor.* "Income Tax Act, 1842" (5 & 6 Vict. 35), § 61, Rule vi.: "Public Libraries Acts, 1855, 1866" [both repealed]— A Municipal Corporation is not, in respect of the ownership of free Libraries, "a literary or scientific institution within the above Rule; nor entitled to the allowance of assessments under Sched. A upon buildings so used. (61 L. J., Q. B., 715; 67 L. T., 618; 56 J. P., 615.)

1889. [2]
A.-G. v. *Croydon, Mayor.* "Public Libraries Acts"—Adoption in Borough— Voting-papers issued to occupiers held properly issued and the occupiers held entitled to vote—Injunction to restrain the Corporation acting on a vote to adopt, refused. (58 L. J., Ch. D., 527; L. R., 42 Ch. D., 178; 61 L. T., 291; 53 J. P., 72.)

1871. [3]
A.-G. v. *Great Eastern Railway Co.* Where a public Body is under an Act Parliament intrusted with powers and duties for a public purpose, the

PART V.—DIGEST OF CASES.   183

Court will give credit to them as being the best judges of what they want for that purpose. (L. R., 6 Ch. App., 572; 19 W. R., 788.)

1876.   [4]
A.-G. v. *Sunderland Corporation.* "Public Health Act, 1848," § 73—Land vested in Corporation for public Pleasure Ground—Injunction granted to restrain the use of a part for erection of Town Offices, etc.—Conservatory, museum, and library allowed. (45 L. J., Ch., 839; L. R., 2 Ch. D., 634; 34 L. T., 921; 40 J. P., 364.)

1868.   [5]
Greig v. *University of Edinburgh.* University property, though dedicated to public purposes, being neither wholly nor in part held by the Crown, is rateable. (L. R., 1 H. L. (Sc.), 348.)

1854.   [6]
Harrison v. *Southampton, Mayor.* 8 & 9 Vict. **43**, extended by 13 & 14 Vict. 65 [and further extended by 18 & 19 Vict. 70]—A Statute authorising a devise of land for a public purpose will be taken to include a bequest of money for the purchase of land—The Court will put a liberal construction on an Act which legalises the gift of property for laudable purposes. (23 L. J., Ch., 919; 2 Sm. & G., 387; 23 L. T. (o. s.), 330.)

1895.   [7]
Holborn District Library Commissioners v. *Bull.* Book borrowed but not returned—Rule that non-return of a book subjected the borrower to a fine—Proceedings in County Court—Judgment for the Commissioners: Defendant to pay 1s. for damages; 2s. 6d. for fines; and all costs, and this notwithstanding that the book had eventually been returned. 99 L. T. Newsp., 295.

1862.   [8]
Liverpool Corporation, In re; Brown, Ex parte. Local Library Act—Rate limited in amount—Distress Warrant against the Overseers refused—Held that the Justices were right—A "penny" Rate means a penny Rate on the nominal rateable property, although part of it is unproductive—A deficiency thus arising cannot be supplied out of the productive part. (31 L. J., M. C., 108; [*Reg.* v. *Liverpool JJ.*] 6 L. T., 241.)

1896.   [9]
Manchester, Mayor v. *McAdam.* "Public Libraries Act, 1892," §§ 4, 11, 12, 14; "Income Tax Act, 1842," § 61—A public Library vested in a Library Authority under the Act of 1892 is "a building, the property of a literary or scientific institution," within the meaning of the said Act of 1842; and therefore the Authority is entitled to exemption from Income Tax in respect of such a Library whoever may be the owners of the buildings, and whether they are supported by Rates or not. (65 L. J., H. L., 672; L. R., A. C., 500; 75 L. T., 229.)

1876.   [10]
Nottingham Corporation v. *Abbott.* "Public Libraries Act, 1855"—Rules framed under the Statute to regulate the user of books borrowed—Acknowledgment of the rules signed by defendant on being admitted as a borrower—Breach of rule requiring a book to be returned within a prescribed time, or a fine of so much a week to be payable—After the lapse of several months beyond the prescribed time, book returned, but payment of the fines refused—Whereupon proceedings taken to enforce fines—Judgment for the plaintiff Corporation with costs. (In the Nottingham County Court, March 14, 1876.—MS.)

184   BOOK I.—LIBRARIES AND MUSEUMS.

1891. [11]
Reg. v. *Blenkinsop.* "Public Libraries Act, 1855," § 13—Proportion of Rate not demanded by Overseers under a mistake as to their legal powers—New Overseers, on discovering the mistake, took proceedings to recover the uncollected sums, treating them as "arrears"—*Mandamus* granted to Justices to enforce the said arrears by Distress. (61 L. J., M. C., 45; L. R., 1 Q.B., 43; 66 L. T., 187; 56 J. P., 246.)

1888. [12]
Reg. v. *Morris.* Poll taken by voting-papers—"Public Libraries Acts" adopted—Commissioners appointed—Application for *Quo Warranto* to question their election on the ground (1) that the Vestry and Guardians were not the prescribed Local Authority; (2) that voting-papers were not issued to each ratepayer; (3) that those issued were not properly collected; (4) that a scrutiny lawfully demanded had been refused; (5) and generally that the result of the voting had not been conclusively ascertained. Application refused. (*Times*, June 13, 1888.)

1876. [13]
Reg. v. *Portsmouth, Mayor.* "Public Libraries Act, 1855"—Meeting convened to consider adoption of Act—The Mayor, not acquainted with the fact that the old provision requiring a two-thirds vote had been repealed and the decision of a simple majority substituted, certified that the Act had not been adopted—Whereupon, Rule absolute for a *Mandamus* commanding him to vary his Certificate, and declare that the Act had been duly adopted. (*Times*, Jan. 25, 1876.)

1875. [14]
Reg. v. *St. Matthew, Bethnal Green, Vestry.* "Public Libraries Act, 1855"—A poll may be demanded by the party defeated on the show of hands on the question whether the Act shall be adopted—The right to demand a poll is a necessary incident to the mode of election by show of hands whenever it is not excluded by special custom. (32 L. T., 558; [*Donovan* v. *St. M.*] 39 J. P., 502.)

1882. [15]
Reg. v. *Wimbledon L. B.* "Public Libraries Act, 1855"—Any qualified person present at a meeting convened under § 6 may, after the show of hands, demand a poll, and the common law right to do this is not affected by 40 & 41 Vict. 54. (51 L. J., Q. B., 219; L. R., 8 Q. B. D., 459; 46 L. T., 47; 46 J. P., 292.)

1879. [16]
Smee v. *Smee and Brighton Corporation.* Bequest in favour of a Free Public Library held void on the ground that Testator was of unsound mind when he made the will. (49 L. J., P. D. A., 8; L. R., 5 P. D., 84; 44 J. P., 220.)

LEGAL DECISIONS IN INFERIOR COURTS.

In addition to the decisions relating to Public Libraries or Museums which have been given from time to time by the Superior Courts, questions of Law connected with the working of these Institutions frequently come before County Court Judges and Benches of Magistrates. In the absence of anything like officially-published records of these decisions it is thought that perhaps a brief digest based on newspaper cuttings, culled though they be haphazard from various sources,

PART V.—DIGEST OF CASES. 185

may not be entirely devoid of use to officials engaged in the management of Public Libraries or Museums.

The paragraphs which follow record some of such decisions which have come under our notice during recent years.

At Richmond proceedings were taken under the "Licensing Act, 1872" (35 & 36 Vict. **94**, 12), against a man who was given into custody and charged with being drunk and disorderly in a public place, to wit, the Richmond Public Library. Fined 20s. and costs.

In another case at Richmond proceedings were taken under the "Metropolitan Police Act, 1839" (2 & 3 Vict. **47**, 54, (13)), where the defendant was also convicted. In this case the offence was laid in the following terms:—" . . . did unlawfully use insulting behaviour in a public place to . . . whereby a breach of the peace might have been occasioned contrary to the form of the statute in such case made and provided."

Several successful prosecutions for thefts from Public Libraries or Museums have taken place. At Stoke-on-Trent a man charged with stealing 37 engravings was committed to gaol for 1 month with hard labour. At Stafford, 2 youths who broke into a case of coins and stole several were both convicted. At Watford, a youth indicted at the Assizes for stealing a Magazine, was sentenced to 2 months' imprisonment with hard labour.

At Manchester, in 1874, a curiously ingenious fraud which had taken place at the Free Library was investigated at the City Police Court. The formal charge was of obtaining a book under false pretences, but the actual conviction was for loitering in the Library for a felonious purpose. The following report is abridged from the *Manchester City News* (May 2, 1874):—"Mr. Talbot, Assistant Town Clerk, attended the City Police Court to prosecute J—— G——, a militiaman, for obtaining a book under false pretences from the Free Library, Campfield. Mr. Talbot said that by filling up a ticket with his name and address any person could obtain a book to read in the Library, and in June, 1873, a volume of the *Illustrated London News* was so obtained by a person who filled up a ticket with the name of Henry Gordon. That book was not returned, and is still missing. On April 22 in this year [1874], a volume of *Fun* was taken out by a person who gave the name of William Brooks, 49 Travis Street, and on Friday last the prisoner came and asked for a volume of *Fun* in the name of Alfred Fordham, 42 Lombard Street.

The librarian, not feeling satisfied, went to Lombard Street, but could find no such house, and therefore gave the man into custody on returning to the Library. The librarian would swear that as far as he was able to judge the handwriting on the tickets referred to was identical, and he (Mr. Talbot) apprehended that if the Court believed that the prisoner obtained a book by giving a false name it might be fairly assumed that he went to the Library for an unlawful purpose.—Mr. Headlam said the prisoner did not get the book on the strength of the name.—Mr. Talbot: That may be so; but does it not alter his position from a lawful to an unlawful one? I think a jury would feel so.—Mr. Headlam: A jury might think he was the man who got the other volumes.—Mr. Talbot: If you are satisfied that the handwriting on the tickets is the same, there will be a case with which you might deal summarily.—The librarian gave evidence in support of Mr. Talbot's statement; the prisoner said he was a labourer out of work, and had no settled residence. He belonged to the 7th Lancashire Militia.—Mr. Headlam said the charge of false pretences was not sustained, but he could convict the prisoner under the "Vagrancy Act" for loitering in the Library for a felonious purpose, and for that offence he should send him to prison for 3 months."

BEGGING, ETC.

1894. Leamington.—Tramp begging in Free Library. Committed to prison. (6 *Library*, p. 89.)

1894. Kensington.—Man who had assaulted an Assistant Librarian. Fined 27s. or 21 days' imprisonment. (6 *Library*, p. 407.)

STEALING.

1892. Kensington.—Man who had stolen a penny local paper. Committed for 21 days with hard labour. (4 *Library*, p. 128.)

1892. Cambridge.—Man who had stolen 15 books from Borough Free Library and 6 from University Library. Sentenced to 8 months' imprisonment. (4 *Library*, p. 190.)

1892. Wandsworth.—Man who had stolen a book. Sentenced to 21 days' imprisonment. (4 *Library*, p. 352.)

1893. Croydon.—Man who had stolen a copy of *Public Opinion*. Fined 5s. and 4s. 6d. costs, or 7 days. (5 *Library*, p. 137.)

PART V.—DIGEST OF CASES. 187

1893. St. Giles'.—Man who had stolen a daily newspaper. Fined 20s. (5 *Library*, pp. 235 and 336.)

1894. Coventry.—Theft of an atlas. Defendant being said to be a person of weak mind, dealt with under "First Offenders' Act." (6 *Library*, p. 253.)

1894. Putney.—Man who had stolen books. Sentenced to 1 month's imprisonment. (6 *Library*, p. 364.)

1896. Liverpool.—Man who had stolen books. Sentenced to 6 months' imprisonment with hard labour. (8 *Library*, p. 127.)

1896. Glasgow.—Man stealing books. Fined 3 guineas or 21 days' imprisonment. (8 *Library*, p. 170.)

MALICIOUS INJURY.

1892. Sheffield.—Man who had mutilated a bound copy of the *Sheffield Telegraph*. Fined 5l. (maximum) with costs, and ordered to pay the damage. (4 *Library*, p. 28.)

1892. Hanley.—Man who had systematically damaged every book got from Library. Fined 20s. and costs in two cases, and money for purchase of two new volumes. (4 *Library*, p. 62.)

1893. Newcastle-on-Tyne.—Man who had torn a plate out of book. Fined 10s. and costs and 6d. damage. (5 *Library*, p. 338.)

1894. Blackburn.—Man who had maliciously damaged a book. Fined 20s. and costs, and the cost of rebinding. (6 *Library*, p. 88.)

1894. Leeds.—Man who had removed a plate out of a book. Fined 1s. and costs, and 40s. for damage. (6 *Library*, p. 178.)

1897. St. Giles's.—Man who had torn a picture from an illustrated weekly newspaper and put the same in his pocket. Sentenced to 7 days' imprisonment with hard labour without the option of a fine. (*Evening Standard*, May 10, 1897.)

UNLAWFUL DETENTION OF LIBRARY PROPERTY.

1896. St. Giles's.—Man had lawfully borrowed a book which he took home to his lodgings. Being in arrear with his rent his landlady locked him out and took possession of his property including the Library book, which she refused to give up to the Librarian, until the lodger had paid his rent. Landlady convicted of illegally detaining the book and ordered to give it up and pay 7s. costs. (*Morning Post*, December 24, 1896.)

BOOK II.
LITERARY AND SCIENTIFIC INSTITUTIONS.

PART I.
DIGEST OF STATUTES.

HAVING in Book I. examined the Law relating to the foundation and maintenance of Public Libraries and Museums supported out of Local Rates, we have now to consider the Law applicable to the foundation and maintenance of other Institutions formed for purposes connected with Literature, Science and Art, and governed, not by any Public Authorities but by private "Committees of Management," "Trustees," or "Managers." These Institutions are not only exceedingly numerous in the United Kingdom—probably there could hardly be found a market town without one of some kind—but they differ greatly among themselves in importance, wealth, usefulness, and popularity. Some, like the Royal Society of London, or the Literary and Philosophical Society of Manchester, or the Royal Irish Academy, have a world-wide reputation, whilst others, under the names of Natural History Societies, Church Institutes, or Village Clubs, are purely local in their operations and influence, but are none the less useful in their way.

(2.) A remark made in the Preface to this volume must be repeated in substance here, to the effect that of Statute Law bearing on Institutions such as those we are now considering there is very little in existence, and in the vast number of

190 BOOK II.—LITERARY AND SCIENTIFIC INSTITUTIONS.

instances these Institutions derive their legal *status* not from Statutes at all, but from Royal charters, voluntary trust deeds, and informal agreements ("simple contracts") between the members.

(3.) The earliest Statute directly designed to promote a taste for books amongst the masses is the "Parochial Libraries Act, 1708:" what its effect was we have not been able to ascertain; indeed it is only by drawing an inference from the language of the preamble that we can suppose it may by chance have had any effect at all. The preamble, after reciting the desirability of assisting the clergy in their studies, proceeds to note that whereas various charitable persons have established Parochial Libraries, "provision is wanting to preserve the same," and the Act proceeds to supply the requisite provision, so far as legislative machinery could do so.

7 Anne, 14.

(4.) This Act has at this time no great practical value; the text of it, however, will be found in Part IV. (*post*).

(5.) By the "Specific Legacies Exemption Act, 1799," it is enacted that "no legacy, consisting of Books, Prints, Pictures, Statues, Gems, Coins, Medals, Specimens of Natural History, or other specific articles, which shall be given or bequeathed to, or in Trust for any Body Corporate whether aggregate or sole, or to the Society of Serjeants' Inn, or of any of the Inns of Court or Chancery, or any Endowed School in order to be kept by such Body Corporate, Society, or School, and not for the purposes of sale, shall be liable to any Duty imposed on legacies by any Law now in force." This enactment seems somewhat limited in its scope, and it appears doubtful whether, if construed literally, it would be available to protect articles bequeathed to many of the Literary and Scientific Institutions which flourish in the present day.

39 Geo. III. 73, 1.

(6.) In 1843 the Legislature indicated its desire to promote the spread of a taste for Science and Art by passing an Act to exempt from County, Borough, and other Local Rates, land and buildings occupied by Scientific or Literary Societies.

6 & 7 Vict. 36.

(7.) Any Society instituted for purposes of Science, Literature, or the Fine Arts exclusively, and occupying, for the transaction of its business, any lands, houses, or buildings, may obtain exemption from Rates on certain conditions. These conditions are (1) that the Society claiming exemption is supported wholly or in part by annual voluntary con-

6 & 7 Vict. 36, 1.

PART I.—DIGEST OF STATUTES. 191

tributions, and does not, and by its Laws may not, make any dividend, gift, division, or bonus in money to its members ; and (2) that it obtains a Certificate of Exemption from, in England, the Barrister appointed to certify the Rules of Friendly Societies, or, in Scotland, from the Lord Advocate.

(8.) The Act provides the machinery requisite for working out this system of Registration. If the Certificate is refused, the Society applying may appeal to the Court of Quarter Sessions for the County or Borough where the land or buildings of the Society are situated. And such Court may, if it thinks fit, allow the appeal and order the Rules to be filed by the Clerk of the Peace, just as if a Certificate had been issued in the usual way. The registration of the Rules of a Society is one of the duties transferred to County Councils by the "Local Government Act, 1888," but the appeal to Quarter Sessions given when a Certificate is refused by Registrar of Friendly Societies does not seem to be affected by that Act. 6 & 7 Vict. 36, 2-4.
6 & 7 Vict. 36, 5.

51 & 52 Vict. 41, 3 (xv).

(9.) During the years immediately after the passing of the Act, appeals under it were frequent, but now the general principles of Law entitling a Society to a Certificate, or the contrary, may be deemed to be settled and understood. Such of the Appeal Cases alluded to as came before the Superior Courts will be found noted in Part V., *Digest of Cases* (*post*). The case of *Reg.* v. *Phillips* decided the important point that a Certificate of exemption is not conclusive proof to the right thereto ; but that a Certificate may be challenged by an aggrieved ratepayer.

(10.) Next in chronological order comes the "Titles of Religious Congregations Act, 1850," the applicability of which to Literary and Scientific Institutions is not generally known, doubtless on account of its quasi-ecclesiastical title. This Act gives great facilities for property conveyed for religious or educational purposes to one set of trustees being transferred to another set of trustees by simple and inexpensive formalities. The appointment of new trustees is to be made to appear by a deed under the hand and seal of the Chairman for the time being of the meeting at which the appointment is made, executed in the presence of the meeting, and attested by two or more credible witnesses. A statutory form of appointment is given in the Schedule to the Act. 13 & 14 Vict. 28.

(11.) In 1854 an Act was passed to afford greater facilities 17 & 18 Vict. 112.

192 BOOK II.—LITERARY AND SCIENTIFIC INSTITUTIONS.

for the establishment of Institutions for the promotion of Literature and Science and the Fine Arts.

17 & 18 Vict. 112, 1.
(12.) Any person seised in fee-simple, fee-tail, or for life, of and in any manor or lands of freehold, copyhold, or customary tenure, and having the present beneficial interest therein, may grant, by way of gift, sale, or exchange, either in fee or for a term of years, any piece of such land not exceeding one acre in extent, whether built upon or not, as a site for any such Institution as described. In the case of a grant by a tenant for life, the remainderman must join, if legally competent. Where the grant is by the Lord of the Manor of waste or commonable land, and gratuitously, the grant operates as a bar to the rights of the Commoners.

17 & 18 Vict. 112, 2-4.
(13.) Special provision is made for grants of land belonging to the Duchies of Lancaster and Cornwall.

17 & 18 Vict. 112, 4.
(14.) If lands granted by way of gift cease to be used for the purposes of the Institution, they are to revert immediately to the Estate, Manor, or Duchy of which they originally formed part; but if the Institution is removed to another site, the land may be sold for its benefit.

17 & 18 Vict. 112, 5.
(15.) Persons not having legal Estates are empowered to convey lands for the purposes of the Act, without the concurrence of their Trustees. And where land is bought which belongs to infants or lunatics, the Guardians or Committees may convey, and give valid discharges for the purchase-money.

17 & 18 Vict. 112, 6
(16.) Corporations, ecclesiastical or lay, sole or aggregate, Officers, Justices of the Peace, Trustees or Commissioners, holding land for public, ecclesiastical, parochial, charitable, or other purposes, may convey lands for the purposes of the Act. But a variety of consents are requisite according to the class of property to be dealt with. For instance, the Bishop of the Diocese, the Parochial Electors in Parish meeting, the Local Government Board, the Guardians of the Poor, or the Charity Commissioners, as the case may be, may severally be required to signify their approval of a grant.

56 & 57 Vict. 73, 52 (1).

17 & 18 Vict. 112, 8, 9.
(17.) Where a part only of lands subject to a rent under a lease is conveyed, the rent and the fine payable upon the renewal of the lease may be apportioned. Provision is made as to the liabilities of tenants, and as to the remedies of landlords in respect of lands not conveyed.

17 & 18 Vict. 112, 10-18.
(18.) The Act contains a variety of minor provisions respecting conveyancing matters, of which it is not necessary to exhibit an abstract here, beyond mentioning that §§ 69–74

PART I.—DIGEST OF STATUTES. 193

and 78 of the "Lands Clauses Act, 1845,", are incorporated. 8 Vict. 18.

(19.) The governing bodies of Institutions established under the Act are invested with various powers and duties with respect to the mortgage or sale of the premises; the vesting of property; actions; judgments; By-Laws; subscriptions of members; and offences by members. Moreover, provision is made for alterations being brought about in the objects of Institutions; for the amalgamation of Institutions; and for the dissolution of Institutions. In the case of proposed alterations, the Board of Trade may interfere to review them, on the application of members aggrieved. 17 & 18 Vict. 112, 19–32.

(20.) The Act is to apply to every Institution for the time being established for the promotion of Science, Literature, the Fine Arts, for Adult Instruction, the diffusion of Useful Knowledge, the foundation or maintenance of Libraries or Reading Rooms for general use among the members or open to the Public, of Public Museums and Galleries of paintings and other works of Art, collections of Natural History, Mechanical and Philosophical Inventions, Instruments, or Designs. The Royal Institution and the London Institution are expressly exempted. 17 & 18 Vict. 112, 33.

(21.) The "Companies Act, 1867," contains a clause applying the principles of that Act and of the "Companies Act, 1862," to Associations formed for Art and Science, but which are not to be carried on for the pecuniary profit of its members. This enactment is coming into very general use for the purposes of Literary and Scientific Societies, presumably for the reason that as the machinery of a trading company is available in great part for the working of Associations formed under it, special safeguards and securities are offered for the protection of the members, especially in regard to the important matter of finance. 30 & 31 Vict. 131, 23.

(22.) The following is an outline of the Section of the Act of 1867 just alluded to:—An Association intended to be formed as a Limited Liability Company under the Acts, and which can prove to the Board of Trade that its object is to promote Commerce, Art, Science, Religion, Charity, or any other useful purpose, and that its intention is to apply its profits solely for such purposes, and to pay no dividend to its members, may obtain from the Board of Trade a licence for registration without the addition to its name of the word "Limited"; and after registration it shall enjoy all the privileges and incur all the obligations granted to and 30 & 31 Vict. 131, 23.

O

imposed on Limited Companies, except that it shall not be required to use the word "Limited," or to publish its name, or send lists of its members or officials to the Registrar. The Board of Trade may impose conditions and require such conditions to be inserted in the Memorandum or Articles of Association.(a)

31 & 32 Vict. 44.

(23.) An Act passed in the year 1868 gives greater facilities for the acquisition of buildings and building sites by Societies or Bodies of persons associated together for Religious, Educational, Literary, Scientific, or other charitable purposes. It relaxed in favour of such objects some of the provisions of the "Charitable Uses Act, 1735," (b) and of the "Charitable Uses Act, 1861." (c) The Act of 1868 was repealed by the "Mortmain and Charitable Uses Act, 1888," with exception of one short section; and that was subsequently repealed by the "Statute Law Revision Act, 1893."

9 Geo. II. 36.
24 & 25 Vict. 9.
51 & 52 Vict. 42.

35 & 36 Vict. 24.

(24.) Another Act on this subject is the "Charitable Trustees Incorporation Act, 1872," the preamble of which recites that " it is expedient to facilitate the Incorporation of the Trustees of Charities established for Religious, Educational, Literary, Scientific, or Public Charitable purposes, and to provide for the due protection and transmission of the property belonging to or vested in such Charities, or Trustees of such Charities, and to diminish the expense of enrolment " under the "Charitable Trusts Act, 1866."(c)

29 & 30 Vict. 57.
35 & 36 Vict. 24, 1

(25.) The Trustees of any Charity for Religious, Educational, Literary, Scientific, or Public Charitable purposes may apply to the Charity Commissioners for a Certificate of registration of such Trustees as a Corporate Body. If the Commissioners, having regard to the extent, nature, and objects and other circumstances of the Charity shall consider such Incorporation expedient they may grant a Certificate on such conditions as they think fit, relating to the qualifications and number of the Trustees, their tenure or avoidance of office, and the mode of appointing new Trustees. The Trustees will thereupon become a Body Corporate, and will have perpetual

(a) In F. B. Palmer's *Company Precedents*, 6th ed. 1895, p. 239, there will be found a very suggestive List of Companies and Associations, etc., which have been registered without the word "Limited." It will be noticed that their defined objects are exceedingly diverse in character.

(b) Better known as the "Mortmain Act." This Act was repealed (with a slight exception) by the "Mortmain and Charitable Uses Act, 1888." (51 & 52 Vict. 42.)

c) This Act was repealed by the "Mortmain and Charitable Uses Act, 1888." (51 & 52 Vict. 42.)

PART I.—DIGEST OF STATUTES. 195

succession and a common seal, and may sue and be sued in their Corporate name, and may hold and acquire and deal with property, real or personal, notwithstanding the Statutes of Mortmain, but with a saving for the "Charitable Uses Act, 1735." 9 Geo. II. 36.

(26.) The Certificate will have the effect of vesting in the new Body Corporate all the property of the Charity, with certain specified exceptions. 35 & 36 Vict. 24, 2.

(27.) The Act contains a large number of miscellaneous regulations relating to the management by the Charity Commissioners of the negotiations for the issue of Certificates, for which the reader is referred to the Act itself. (See Book IV., *post.*) 35 & 36 Vict. 24, 3–15.

(28.) By far the most important existing Statute bearing on facilities for the establishment of Literary and Scientific Institutions by gift is the "Mortmain and Charitable Uses Act, 1888," which consolidates all the previous Statute Law, repealing what is obsolete, and amending and extending what is useful. But even this Act has already been twice amended. 51 & 52 Vict. 42. 54 & 55 Vict. 73 : 55 & 56 Vict. 11.

(29.) §§ 6 and 7 of the Act of 1888 by granting exemptions of a certain character facilitate indirectly the provision of sites for Museums and Institutions designed to promote Art, Literature, Science, etc. But there are conditions prescribed which must be carefully borne in mind by testators and their legal advisers. (See the Act in Book IV., *post.*)

PART II.

PRECEDENTS OF FORMAL DOCUMENTS.

I.

OFFICIAL CIRCULAR OF THE BOARD OF TRADE.

(A.)

Procedure in cases of Application to the Board of Trade for a Licence under § 23 of the " Companies Act, 1867."

1. The accompanying drafts have been prepared to show generally the manner in which the Memorandum and Articles of Association should be framed where it is proposed to apply to the Board of Trade for a licence under the 23rd section of the " Companies Act, 1867."

2. Under this section any Chamber, Institute, Society, or other Association formed for the purpose of promoting Commerce, Art, Science, Religion, Charity, or any other useful object which does not involve the division of profit, may, if it obtains the Licence of the Board of Trade, be incorporated by registration with limited liability, but without the addition of the word "Limited" to its name. Attention is drawn to the substitution in the drafts of the words "Association," " Chamber," etc., for the word "Company."

3. It is to be understood that the drafts of the Memorandum and Articles of Association are subject to such additions, alterations, and omissions as the circumstances of the Association desiring incorporation may render necessary, or the Board of Trade may require.

4. An Association desiring to be incorporated in this manner should make a written application to the Board of Trade for a licence, and, together with such application,

PART II.—PRECEDENTS OF FORMAL DOCUMENTS. 197

should transmit for consideration a *draft* (a) in duplicate of the proposed Memorandum of Association and Articles of Association, together with a list of the promoters and proposed Managing Body of the Association, and any report or statement of its proceedings. If the Board of Trade are satisfied that the application may be entertained, they will furnish a notice of such application, to be inserted in a local newspaper for the information of the public, and if after the expiration of a limited time there appears to be no sufficient reason why the Licence should not be granted, the Board of Trade will accept the Memorandum and Articles of Association with such amendment, if any, as may be necessary, and grant a licence.

5. The Board of Trade will require to have the Memorandum and Articles of Association settled on their behalf by counsel, at the expense of the applicants, for which purpose a fee of £5 5s. must accompany the application.(b) The Board of Trade will not, however, be responsible for the Memorandum or Articles being properly framed as regards the interest of the Association.

(B.)

[DRAFT.]

MEMORANDUM OF ASSOCIATION.

1. The name of the Association is "The   ."
2. The registered office of the Association will be situate in [England].
3. The objects for which the Association is established are: [Here express objects shortly.]
 (1.) The
 (2.) The
 (3.) The doing all such other lawful things as are incidental or conducive to the attainment of the above objects.

4. The income and property of the Association, whencesoever derived, shall be applied solely towards the promotion of the objects of the Association as set forth in this Memo-

---

(a) It is requested that the draft, and any subsequent revisions that may be required, may, whether in print or manuscript, be of foolscap-sized paper, being the size most convenient for registration.

(b) A cheque for the amount of this fee should be made payable to an "Assistant Secretary of the Board of Trade."

randum of Association; and no portion thereof shall be paid or transferred directly or indirectly, by way of dividend, bonus, or otherwise howsoever by way of profit, to the members of the Association.

Provided that nothing herein shall prevent the payment, in good faith, of remuneration to any officers or servants of the Association, or to any member of the Association, or other person, in return for any services actually rendered to the Association.

5. The fourth paragraph of this Memorandum is a condition on which a licence is granted by the Board of Trade to the Association in pursuance of Section 23 of the Companies Act, 1867.

6. If any member of the Association pays or receives any dividend, bonus, or other profit, in contravention of the terms of the fourth paragraph of this Memorandum, his liability shall be unlimited.

7. Every member of the Association undertakes to contribute to the assets of the Association, in the event of the same being wound up during the time that he is a member, or within one year afterwards, for payment of the debts and liabilities of the Association contracted before the time at which he ceases to be a member, and of the costs, charges, and expenses of winding up the same, and for the adjustment of the rights of the contributories amongst themselves, such amount as may be required not exceeding [pounds], or in case of his liability becoming unlimited, such other amount as may be required in pursuance of the last preceding paragraph of this Memorandum.

8. If upon the winding up or dissolution of the Association there remains, after the satisfaction of all its debts and liabilities, any property whatsoever, the same shall not be paid to or distributed among the members of the Association, but shall be given or transferred to some other institution or institutions, having objects similar to the objects of the Association, to be determined by the members of the Association at or before the time of dissolution, or in default thereof by such Judge of the High Court of Justice as may have or acquire jurisdiction in the matter.

9. True accounts shall be kept of the sums of money received and expended by the Association, and the matter in respect of which such receipt and expenditure takes place, and of the property, credits, and liabilities of the Association; and, subject to any reasonable restrictions as to the time and

PART II.—PRECEDENTS OF FORMAL DOCUMENTS. 199

manner of inspecting the same that may be imposed in accordance with the regulations of the Association for the time being, shall be open to the inspection of the members. Once at least in every year the accounts of the Association shall be examined, and the correctness of the balance-sheet ascertained by one or more properly qualified Auditor or Auditors.

We, the several persons whose names and addresses are subscribed, are desirous of being formed into an Association in pursuance of this Memorandum of Association.

	(a) Names, Addresses, and Descriptions of Subscribers.
1.	
2.	
3.	
4.	
5.	
6.	
7.	

Dated   day of   18
Witness to the above signatures,
A. B.

(C.)

[DRAFT.]

ARTICLES OF ASSOCIATION.

1. For the purposes of registration, the number of the members of the Association is declared not to exceed [   ].

2. These Articles shall be construed with reference to the provisions of the Companies Act, 1862, and the Companies Act, 1867, and terms used in these Articles shall be taken as having the same respective meanings as they have when used in those Acts.

3. The chamber (*b*) [institute or society, as the case may be] is established for the purposes expressed in the Memorandum of Association.

4. Qualification of members.

5. Admission of members.

(*a*) All the names should be in full, the addresses should be definite, giving, where practicable, the name of the street and the number of the house.
(*b*) It is proposed to adopt the style of "chamber," "society," etc., throughout, and to avoid the use of the word "company."

200 BOOK II.—LITERARY AND SCIENTIFIC INSTITUTIONS.

6. Retirement of members.
7. Rights of members.
8. Honorary officers and their elections.
9. Management of chamber.
10. Powers of chamber [or of the council or governing body thereof].
11. Meetings, proceedings, etc.
12. Accounts, audit, etc., and so forth.

Names, addresses, and descriptions of subscribers [as in Memorandum of Association].

Dated the   day of

Witness,

II.

LITERARY OR SCIENTIFIC SOCIETY UNDER THE "COMPANIES ACTS, 1862, 1867, AND 1877."

Draft Memorandum of Association, and Articles of Association.

The   Society.

MEMORANDUM OF ASSOCIATION.

1. The name of the Society [Association, Institution] is "The   Society" [Association, Institution].
2. The registered office of the [Society] will be situated in England.
3. The objects for which the [Society] is established are to promote the advancement and diffusion of a knowledge of   and for this purpose especially:
    (1.) To invite from the members and others, communications, written or oral, relating to   and to receive, hear, and discuss such communications at Meetings of the [Society].
    (2.) To invite the exhibition of and to exhibit, at Meetings of the [Society], any new, improved, or other apparatus for   and any new or other experiments illustrative of
    (3.) To print and publish, and to sell, lend, and distribute, any communications made to the [Society] or any other papers, treatises, or communications relating to   and any reports of the pro-

ceedings and accounts of the [Society], and for this purpose to cause translations to be made of any such papers, treatises, or communications as shall be in a foreign language, and to illustrate any of the publications.

(4.) To purchase, take on lease, or otherwise acquire, and also to dispose of, any premises and other property for the purposes of the [Society], subject to the provisions of § 23 of the " Companies Act, 1862."

(5.) To do all such other lawful things as are incidental or conducive to the attainment of the above objects.

4. The income and property of the [Society], whencesoever derived, shall be applied solely towards the promotion of the objects of the [Society] as set forth in this Memorandum of Association; and no portion thereof shall be paid or transferred directly or indirectly by way of dividend or bonus or otherwise howsoever by way of profit, to any person who is or has been a Member of the [Society], or to any person claiming through him: Provided that nothing herein contained shall prevent the payment of just remuneration to any officers or servants of the [Society] or to anyone, although a member of the [Society], for services rendered to the [Society].

5. The 4th paragraph of this Memorandum is a condition on which a licence is granted by the Board of Trade to the [Society] in pursuance of § 23 of the " Companies Act, 1867." For the purpose of preventing any evasion of the terms of the said 4th paragraph, the Board of Trade may from time to time, on the application of any member of the [Society], impose further conditions which shall be duly observed by the [Society].

6. If the [Society] act in contravention of the 4th paragraph of this Memorandum or of any such further conditions, the liability of every Member of the Council [Director, Manager] of the [Society] shall be unlimited, and the liability of every Member of the [Society] who has received any such dividend, bonus, or other profit as aforesaid shall likewise be unlimited.

7. Every Member of the [Society] undertakes to contribute to the assets of the [Society] in the event of the same being wound up during the time that he is a Member, or within one year afterwards, for payment of the debts and liabilities of the [Society] contracted before the time at which he ceases

to be a Member, and of the costs, charges, and expenses of winding up of the same, and for the adjustment of the rights of the contributories amongst themselves, such amount as may be required, not exceeding £1, or in case of his liability becoming unlimited, in pursuance of the last preceding paragraph of this Memorandum, such amount as may be required: Provided always that every Member of the [Society] whose liability remains limited, shall be called on to contribute to the full extent of his liability before any greater contribution is made by any Member of the [Society] whose liability has become unlimited.

8. If upon the winding-up or dissolution of the [Society] there remains after the satisfaction of all its debts and liabilities any property whatsoever, the same shall be applied in the first place to the reimbursement of Members who may have made payments under the provisions of the last preceding paragraph, and the surplus shall not be paid to or distributed among the members of the [Society], but shall be given or transferred to some other Institution or Institutions having objects similar to the objects of the [Society] to be determined by the members of the Society of or before the time of dissolution, or in default thereof by such Judge of the High Court of Justice as may have or acquire jurisdiction in the matter.

WE, the several persons whose names and addresses are subscribed, are desirous of being formed into a [Society] in pursuance of this Memorandum of Association.

	Names, Addresses, and Descriptions of Subscribers.
1.	
2.	
3.	
4.	
5.	
6.	
7.	

Dated the   day of   18

Witness to the above signatures:

PART II.—PRECEDENTS OF FORMAL DOCUMENTS. 203

ARTICLES OF ASSOCIATION.

IT IS AGREED AS FOLLOWS:
1. For the purposes of registration the number of the members of the [Society] is declared not to exceed [500].
2. These Articles shall be construed with reference to the provisions of the "Companies Acts, 1862, 1867, and 1877," and terms used in these Articles shall be taken as having the same respective meanings as they have when used in those Acts. In these Articles words importing the masculine gender only shall be taken to include the feminine gender.
3. The [Society] is established for the purposes expressed in the Memorandum of Association.

Members.

4. The [Society] shall consist of ordinary members, *ex officio* members, and honorary members.
5. The persons whose names are set forth in the second Schedule hereto, and any other persons who shall be elected ordinary members, as hereinafter provided, shall be ordinary members of the [Society].
6. The Presidents [Chairmen] for the time being of such [Societies] as the Council may from time to time recommend, may, with the approval of a general meeting of the [Society], be nominated as *ex officio* members. They shall receive all the publications issued by the [Society] during their term of membership, and enjoy all other privileges of members, but shall not be liable to pay any subscription.
7. Honorary members shall be such persons distinguished for their attainments in   , and not being British subjects, as shall be elected honorary members in the manner hereinafter provided.
8. The number of honorary members shall not exceed [12] at any one time.
9. The rights and privileges of every ordinary, *ex officio*, and honorary member shall be personal to himself; they shall not be transferable by his own act, or by operation of law, and shall cease upon his death.

Election, Admission, Retirement and Expulsion of Members.

10. No person shall be qualified for election as an ordinary member unless he be recommended as a candidate by not less than 3 members, to 2 of whom he must be personally known.

Such recommendation shall be made by the signature of such members to the following form:—

Name..

Occupation or Qualification ....

Residence...

Being desirous of becoming a member of the   Society we, the undersigned, being members, recommend him as a proper person to be elected a member thereof.

Dated the   day of   18

From personal knowledge. | From general knowledge.

11. The names of candidates so recommended shall be submitted to the Council hereinafter mentioned. The Council shall, at their next meeting after a name has been submitted to them, either approve or reject the same.(a) The Council may in their discretion reject the name of any candidate.

12. The names of such candidates as shall be approved by the Council shall be submitted to the [Society] at the meeting held next after such approval shall have been given; and for this purpose the names of the candidates and of the members who recommend them shall be read at such meeting by one of the Secretaries. The names shall then be submitted for ballot at the next following meeting of the Society.

13. Honorary members shall be nominated by the Council, and shall be elected by the [Society] at the annual general meeting. An honorary member shall be deemed to be nominated by the Council when his name has been submitted to one meeting of the Council and accepted upon ballot at a second meeting thereof.

14. A list of the names of persons nominated by the Council as honorary members shall be sent to every ordinary member, by being posted to his registered address, at least 14 days before the annual general meeting. The names shall then be submitted for ballot at the annual general meeting.

15. At every ballot, whether for the election of an ordinary member or for the nomination or election of an honorary member, one black ball in 4 shall exclude.

16. Every member who is elected shall be informed of his

(a) If it should be thought that too much elective power is here conferred on the governing body, it may be provided that the name of any candidate duly nominated shall go at once to the general body of members.

election by one of the Secretaries, who shall also send him a copy of the Memorandum and Articles of Association of the [Society], together with a blank obligation in the following form: —

> I, the undersigned, having been elected an (ordinary, *ex officio*, or honorary, as the case may be) member of the [Society] do hereby engage that I will endeavour to promote its interests and welfare, and will observe its laws as long as I shall continue a member thereof.
>
> (Signed)
>
> Dated the   day of   18

17. Every person elected, whether as an ordinary, an *ex officio*, or an honorary member, shall within one calendar month, or such extended or other time as the Council shall in any particular case direct, sign and return the said form to one of the Secretaries; and every person elected as an ordinary member shall, within 3 calendar months from the date of his election, pay the entrance fee and the first annual subscription, according to the scale hereinafter mentioned.

18. If any member shall fail to comply with so much of the last preceding article as applies to his case, the Council may, at any time after 3 calendar months from the date of his election, declare his election void.

19. At the first meeting at which a member is present after he has complied with the provisions of Article 17, he shall be admitted according to the following form:—He shall first sign his name in a book to be kept for that purpose, and shall then be presented to the President or other member in the chair by one of the Secretaries; and the President (or Chairman), addressing him by name, shall say, " In the name of the [Society], I admit you a member thereof."

20. If any member, after returning to the registered office all books or other property of the [Society] in his hands, shall leave at or send by Post to the registered office a notice in writing signed by himself, stating that he resigns his membership in the [Society] he shall thereupon cease to be a member.

21. Upon the recommendation of the Council the [Society] may, by a resolution passed at a special general meeting, expel any member from the [Society], provided that at such meeting not less than 20 members shall be present, and that of those who vote at least three-fourths shall be in favour of the resolution.

22. In any case in which the Council may think it proper

to recommend the expulsion of a member, the President shall call a special general meeting to consider the matter. At such meeting the voting upon the question shall be by ballot.

23. If any member fails to pay any subscription within 6 months of the same becoming due from him, the Treasurer shall serve him with notice that he is in arrear, and that in the event of non-payment before a day to be named in the notice, and not being less than 24 months from the date at which the subscription became due, he will be liable to be removed from the [Society].

24. In the event of non-payment before the day named in such notice as aforesaid, the member so in arrear may be removed from the [Society] by a resolution of the Council to that effect.

25. The last 2 preceding Articles shall be additional to, and not in substitution for, the power given by Article 18.

26. Any member who shall retire, be expelled, or be removed from the [Society], shall remain liable for the payment of all moneys due from him at the date of his retirement, expulsion, or removal.

Payments by Members.

27. The persons whose names are set forth in the 2nd Schedule hereto, other than those whose names are marked thus *, shall pay an annual subscription of   each.

28. The persons whose names are marked thus * in the said 2nd Schedule are members who have compounded for their annual subscriptions. They shall not be liable to pay any further annual subscriptions.

29. Every ordinary member hereafter to be elected shall pay an entrance fee of   , and an annual subscription of   .

30. Subscriptions shall be payable in advance, and shall become due on the [1st day of January] in each year.

31. The entrance fee and subscription shall become due from every ordinary member immediately upon his election; but any ordinary member elected on or after the [1st of November] in any year shall not be liable to pay his subscription for that year. For the purpose of subscriptions a year shall be the period between the [1st day of January] and the [31st day of December].

32. Any member may, at any time, compound for all annual subscriptions thereafter to become due from him by the payment of   in one sum.

PART II.—PRECEDENTS OF FORMAL DOCUMENTS. 207

33. The Council may, under the authority of a special resolution, as defined in the " Companies Act, 1862," from time to time reduce the annual subscription, and the amount to be paid for compounding.

34. Neither *ex officio* nor honorary members shall be liable to pay any entrance fee, or annual or other subscription.

Council. [Committee.]

35. The affairs of the [Society] shall be managed by a Council, consisting of a President [Chairman], not more than   nor less than   Vice-Presidents (exclusive of the *ex officio* Vice-Presidents presently mentioned),   Secretaries, a Treasurer, and not more than   other persons, all of whom must be ordinary members of the [Society].

36. The first Council shall be composed of the persons whose names and addresses are set forth in the 1st Schedule hereto, and they shall hold the several offices set opposite to their respective names therein.

37. Subsequent Councils shall be elected by the Society annually by ballot at the annual general meeting.

38. At each annual general meeting [all] the members of the Council shall retire from office, and the [Society] shall elect a new Council in manner herein provided.

39. It shall be the duty of the Council before each annual general meeting to prepare a list containing the names of the members whom they recommend for election to the respective offices of [President, Vice-Presidents, Secretaries, and Treasurer], and the names of   other members whom they recommend for election as ordinary members of the Council.

40. Names recommended by the Council shall be names proposed at one meeting of the Council and agreed to at a subsequent meeting.

41. A copy of the list so prepared shall be sent to every ordinary member by being posted to his registered address at least 14 days before the annual general meeting.

42. Every ordinary member shall have power to alter the list so sent by the removal or addition of the name of any ordinary member, or as regards the name of any member already included in the list by removing the same from the office for which the member has been recommended by the Council, or inserting such name under a different office, and he shall use the list with such alterations (if any) as a balloting-list at the annual general meeting.

208 BOOK II.—LITERARY AND SCIENTIFIC INSTITUTIONS.

43. Any balloting-list which (as altered) shall contain the names of more than   President,   Vice-Presidents, Secretaries,   Treasurer, and   ordinary members of the Council, shall be null and void.

44. On the day of election the Chairman shall nominate 2 Scrutineers, to be approved by the meeting, to assist the Secretaries in examining the balloting-lists. Each ordinary member present and voting shall deliver his list to one of the Scrutineers, and the names of the members so voting shall be recorded by one of the Secretaries. Ordinary members who are not able to be present may vote by sending their balloting-lists in a sealed envelope addressed to the Scrutineers, enclosed in a letter addressed to the Secretaries at the registered office of the [Society], so as to be delivered before the time of meeting. The members whose names shall be reported to the President by the Scrutineers as having received the majority of votes for filling the offices of President, Vice-Presidents, Secretaries, Treasurer, and ordinary members of Council respectively, shall be deemed to be elected to those several offices, and their names shall be announced from the Chair as those of the persons elected to serve for the ensuing year.

45. A retiring member of the Council shall be re-eligible provided that—

(*a*) The same person shall not be eligible as [President] for more than 2 years in succession.

(*b*) At least   persons shall be elected to the new Council who were not members of the retiring Council.

46. Any casual vacancy occurring in the Council may be filled up by the Council.

47. Every [President] shall, during the 2 years next following his ceasing to be [President], be an *ex officio* [Vice-President] and member of the Council in addition to the members elected in manner aforesaid. Provided always that if any such *ex officio* member shall, during the said 2 years, be elected to any office on the Council, he shall upon such election cease to be an *ex officio* Vice-President and member.

Meetings of the [*Society*].

48. The Meetings of the [Society] shall be of two kinds—

(*a*) General meetings, including annual and special general meetings.

(*b*) Monthly meetings.

PART II.—PRECEDENTS OF FORMAL DOCUMENTS. 209

49. The word "meeting," when standing alone in these Articles, and referring to a meeting of the [Society], shall include as well a monthly meeting as a general meeting, unless such construction would be repugnant to the subject or context.

(a) *General Meetings.*

50. The first general meeting shall be held at such time, not more than 4 months after the registration of the [Society], and at such place, as the Council shall determine.

51. Subsequent general meetings shall be held once in every calendar year at such time and place as may be prescribed by the [Society] in general meeting; and if no other time is prescribed, a general meeting shall be held on the day of the first meeting in the month of   , or if there be no meeting in that month, then on the   .

52. The above-mentioned general meetings shall be called annual general meetings; all other general meetings shall be called special general meetings.

53. The [President] or the Council may, whenever he or they think fit, and the [President] shall, upon receiving a written requisition signed by not less than   members, convene a special general meeting.

54. Any such requisition shall state the object for which the meeting is required, and shall be addressed to the [President], and left at or sent by post to the registered office.

55. Upon receiving the requisition, the [President] shall forthwith convene a special general meeting, to be held within 14 days from the receipt of the requisition. If he do not so convene the same, the requisitionists or any other members, not less than   in number, may themselves convene a special general meeting.

56. Seven days' notice at the least, exclusive of the day of giving the notice, but inclusive of the day for which the notice is given, specifying the place, the day, and the hour of meeting, and, in case of special business, the general nature of such business, shall be given to each ordinary member by circular posted to him at his registered address. Honorary and *ex officio* members shall not be entitled to receive any such notice.

57. All business that is transacted at a special general meeting shall be deemed special; and likewise all business that is transacted at an annual general meeting, with the

P

exception of the consideration of the Accounts, Balance-sheets, and ordinary reports of the Council, Treasurer, and Auditors respectively, and business immediately relating thereto.

58. No business, of which notice has not been given in manner aforesaid, shall be dealt with in any way at a general meeting.

59. At every general meeting (except where by these Articles a larger quorum is expressly required) members shall form a quorum. If at any general meeting a quorum is not present within half-an-hour of the time appointed for holding the meeting, the meeting, if convened upon the requisition of members, shall be dissolved. In any other case it shall stand adjourned to the same day in the next week, at the same time and place; and if at such adjourned meeting a quorum is not present, the meeting shall be deemed to stand adjourned *sine die*.

60. The Chairman of any general meeting may, with the consent of the meeting, adjourn the meeting from time to time, and from place to place.

61. Every ordinary member shall have one vote. Neither *ex officio* nor honorary members shall be entitled to a vote.

62. Votes may be given either personally or by proxy, in such a form (*a*) as may be from time to time prescribed by the Council.

63. At any general meeting, unless a poll is demanded by at least 5 members, a declaration by the Chairman that a resolution has been carried and an entry to that effect in the minute book of proceedings, shall be sufficient evidence of the fact, without proof of the number or proportion of the votes recorded in favour of or against such Resolution.

64. If a poll is duly demanded, it shall take place at such time and place, and either by open voting or by ballot, as the Chairman directs, and the result of the poll shall be deemed the Resolution of the meeting at which the poll is demanded. The Chairman of a general meeting shall, in case of an equality of votes at the meeting, or at the poll, if a poll is demanded, be entitled to a casting vote in addition to the vote or votes to which he is entitled as a member.

(*a*) But in the case of a Body formed under Act of Parliament in the way now contemplated, every Proxy-paper must bear a 1*d*. stamp. (See 34 Vict. **4**, 4.)

PART II.—PRECEDENTS OF FORMAL DOCUMENTS. 211

(b) *Monthly Meetings.*

65. The Council shall from time to time appoint the times and places for holding the ordinary monthly meetings of the [Society], to hear and discuss communications relating to , and generally to proceed with the literary or scientific business of the [Society]. The meetings so appointed shall be called monthly meetings.

66. Monthly meetings shall, unless the Council shall otherwise appoint, be held at least once in every calendar month during the months from November to June inclusive; and that period, or such other period as the Council shall from time to time appoint for holding such meetings, is in these Articles referred to as a " Session."

67. At any monthly meeting the names of candidates for ordinary membership may be read, new ordinary members may be elected, and new members admitted.

68. No notice shall be required of the business to be transacted at a monthly meeting.

69. Persons not members of the [Society] may attend these meetings as Visitors upon the introduction of members. Each member shall be at liberty to introduce not more than 2 Visitors at any monthly meeting by giving or sending to the Chairman of the meeting, or to any Secretary who may be present, the names of the Visitors and the name of the member introducing them.

70. The Council may in their discretion grant to persons not members of the Society admission to all or any of the monthly meetings of a Session.

71. At a monthly meeting the ordinary course of business shall, subject to the control of the Chairman, be as follows :—

(1.) The names of Visitors and those of the members by whom they are introduced shall be announced from the chair, if the Chairman thinks fit to do so.

(2.) The minutes of the previous meeting shall be read and be submitted for confirmation.

(3.) New members shall be admitted.

(4.) Presents made to the [Society] since its last meeting shall be announced from the chair, and, so far as the Chairman may deem expedient, shall be exhibited.

(5.) The names of candidates for election as ordinary members shall be read.

(6.) The literary or scientific business of the meeting shall be proceeded with.

(7.) The matter to be brought before the next meeting shall be announced from the chair.

(8.) The ballot for new ordinary members shall take place.

72. Every person who shall desire to bring a communication before the [Society] shall give notice thereof in writing to one of the Secretaries, stating the nature of the communication. In all cases it shall rest with the Council to decide whether any paper shall or shall not be read.

73. Written or oral communication shall be accompanied whenever it is practicable by experimental illustration, and the exhibition and use of the apparatus referred to in them.

74. All papers or communications which have been read to the [Society], with or without the explanatory drawings, shall become the property of the [Society]. The Council shall have power to publish [in the "Proceedings" of the Society] such of the papers or abstracts of them as they may deem fit; but any paper not published in full by the Council shall remain at the absolute disposal of the author.

75. No report of any written or oral communication made to or proceedings had by the [Society] at a meeting shall be published except under the authority or by the permission of the Council. (a)

Duties of Officers and Council.—(a) *Of the President and Vice-Presidents.*

76. The President shall act as Chairman at all meetings of the [Society] or of the Council at which he is present. In his absence one of the Vice-Presidents according to seniority of appointment shall discharge the functions of the President. If, at any meeting whether of the [Society] or of the Council, neither the President nor any Vice-President is present, some other member shall be chosen Chairman for the occasion.

77. The President and Vice-Presidents shall discharge the several duties herein assigned to him or them.

(b) *Of the Secretaries.*

78. It shall be the duty of the Secretaries (or of one of them) to attend every meeting of the [Society] and of the Council; to record the minutes of proceedings; and to read those minutes at the next meeting. They shall, under the direction of the President and Council, conduct the corre-

---

(a) There will often be cases in which it will be desirable to relax, formally or informally, the stringency of such a rule as this.

PART II.—PRECEDENTS OF FORMAL DOCUMENTS. 213

spondence of the [Society], and issue all requisite notices to the members for convening meetings or otherwise, and perform such other duties as the President or Council shall assign to them.

(c) *Of the Treasurer.*

79. The Treasurer shall keep a proper account of the income and expenditure of the [Society] in books to be provided for the purpose. He shall submit his accounts, with vouchers for payments made by him, to be audited once in each year, and shall produce the account-books, properly posted up, when required by the Council. He shall present to the [Society] at the annual general meeting a Balance-sheet and Report signed by the Auditors.

80. He shall keep an account of such members as shall have paid their annual subscriptions, and also of those who have paid a composition in lieu thereof. In this account shall be noted the times up to which the annual payments have been made, and the arrears of each member.

81. Six weeks at least before the day appointed for holding the annual general meeting the Council shall appoint 2 members of the [Society], not being members of the Council, to audit the Treasurer's accounts and balance-sheet, and report thereon to the [Society].

(d) *Of the Council.*

82. The Council shall make provision for carrying out the objects of the [Society], and for conducting its affairs in accordance with the Memorandum or Articles of Association. They shall, subject to the regulations of the [Society] for the time being, have the sole control and management of the income, property, and affairs of the [Society], and may appoint and dismiss any paid officers and servants.

83. Meetings of the Council shall be summoned by the Secretaries, under the direction of the President. Five members shall form a quorum.

84. The Council shall meet at least once in each calendar month during a session.

85. In addition to meetings mentioned in the last article, the President may at any time direct the Secretaries to summon a special meeting of the Council; and he shall direct a special meeting thereof to be summoned at any time upon a requisition addressed to him by 3 members of the Council.

86. Questions arising at a meeting of the Council shall be decided by a show of hands, except in any case in which a ballot shall be demanded, or in which a ballot is required by these Articles. In case of an equality in votes, the Chairman shall have a second or casting vote.

87. Any member of the Council who shall be personally or pecuniarily interested in a question under consideration shall retire during the discussion and determination of the same.

88. If at any meeting of the Council business be introduced of which notice has not been given either at the previous meeting, or in the summons calling the meeting, any member present shall be entitled to require that no vote or decision shall be taken on such business until the next meeting; but, subject as aforesaid, any business may be transacted at a meeting of the Council without notice of such business having been given.

89. The Council shall, at the annual general meeting, present to the [Society] a report on the position of the [Society], financially and otherwise, and on the affairs and proceedings of the [Society] generally during the previous year.

90. A notice may be served by the [Society] upon any member, either personally or by sending it through the Post in a prepaid letter addressed to such member at his registered address.

91. Any notice sent by post shall be deemed to have been served at the time when the letter containing the same would be delivered in the ordinary course of the Post; and in proving such service it shall be sufficient to prove that the letter containing the notice was properly addressed and put into the Post-Office in sufficient time.

Time and Place of Monthly Meetings.

Monthly meetings of the [Society] are held at on days during the months of [November to June inclusive], at the hour of P.M.

Office of the Society.

The registered office of the [Society] is at .

PART II.—PRECEDENTS OF FORMAL DOCUMENTS. 215

THE FIRST SCHEDULE ABOVE REFERRED TO.

Members of the Council.
President ....
Vice-Presidents ....
Secretaries ....,..................
Treasurer...
Ordinary members of Council ....

THE SECOND SCHEDULE ABOVE REFERRED TO.

Members of the Society.

* Denotes Life Members.

Names, addresses, and Descriptions of Subscribers :

Dated the   day of   , 18 .

III.

LITERARY OR SCIENTIFIC SOCIETY UNDER THE " COMPANIES
Act, 1867," § 23.

Newspaper Advertisement of Application having been made to the Board of Trade.

APPLICATION for a LICENCE of the BOARD OF TRADE.—Notice is hereby given, that in pursuance of the 23rd Section of the " Companies Act, 1867," application has been made to the Board of Trade for a Licence directing an Association about to be formed under the name of the   SOCIETY [Association, Institution] to be registered with limited liability, without the addition of the word " Limited " to its name.

The objects for which the [Society] is proposed to be established are :—

1. To invite from the members and others, communications, written or oral, relating to   , and to receive, hear, and discuss such communications at meetings of the [Society].

2. To invite the exhibition of, and to exhibit at meetings

of the [Society], any new, improved, or other apparatus for , and any new or other experiments illustrative of .

3. To print and publish and to sell, lend, and distribute any communications made to the [Society], or any other papers, treatises, or communications relating to , and any reports of the proceedings and accounts of the [Society], and for this purpose to cause translations to be made of any such papers, treatises, or communications as shall be in a foreign language, and to illustrate any of the publications.

4. To purchase, take on lease, or otherwise acquire, and also to dispose of, any premises and other property for the purposes of the [Society], subject to the provisions of § 21 of the "Companies Act, 1862."

5. To do all such other lawful things as are incidental or conducive to the attainment of the above objects.

Notice is hereby further given, that any person, Company, or Corporation objecting to this application may bring such objection before the Board of Trade on or before the day of next, by a letter addressed to the Assistant-Secretary, Railway Department, Board of Trade, Whitehall, London, S.W.

Dated this day of , 18 .

Solicitors for the said [Society].

IV.

PAROCHIAL INSTITUTE UNDER THE "COMPANIES ACT, 1867," § 23.

[Begin as in No. 2 or 3, and then proceed (a) to define the objects of the Institute as follows :—]

1. To establish a Library and Reading Rooms at , in the County of , and to provide a large hall or room for entertainments, lectures, and meetings.

2. To promote mental culture, and to encourage habits of temperance, industry, and application, and with a view thereto, among other things, to offer and give prizes and rewards.

(a) In F. B. Palmer's *Company Precedents*, 6th edit. 1895, pp. 271-94, there will be found a large number of useful precedents. Amongst them are the titles: "Cricket Club," "Coffee Tavern," "Public Hall," "Circulating Library," "School or College," "Club," "Club-House," "Political Club," "Musical Society."

3. To purchase, hire, or otherwise acquire, for the purposes of the Institute, any real or personal property, and in particular any lands, buildings, furniture, books, newspapers, periodicals, and musical instruments.

4. To invest the moneys of the Institute, not immediately required, in such manner as may be determined.

5. To accept and hold any money or property upon trust for any charitable purposes for the benefit of the inhabitants of the Parish of   , or any class or section thereof, and to execute such trusts.

6. To borrow or raise money by the issue of, or upon, bonds, debentures, bills of exchange, promissory notes, or other obligations or securities of the Institute, or by mortgage or charge of all or any part of the property of the Institute, or of its uncalled capital, or in such other manner as the Committee of Management shall think fit.

7. To sell, improve, manage, develope, lease, mortgage, dispose of, or otherwise deal with all or any part of the property of the Institute.

8. To do all such other things as are incidental or conducive to the attainment of the above objects.

V.

MEMORANDUM AND ARTICLES OF ASSOCIATION SUITED FOR A COUNTRY TOWN CLUB FOR GENTLEMEN.

" *The Companies Acts*, 1862, 1867, and 1877."

COMPANY LIMITED BY SHARES.

The   Club, Limited.

MEMORANDUM OF ASSOCIATION.

1. The name of the Company is the " '   Club,' Limited."

2. The registered office of the Company will be situate in England.

3. The objects for which the Company is established are :—

To provide, and at the discretion of the Company to carry on, an Institution at   , in the County of

, embodying, at the discretion of the Committee, all or any of the leading features of a first-class London Club; including the supply of refreshments, of such kinds as are usually provided at London Clubs [and, either in conjunction with or distinct from the Club, to provide a Subscription Library and Reading Room].

To acquire by purchase, lease, or otherwise, any lands, buildings, and hereditaments of any tenure in , and to erect, finish, or complete any buildings, and to fit up and furnish such buildings or any parts thereof with fixtures, or furniture, appliances for the purposes first above mentioned, or any or either of them, and to mortgage, sell, or otherwise dispose of the whole or any part or parts of such land, buildings, or hereditaments, and also to let or demise the same or any part or parts thereof, either furnished or unfurnished, and either for the purposes first above mentioned or for any other purposes, and upon such terms and conditions as the Company shall from time to time determine.

And the doing of all such other things as are incidental or conducive to the attainment of the above objects.

4. The liability of the members is limited.

5. The nominal capital of the Company is   POUNDS, divided into   shares of   POUNDS each, to be increased, if needs be, to an amount not exceeding POUNDS, by the creation of such number of additional shares of   POUNDS each as may be deemed expedient.

We, the several persons whose names and addresses are subscribed, are desirous of being formed into a Company in pursuance of this Memorandum of Association, and we respectively agree to take the number of shares in the capital of the Company set opposite our respective names.

Names, Addresses, and Description of Subscribers	Number of Shares taken by each Subscriber

Dated the   day of   , 18 .

Witness to the above signatures   .

PART II.—PRECEDENTS OF FORMAL DOCUMENTS. 219

ARTICLES OF ASSOCIATION.

IT IS AGREED AS FOLLOWS :—

Table A. partially to apply.

1. The provisions of Table A., in the 1st Schedule of the "Companies Act, 1862," as qualified, altered, or added to either by the "Companies Acts, 1867 and 1877," or by the Articles, provisions and clauses hereinafter contained, shall be the regulations for the management of this Company unless and until the same, or any of them, shall be annulled, superseded, varied, or added to by any special Resolution of the Company in general meeting; but the provisions of Table A. shall not apply if and whenever the same are inconsistent with the provisions herein contained.

Interpretation Clause.

2. The expression "The Committee," used in the Memorandum of Association, and hereinafter used, or used in any prospectus or other document of the Company, is equivalent to the expression "Directors," used in the "Companies Act, 1862," and in any subsequent Act or Acts relating to Joint-Stock Companies. The expression "Member of the Club" shall mean a person who shall have been duly admitted or elected a member of the Club in conformity with the Rules or Regulations for the time being in force with respect to the admission of members of the Club. The word "Shareholder" shall have the same meaning as the word "Member," as determined by the "Companies Act, 1862." The expression "Register of Shareholders" shall bear the same meaning as the expression "Register of Members," as used in the said Act. Words importing the masculine gender shall be deemed and taken to include females, and the singular to include the plural and the plural the singular, unless repugnant to the context, or to any express provision herein contained.

Company to have lien upon Shares.

3. The Company shall have a lien upon the shares of any debtor to the Company on any account whatever, and may make such lien available in like manner as for calls in arrear.

Committee may refuse to register Transfer.

4. The Committee may decline to register a transfer of shares to any person unless they shall have previously approved of such person as a transferee, and no person (other than a Vice-President for the time being) who shall not have been so previously approved, shall be entitled to become the transferee of any shares in the Company; and the Committee shall not be bound to assign any reason for withholding approval.

Fee on Registration of Transfer.

5. A fee of 2s. 6d. shall be charged for the registration of every transfer of shares.

Females not to be members of the Club.

6. Females may be shareholders in the Company, but not members of the Club.

Borrowing powers.

7. The Committee may, but subject to the proviso hereinafter contained, raise or borrow for the purposes of the Company, such sum or sums of money as they may from time to time think expedient, either by way of mortgage of the whole or any part of the property of the Company, or by bonds or debentures, or in such manner as they deem best, and so that any mortgage or other security made under this power may contain a power of sale of the property comprised therein and such other powers and provisions as the Committee may think fit; provided that the total amount of such mortgages, debentures, bonds or other securities shall not at any time exceed the sum of   pounds, without the sanction previously given of an extraordinary general meeting.

General Meetings.

8. The 1st general meeting shall be held at such time, not being more than 4 months after the registration of the Company, and at such place as the Committee shall determine; subsequent general meetings shall be held on the 1st or some other Saturday in February in every year, at such time and place as the Committee may appoint. The above-mentioned general meetings shall be called ordinary meetings. All other general meetings shall be called extraordinary.

PART II.—PRECEDENTS OF FORMAL DOCUMENTS. 221

Classes of Members of the Club.

9. There shall be 2 classes of members of the Club, namely, annual members, and members for periods less than a year. Sons between the ages of 18 and 25, of annual members, will be admissible as annual members, but subject to the regulations for the time being in force relative to the admission or election of annual members, on paying the entrance fee for the time being payable, and one-half of the annual subscription for the time being payable. This privilege is to cease either on the father of such member ceasing to be a member of the Club, or the son ceasing to reside with him, in which case, however, the son may continue an ordinary member on paying for the current year the difference between his special and the ordinary subscription, and thenceforward paying the ordinary subscription.

Members for less than a year.

10. Persons desirous of becoming Members of the Club for any period less than a year will be admitted at the discretion of the Committee, and upon such conditions as the Committee may from time to time prescribe.

Subscriptions of Annual Members.

11. The subscription of every annual member shall be deemed to expire on the 31st day of December in each year, and no annual member shall be entitled to any abatement from his subscription for the current year, by reason of the fact that he was elected or became an annual member of the Club at some period intermediate between the 1st day of January and the 31st day of December: Provided that the Committee may, if they think fit, remit a portion of the annual subscription of persons elected or becoming annual members after the 1st day of July in any year.

Permanent Residents in the locality.

12. No person being a permanent resident in will be eligible for admission as a member of the Club for less than a year, or be eligible as a subscriber to the Visitors' Reading Room.

Admission of 100 Members.

13. The first 100 annual members are to be admitted at the discretion of the Committee. When that number shall

have been reached, the election of persons proposed as annual members (who must in all cases be personally known to either their proposers or seconders), shall be by ballot of the then annual members, in conformity with the regulations for the time being in force with respect to the admission of members of the Club. Shareholders will not be admissible as members of the Club, except in conformity with the regulations for the time being in force with respect to the admission of members of the Club.

Admission of Visitors.

14. Visitors to , or the neighbourhood, may be admitted to such of the privileges of the Club on payment of such entrance fee or subscription, or both, as the Committee shall from time to time determine. The admission of any person to such privileges shall be wholly in the discretion of the Committee.

Days of opening.

15. The Club shall be open every week day during such hours as the Committee shall from time to time prescribe. The Club shall be closed on Sundays, Good Friday, and Christmas Day.

Election of President and Vice-Presidents.

16. The Committee for the time being may, if they think fit, appoint a President of the Club, who will be an honorary member of the Club, and who shall, if a shareholder, be *ex officio* a member of the Committee, with the same or like powers as if he had been elected a member of the Committee by a general meeting of the Company. The first Honorary President shall be .

Vice-Presidents.

17. The Committee for the time being may also appoint such persons as they may think fit to be Vice-Presidents for such period, not being less than one year, as the Committee shall from time to time determine. Such appointments may, however, be at any time rescinded by the Committee. Vice-Presidents will not be *ex officio* members of the Committee, but if not already members of the Club, they may become such without ballot or election, on paying the usual entrance fee and subscription, and they may also (while they continue to be Vice-Presidents) become transferees of shares in the Company without the consent of the Committee.

PART II.—PRECEDENTS OF FORMAL DOCUMENTS. 223

Annual Members of the Club may attend General Meetings.

18. Every annual member of the Club, although not a shareholder, shall be entitled to be present at general meetings, whether ordinary or extraordinary, of the Company, and he may speak upon any question at such meetings, and may vote upon the election of members of the Committee, but not upon any other matter or question.

Votes of Annual Members of the Club.

19. Every annual member of the Club shall be entitled to one vote, the same to be given personally, and not by proxy. Provided that if such member of the Club be also a shareholder, he shall vote only in the capacity of shareholder. Every annual member of the Club shall also be entitled to receive a copy of the Company's balance-sheet on application.

Number of the Committee.

20. The Committee shall not, without the consent of a general meeting, consist of more than 15 or less than 9 members.

First Members.

21. The first Members of the Committee shall be:— and such others not exceeding in the whole 15, as the Committee for the time being shall at any time prior to the ordinary general meeting of the year 189 , appoint. All members of the Committee shall continue in office until the ordinary general meeting last mentioned, except in case of death, resignation, or disqualification, in either of which events the Committee for the time being may appoint any person to supply the vacancy so occasioned.

Qualification of Members of the Committee.

22. Every member of the Committee must be the holder of at least one share, on which all calls for the time being must have been paid, as well as be an annual member of the Club, and he will become disqualified from acting as a member of the Committee if he should cease to be a shareholder or cease to be a member of the Club.

Committee may make By-Laws.

23. The Committee may from time to time make such By-Laws, Rules and Regulations for the management of the

Club-house and premises, and for observance by members and visitors, as the Committee shall think fit, the same not being inconsistent with the Articles and Regulations of the Company for the time being.

Powers of Committee.

24. The Committee may do all acts which in their judgment shall be necessary or expedient for carrying out the objects or purposes for which the Company is established, and particularly for obtaining at such price and generally upon such terms and conditions as they shall deem reasonable, a house with land appurtenant thereto, situate in the Parish of aforesaid, and suitable for the purposes of the Company, and may finish, alter, or adapt, or cause to be finished, altered, or adapted, such building, for the purposes of the Company, in such manner as they shall deem expedient, and may fit up and furnish the same or any part or parts thereof for the purposes of the Company, and may let or demise such part or parts of such building as they think proper to any person or persons for such term or period, and at such rent or rents, and generally with such rights and upon such conditions, and subject to such restrictions as the Committee in their sole discretion shall think proper.

Committee may enter into Agreements, etc.

25. The Committee may enter into any agreement for any of the purposes aforesaid, and may accept a lease or conveyance on behalf of the Company, and either in the name of the Company or in the names or name of any persons or person who shall be willing to undertake responsibility in that behalf, and any such person shall be indemnified by the Company against such responsibility. The Committee may pay out of the funds of the Company all outlays, costs, and expenses which they may have incurred for any of the purposes of the Company.

Chairman of Committee.

26. There shall be a chairman of the Committee. The first chairman shall be   .

Continuation in office of Chairman.

27. The first chairman shall remain in office until the first Committee meeting next after the ordinary general meeting

PART II.—PRECEDENTS OF FORMAL DOCUMENTS. 225

of 18 . All subsequent chairmen shall be elected by the Committee out of their own body, at the first meeting of the Committee subsequent to the ordinary general meeting. No chairman shall remain continuously in office for more than 2 years.

Officers.

28. The Company shall have a Secretary and a Solicitor.

Secretary and Solicitor.

29. Mr.   is hereby appointed Secretary, and Mr.   Solicitor, of the Company. Neither of them shall be removed from office except by a resolution passed by the Committee at a meeting specially convened to consider the question.

Reserve Fund.

30. The Committee may set apart and include under the name of "Reserve Fund," moneys for repairing and maintaining the Club-house, the furniture, and the property of the Company generally.

	Names, Addresses, and Descriptions of Subscribers.
1.	
2.	
3.	
4.	
5.	
6.	
7.	

Dated the   day of   , 18 .
Witness to the above signatures :

VI.

DRAFT ROYAL CHARTER TO THE NORTH OF ENGLAND INSTITUTE OF MINING AND MECHANICAL ENGINEERS (*a*).

VICTORIA, by the grace of God, of the United Kingdom of Great Britain and Ireland, Queen, Defender of the Faith, to all to whom these presents shall come, greeting :

(*a*) This Royal Charter is here given as an example of the usual form of such documents when granted to Institutions of a Literary and Scientific

Q

Whereas it has been represented to us that Nicholas Wood, of Hetton, in the County of Durham, Esquire (since deceased); Thomas Emerson Forster, of Newcastle-upon-Tyne, Esquire (since deceased); Sir George Elliott, Baronet (then George Elliott, Esquire), of Houghton Hall, in the said county of Durham, and Edward Fenwick Boyd, of Moor House, in the said county of Durham, Esquire, and others of our loving subjects, did, in the year 1852, form themselves into a Society, which is known by the name of "The North of England Institute of Mining and Mechanical Engineers," having for its objects the prevention of accidents in mines and the advancement of the Sciences of Mining and Engineering generally, of which Society Lindsay Wood, of South Hill, Chester-le-Street, in the county of Durham, Esquire, is the present President.

And whereas it has been further represented to us that the Society was not constituted for gain, and that neither its projectors nor members derive nor have derived pecuniary profit from its prosperity; that it has during its existence of a period of nearly a quarter of a century steadily devoted itself to the preservation of human life and the safer development of mineral property; that it has contributed substantially and beneficially to the prosperity of the country and the welfare and happiness of the working members of the community; that the Society has since its establishment diligently pursued its aforesaid objects, and in so doing has made costly experiments and researches with a view to the saving of life by improvements in the ventilation of mines, by ascertaining the conditions under which the safety lamp may be relied on for security; that the experiments conducted by the Society have related to accidents in mines of every description, and have not been limited to those proceeding from explosions; that the various modes of getting coal, whether by mechanical appliances or otherwise, have received careful and continuous attention, while the improvements in the mode of working and hauling below ground, the machinery employed for preventing the disastrous falls of roof underground, and the prevention of spontaneous combustion in seams of coal as well as in cargoes, and the

character; but it is to be understood by Promoters that since the passing of the "Companies Act, 1867," Royal Charters have been very rarely granted, and only for very exceptional reasons, § 23 of the Act alluded to being deemed in high official circles to be a substitute for the Charter system.

PART II.—PRECEDENTS OF FORMAL DOCUMENTS. 227

providing additional security for the miners in ascending and descending the pits, the improvements in the cages used for this purpose, and in the safeguards against what is technically known as "over winding," have been most successful in lessening the dangers of mining, and in preserving human life; that the Society has held meetings at stated periods, at which the results of the said experiments and researches have been considered and discussed, and has published a series of *Transactions* filling many volumes, and forming in itself a highly valuable library of scientific reference, by which the same have been made known to the public, and has formed a library of Scientific Works and collections of models and apparatus, and that distinguished persons in foreign countries have availed themselves of the facilities afforded by the Society for communicating important scientific and practical discoveries, and thus a useful interchange of valuable information has been effected; that in particular, with regard to ventilation, the experiments and researches of the Society, which have involved much pecuniary outlay and personal labour, and the details of which are recorded in the successive volumes of the Society's *Transactions*, have led to large and important advances in the practical knowledge of that subject, thus the Society's researches have tended largely to increase the security of life; that the members of the Society exceed 800 in number, and include a large proportion of the leading Mining Engineers in the United Kingdom.

And whereas in order to secure the property of the Society, and to extend its useful operations, and to give it a more permanent establishment among the Scientific Institutions of our kingdom, we have been besought to grant to the said Lindsay Wood, and other the present members of the Society, and to those who shall hereafter become members thereof, our Royal Charter of Incorporation.

Now know ye that we, being desirous of encouraging a design so laudable and salutary, of our especial grace, certain knowledge, and mere motion, have willed, granted, and declared, and do, by these presents, for us, our heirs, and successors, will, grant, and declare, that the said Lindsay Wood, and such others of our loving subjects as are now members of the said Society, and such others as shall from time to time hereafter become members thereof, according to such By-Laws as shall be made as hereinafter mentioned, and their successors, shall for ever hereafter be, by virtue of these presents, one body, politic and corporate, by the name of " The North of England Institute of Mining and Mechanical Engineers," and by the name aforesaid shall have perpetual succession and a common Seal, with full power and authority to alter, vary, break, and renew the same at their discretion, and by the same name to sue and be sued, implead and be impleaded, answer and be answered unto, in every Court of us, our heirs and successors, and be for ever able and capable in the Law to purchase, acquire, receive, possess, hold and enjoy to them and their successors any goods and chattels whatsoever, and also be able and capable in the Law (notwithstanding the Statutes of Mortmain) to purchase, acquire, possess, hold and enjoy to them and their successors a hall or house, and any such other lands, tenements, or hereditaments whatsoever, as they may deem requisite for the purposes of the Society, the yearly value of which, including the site of the said hall, or house, shall not exceed in the whole the sum of £3000, computing the same respectively at the rack rent which might have been had or gotten for the same respectively at the time of the purchase or acquisition thereof.

And we do hereby grant our especial licence and authority unto all and every person and persons and bodies politic and corporate, otherwise competent, to grant, sell, alien, convey or devise in Mortmain unto and to the use of the said Society and their successors, any lands, tenements, or hereditaments, not exceeding with the lands, tenements, or hereditaments so purchased or previously acquired such annual value as aforesaid, and also any moneys, stocks, securities, and other personal estate to be laid out and disposed of in the purchase of any lands, tenements, or hereditaments not exceeding the like annual value.

And we further will, grant, and declare that the said Society shall have full power and authority, from time to time, to sell, grant, demise, exchange and dispose of absolutely, or by way of mortgage, or otherwise, any of the lands, tenements, hereditaments and possessions, wherein they have any estate or interest, or which they shall acquire as aforesaid, but that no sale, mortgage or other disposition of any lands, tenements, or hereditaments, of the Society shall be made, except with the approbation and concurrence of a general meeting.

And our will and pleasure is, and we further grant and declare that for the better rule and government of the

PART II.—PRECEDENTS OF FORMAL DOCUMENTS. 229

Society, and the direction and management of the concerns thereof there shall be a Council of the Society, to be appointed from among the members thereof, and to include the President and the Vice-Presidents, and such other officebearers or past office-bearers as may be directed by such By-Laws as hereinafter mentioned, but so that the Council, including all *ex officio* members thereof, shall consist of not more than 40 or less than 12 members, and that the Vice-Presidents shall be not more than 6 or less than 2 in number.

And we do hereby further will and declare that the said Lindsay Wood shall be the first President of the Society, and the persons now being the Vice-Presidents, and the Treasurer and Secretary, shall be the first Vice-Presidents, and the first Treasurer and Secretary, and the persons now being the members of the Council shall be the first members of the Council of the Society, and that they respectively shall continue such until the first election shall be made at a general meeting in pursuance of these presents.

And we do hereby further will and declare that, subject to the powers by these presents vested in the general meetings of the Society, the Council shall have the management of the Society, and of the income and property thereof, including the appointment of officers and servants, the definition of their duties, and the removal of any of such officers and servants, and generally may do all such acts and deeds as they shall deem necessary or fitting to be done, in order to carry into full operation and effect the objects and purposes of the Society, but so always that the same be not inconsistent with, or repugnant to, any of the provisions of this our Charter, or the laws of Our Realm, or any By-Law of the Society in force for the time being.

And we do further will and declare that at any general meeting of the Society, it shall be lawful for the Society, subject as hereinafter mentioned, to make such By-Laws as to them shall seem necessary or proper for the regulation and good government of the Society, and of the Members and affairs thereof, and generally for carrying the objects of the Society into full and complete effect, and particularly (and without its being intended hereby to prejudice the foregoing generality) to make By-Laws for all or any of the purposes hereinafter mentioned, that is to say: for fixing the number of Vice-Presidents, and the number of members of which the Council shall consist, and the manner of electing the President and Vice-Presidents, and other members of the Council, and the period of their continuance in office, and the manner and time of supplying any vacancy therein, and for regulating the times at which general meetings of the Society and meetings of the Council shall be held, and for convening the same and regulating the proceedings thereat, and for regulating the manner of admitting persons to be members of the Society, and of removing or expelling members from the Society, and for imposing reasonable fines or penalties for non-performance of any such By-Laws, or for disobedience thereto, and from time to time to annul, alter, or change any such By-Laws; so always that all By-Laws to be made as aforesaid be not repugnant to these presents, or to any of the laws of our Realm.

And we do further will and declare that the present Rules and Regulations of the Society, so far as they are not inconsistent with these presents, shall continue in force, and be deemed the By-Laws of the Society until the same shall be altered by a general meeting. Provided always that the present Rules and Regulations of the Society, and any future By-Laws of the Society so to be made as aforesaid, shall have no force or effect whatsoever until the same shall have been approved in writing by our Secretary of State for the Home Department. In witness whereof we have caused these our letters to be made Patent.

   Witness ourself at our Palace, at Westminster, this   day of   in the   year of our reign.

VICTORIA R.

231

PART III.

PRECEDENTS OF BY-LAWS AND REGULATIONS.

I.

RULES FOR A COUNTRY TOWN CLUB FOR GENTLEMEN, FORMED UNDER THE "COMPANIES ACTS, 1862, 1867, AND 1877."

RULES OF THE   CLUB, LIMITED.

1. The "   Club,"   is a non-political Club.
2. It shall consist of not more than   members, but this number may be increased from time to time as the Committee may determine.
3. The Club shall be under the management of a Committee appointed according to the provisions of the Articles of Association.
4. Candidates must be proposed by one member of the Club and seconded by another. The candidate's name, rank, residence, and profession or occupation (if any) must, together with the names of his proposer and seconder, be entered upon a form provided for the purpose, which form, dated and countersigned by the Secretary, shall be exhibited in the principal room of the Club-house at least 7 days previously to the day of ballot. The names of the proposer and seconder must be either in their own handwriting or in that of the Secretary, duly authorised in writing. The proposer must certify to a personal knowledge of the candidate.
5. No candidate shall be elected until he shall have attained the age of 18 years.
6. The election of members, after the first 100, is vested in the members generally, and shall be by ballot. Fifteen

members of the Club shall be a quorum for such ballot, and *one* black ball in every five balls shall exclude. A candidate who may be rejected can only be ballotted for once again, except with the sanction of the Committee.

7. Ballots for the election of members shall take place under the superintendence of at least one member of the Committee, on Saturdays, between the hours of 3 and 4 P.M. The member of the Committee in attendance for this purpose shall declare the opening and closing of the ballot, and the result.

8. The entrance fee on admission to the Club is for the present   guineas, but power is vested in the Committee to increase the entrance fee if they shall see fit.

9. The annual subscription is   guineas for the first 100 members, but power having been vested in the Committee to increase the annual subscription when the number of 100 members was made up, it is for the present fixed at   guineas.

10. The subscription of every member is payable in advance; and in the case of annual members, is due on the 1st day of January in each year.

11. No newly-elected member shall be eligible to participate in any of the advantages or privileges of the Club until he has paid the sum due from him on his admission.

12. Members elected after the 1st day of July in any year will be called upon to pay only one-half the ordinary annual subscription for the current year.

13. Members who shall reside out of England for more than six months, and who shall have previously given notice to the Secretary of their intention to do so, shall be entitled to have the proportionate part of their subscription remitted for every whole period of six months during which they are so absent.

14. Every member failing to pay his annual subscription, due on the 1st of January, shall, on the first Monday in February following, be applied to by the Secretary; and if his subscription be not paid on or before the 1st of March, his name shall be exhibited in a conspicuous place in the principal room of the Club-house; and if his subscription be not paid on or before the 1st of April, the said member shall cease to be a member of the Club, but the Committee may re-admit him as a member if they think fit.

15. Members wishing to resign must notify their wish by a letter to the Secretary not later than the 31st day of December.

PART III.—PRECEDENTS OF BY-LAWS, ETC.

16. Any member who shall use the Club-house after the 1st of January, in any year, shall be liable to pay his subscription for that year.

17. An ordinary annual member shall have the privilege of introducing from time to time to the Club *one* friend, not being a resident at   or within 10 miles; but this privilege, so far as regards one and the same person, is only to last for 4 consecutive days (Sunday not counting), and is not to be exercised more than twice in the course of the year in favour of the same person, and provided that such friend shall not have been so introduced by any other member of the Club during 3 months previously. The names and addresses of persons thus introduced to the Club-house, together with the names of the members introducing them, shall be entered in a book, to be called the "Strangers' Book," kept for that purpose.

18. Sons of members shall be admissible as members of the Club upon paying the usual entrance fee and *one-half* the usual annual subscription during the time of their father's membership and whilst they reside with him, and are under 25 years of age.

19. A candidate for admission as a member for a period less than a year must not be resident in   nor within 10 miles of the Club-house. When his nomination paper has been duly signed by his proposer and seconder, he may, provided 2 members of the Committee (not being either the proposer or seconder), countersign it, temporarily use the Club-house on depositing his subscription with the Secretary, pending an opportunity for his name to be put up for ballot on the customary balloting day. A candidate who pays his subscription, and is afterwards rejected on the ballot, shall have the subscription which he has paid returned to him. A short-period member, at the expiration of the period for which he has been admitted, may renew his subscription from time to time if the Committee think fit, in which case he will be called upon to pay only the difference between the sum he has already paid and that payable under Rule 20 for the period to which he purposes to extend his membership. A short-period member has not the privilege of introducing a friend or of voting at a ballot for annual members; he may, however, nominate short-period members.

20. Short-period members shall pay according to the following scale :

	£	s.	d.
For a fortnight	0	10	6
For 2 months	1	1	0
For 3 months	1	11	6
For 4 months	2	2	0
For 6 months	3	3	0

21. A book shall be kept in the principal room, in which members may enter complaints and suggestions; and this book shall be laid before the Committee at every ordinary meeting.

22. Any member who shall cease to belong to the Club, either by resignation or otherwise, shall not have any part of his annual subscription for the current year returned to him.

23. In case the conduct of any member, either in or out of the Club-house, shall, in the opinion of the Committee, be injurious to the character and interests of the Club, the Committee is empowered to call upon such member to resign; and if he should not do so, the Committee may erase his name from the list of members, and he shall thenceforth be ineligible to enter the Club-house.

24. Every member shall discharge all expenses which he may have incurred in the Club-house before leaving it. Any breach of this rule shall be reported to the Committee at its next meeting.

25. No member of the Club shall individually give orders for any article to be supplied to the Club, or in any other way pledge the credit of the Club.

26. No smoking shall be allowed in the Club-house except in the billiard-room, and in such other room (if any) as the Committee may set apart for that purpose.

27. The conduct of a servant of the Club shall in no case be made a matter of personal reprimand by any member; but all complaints against servants shall be made by a letter to the Secretary, signed by the member complaining.

28. No placard or paper of any sort, whether written or printed, shall be exhibited in any part of the Club-house without the sanction of the Committee.

29. No member shall give any money or gratuity to any servant of the Club upon any pretence whatsoever.

30. No member is on any account to bring a dog or any other animal into the Club-house.

31. No member shall take or permit to be taken from the Club-house, upon any pretence whatsoever, any newspaper, pamphlet, or other article, which is the property of the Club.

PART III.—PRECEDENTS OF BY-LAWS, ETC. 235

32. No game of hazard shall on any account be played nor dice be used in the Club-house, except for Backgammon.

33. Any deviation from the 2 last-mentioned rules shall, on satisfactory proof being laid before the Committee, involve the immediate expulsion of the offending member or members.

34. The Club-house shall be opened at 9 A.M., from May to September inclusive; during the remainder of the year at 10 A.M. The Club shall be closed all the year round at 10 P.M. The Club-house shall not be opened at all on Sundays, Good Friday, and Christmas-Day.

35. The permanent library of the Club shall be under the direction of the Committee, and shall be open to the contributions of the members, whose names will be recorded.

36. The general business of the Club shall be managed by the Committee, who may make all such regulations (not inconsistent with the "Companies Acts, 1862, 1867, and 1877," the Articles of Association, or these General Rules) as they shall from time to time think necessary for the internal management and well-being of the Club, and the decision of the Committee thereon shall be binding upon all the members of the Club.

37. Members of the Club who are not shareholders are entitled to attend the annual meetings of the Company and to speak thereat, but they are not entitled to take part in any vote save as to the election of members of the Committee.

38. No subject which does not relate to the business of the Club shall be brought forward for discussion at any annual general meeting; and notice of any subject which is to be brought forward by a member of the Club shall be given in writing to the Secretary, and shall be posted up in the principal room of the Club-house at least 7 days previous to the meeting.

39. Every member shall keep the Secretary informed from time to time as to his address, and all notices sent by Post to such address shall be deemed to be duly delivered.

40. These Rules shall be printed, and, together with a list of the Committee and members, shall be transmitted to every member on his election, but no member shall be absolved from the effect of these rules on the ground that he has not received a copy of them.

II.

RULES FOR A CHURCH INSTITUTE OR READING ROOMS, UNDER A TRUST.

RULES OF THE   CHURCH INSTITUTE.

Name and Objects of the Institute.

1. This Society shall be called "The   Church Institute"; its objects being the maintenance and advancement of the principles of the Church of England, the promotion of general knowledge in subordination to Religion, and the encouragement of kindly intercourse among all members of the Church of England.

Means of advancing the Objects.

2. The means proposed for carrying out the above-mentioned objects are, providing and maintaining suitable premises, to contain Library, Reading, and Class Rooms; the delivery of Lectures, and the formation of Classes for religious and general instruction; the establishment of a Reference Library for the use of Sunday School teachers, and to promote the efficiency of Sunday Schools; also to promote the formation of Branch Institutes within the Deanery.

Trustees and Property.

3. The property of the Institute, as acquired, is and shall be vested in [6] Trustees, to be elected by the Council; and when any Trustee or Trustees of the property of the Institute shall die, or desire to be discharged, or refuse or decline or become incapable to act, or shall cease to be a member of the Church of England, the Council of the said Institute shall have power to appoint a new Trustee or Trustees; and, upon every such appointment, the number of Trustees may be increased or reduced, so that the number be not reduced below 3.

4. The property of the Institute shall not be alienated or disposed of, except by the direction of the Council for the time being, of which contemplated alienation or disposition notice shall have been posted in the Library 14 days previous to such alienation or disposition.

5. The Council may, so often as occasion shall require, purchase any land or property within the Parish of

PART III.—PRECEDENTS OF BY-LAWS, ETC. 237

for the purposes of the Institute, out of the funds of the Institute, or any moneys given or subscribed to it, and shall cause such land or property to be conveyed to the Trustees of the property of the Institute, upon trust for promoting the objects of the Institute, and in such manner and form, and with and subject to such trusts, powers, and provisions as shall be judged by the Council for the time being to be expedient; and the signature of the President for the time being (if it shall be considered desirable that it should be given) to any deed or deeds shall be deemed conclusive evidence that the trusts, powers, and provisions contained therein have been approved of, and judged expedient by the Council; but such signature shall not be essential or necessary to be required.

Government.

6. The Rector [Vicar] of   for the time being shall be, *ex officio*, President, if willing to act.

7. The affairs of the Institute shall be under the management of a President, [6] Vice-Presidents (3 clerical and 3 lay), a Treasurer, [3] Honorary Secretaries (1 clerical and 2 lay), 2 Auditors, and an Executive Council, consisting of the Vicar of every parish in the Deanery, and [2] lay members from each such parish, and a number not exceeding [20] of the other lay members, every such person being a subscriber.

Retirement of Officers.

8. That the Vice-Presidents, Treasurer, Honorary Secretaries, Auditors, and Lay Members of the Executive Council shall retire annually, but shall be eligible for re-election.

Members eligible for Office, or to vote.

9. Members above 20 years of age shall alone be eligible for office, or to vote. A list of those thus qualified shall be placed in the reading-room 14 days previous to the annual meeting. Each person proposed for office must have been a member of the Institute for at least 6 months previously.

Vacancies.

10. The Council shall have power to supply any vacancy which may occur in any office during the year, by electing some other member of the Institute.

Annual General Meeting.

11. A General Meeting shall be held each year, within 30 days after Easter, of which notice shall be given in the local newspapers and on the notice board of the Institute. At this meeting a report of the past year's proceedings shall be presented by the retiring Council, and the Council for the ensuing year elected.

Meetings of the Council.

12. The Council shall meet on the [third Tuesday] in each month, without being specially summoned. Any Member of the Executive Council, residing within the Borough, neglecting to attend 3 successive meetings, shall receive notice of such neglect from the Secretaries; and if he fail to attend the next meeting, he shall be considered to have resigned his office unless he shows satisfactory cause for such absence.

Committees.

13. At the first meeting of the Council, after the Annual Meeting, Committees shall be appointed out of its members for the efficient working of the various departments of the Institute; each Committee shall consist of not less than 5 members of the Council. The proceedings of each Committee shall be subject to the approval of the Council. The President and Vice-Presidents of the Institute, Treasurer, the Honorary Secretaries and Auditors shall be, *ex officio*, members of each Committee.

Special General Meeting.

14. The President may, whenever he considers it necessary, or on the requisition in writing of [15] members of the Council, or of [25] members of the Institute, call a special general meeting of the members of the Institute, and the object of such meeting shall be stated in the notice calling such meeting.

Membership.

15. Members shall be of two classes—honorary members subscribing not less than [one guinea], and ordinary members not less than [5s.] per annum. Subscriptions shall be due in advance, and may be paid in one amount on the 1st of April in each year, or in·two sums on the 1st of April and the 1st of October, and this subscription shall entitle members to all privileges. Any member neglecting to pay his or her sub-

PART III.—PRECEDENTS OF BY-LAWS, ETC. 239

scription for six weeks after the same shall be due shall, after receiving notice from the Librarian (unless it be paid within a week of such notice), cease to be a member of the Institute. Candidates for admission to the Institute, on depositing with the Librarian the amount of their subscriptions, may be admitted provisionally, subject to confirmation. The Council may reject or confirm the admission, from time to time, of members, and shall have power to expel anyone. Any person so expelled shall forfeit any privileges to which his subscription would have entitled him.

Members' Privileges.

16. Members paying annually half-a-guinea shall be entitled to one extra ticket of admission to all Lectures of the Institute.

Members' Cards.

17. Every person, on admission, shall be furnished with a copy of the Rules gratis, and a card, which shall entitle such person to the privileges of the Institute, in accordance with its Rules and Regulations. Such cards must be produced (if required) before admission to the Institute or its privileges.

Admission to Lectures.

18. Non-members may be admitted to attend the Lectures or entertainments provided at the expense of the Institute, on the payment of such sum as shall from time to time be determined by the Council. The Council shall also have power to make a charge to members for admission to lectures or entertainments when they find it necessary or expedient to do so.

Duties of Honorary Secretaries.

19. The Honorary Secretary shall enter Minutes of all meetings of the Council in a Minute-book, which shall be read at the next meeting, and signed by the Chairman, and shall discharge such other duties as the Council may from time to time appoint.

Duties of the Treasurer.

20. The Treasurer shall receive all moneys from the officer of the Institute duly authorised to collect the same; he shall have charge of all funds, and make all payments on account of the Institute, according to the orders of the Council, to

whom also his books shall at all times be open for inspection. He shall keep fair and accurate accounts of his receipts and disbursements. He shall not retain in his hand any sum exceeding [£10], but when the balance in hand exceeds that amount, he shall pay it to the account of the Institute in such bank as the Council may appoint.

Duties of the Auditors.

21. The Auditors shall audit and sign the Treasurer's accounts previously to their being laid before the annual meeting.

Duties of the Librarian.

22. The Librarian shall, under the Council, have the charge and control of the Institute; he shall collect the subscriptions, contributions, and other moneys, and hand over all sums received to the Treasurer at least once a week; he shall keep the books and accounts of the Institute, attend meetings, and, in the absence of the Honorary Secretaries, take and preserve the Minutes of meetings, enrol the names of members, issue cards of membership, and transact the general business of the Institute.

Accounts.

23. The accounts of the Institute shall be made up to the end of March in each year, and together with all books of accounts, bills, vouchers, receipts, and other documents relating thereto, shall be laid before the Auditors one week before the annual meeting.

Register of Members.

24. The name and residence of each member shall be entered in a book, to be kept for the purpose; and when any member changes his or her residence, such change shall be signified to the Librarian.

Formation of Special Classes.

25. The Council shall, as they may deem necessary, form classes, and appoint teachers; they shall also fix the contributions of members who take advantage of them.

Admission to Special Classes.

26. Members may, by applying to the Librarian, be admitted to any classes of the Institute, on paying the con-

PART III.—PRECEDENTS OF BY-LAWS, ETC. 241

tribution specified. They shall also be at liberty, under the sanction of the Council, to form themselves into classes for mutual benefit and improvement.

Rooms may be used for Meetings, etc., not connected with the Institute.

27. The Council shall have power to grant the use of any of the rooms of the Institute for entertainments and meetings not connected with the Institute, on such terms as they may from time to time determine.

Privileges of Members of other Church Institutes.

28. Members of Church Institutes beyond the limits of the Deanery are allowed to avail themselves of this Institute during their temporary residence in the town, on producing their cards of membership to the Librarian, and entering their names in a book kept for that purpose.

By-Laws.

29. The Council shall have power from time to time to make By-Laws and Regulations, so that the same be not inconsistent with these Rules; and should any case of doubt or difficulty occur, which is not provided for by any Rule or By-Law, it shall be determined by resolution of the Council. A copy of the By-Laws is to be exhibited in each department to which the same may have reference.

Alteration of Rules.

30. No proposition for any new Rule, or for altering or repealing any existing Rule of the Institute, shall be entertained, unless it be in writing, and either recommended by the Council or signed by at least [25] members of the Institute, and delivered to the President, who shall thereupon call a special general meeting not less than [14] days after the receipt thereof. And no Rule shall be repealed or altered, or any new Rule adopted, except by [two-thirds] of those members present at such meeting.

Dissolution of the Institute.

31. No resolution for dissolving the Institute shall be passed, unless it be proposed in the manner prescribed for the alteration of Rules, and be passed at 2 successive special general meetings, nor unless at least [four-fifths] of the members be present.

R

III.
RULES FOR A VILLAGE WORKMEN'S CLUB.

Name.

1. The Club shall be called the "   Workmen's Club."

Constitution.

2. The Club shall consist of all members elected according to the following Rules, who shall pay the subscription fixed, and conform to the Rules.

Objects.

3. The objects aimed at shall be social intercourse and healthy recreation, and the mental, moral, and spiritual improvement of the members.

Management.

4. The Club shall be under the management of a Committee of 12 persons, 8 of whom must be working men, chosen by the members, whilst the other 4 may be nominated by the Trustees of the Club for the time being. In default of such nomination at or prior to the annual general meeting, these 4 members shall be chosen by the members either from the ordinary or from the honorary members. The elected members shall retire annually, but shall be eligible for re-election. Should any member absent himself from 3 Committee meetings in succession without giving a sufficient reason, his seat shall be deemed vacant, and the vacancy shall be filled by the Committee. The Committee shall meet for the transaction of ordinary business on the 1st [Monday] in every month, or on such other day as may be considered desirable by the Committee, 3 to form the quorum. For special business, of which 3 clear days' notice shall be given by the Secretary, 5 members are to form the quorum.

Election of Members.

5. A member may introduce to the Club a candidate for membership (not, however, under 19 years of age, except with the special permission of the Committee), by writing the candidate's name, together with his own, in a book kept for

PART III.—PRECEDENTS OF BY-LAWS, ETC. 243

the purpose. By paying his subscription, such candidate shall become entitled to all the privileges of membership till the next Committee meeting, when he will be ballotted for.

Terms of Membership.

6. Members are to be of 2 classes : ordinary and honorary. Ordinary members shall be working men, and pay 2d. per week, 8d. per month, 1s. 9d. per quarter, 3s. 6d. per half-year, or 7s. per year—*in advance*. Holders of quarterly, half-yearly, and annual tickets are to be admitted free to the gallery, and at half-price to the body of the hall, to the Popular Readings or any other entertainments. Cards of membership will be provided. Those for half-yearly and annual members will be coloured, and such cards must be shown at the doors at each entertainment to ensure free admission, and as often as demanded by any member of the Committee or officer of the Club. All persons who have been members for at least 3 months shall be entitled to vote at the annual meeting. Honorary members shall subscribe not less than 10s. 6d. per annum. A list of the honorary members will be posted in the Reading Room.

Hours of Opening.

7. The Club shall be opened daily (Sundays excepted) from 5.30 A.M. to 10 P.M. from March to October, and from 6.30 A.M. to 10 P.M. from November to February.

Games.

8. Neither betting, gambling, cards, nor dice shall be allowed; but Bagatelle, Dominoes, Draughts, Chess, Solitaire, and Fox-and-Geese shall be provided by the Committee. No other games shall be used without being first sanctioned by the Committee.

Steward of the Club.

9. The Steward shall be nominated by the Committee, and the nomination shall then be submitted to the Trustees for the time being for approval. If such approval is given, the appointment shall be considered complete; otherwise a fresh nomination must be made by the Committee, and submitted in like manner, until some nominee is approved as aforesaid. Any complaint against the management of the Steward shall be made to the Committee, in writing, at their next meeting,

and, if they consider it necessary, they shall report thereon to the Trustees.

Use of the Lecture Room.

10. The Committee shall be empowered to make arrangements for the loan or letting of the Lecture Room for purposes not inconsistent with the fundamental principles of the Club.

Annual General Meeting.

11. An annual general meeting of the members for the election of the Committee shall be held in the 1st week in [October], when a Statement of Accounts for the past year, ending on the [29th day of September], shall be produced.

Alteration of Rules.

12. No new Rule shall be made, or old one altered, without the consent of three-fourths of the Committee, at a special meeting called for the purpose of considering the matter.

Construction of Rules.

13. Should any dispute arise as to the meaning of any of these Rules, the decision of the Committee thereon shall be final.

Miscellaneous Rules.

14. Any 2 members of the Committee shall have power to remove from the building any member who conducts himself offensively.

15. No bad language or quarrelling shall be permitted.

16. No intoxicated person shall be admitted, and no intoxicating drinks shall be brought on to the premises.

17. All wilful damage done to the property of the Club shall be paid for by the offender.

18. No smoking shall be allowed except in the room or rooms set apart for the purpose.

19. Every member playing at any game shall count the pieces before returning them, and shall be liable for any that are lost or damaged by him. No one shall play more than 2 games in succession if any other members are waiting to play.

20. Every member shall assist in carrying out the Rules, in keeping order, and in protecting the property of the Club.

PART III.—PRECEDENTS OF BY-LAWS, ETC.

21. A book shall be kept wherein may be entered remarks and suggestions by members; and also a box to receive donations from visitors interested in the welfare of the Club.

22. The outgoing Committee shall take stock of all the property of the Club, preparatory to handing the same over to the incoming Committee.

23. A copy of this code of Rules shall be printed in large type, and shall be posted in every room.

PART IV.

STATUTES RELATING TO LITERARY AND SCIENTIFIC INSTITUTIONS.

FOR a statement of the principles upon which these Statutes have been arranged and printed, see the Introduction to Part IV. of Book I. (*ante*, p. 70).

1708. [7 Anne] *Parochial Libraries.* [c. 14]

7 ANNE, 14.

Revised Statutes, 2nd ed. vol. i. p. 840.

Reasons for Act.

An Act for the better preservation of Parochial Libraries in that part of Great Britain called England. 1708.

WHEREAS in many places in the south parts of Great Britain called England and Wales the provision for the clergy is so mean that the necessary expense of books for the better prosecution of their studies cannot be defrayed by them. And whereas of late years several charitable and well-disposed persons have by charitable contributions erected Libraries within several Parishes and Districts in England and Wales, but some provision is wanting to preserve the same and such others as shall be provided in the same manner from embezzlement: Be it therefore enacted, etc.

1. In every Parish or place where such a Library is or shall be erected, the same shall be preserved for such use and uses as the same is and shall be given, and the orders and rules of the founder or founders of such Libraries shall be observed and kept.

PART IV.—STATUTES.—7 ANNE, c. 14. 247

2. And for the encouragement of such founders and bene- Incumbent
factors, and to the intent they may be satisfied that their into se-
pious and charitable intent may not be frustrated, be it also curity for
enacted, by the authority aforesaid, that every Incumbent, tion of
Rector, Vicar, Minister, or Curate of a Parish, before he shall Library.
be permitted to use and enjoy such Library, shall enter into
such security, by bond or otherwise, for preservation of such
Library and due observance of the rules and orders belonging
to the same, as the proper Ordinaries, within their respective
jurisdictions, in their discretion shall think fit, and in case
any book or books belonging to the said Library shall be
taken away and detained, it shall and may be lawful for the
said Incumbent, Rector, Vicar, Minister, or Curate for the
time being, or any other person or persons, to bring an
Action of Trover and Conversion in the name of the proper Action for
Ordinaries, within their respective jurisdictions, whereupon tained.
treble damages shall be given, with full costs of suit, as if the
same were his or their proper book or books, which damages
shall be applied to the use and benefit of the said Library.

3. And it is further enacted, by the authority aforesaid, Power to
that it shall and may be lawful to and for the proper Ordinary to inquire
or his Commissary or official in his respective jurisdiction, into
or the Archdeacon, or, by his direction, his official or Surro- Libraries
gate, if the said Archdeacon be not the Incumbent of the
place where such Library is, in his or their respective Visita-
tion, to inquire into the state and condition of the said
Libraries, and to amend and redress the grievances and
defects of and concerning the same, as to him or them shall
seem meet, and it shall and may be lawful to and for the
proper Ordinary from time to time, as often as shall be
thought fit, to appoint such person or persons as he shall
think fit to view the state and condition of such Libraries,
and the said Ordinaries, Archdeacons, or officials respectively
shall have free access to the same at such times as they shall
respectively appoint.

4. And be it also further enacted, by the authority afore- Incumbent
said, that where any Library is appropriated to the use of the and sign a
Minister of any Parish or place, every Rector, Vicar, Minister, Catalogue.
or Curate of the same, within 6 months after his institution,
induction, or admission, shall make or cause to be made a
new catalogue of all books remaining in or belonging to such
Library, and shall sign the said catalogue, thereby acknowledging the custody and possession of the said books, which
said catalogue so signed shall be delivered to the proper

248   BOOK II.—LITERARY AND SCIENTIFIC INSTITUTIONS.

Ordinary within the time aforesaid, to be kept or registered in his Court, without any fee or reward for the same.

Catalogue to be delivered to Ordinary.   5. And be it further enacted by the authority aforesaid, that where there are any parochial libraries already erected, the Incumbent, Rector, Vicar, Minister, or Curate of such Parish or place may make or cause to be made a catalogue of all books in the same, thereby acknowledging the custody and possession thereof, which catalogue so signed shall be delivered to the proper Ordinary on or before the 29th day of September, which shall be in the year of our Lord 1709, and where any Library shall at any time hereafter be given and appropriated to the use of any Parish or place where there shall be an Incumbent, Rector, Vicar, Minister, or Curate in possession, such Incumbent, Rector, Vicar, Minister, or Curate, shall make or cause to be made a catalogue of all the books, and deliver the same as aforesaid, within 6 months after he shall receive such Library.

Upon death or removal of Rector, the Library to be locked, etc., by Churchwarden.   6. And to prevent any embezzlement of books upon the death or removal of any Incumbent, be it also enacted by the authority aforesaid that immediately after the death or removal of any Incumbent, Rector, Vicar, Minister, or Curate, the Library belonging to such Parish or place shall be forthwith shut up and locked or otherwise secured by the Churchwarden or Churchwardens for the time being, or by such person or persons as shall be authorised or appointed by the proper Ordinary or Archdeacon respectively, so that the same shall not be opened again till a new Incumbent, Rector, Vicar, Minister, or Curate, shall be inducted or admitted into the Church of such Parish or place.

Proviso when Library is used for public business.   7. Provided always that in case the place where such Library is or shall be kept, shall be used for any publick occasion, for meeting of the Vestry or otherwise, for the dispatch of any business of the said Parish or for any other publick occasion for which the said place hath been ordinarily used, the place shall nevertheless be made use of as formerly for such purposes, and after such business despatched shall be again shut and lockt up or otherwise secured as is before directed.

Register of books given, etc., to be kept.   8. And be it also further enacted by the authority aforesaid that for the better preservation of the books belonging to such Libraries, and that the benefactions given towards the same may appear; a book shall be kept within the said Library for the entering and registering of all such benefactions, and such books as shall be given towards the same, and therein the Minister, Rector, Vicar, or Curate of the said Parish or place shall enter or cause to be fairly entered such benefaction, and an account of all such books as shall from time to time be given, and by whom given.

9. And for the better governing the said Libraries and preserving of the same, it is hereby further enacted by the authority aforesaid, that it shall and may be lawful to and for the proper Ordinary together with the donor of such benefaction (if living), and after the death of such donor for the proper Ordinary alone, to make such other rules and orders concerning the same over and above and besides but not contrary to such as the donor of such benefaction shall in his discretion judge fit and necessary, which said orders and rules so to be made from time to time be entered in the said book or some other book to be prepared for that purpose and kept in the said Library. Ordinary may make rules and orders concerning Library.

10. And it is further enacted and declared by the authority aforesaid that none of the said books shall in any case be alienable nor any book or books that shall hereafter be given by any benefactor or benefactors shall be alienated without the consent of the proper Ordinary, and then only when there is a duplicate of such book or books, and that in case any book or books be taken or otherwise lost out of the said Library, it shall and may be lawful to and for any Justice of Peace within the said County, Riding, or Division, to grant his warrant to search for the same, and in case the same be found, such book or books so found shall immediately by order of such Justice be restored to the said Library, any law, statute, or usage to the contrary in anywise notwithstanding. Books not alienable.

11. Provided always that nothing in this Act contained shall extend to a Publick Library lately erected in the Parish of Ryegate, in the County of Surrey, for the use of the freeholders, Vicar, and inhabitants of the said Parish, and of the gentlemen and clergymen inhabiting in parts thereto adjacent, the said Library being constituted in another manner than the Libraries provided for by this Act.(a) Proviso as to Library at Riegate.

(a) Annexed to the original Act by a separate Schedule.

250 BOOK II.—LITERARY AND SCIENTIFIC INSTITUTIONS.

1799.   [39 Geo. III.]   *Specific Legacies Exemption.*   [c. 73]

39 GEO. III. 73.

Revised Statutes, 2nd ed. vol. ii. p. 841.

An Act for exempting certain specifick Legacies which shall be given to Bodies Corporate or other Public Bodies from the payment of Duty. [12th July, 1799.

WHEREAS it is expedient that certain specifick legacies given to Bodies Corporate and other Public Bodies and Societies should be exempted from the Duties imposed on legacies: Be it enacted, etc.

Exemption of certain legacies from Duty.

From and after the passing of this Act no legacy consisting of books, prints, pictures, statues, gems, coins, medals, specimens of Natural History, or other specifick articles, which shall be given or bequeathed to or in trust for any Body Corporate, whether aggregate or sole, or to the Society of Serjeants Inn, or any of the Inns of Court or Chancery, or any endowed school, in order to be kept and preserved by such Body Corporate, Society, or School, and not for the purposes of Sale, shall be liable to any Duty imposed on legacies by any law now in force.

*   *   *   *   *   *

1843.   [6 & 7 Vict.]   *Scientific Societies Exemption.*   [c. 36]

6 & 7 VICT. 36.

Revised Statutes, 2nd ed. vol. vii. p. 56.

An Act to exempt from County, Borough, Parochial, and other Local Rates, Land and Buildings occupied by Scientific or Literary Societies. [28th July, 1843.

Scientific Societies exempted from Rates upon obtaining a Certificate.

1. No person or persons shall be assessed or rated, or liable to be assessed or rated, or liable to pay, to any County, Borough, Parochial, or other Local Rates or Cesses, in respect of any land, houses, or buildings, or parts of houses or buildings, belonging to any Society instituted for purposes of Science, Literature, or the Fine Arts exclusively, either as tenant or as owner, and occupied by it for the transaction of its busi-

PART IV.—STATUTES.—6 & 7 VICT. c. 36.   251

ness, and for carrying into effect its purposes, provided that
such Society shall be supported wholly or in part by annual
voluntary contributions, and shall not, and by its laws may
not, make any dividend, gift, division, or bonus in money
unto or between any of its members, and provided also that
such Society shall obtain the Certificate of the Barrister-at-
Law or Lord Advocate, as hereinafter mentioned.

2. Provided always that before any Society shall be entitled Scientific
to the benefit of this Act such Society shall cause 3 copies of Societies to cause
all laws, rules, and regulations for the management thereof, Copies of
signed by the President or other chief officer and 3 members their Rules to be sub-
of the Council or Committee of Management, and counter- mitted to
signed by the Clerk or Secretary of such Society, to be sub- the person appointed
mitted, in England, Wales, and Berwick-upon-Tweed, to the to certify
Barrister-at-Law for the time being appointed to certify the the Rules of Friendly
Rules of Friendly Societies there, and in Scotland to the Societies.
Lord Advocate, or any Depute appointed by him to certify
the Rules of Friendly Societies there, and in Ireland to the
Barrister for the time being appointed to certify the Rules of
Friendly Societies there, for the purpose of ascertaining
whether such Society is entitled to the benefit of this Act;

And such Barrister or Lord Advocate, as the case may be,
shall give a Certificate on each of the said copies that the
Society so applying is entitled to the benefit of this Act, or
shall state in writing the grounds on which such Certificate
is withheld;

And one of such copies, when certified by such Barrister Disposition
or Lord Advocate, shall be returned to the Society, another of such copies.
copy shall be retained by such Barrister or Lord Advocate,
and the other of such copies shall be transmitted by such
Barrister or Lord Advocate to the Clerk of the Peace for the
Borough or County where land or buildings of such Society
in respect of which such exemption is claimed shall be
situated, and shall by him be laid before the Recorder or
Justices for such Borough or County at the General Quarter
Sessions, or adjournment thereof, held next after the time
when such copy shall have been so certified, and transmitted
to him as aforesaid, and the Recorder or Justices then and
there present are hereby authorised and required, without
motion, to allow and confirm the same; and such copy shall
be filed by such Clerk of the Peace with the Rolls of the
Sessions of the Peace in his custody, without fee or reward.

3. If the laws, rules, and regulations of any such Society Certain
shall be altered, so as to affect or relate to the property or alterations in the

252   BOOK II.—LITERARY AND SCIENTIFIC INSTITUTIONS.

Rules to be certified and deposited in like manner.

constitution of such Society, such alterations shall, within one calendar month after the same shall have been made, be submitted to such Barrister or Lord Advocate, and such Barrister or Lord Advocate shall certify as aforesaid; and such rules, when so certified, shall be filed with the Clerk of the Peace as aforesaid; and in the meantime such Society shall be entitled to the benefit of this Act, as if no such alterations had been made:

In case of refusal to certify.

Provided always, that if the said Barrister or Lord Advocate shall refuse to certify, that then, subject to such appeal as is hereinafter provided, the said Society shall cease to be entitled to the benefit of this Act from the time when such alterations shall come into operation.

Fee for Certificate.

4. Provided always that the fee payable to such Barrister or Lord Advocate for perusing the laws, rules, and regulations of each Society, or the alterations made therein, and giving such Certificate or Statement as aforesaid, shall not at any one time exceed the sum of one guinea, which, together with the expense of transmitting the rules to and from the said Barrister or Lord Advocate, shall be defrayed by each Society respectively.

Where Certificate is refused.

5. Provided always that in case any such Barrister or Lord Advocate shall refuse to certify that any such Society is entitled to the benefit of this Act, it shall then be lawful for any such Society to submit the laws, rules, and regulations thereof to the Court of Quarter Sessions for the Borough or County where the land or buildings of the Society shall be situated, together with the reasons so assigned by the said Barrister or Lord Advocate as aforesaid;

And the Recorder or Justices at such Quarter Sessions shall and may, if he or they think fit, order the same Rules to be filed, notwithstanding such refusal as aforesaid; and such filing shall have the same effect as if the said Barrister or Lord Advocate had certified as aforesaid.

Appeal to Quarter Sessions.

6. Provided always that any person or persons assessed to any Rate from which any Society shall be exempted by this Act may appeal from the decision of the said Barrister or Lord Advocate in granting such Certificate as aforesaid to the said Court of Quarter Sessions, within 4 calendar months next after the first assessment of such Rate made after such Certificate shall have been filed as aforesaid, or within 4 calendar months next after the first assessment of such Rate made after such exemption shall have been claimed by such Society, such appellant first giving to the Clerk or

Secretary of the Society in question, 21 days previously to the sitting of the said Court, notice in writing of his intention to bring such appeal, together with a statement in writing of the grounds thereof, and within 4 days after such notice entering into a recognizance before some Justice, with 2 sufficient sureties, to try such appeal at and abide the Order of and pay such costs as shall be awarded by the Recorder or Justices at such Quarter Sessions;

And at such Quarter Sessions such Recorder or Justices shall, on its being proved that such notice and statement have been given as aforesaid, proceed to hear such appeal, according to the grounds set forth in such statement, and not otherwise, and if the Certificate of the said Barrister or Lord Advocate shall appear to him or them to have been granted contrary to the provisions of this Act, shall and may annul the same, and shall and may, according to their discretion, award such costs to the party appealing or appealed against as he or they shall think proper, and his or their determination concerning the premises shall be conclusive and binding on all parties to all intents and purposes whatsoever.

[13 & 14 Vict.] *Titles of Religious Congregations.* [c. 28] 1850.

13 & 14 VICT. 28.

An Act to render more simple and effectual the Titles by which Congregations or Societies for Purposes of Religious Worship or Education in England and Ireland hold Property for such Purposes. [15th July, 1850.]

Revised Statutes, 2nd ed. vol. viii. p. 634.

1. Wherever Freehold, Leasehold, Copyhold, or Customary Property in England or Wales has been or hereafter shall be acquired by any Congregation or Society or body of persons associated for Religious purposes or for the promotion of Education, as a Chapel, Meeting House, or other place of Religious Worship, or as a Dwelling House for the Minister of such Congregation, with offices, garden, and glebe, or land in the nature of glebe, for his use, or as a School-house, with schoolmaster's house, garden, and playground, or as a College, Academy, or Seminary, with or without grounds for air, exercise, or recreation, or as a hall or rooms for the meeting

Property conveyed for Religious or Educational purposes to vest in Successors without Conveyance.

254 BOOK II.—LITERARY AND SCIENTIFIC INSTITUTIONS.

or transaction of the business of such Congregation or Society or body of persons, and wherever the conveyance, assignment, or other assurance of such property has been or may be taken to or in favour of a trustee or trustees to be from time to time appointed, or of any party or parties named in such conveyance, assignment, or other assurance, or subject to any trust for the Congregation or Society or body of persons, or of the individuals composing the same, such conveyance, assignment, or other assurance shall not only vest the Freehold, Leasehold, Copyhold, or Customary Property thereby conveyed or otherwise assured in the party or parties named therein, but shall also effectually vest such Freehold, Leasehold, Copyhold, or Customary Property in their successors in office for the time being and the old continuing trustees, if any, jointly, or if there be no old continuing trustees, then in such successors for the time being wholly chosen and appointed in the manner provided or referred to in or by such conveyance, assignment, or other assurance, or in any separate deed or instrument declaring the trust thereof;

Or if no mode of appointment be therein set forth, prescribed, or referred to, or if the power of appointment be lapsed, then in such manner as shall be agreed upon by such Congregation or Society or body of persons, upon such and the like trusts, and with, under, and subject to the same powers and provisions, as are contained or referred to in such conveyance, assignment, or other assurance, or in any such separate deed or instrument, or upon which such property is held, and that without any transfer, assignment, conveyance, or other assurance whatsoever, anything in such conveyance, assignment, or other assurance, or in any such separate deed or instrument, contained to the contrary notwithstanding :

Provided always, that in case of any appointment of a new trustee or trustees of or the conveyance of the legal estate in any such property being made as heretofore was by law required, the same shall be as valid and effectual to all intents and purposes as if this Act had not been passed.

Providing for payment in lieu of fines on death or alienation of property of copyhold or

2. Where such property shall be of copyhold or customary tenure, and liable to the payment of any fine, with or without a heriot, on the death or alienation of the tenant or tenants thereof, it shall be lawful for the lord or lady of the manor of which such property shall be holden, on the next appointment of a new trustee or trustees thereof, and at the expiration of every period of 40 years thereafter, so long as such property

PART IV.—STATUTES.—13 & 14 VICT. c. 28.   255

shall belong to or be held in trust for such Congregation or Customary
Society or body of persons or other party or parties to whom tenure.
such property may have been or shall be conveyed for their
benefit, to receive and take a sum corresponding to the fine
and heriot, if any, which would have been payable by law
upon the death or alienation of the tenant or tenants thereof;

And such payments shall be in full of all fines payable to
the lord or lady of the manner of which such property is
holden, while the same shall remain the property or be held
in trust for such Congregation or Society or body of persons;

And the lord or lady of such manor shall have all such
powers for the recovery of such sums as such lord or lady could
have had in the event of the tenant or tenants of such property
having died or having alienated the same.

3. For the purpose of preserving evidence of every such Appointment of
choice and appointment of a new trustee or new trustees, and new
of the person and persons in whom such charitable estates trustees to
and property shall so from time to time become legally be made
vested, every such choice and appointment of a new trustee deed.
or new trustees shall be made to appear by some deed under
the hand and seal of the chairman for the time being of the
meeting at which such choice and appointment shall be made,
and shall be executed in the presence of such meeting, and
attested by two or more credible witnesses, which deed may
be in the form or to the like effect of the Schedule to this Act
annexed, or as near thereto as circumstances will allow, and
may be given and shall be received as evidence in all courts
and proceedings in the same manner and on the like proof as
deeds under seal, and shall be evidence of the truth of the
several matters and things therein contained.

4. The provisions of this Act shall extend to that part of Act extended to
the United Kingdom called Ireland.   Ireland.

*   *   *   *   *   *

[§ 5 is repealed by the " Statute Law Revision Act, 1875,"
38 & 39 Vict. **66.**]

SCHEDULE to which this Act refers.

MEMORANDUM of the choice and appointment of new trustees
of the [*describe the chapel, school, or other buildings and
property*] situate   in the parish [*or township*] of
       in the county [*riding, division, city or place*] of
   .   at a meeting duly convened and held for that

purpose [*in the vestry of the said chapel*] on the [*25th*] day of [*April*, 1850], *A. B.* of chairman.

Names and descriptions of all the trustees on the constitution or last appointment of trustees made the day of
*Adam Bell of
Charles Dixon of
Edward Foster of
George Hurst of
John Jackson of
Kenneth Lucas of
Matthew Norman of
Octavius Parker of*

Names and descriptions of all the trustees in whom the said [*chapel*] and premises now become legally vested.

First.—Old continuing trustees:
*John Jackson, now of
Matthew Norman, now of
Octavius Parker, now of*

Second.—New trustees now chosen and appointed:
*Benjamin Adams of
Charles Bell of
Jonathan Edmonds of
Richard Baxter of
John Home of*

Dated this day of
William Hicks, (L.S.)
Chairman of the said meeting.

Signed, sealed, and delivered by the said *William Hicks*, as Chairman of the said meeting, at and in the presence of the said meeting, on the day and year aforesaid, in the presence of
*C. D.
E. F.*

[*The blanks, and parts in italics, to be filled up as the case may be.*]

PART IV.—STATUTES.—16 & 17 VICT. c. 51.

[16 & 17 Vict.]   *Succession Duty.*   [c. 51] 1853.

16 & 17 VICT. 51.

An Act for granting to Her Majesty Duties on Succession to Property, and for altering certain Provisions of the Acts charging Duties on Legacies and Shares of Personal Estates. [4th August, 1853.]

Revised Statutes, 2nd ed. vol. ix. pp. 45, 50.

16. Where property shall become subject to a Trust for any charitable or public purposes, under any past or future disposition, which, if made in favour of an individual, would confer on him a succession, there shall be payable in respect of such property, upon its becoming subject to such Trusts, a Duty at the rate of £10 per centum upon the amount or principal value of such property;

Succession subject to Trusts for charitable or public purposes chargeable with Duty.

And it shall be lawful for the Trustee of any such property to raise the amount of any Duty due in respect thereof, with all reasonable expenses, upon the security of the Charity property, at interest, with power to him to give effectual discharges for the money so raised.

[17 & 18 Vict.]   *Literary and Scientific Institutions.*   [c. 112] 1854.

17 & 18 VICT. 112.

An Act to afford greater Facilities for the Establishment of Institutions for the Promotion of Literature and Science and the Fine Arts, and to provide for their better Regulation. [11th August, 1854.]

Revised Statutes. 2nd ed. vol. ix. p. 458.

1. Any person in England, Wales, or Ireland, being seised in fee simple, fee tail, or for life of and in any manor or lands of freehold, copyhold, or customary tenure, and having the present beneficial interest therein, may grant, convey, or enfranchise, by way of gift, sale, or exchange, in fee simple or for a term of years, any quantity not exceeding one acre of such land, whether built upon or not, as a site for any such Institution as hereinafter described;

Lands to be used as sites for Institutions, etc.

S

258 BOOK II.—LITERARY AND SCIENTIFIC INSTITUTIONS.

Provided that no such grant made by any person seised only for life of and in any such manor or lands shall be valid, unless, if there be any person next entitled to the same in remainder in fee simple or fee tail, and if such person be legally competent, he shall be a party to and join in such grant;

Provided also, that where any portion of waste or commonable land shall be gratuitously conveyed by any Lord of a Manor for any such purpose as aforesaid, the rights of all commoners and others having interest of a like nature in the said land shall be barred and divested by such conveyance.

Chancellor and Council of the Duchy of Lancaster empowered to grant land for the site of an Institution.

2. The Chancellor and Council of Her Majesty's Duchy of Lancaster for the time being, by any deed or writing under the hand and seal of the Chancellor of the said Duchy for the time being, attested by the clerk of the council of the said Duchy for the time being for and in the name of Her Majesty, her heirs and successors, may, if they see fit, grant, convey, or enfranchise, to or in favour of such Institution, any land forming part of the possessions of the said Duchy, not exceeding in the whole one acre in any one Parish, upon such terms and conditions as to the said Chancellor and Council shall seem meet;

And where any sum or sums of money shall be paid for the purchase or consideration of such land so to be granted, conveyed, or enfranchised as aforesaid, the same shall be paid into the hands of the Receiver General for the time being of the said Duchy, or his deputy, and shall be by him paid, applied, and disposed of according to the provisions and regulations contained in an Act of the 48th year of the reign of His late Majesty King George III., chapter 73, or any other Act or Acts now in force for that purpose.

Officers of the Duchy of Cornwall empowered to grant land for site of an Institution.

3. Any 3 or more of the principal officers of the Duchy of Cornwall, under the authority of a Warrant issued for that purpose under the hands of any 3 or more of the Special Commissioners for the time being for managing the affairs of the Duchy of Cornwall, or under the hands of any 3 or more of the persons who may hereafter for the time being have the immediate management of the said Duchy, if the said Duchy shall be then vested in the Crown, or if the said Duchy shall be then vested in a Duke of Cornwall, then under the hands of any 3 or more of the principal officers of the said Duchy, or under the hands of any 3 or more of the persons for the time being having the immediate management of the said Duchy, may, if they think fit, and are so

PART IV.—STATUTES.—17 & 18 VICT. c. 112.   259

authorised, by deed grant, convey, or enfranchise to or in favour of any existing or intended Institution any land forming part of the possessions of the said Duchy of Cornwall, not exceeding in the whole one acre in any one Parish, upon such terms and conditions as to the said Special Commissioners or principal officers, or such other person as aforesaid, as shall seem meet.

4. Provided, that upon any land so granted by way of gift as aforesaid, or any part thereof, ceasing to be used for the purposes of the Institution, the same shall thereupon immediately revert to and become again a portion of the estate or manor or possessions of the Duchy, as the case may be, to all intents and purposes as fully as if this Act or any such grant as aforesaid had not been passed or made, except that where the Institution shall be removed to another site the land not originally part of the possessions of either of the Duchies aforesaid may be exchanged, or sold for the benefit of the said Institution, and the money received for equality of exchange or on the sale may be applied towards the erection or establishment of the Institution upon the new site. *Lands ceasing to be used for the purposes of the Act to revert.*

5. Where any person shall be equitably entitled to any manor or land, but the legal estate therein shall be vested in some Trustee or Trustees, it shall be sufficient for such person to convey the land proposed to be granted for the purpose of this Act, without the Trustee or Trustees being party to the conveyance thereof. *Persons not having legal estates empowered to convey land without the concurrence of their Trustees.*

And where it is deemed expedient to purchase for the purpose aforesaid any land belonging to or vested in any infant or lunatic, such land may be conveyed by the Guardian or Curator of such infant or the Committee of such lunatic respectively, who may receive the purchase-money for the same, and give valid and sufficient discharges to the party paying such purchase-money, who shall not be required to see to the application thereof.

6. Any Corporation, ecclesiastical or lay, whether sole or aggregate, and any Officers, Justices of the Peace, Trustees or Commissioners, holding land for public, ecclesiastical, parochial, charitable, or other purposes or objects, may, subject to the provisions hereinafter mentioned, grant, convey, or enfranchise for the purpose of this Act, such quantity of land as aforesaid, in any manner vested in such Corporation, Officers, Justices, Trustees, or Commissioners. *Corporation, Justices, Trustees, etc., may convey lands for the purposes of the Act.*

Provided that no Ecclesiastical Corporation sole, being below the dignity of a Bishop, shall be authorised to make

s 2

such grant without the consent in writing of the Bishop of the Diocese to whose jurisdiction the said Ecclesiastical Corporation shall be subject.

Provided also, that no Parochial property shall be granted for such purpose without the consent of a majority of the ratepayers and owners of property in the Parish to which the same belongs, assembled at a meeting (a) to be convened according to the mode pointed out in the Act passed in the 6th year of the reign of His late Majesty, intituled "An Act to facilitate the conveyance of work-houses and other property of Parishes and of Incorporations or Unions of Parishes in England and Wales," and without the consent of the *Poor Law Board* (b) to be testified by their seal being affixed to the deed of conveyance, and of the Guardians of the Poor of the Union within which the said Parish may be comprised, or of the Guardians of the Poor of the said Parish where the administration of the relief of the poor therein shall be subject to a Board of Guardians, testified by the Guardians of such Union or Parish being the parties to convey the same:

5 & 6 Will. IV. 69.

And that no property held upon trust for charitable purposes shall be granted without the consent of the Charity Commissioners.

(a) By the "Local Government Act, 1894"—56 & 57 Vict. 73, 53 (1)—the meeting to deal with Parochial property under the Act of 1854 will now be the "Parish Meeting" created by the Act of 1894.

(b) Now the Local Government Board (34 & 35 Vict. 70, 2).

How such parties may convey.

7. Where any Officers, Trustees, or Commissioners, other than Parochial Trustees, shall make any such grant, it shall be sufficient if a majority or quorum authorised to act of such Officers, Trustees, or Commissioners, assembled at meeting duly convened, shall assent to such grant, and shall execute the deed of conveyance, although they shall not constitute a majority of the actual body of such Officers, Trustees, or Commissioners;

And the Justices of the Peace may give their consent to the making any grant of land or premises belonging to any County, Riding, or Division by vote at their General Quarter Sessions, and may direct the same to be made in the manner directed to be pursued on the sale of the sites of Gaols by an Act passed in the 7th year of the reign of His late Majesty George IV., intituled "An Act to authorise the disposal of unnecessary Prisons in England."

7 Geo. IV. 18.

Where part only of lands

8. If part only of any land held in fee subject to a perpetual rent, or comprised in a lease for a term of years unexpired,

PART IV.—STATUTES.—17 & 18 VICT. c. 112. 261

shall be conveyed or agreed to be conveyed for the purpose of this Act, the rent payable in respect of the lands subject thereto, and any fine certain or fixed sum of money to be paid upon any renewals of the lease, or either of such payments, may be apportioned between the part of the said land so conveyed or agreed to be conveyed and the residue thereof, and such apportionment may be settled by agreement between the parties following; subject to a rent under lease is conveyed, the rent and fine upon renewal of lease may be apportioned.

That is to say, the person for the time being entitled to the rent where the land is held in fee or the lessor or other the owner subject to such lease of the lands comprised therein, the person entitled to the fee subject to the rent, or the lessee or other party entitled to the land by virtue of such lease or any assignment thereof for the residue of the term thereby created, and the party to whom such conveyance as aforesaid for the purpose of this Act is made or agreed to be made;

And when such apportionment shall so be made it shall be binding on all under-lessees and other persons and Corporations whatsoever, whether parties to the said agreement or not.

9. In case of any such apportionment as aforesaid, and after the lands so conveyed or agreed to be conveyed as aforesaid shall have been conveyed, the person entitled to the fee or other estate in the lands subject to the rent, the lessee, and all parties entitled under him to the lands not included in such conveyance, shall, as to all future accruing rent, and all future fines certain or fixed sums of money to be paid upon renewals, be liable only to so much of the rent or of such fines or sums of money as shall be apportioned in respect of such last-mentioned lands; Liabilities of tenants, and remedies of landlords as to lands not conveyed.

And the party entitled to the rent charged or reserved shall have all the same rights and remedies for the recovery of such portion of the rent as last aforesaid as previously to such apportionment he had for the recovery of the whole rent charged or reserved;

And all the covenants, conditions, and agreements, except as to the amount of rent to be paid, and of the fines or sums of money to be paid upon renewals, in case of any apportionment of the same respectively, shall remain in force with regard to that part of the land which shall not be so conveyed as aforesaid, in the same manner as they would have done in case such part only of the land had been subject to the rent or included in the lease.

262 BOOK II.—LITERARY AND SCIENTIFIC INSTITUTION

Any number of sites may be granted.

10. Any person or Corporation may grant any number of sites for distinct and separate Institutions, although the aggregate quantity of land thereby granted by such person or Corporation shall exceed the extent of one acre, provided that the site of each Institution do not exceed that extent.

Grants of sites may be made to Corporations or Trustees for the purposes of an Institution.

11. Where the Institution shall not be incorporated, the grant of any land for the purpose of such Institution, whether taking effect under the Authority of this Act or any other authority, may be made to any Corporation sole or aggregate, or to several Corporations sole, or to any Trustees whatsoever, to be held by such Corporation or Corporations or Trustees for the purpose of such Institution.

Incorporation of 13 & 14 Vict. 28.

12. The provisions of the Act of the 14th Victoria, chapter 28, shall be applicable to the conveyances of lands in England, Wales, and Ireland, made or to be made to Trustees, not being Corporations, for the purposes of such Institutions. (*a*)

(*a*) This is "An Act to render more simple and effectual the Titles by which Congregations or Societies for the purposes of Religious Worship or Education hold property for such purposes." (See p. 253, *ante*.)

Form of grants, etc.

13. All grants, conveyances, and assurances of any site for an Institution under the provisions of this Act may be made according to the form following, or as near thereto as the circumstances of the case will admit; (that is to say,)

"I, or we [*or the corporate title of a Corporation,*] under the authority of an Act passed in the   year of the reign of Her Majesty Queen Victoria, intituled   do hereby freely and voluntarily, and without any valuable consideration [*or* do in consideration of the sum of   to me, *or* us, *or* the said   paid], grant and convey [*add if necessary*, enfranchise] to   all [*Description of the Premises*] and all my, *or* our, *or* the right, title, and interest of the   to   and in the same and every part thereof, to hold unto and to the use of the said Corporation and their successors, *or* of the said ·   and his, *or* their [heirs *or* executors *or* administrators *or* successors], for the purposes of the said Act, and to be applied as a site for   and for no other purpose whatever; such   to be under the management and control of [*set forth the mode in which and the persons by whom the Institution is to be managed and directed; in cases where the land is purchased, exchanged or demised, usual covenants or obligations for title may be added*]. In witness whereof the conveying and other parties

PART IV.—STATUTES.—17 & 18 VICT. c. 112.

have hereunto set their hands and seals, [*or seals only, as the case may be,*] this   day of   . Signed, sealed, and delivered by the said   in the presence of   of   ."

And no bargain and sale or livery of seisin shall be requisite in any conveyance intended to take effect under the provisions of this Act, nor more than one witness to the execution by the conveying party.

14. Any deed executed for the purposes of any Institution to which this Act applies, without any valuable consideration, shall continue valid, if otherwise lawful, although the donor or grantor shall die within twelve calendar months from the execution thereof. Death of donor within 12 months not to invalidate grant.

15. Where land of copyhold or customary tenure shall have been or shall be granted for the purpose of such Institution, the conveyance of the same by any deed wherein the copyholder shall grant and convey his interest, and the Lord shall also grant and convey his interest, shall be deemed to be valid and sufficient to vest the freehold interest in the grantee or grantees thereof without any surrender or admittance or enrolment in the Lord's Court, but the fees (if any) payable by the custom of the manor upon enfranchisement shall be paid to the Steward. Mode of conveying interest in copyhold land.

16. Where any land shall be sold by any Ecclesiastical Corporation sole for the purpose of this Act, and the purchase-money to be paid shall not exceed the sum of £20, the same may be retained by the party conveying for his own benefit, but when it shall exceed the sum of £20 it shall be applied for the benefit of the said Corporation in such manner as the Bishop in whose Diocese such land shall be situated shall, by writing under his hand, to be registered in the registry of his Diocese, direct and appoint; Application of purchase money of land sold by Ecclesiastical Corporation sole.

But no person purchasing such land for the purpose aforesaid shall be required to see to the due application of any such purchase-money.

17. In cases not otherwise provided for in this Act, the clauses 69, 70, 71, 72, 73, 74, and 78 of the "Lands Clauses Consolidation Act, 1845," being the 8th and 9th Victoria, chapter 18, shall apply in respect of the application of the purchase-money of all sites purchased from incapacitated persons, Corporations, and Trustees, hereby empowered to sell, other than the Chancellor and Council of the Duchy of Lancaster and the officers of the Duchy of Cornwall. Certain clauses of 8 Vict. 18, incorporated.

264 BOOK II.—LITERARY AND SCIENTIFIC INSTITUTIONS.

Trustees may sell or exchange lands or buildings;

18. If it shall be deemed advisable to sell any land or building not previously part of the possessions of the Duchy of Lancaster or Cornwall held in trust for any Institution, or to exchange the same for any other site, the trustees in whom the legal estate in the said land or building shall be vested may, by the direction or with the consent of the Governing Body of the said Institution, if any such there be, sell the said land or building, or part thereof, or exchange the same for other land or building suitable to the purposes of their trust, and receive on any exchange any sum of money by way of effecting an equality, and apply the money arising from such sale or given on such exchange in the purchase of another site, or in the improvement of other premises used or to be used for the purposes of such trust;

Or may let.

And such Trustees may, with like direction or consent, let portions of the premises belonging to the Institution not required for the purposes thereof, for such term, and under such covenants, or agreements, as shall be deemed by such Governing Body to be expedient, and apply the rents thereof to the benefit of the Institution.

Trustees to be indemnified from charges; in default thereof empowered to mortgage or sell the premises.

19. The Trustees of such Institution who, by reason of their being the legal owner of the building or premises, shall become liable to the payment of any Rate, Tax, charge, costs, or expenses, shall be indemnified and kept harmless by the Governing Body thereof from the same, and in default of such indemnity shall be entitled to hold the said building or premises and other property vested in them as a security for their reimbursement and indemnification, and, if necessity shall arise, may mortgage or sell the same, or part thereof, free from the trusts of the Institution, and apply the amount obtained by such mortgage or sale to their reimbursement, and the balance (if any) to the benefit of the Institution, subject to the restrictions hereinbefore contained with regard to lands given and lands belonging to the Duchies aforesaid.

Vesting of property of Institution.

20. Where any Institution shall be incorporated, and have no provision applicable to the personal property of such Institution, and in all cases where the Institution shall not be incorporated, the money, securities for money, goods, chattels, and personal effects belonging to the said Institution, and not vested in Trustees, shall be deemed to be vested for the time being in the Governing Body of such Institution, and in all proceedings, civil and criminal, may be described as the moneys, securities, goods, chattels, and effects of

the Governing Body of such Institution by their proper title.

21. Any Institution incorporated which shall not be entitled to sue and be sued by any corporate name, and every Institution not incorporated, may sue or be sued in the name of the President, Chairman, principal Secretary, or Clerk, as shall be determined by the rules and regulations of the Institution, and, in default of such determination, in the name of such person as shall be appointed by the Governing Body for the occasion ; {Suits by and against Institutions.}

Provided, that it shall be competent for any person having a claim or demand against the Institution to sue the President or Chairman thereof, if, on application to the Governing Body, some other officer or person be not nominated to be the defendant.

22. No suit or proceeding in any Civil Court shall abate or discontinue by reason of the person by or against whom such suit or proceedings shall have been brought or continued dying or ceasing to fill the character in the name whereof he shall have sued or been sued, but the same suit or proceeding shall be continued in the name of or against the successor of such person. {Suits not to abate or discontinue.}

23. If a judgment shall be recovered against the person or officer named on behalf of the Institution, such judgment shall not be put in force against the goods, chattels, or lands, or against the body of such person or officer, but against the property of the Institution, and a Writ of Revivor shall be issued setting forth the judgment recovered, the fact of the party against whom it shall have been recovered having sued or having been sued, as the case may be, on behalf of the Institution only, and requiring to have the judgment enforced against the property of the Institution. {Enforcement of Judgment.}

24. In any Institution, the Governing Body, if not otherwise legally empowered to do so, may, at any meeting specially convened according to its regulations, make any By-Law for the better governance of the Institution, its members or officers, and for the furtherance of its purpose and object, and may impose a reasonable pecuniary penalty for the breach thereof, which penalty, when accrued, may be recovered in any local Court of the District wherein the defendant shall inhabit or the Institution shall be situated, as the Governing Body thereof shall deem expedient: {Institution may make By-Laws.}

Provided always, that no pecuniary penalty imposed by any By-Law for the breach thereof shall be recoverable unless

266 BOOK II.—LITERARY AND SCIENTIFIC INSTITUTIONS.

the By-Law shall have been confirmed by the votes of three-fifths of the members present at a meeting specially convened for the purpose.

Members may be sued. 25. Any member who may be in arrear of his subscription according to the rules of the Institution, or may be or shall possess himself of or detain any property of the Institution in a manner or for a time contrary to such rules, or shall injure or destroy the property of the Institution, may be sued in the manner hereinbefore provided;

But if the defendant shall be successful in any Action or other proceeding at the instance of the Institution, and shall be adjudged to recover his costs, he may elect to proceed to recover the same from the officer in whose name the suit shall be brought, or from the Institution, and in the latter case shall have process against the property of the said Institution in the manner above described.

Offences by members. 26. Any member of the Institution who shall steal, purloin, or embezzle the money, securities for money, goods, and chattels of the Institution, or wilfully and maliciously, or wilfully and unlawfully, destroy or injure the property of such Institution, or shall forge any deed, bond, security for money, receipt, or other instrument, whereby the funds of the Institution may be exposed to loss, shall be subject to the same prosecution, and if convicted shall be liable to be punished in like manner, as any person not a member would be subject and liable to in respect of the like offence.

Institutions may alter, extend, or abridge their purposes, or amalgamate. 27. Whenever it shall appear to the Governing Body of any Institution (not having a Royal Charter, nor established by nor acting under any Act of Parliament), which has been established for any particular purpose or purposes, that it is advisable to alter, extend, or abridge such purpose, or to amalgamate such Institution, either wholly or partially, with any other Institution or Institutions, such Governing Body may submit the proposition to their members in a written or printed report, and may convene a special meeting for the consideration thereof according to the regulations of the Institution;

But no such proposition shall be carried into effect unless such report shall have been delivered or sent by post to every member 10 days previous to the special meeting convened by the Governing Body for the consideration thereof, nor unless such proposition shall have been agreed to by the votes of three-fifths of the members present at such meeting, and confirmed by the votes of three-fifths of the members present

PART IV.—STATUTES.—17 & 18 VICT. c. 112. 267

at a second special meeting convened by the Governing Body at an interval of one month after the former meeting. (a)

(a) By the "Schools for Science and Art Act, 1891" (54 & 55 Vict. 61), the Managers of any Institution to which this Act of 1854 applies may transfer it to a Local Authority under the "Technical Instruction Acts."

28. If any members of the Institution, being not less than two-fifths in number, consider that the proposition so carried is calculated to prove injurious to the Institution, they may, within 3 months after the confirmation thereof, make application in writing to the Lords of the Committee of Her Majesty's Privy Council for Trade and Foreign Plantations, who, at their discretion, shall entertain the application, and if, after due inquiry, they shall decide that the proposition is then calculated to prove injurious to the Institution, the same shall not be then carried into effect; Board of Trade may suspend such alteration, etc., if applied to by two-fifths dissentients.

But such decision shall not prevent the members of such Institution from reconsidering the same proposition on a future occasion.

29. Any number not less than three-fifths of the members of any Institution may determine that it shall be dissolved, and thereupon it shall be dissolved forthwith, or at the time then agreed upon, and all necessary steps shall be taken for the disposal and settlement of the property of the Institution, its claims and liabilities, according to the rules of the said Institution applicable thereto, if any, and if not, then as the Governing Body shall find expedient; Dissolution of Institutions and adjustment of their affairs.

Provided, that in the event of any dispute arising among the said Governing Body or the members of the Institution the adjustment of its affairs shall be referred to the Judge of the County Court of the District in which the principal building of the Institution shall be situated, and he shall make such order or orders in the matter as he shall deem requisite, or, if he find it necessary, shall direct that proceedings shall be taken in the Court of Chancery for the adjustment of the affairs of the Institution.

30. If upon the dissolution of any Institution there shall remain, after the satisfaction of all its debts and liabilities, any property whatsoever, the same shall not be paid to or distributed among the members of the said Institution or any of them, but shall be given to some other Institution to be determined by the members at the time of the dissolution, or in default thereof by the Judge of the County Court aforesaid; Upon a dissolution, no member to receive profit.

268 BOOK II.—LITERARY AND SCIENTIFIC INSTITUTIONS.

Proviso for Joint Stock Companies. Provided, however, that this clause shall not apply to any Institution which shall have been founded or established by the contributions of shareholders in the nature of a Joint Stock Company.

Definition of "Member." 31. For the purposes of this Act, a member of an Institution shall be a person who, having been admitted therein according to the rules and regulations thereof, shall have paid a subscription, or shall have signed the roll or list of members thereof;

But in all proceedings under this Act no person shall be entitled to vote or be counted as a member whose current subscription shall be in arrear at the time.

Definition of "Governing Body." 32. The Governing Body of the Institution shall be the Council, Directors, Committee, or other body to whom by Act of Parliament, charter, or the rules and regulations of the Institution, the management of its affairs is entrusted; and if no such body shall have been constituted on the establishment of the Institution, it shall be competent for the members thereof, upon due notice, to create for itself a Governing Body to act for the Institution thenceforth.

To what Institutions Act to apply. 33. The Act shall apply to every Institution for the time being established for the promotion of Science, Literature, the Fine Arts, for adult instruction, the diffusion of useful knowledge, the foundation or maintenance of Libraries or Reading Rooms for general use among the members or open to the public, of public museums and galleries of paintings and other works of Art, collections of Natural History, mechanical and philosophical inventions, instruments, or designs;

Provided, that the Royal Institution, and the London Institution for the advancement of literature and the diffusion of useful knowledge, shall be exempt from the operation of this Act.

Parish defined. 34. The term "Parish" shall signify herein any place separately maintaining its own poor.

Short title. 35. In all deeds, documents, proceedings, suits, and prosecutions this Act may be cited and described by the name of the "Literary and Scientific Institutions Act, 1854."

[24 & 25 Vict.] *Malicious Damage.* [c. 97] 1861.

24 & 25 VICT. 97.

An Act to consolidate and amend the Statute Law of England and Ireland relating to Malicious Injuries to Property. [6th August, 1861.

<small>Revised Statutes, 2nd ed., vol. x. pp. 701, 711.</small>

39. Whosoever shall unlawfully and maliciously destroy or damage any book, manuscript, picture, print, statue, bust, or vase, or any other article or thing kept for the purposes of Art, Science, and Literature, or as an object of curiosity, in any museum, gallery, cabinet, library, or other repository, which museum, gallery, cabinet, library, or other repository is either at all times or from time to time open for the admission of the public or of any considerable number of persons to view the same, either by the permission of the proprietor thereof or by the payment of money before entering the same, or any picture, statue, monument, or other memorial of the dead, painted glass, or other ornament or work of art, in any Church, Chapel, meeting house, or other place of divine worship, or in any building belonging to the Queen, or to any County, Riding, Division, City, Borough, Poor Law Union, Parish, or Place, or to any University, or College or Hall of any University, or to any Inn of Court, or in any street, square, churchyard, burial ground, public garden or ground, or any statue or monument exposed to public view, or any ornament, railings, or fence surrounding such statue, shall be guilty of a misdemeanour, and being convicted thereof shall be liable to be imprisoned for any term not exceeding 6 months, with or without hard labour, and, if a male under the age of 16 years, with or without whipping; provided that nothing herein contained shall be deemed to affect the right of any person to recover, by action at law, damages for the injury so committed.

<small>Destroying or damaging Works of Art in Museums, Libraries or other places.</small>

1867. [30 & 31 Vict.] *Companies.* [c. 131]

30 & 31 VICT. 131.

An Act to amend the "Companies Act, 1862."

[20th August, 1867.

Revised Statutes, 2nd ed., vol. xi. pp. 1149, 1155.

Association not formed for purposes of gain

23. Where any Association is about to be formed under the principal Act as a limited Company, if it proves to the Board of Trade that it is formed for the purpose of promoting commerce, art, science, religion, charity, or any other useful object, and that it is the intention of such Association to apply the profits (if any), or other income of the Association, in promoting its objects, and to prohibit the payment of any dividend to the members of the Association, the Board of Trade may, by licence, under the hand of one of the Secretaries or Assistant Secretaries, direct such Association to be registered with limited liability, without the addition of the word "limited" to its name, and such Association may be registered accordingly, and upon registration shall enjoy all the privileges and be subject to the obligations by this Act imposed on limited Companies, with the exceptions that none of the provisions of this Act that require a limited Company to use the word "limited" as any part of its name, or to publish its name, or to send a list of its members, directors, or managers to the Registrar, shall apply to an Association so registered.

The licence by the Board of Trade may be granted upon such conditions and subject to such regulations as the Board think fit to impose; and such conditions and regulations shall be binding on the Association, and may, at the option of the said Board, be inserted in the Memorandum and Articles of Association, or in both or one of such documents.(*a*)

(*a*) The Board of Trade has published a Circular, and Forms to carry out this provision. (See pp. 196 *et seq., ante.*)

[35 & 36 Vict.] *Charitable Trustees Incorporation.* [c. 24] 1872.

35 & 36 VICT. 24.

An Act to facilitate the incorporation of Trustees of Charities for religious, educational, literary, scientific, and public charitable purposes, and the enrolment of certain charitable trust deeds. [27th June, 1872.

Revised Statutes, 2nd ed., vol. xiii. p. 34.

1. It shall be lawful for the Trustees or Trustee for the time being of any charity for religious, educational, literary, scientific, or public charitable purposes, to apply, in manner hereinafter mentioned, to the Charity Commissioners for England and Wales for a Certificate of registration of the Trustees of any such charity as a Corporate Body;

And if the Commissioners, having regard to the extent, nature, and objects and other circumstances of the charity, shall consider such incorporation expedient, they may grant such Certificate accordingly, subject to such conditions or directions as they shall think fit to insert in their Certificate relating to the qualifications and number of the Trustees, their tenure or avoidance of office, and the mode of appointing new Trustees, and the custody and use of the common seal; and the Trustees of such charity shall thereupon become a Body Corporate by the name described in the Certificate, and shall have perpetual succession and a common seal, of which the device shall be approved by the Commissioners, and power to sue and be sued in their corporate name, and to hold and acquire, notwithstanding the Statutes of Mortmain, and by instruments under their common seal to convey, assign, and demise, any present or future property, real or personal, belonging to, or held for the benefit of such charity, in such and the like manner, and subject to such restrictions and provisions, as such Trustees might, without such incorporation, hold or acquire, convey, assign, or demise the same for the purposes of such charity. . . .

[Remainder of section repealed by "Statute Law Revision Act (No. 2), 1893."]

Upon application of Trustees of any charity, Commissioners may grant Certificate of registration as a corporate body.

2. The Certificate of incorporation shall vest in such Body Corporate all real and personal estate, of what nature or tenure soever, belonging to or held by any person or persons in trust for such charity, and thereupon any person or

Estate to vest in body corporate.

persons in whose name or names any stocks, funds, or securities, shall be standing in trust for the charity, shall transfer the same into the name of such Body Corporate, except as hereinafter provided;

And all covenants and conditions relating to any such real estate enforceable by or against the Trustees thereof before their incorporation shall be enforceable to the same extent and by the same means by or against them after their incorporation;

Provided always, that if such property shall be of copyhold or customary tenure, and liable to the payment of any fine or heriot on the death or alienation of the tenant or tenants thereof, it shall be lawful for the lord or lady of the manor of which such property shall be holden, on the granting of the said Certificate, and at the expiration of every period of 40 years thereafter so long as such property shall belong to such Body Corporate, to receive and take a sum corresponding to the fine and heriot, if any, which would have been payable by law upon the death or alienation of the tenant or tenants thereof, and to recover the same by any means which such lord or lady could have used in the event of the death or alienation of the tenant or tenants of such property, such payments to be in full of all fines and heriots payable in respect of the same property;

Provided also that such Certificate shall not have the effect of summarily transferring or directing the transfer to the incorporated Trustees any stocks, funds, or securities held by the Official Trustees of Charitable Funds for the benefit of the charity, but the same shall be transferable only by the Official Trustees to the incorporated Trustees under the discretionary order of the Commissioners, and by the ordinary means of transfer or assignment.

Particulars respecting application.

3 Every application to the Commissioners for a Certificate under this Act shall be in writing, signed by the person or persons making the same, and shall contain the several particulars specified in the Schedule hereto, or such of them as shall be applicable to the case.

The said Commissioners may require such declaration or other evidence in verification of the statements and particulars in the application, and such other particulars, information, and evidence, if any, as they may think necessary or proper.

Nomination of Trustees, and filling

4. Before a Certificate of incorporation shall be granted, Trustees of the charity shall have been effectually appointed to the satisfaction of the Commissioners, and where a

PART IV.—STATUTES.—35 & 36 VICT. c. 24. 273

certificate of incorporation shall have been granted vacancies in the number of Trustees of such charity shall from time to time be filled up so far as shall be required by the constitution or settlement of the charity, or by any such conditions or directions as aforesaid, by such legal means as would have been available for the appointment of new Trustees of the charity if no Certificate of incorporation had been granted, or otherwise as shall be required by such conditions' or directions as aforesaid, and the appointment of every new Trustee shall be certified by or by the direction of the Trustees to the Commissioners, either upon the completion of such appointment or when the next return of the yearly income and expenditure of the charity shall or ought to be made to the Commissioners under the general law, with which the certificate of such appointment shall be sent, and within one month after the expiration of each period of 5 years after the grant of a Certificate of incorporation, or whenever required by the Commissioners, a return shall be made to the said Commissioners by the then Trustees of the names of the Trustees at the expiration of each such period, with their residences and additions. up vacancies.

5. After a Certificate of incorporation has been granted under the provisions of this Act, all Trustees of the charity, notwithstanding their incorporation, shall be chargeable for such property as shall come into their hands, and shall be answerable and accountable for their own acts, receipts, neglects, and defaults, and for the due administration of the charity and its property, in the same manner and to the same extent as if no incorporation had been effected, and nothing herein contained shall diminish or impair any control or authority exerciseable by the Commissioners over the Trustees who shall be so incorporated, but they shall remain subject jointly and separately to such control and authority as if they were not incorporated. Liability of Trustees and others, notwithstanding incorporation.

6. A Certificate of incorporation so granted shall be conclusive evidence that all the preliminary requisitions herein contained and required in respect of such incorporation have been complied with, and the date of incorporation mentioned in such Certificate shall be deemed to be the date at which incorporation has taken place. Certificate to be evidence of compliance with requisitions.

7. The said Commissioners shall keep a record of all such applications for, and certificates of incorporation, and shall preserve all documents sent to them under the provisions of this Act, and any person may inspect such documents, under Commissioners to record applications for certifi-

T

274 BOOK II.—LITERARY AND SCIENTIFIC INSTITUTIONS.

cates, etc., and charge for copies. the direction of the Commissioners, and any person may require a copy or extract of any such document to be certified under the hand of the Secretary or Chief Clerk of the said Commissioners, and there shall be paid for such certified copy or extract a fee, to be fixed by the Commissioners, not exceeding 4*d.* for each folio of such copy or extract.

Enforcement of orders and directions of Commissioners. 8. All conditions and directions inserted in any Certificate of incorporation shall be binding upon and performed or observed by the Trustees as trusts of the charity, and shall also be enforceable by the same means or in the same manner as any orders made by the Commissioners under their ordinary jurisdiction may now be enforced.

Applications and certificates to be stamped. 9. Every application for a Certificate of incorporation under this Act, and every such Certificate, shall be charged with a Stamp Duty of 10*s.* and a stamp denoting the payment of that duty shall be impressed or fixed upon such application or Certificate.

Gifts to charity before incorporation to have same effect afterwards. 10. After the incorporation of the Trustees of any charity, pursuant to this Act, every donation, gift, and disposition of property, real or personal, theretofore lawfully made (but not having actually taken effect), or thereafter lawfully made by deed, will, or otherwise to or in favour of such charity, or the Trustees thereof, or otherwise for the purposes thereof, shall take effect as if the same had been made to or in favour of the incorporated Body, or otherwise for the like purposes.

Contracts not under seal to be binding in certain cases. 11. Every contract made or entered into by the Trustees of a charity, which would be valid and binding according to the constitution, settlement, or rules of the charity, if no such incorporation had taken place as aforesaid, shall be valid and binding although the same shall not have been made or entered into under the common seal of the Trustees.

Payments on transfers in reliance in corporate seal protected. 12. Any Company or person who shall make or permit to be made any transfer or payment *bonâ fide* in reliance on any instruments to which the common seal of any Body Corporate created under this Act is affixed, shall be indemnified and protected in respect of such transfer or payment, notwithstanding any defect or circumstance affecting the execution of the instrument.

[§ 13 is repealed by the "Mortmain and Charitable Uses Act, 1888" (51 & 52 Vict. 42, 13), and other provisions substituted.]

Definition of terms "public charitable purposes;" 14. The words "public charitable purposes" shall mean all such charitable purposes as come within the meaning, purview, or interpretation of the Statute of the 43rd year of Queen Elizabeth, chapter 4, or as to which, or the administration of the revenues or property applicable to which, the Court of Chancery has or may exercise jurisdiction;

And the word "Trustees" shall include the Governors, Managers, or other persons having the conduct or management of any charity. *"Trustees."*

15. This Act may be cited for all purposes as the "Charitable Trustees Incorporation Act, 1872." *Short title.*

SCHEDULE.

The objects of the charity and the rules and regulations of the same, together with the date of and parties to every deed, will, or other instrument, if any, creating, constituting or regulating the same.

A statement and short description of the property, real and personal, which at the date of the application is possessed by or belonging to or held on behalf of such charity.

The names, residences, and additions of the Trustees of such charity.

The proposed title of the corporation, of which title the words "Trustees" or "Governors" and "Registered" shall form part.

The proposed device of the common seal, which shall in all cases bear the name of incorporation.

The regulations for the custody and use of the common seal.

[51 & 52 Vict.] *Mortmain and Charitable Uses.* [c. 42]

51 & 52 VICT. 42.

An Act (a) to consolidate and amend the Law relating to Mortmain and to the disposition of Land for Charitable Uses. [13th August, 1888. *Law Reports Statutes, vol. xxv. p. 330.*

(a) The Sections and Parts of Sections not reprinted here are omitted because they are not of importance for the purposes of this work. It may be added that Parts I. and II. are amended by 53 & 54 Vict. 16, but as these amendments only concern land set apart for Working Men's Dwellings they are outside the purview of this volume.

BE it enacted, etc.

PART I.

MORTMAIN.

1.—(1.) Land shall not be assured to or for the benefit of, or acquired by or on behalf of, any corporation in mortmain, *Forfeiture on unlawful assurance*

276 BOOK II.—LITERARY AND SCIENTIFIC INSTITUTIONS

or acquisition in mortmain. otherwise than under the authority of a licence from Her Majesty the Queen, or of a statute for the time being in force, and if any land is so assured otherwise than as aforesaid the land shall be forfeited to Her Majesty from the date of the assurance, and Her Majesty may enter on and hold the land accordingly:

* * * * * * *

PART II.

CHARITABLE USES.

Conditions under which assurances may be made to charitable uses. 4.—(1.) Subject to the savings and exceptions contained in this Act, every assurance of land to or for the benefit of any charitable uses, and every assurance of personal estate to be laid out in the purchase of land to or for the benefit of any charitable uses, shall be made in accordance with the requirements of this Act, and unless so made shall be void.

(2.) The assurance must be made to take effect in possession for the charitable uses to or for the benefit of which it is made immediately from the making thereof.

(3.) The assurance must, except as provided by this section, be without any power of revocation, reservation, condition, or provision for the benefit of the assuror or of any person claiming under him.

(4.) Provided that the assurance, or any instrument forming part of the same transaction, may contain all or any of the following provisions, so, however, that they reserve the same benefits to persons claiming under the assuror as to the assuror himself; namely,

(i.) The grant or reservation of a peppercorn or other nominal rent;
(ii.) The grant or reservation of mines or minerals;
(iii.) The grant or reservation of any easement;
(iv.) Covenants or provisions as to the erection, repair, position, or description of buildings, the formation or repair of streets or roads, drainage or nuisances, and covenants or provisions of the like nature for the use and enjoyment as well of the land comprised in the assurance as of any other adjacent or neighbouring land;
(v.) A right of entry on nonpayment of any such rent or on breach of any such covenant or provision;
(vi.) Any stipulation of the like nature for the benefit of the assuror or of any person claiming under him.

PART IV.—STATUTES.—51 & 52 VICT. c. 42. 277

(5.) If the assurance is made in good faith on a sale for full and valuable consideration, that consideration may consist wholly or partly of a rent, rent-charge, or other annual payment reserved or made payable to the vendor, or any other person, with or without a right of re-entry for non-payment thereof.

(6.) If the assurance is of land, not being land of copyhold or customary tenure, or is of personal estate, not being stock in the public funds, it must be made by deed executed in the presence of at least two witnesses.

(7.) If the assurance is of land, or of personal estate, not being stock in the public funds, then, unless it is made in good faith for full and valuable consideration, it must be made at least twelve months before the death of the assuror, including in those twelve months the days of the making of the assurance and of the death.

(8.) If the assurance is of stock in the public funds, then, unless it is made in good faith for full and valuable consideration, it must be made by transfer thereof in the public books kept for the transfer of stock at least six months before the death of the assuror, including in those six months the days of the transfer and of the death.

(9.) If the assurance is of land, or of personal estate other than stock in the public funds, it must, within six months after the execution thereof, be enrolled in the Central Office of the Supreme Court of Judicature, unless in the case of an assurance of land to or for the benefit of charitable uses those uses are declared by a separate instrument, in which case that separate instrument must be so enrolled within six months after the making of the assurance of the land.

5.—(1.) Where an instrument, the enrolment whereof is required under this Part of this Act for the validation of an assurance, is not duly enrolled within the requisite time, Her Majesty's High Court of Justice, or the officer having control over the enrolment of deeds in the Central Office, may, on application in such manner and on payment of such fee as may be prescribed by rules of the Supreme Court, and on being satisfied that the omission to enrol the instrument in proper time has arisen from ignorance or inadvertence, or through the destruction or loss of the instrument by time or accident, and that the assurance was of a nature to be validated under this section, order or cause the instrument to be enrolled. *Power to remedy omission to enrol within requisite time.*

(2.) Thereupon, if the assurance to be validated was made

in good faith and for full and valuable consideration, and was made to take effect in possession immediately from the making thereof without any power of revocation, reservation, condition, or provision, except such as is authorised by this Act, and if at the time of the application possession or enjoyment was held under the assurance, then enrolment in pursuance of this section shall have the same effect as if it had been made within the requisite time :

(3.) Provided that if at the time of the application any proceeding for setting aside the assurance, or for asserting any right founded on the invalidity of the assurance, is pending, or any decree or judgment founded on such invalidity has been then obtained, the enrolment under this section shall not give any validity to the assurance.

(4.) Where the instrument omitted to be enrolled in proper time has been destroyed or lost by time or accident and the trusts thereof sufficiently appear by a copy or abstract thereof or some subsequent instrument, such copy, abstract, or subsequent instrument may be enrolled under this section in like manner and with the like effect as if it were the instrument so destroyed or lost.

(5.) An application under this section may be made by any trustee, governor, director, or manager of, or other person entitled to act in the management of or otherwise interested in, any charity or charitable trust intended to be benefited by the uses declared by the instrument to be enrolled.

PART III.

EXEMPTIONS.

Assurances for a public park, elementary school, or public museum.

6.—(1.) Parts One and Two of this Act shall not apply to an assurance by deed of land of any quantity or to an assurance by will of land of the quantity hereinafter mentioned for the purposes only of a public park, a schoolhouse for an elementary school, a public museum, or an assurance by will of personal estate to be applied in or towards the purchase of land for all or any of the same purposes only :

(2.) Provided that a will containing such an assurance, and a deed containing such an assurance and made otherwise than in good faith for full and valuable consideration, must be executed not less than twelve months before the death of the assuror, or be a reproduction in substance of a devise made in a previous will in force at the time of such re-

PART IV.—STATUTES.—51 & 52 VICT. c. 42. 279

production, and which was executed not less than twelve months before the death of the assuror, and must be enrolled in the books of the Charity Commissioners within six months after the death of the testator, or in case of a deed the execution of the deed.

(3.) The quantity of land which may be assured by will under this section shall be any quantity not exceeding twenty acres for any one public park, and not exceeding two acres for any one public museum, and not exceeding one acre for any one schoolhouse.

(4.) In this section :—
(i.) "public park" includes any park, garden, or other land dedicated or to be dedicated to the recreation of the public;
(ii.) "elementary school" means a school or department of a school at which elementary education is the principal part of the education there given, and does not include any school or department of a school at which the ordinary payments in respect of the instruction from each scholar exceed ninepence a week ;
(iii.) "school house" includes the teacher's dwelling-house, the playground (if any), and the offices and premises belonging to or required for a school ;
(iv.) "public museum" includes buildings used or to be used for the preservation of a collection of paintings or other works of art, or of objects of natural history, or of mechanical or philosophical inventions, instruments, models, or designs, and dedicated or to be dedicated to the recreation of the public, together with any libraries, reading rooms, laboratories, and other offices and premises used or to be used in connection therewith. (*a*)

(*a*) This section is almost identical with the provisions of the "Public Parks Act, 1871 " (34 Vict. 13), now repealed (see Sched.). The term "will" includes a codicil (see § 10). As in the Act of 1871, so in this enactment, the limit of acreage is confined to gifts by will, but gifts by deed may be of any quantity, provided the formalities of enrolment and execution are observed. The section generally is extended by 55 & 56 Vict. 11, so as to give further powers to certain Local Authorities for general purposes.

7. Part Two of this Act shall not apply to the following assurances: Assurances for certain universities, colleges, and societies.

* * * * * * *

(ii.) An assurance, otherwise than by will, to trustees on behalf of any society or body of persons associated together for religious purposes or for the promotion of education, art, literature, science, or other like purposes, of land not exceeding two acres for the erection thereon of a building for such purposes, or any of them, or whereon a building used or intended to be used for such purposes, or any of them, has been erected, so that the assurance be made in good faith for full and valuable consideration :

Provided that the trustees of the instrument containing any assurance to which this section applies or declaring the trusts thereof, may, if they think fit, at any time cause the instrument to be enrolled in the Central Office of the Supreme Court of Judicature.

* * * * * *

PART IV.

SUPPLEMENTAL.

Adaptation of law to system of land registration. 38 & 39 Vict. 87.
9. Any assurance of land which is by this Act required to be made by deed may be made by a registered disposition under the provisions of the "Land Transfer Act, 1875," or of any Act amending the same, and any assurance so made shall be exempt from the provisions of this Act as to execution in the presence of witnesses, and as to enrolment in the Central Office of the Supreme Court.

Definitions.
10. In this Act, unless the context otherwise requires—

(i.) " Assurance " includes a gift, conveyance, appointment, lease, transfer, settlement, mortgage, charge, incumbrance, devise, bequest, and every other assurance by deed, will, or other instrument; and "assure" and "assuror" have meanings corresponding with assurance.

(ii.) "Will" includes codicil.

[Sub-section iii. is repealed by 54 & 55 Vict. 73, 3, and another definition of " land " substituted.]

(iv.) " Full and valuable consideration " includes such a consideration either actually paid upon or before the making of the assurance, or reserved or made payable to the vendor or any other person by way of rent, rentcharge, or other annual payment in perpetuity, or for any term of years or other period, with or without a right of re-entry for nonpayment thereof, or partly paid and partly reserved as aforesaid.

Extent of Act.
11. This Act shall not extend to Scotland or Ireland.

12. Nothing in this Act shall affect the operation or

PART IV.—STATUTES.—51 & 52 VICT. c. 42.

validity of any charter, licence, or custom in force at the passing of this Act enabling land to be assured or held in mortmain. {Savings for existing customs, etc.

* * * * * *

14. This Act may be cited as the "Mortmain and Charitable Uses Act, 1888." {Short title.

SCHEDULE. §13.

Acts Repealed.

Note.—This Schedule is to be read as referring to the Revised Edition of the Statutes prepared under the direction of the Statute Law Committee in all cases of statutes included in that edition as already published.

The chapters of the statutes (before the division into separate Acts) are described by the marginal abstracts given in that edition.

Session and Chapter.	Title.	Extent of Repeal.
7 Edw. 1 . . .	*Statut' de Viris Religiosis* . .	The whole Act.
13 Edw. 1, 32 . .	Remedy in case of mortmain under judgements by collusion.	The whole chapter.
18 Edw. 3, st. 3, 3	Prosecutions against religious persons for purchasing lands in mortmain.	The whole chapter.
15 Ric. 2, 5 . .	St. 7 Edw. 1, de Religiosis. Converting land to a churchyard declared to be within that statute. Mortmain where any is seised of lands to the use of spiritual persons. Mortmain to purchase lands in gilds, fraternities, offices, commonalties, or to their use.	The whole chapter.
23 Hen. 8, 10 . .	An Acte for feoffments and assuraunce of landes and tenements made to the use of any parisshe Churche, Chapell, or suche like.	The whole Act.
43 Eliz. 4 . . .	An Acte to redresse the misemployment of landes, goodes, and stockes of money heretofore given to charitable uses.	The whole Act.
7 & 8 Will. 3, 37 .	An Acte for the encouragement of charitable gifts and dispositions.	The whole Act,

BOOK II.—LITERARY AND SCIENTIFIC INSTITUTIONS.

Session and Chapter.	Title.	Extent of Repeal.
9 Geo. 2, 36 ..	An Act to restrain the disposition of lands whereby the same become unalienable.	The whole Act, except so much of § 5 as is unrepealed.
9 Geo. 4, 85 ..	An Act for remedying a defect in the titles of land purchased for charitable purposes.	The whole Act.
24 & 25 Vict. 9 .	An Act to amend the law relating to the conveyance of land for charitable uses.	The whole Act.
25 & 26 Vict. 17 .	An Act to extend the time for making enrolments under the Act passed in the last session of Parliament, intituled "An Act to amend the law relating to the conveyance of land for charitable uses, and to explain and amend the said Act."	The whole Act.
27 & 28 Vict. 15 .	An Act to further extend the time for making enrolments under the Act passed in the twenty-fourth year of the reign of Her present Majesty, intituled, "An Act to amend the law relating to the conveyance of lands for charitable uses, and otherwise to amend the said law."	The whole Act.
29 & 30 Vict. 57 .	An Act to make further provision for the enrolment of certain deeds, assurances, and other instruments relating to charitable trusts.	The whole Act.
31 & 32 Vict. 44 .	An Act for facilitating the acquisition and enjoyment of sites for buildings for religious, educational, literary, scientific, and other charitable purposes.	§§ one and two.
34 & 35 Vict. 13 .	An Act to facilitate gifts of land for public parks, schools, and museums.	The whole Act.
35 & 36 Vict. 24 .	An Act to facilitate the incorporation of trustees of charities for religious, educational, literary, scientific, and public charitable purposes, and the inrolment of certain charitable trust deeds.	§ thirteen.

[54 & 55 Vict.] *Schools for Science and Art Act,* [c. 61]
1891.

54 & 55 VICT. 61.

An Act to facilitate the transfer of Schools for Science and Art to Local Authorities. [5th August, 1891.]

BE it enacted, etc.

1.—(1.) The managers of any school for science and art, or for science, or for art, or of any institution to which the "Literary and Scientific Institutions Act, 1854," applies, may make an arrangement with any local authority within the meaning of the "Technical Instruction Act, 1889," for transferring the school or institution to that authority, and the local authority may assent to any such arrangement and give effect thereto, subject to the provisions of that Act.

(2.) The provisions of § 23 of the "Elementary Education Act, 1870," with respect to arrangements for the transfer of schools shall apply in the case of arrangements for the transfer of schools or institutions in pursuance of this section, with this modification, that for the purposes of transfers to a local authority references to the school board shall be construed as references to the local authority and references to the Education Department as references to the Department of Science and Art, and references to a school shall, in the case of an institution not being a school, be construed as references to the institution.

(3.) In this section the expression "managers" includes all persons who have the management of any school or institution, whether the legal interest in the site and buildings of the school or institution is or is not vested in them.

2. This Act may be cited as the "Schools for Science and Art Act, 1891."

1891. [54 & 55 Vict.] *Mortmain and Charitable Uses Act,* [c. 73] 1891.

54 & 55 VICT. 73.

Law Reports Statutes, vol. xxviii. p. 458.

An Act to amend the Mortmain and Charitable Uses Act, 1888, and the Law relating to Mortmain and Charitable Uses. [5th August, 1891.

BE it enacted, etc.

Short title. **1.** This Act may be cited as the " Mortmain and Charitable Uses Act, 1891."

Extent of Act. **2.** This Act shall not extend to Scotland or Ireland.

Definition of "land." 51 & 52 Vict. 42. **3.** " Land " in the " Mortmain and Charitable Uses Act, 1888," and in this Act, shall include tenements and hereditaments, corporeal or incorporeal, of any tenure, but not money secured on land or other personal estate arising from or connected with land; and the definition of land contained in the " Mortmain and Charitable Uses Act, 1888," is hereby repealed.

Meaning of "assurance." **4.** In this Act the word " assurance " shall have the same meaning as in the " Mortmain and Charitable Uses Act, 1888."

Land assured by will for a charitable purpose to be sold. **5.** Land may be assured by will to or for the benefit of any charitable use, but, except as hereinafter provided, such land shall, notwithstanding anything in the will contained to the contrary, be sold within one year from the death of the testator, or such extended period as may be determined by the High Court, or any judge thereof sitting at chambers, or by the Charity Commissioners.

Land after expiration of time limited for sale to be sold by order of Charity Commissioners. **6.** So soon as the time limited for the sale of any lands under any such assurance shall have expired without completion of the sale of the land, the land unsold shall vest forthwith in the official trustee of charity lands, and the Charity Commissioners shall take all necessary steps for the sale or completion of the sale of such land to be effected with all reasonable speed by the administering trustees for the time being thereof, and for this purpose the said Commissioners may make any order under their seal directing such trustees to proceed with the sale or completion of the sale of the said land or removing such trustees and appointing others, and may provide by any such order for the payment of the proceeds of sale to the official trustees of charitable

PART IV.—STATUTES.—54 & 55 VICT. c. 73.   285

funds in trust for the charity, and for the payment of the costs and expenses incurred by the said administering trustees in or connected with such sale, and every such order shall be enforceable by the same means and be subject to the same provisions as are applicable under the "Charitable Trusts Act, 1853," and the Acts amending the same, respectively, to any orders of the said Commissioners made thereunder. 16 & 17 Vict. 137.

7. Any personal estate by will directed to be laid out in the purchase of land to or for the benefit of any charitable uses shall, except as hereinafter provided, be held to or for the benefit of the charitable uses as though there had been no such direction to lay it out in the purchase of land. Personal estate by will directed to be laid out in land not to be so laid out.

8. It shall be lawful for the High Court, or any judge thereof sitting at chambers, or for the Charity Commissioners, if satisfied that land assured by will to or for the benefit of any charitable use, or proposed to be purchased out of personal estate by will directed to be laid out in the purchase of land, is required for actual occupation for the purposes of the charity and not as an investment, by order to sanction the retention or acquisition, as the case may be, of such land. Power to retain land in certain cases.

9. This Act shall only apply to the will of a testator dying after the passing of this Act. Application of Act.

10. Nothing in this Act contained shall limit or affect the exemptions contained in Part III. of the "Mortmain and Charitable Uses Act, 1888," or apply to any land or personal estate to be laid out in the purchase of land acquired under any assurance to which such exemptions or any of them apply, or shall exclude or impair any jurisdiction or authority which might otherwise be exercised by a court or judge of competent jurisdiction or by the Charity Commissioners. Saving.

[55 & 56 Vict.]   *Mortmain and Charitable Uses*   [c. 11]   1892.
Amendment Act, 1892.

55 & 56 VICT. 11.

An Act to amend the Mortmain and Charitable Uses Act, 1888.   [20th June, 1892. Law Reports Statutes, vol. xxix. p. 118.

BE it enacted, etc.

1. Section 6 of the "Mortmain and Charitable Uses Act, 1888" (except so much of sub-section (2) thereof as provides Extension of 51 & 52 Vict. 42, c.

that an assurance by deed, made otherwise than in good faith for full and valuable consideration, must be executed not less than twelve months before the death of the assuror), shall apply to any assurance by deed of land to any local authority for any purpose or purposes for which such authority is empowered by any Act of Parliament to acquire land.

Definitions.
2. For the purpose of this Act " Local Authority " means any County Council, Council of a municipal borough, Sanitary Authority, or any body having power to make a rate for public purposes or by the issue of any precept, certificate, or other document to require payment from some authority or officer of money which may render necessary the making of any such rate; and "assurance" has the same meaning as in the "Mortmain and Charitable Uses Act, 1888."

Extent of Act.
3. This Act shall not apply to Scotland or Ireland.

Short title.
4. This Act may be cited as the "Mortmain and Charitable Uses Act Amendment Act, 1892."

287

PART V.
DIGEST OF CASES.

THIS Digest has been compiled with the view of laying before the reader handy notes of such Cases, decided, for the most part, in the Superior Courts, as may be useful for the guidance of persons connected with Literary and Scientific Institutions.

For an account of the general principles on which the details of the Digest have been worked out, see the Introduction to Part V. of Book I. (*ante*, p. 181).

As regards the Cases relating to Charities, many of which involve matters connected with the Laws of Mortmain, it must be understood that the selection is by no means intended to be exhaustive; but that only a moderate number of the reported Cases connected with such subjects are given, being those likely to be of general usefulness for the guidance of intending Testators, Solicitors, and Trustees and Managers of Literary Institutions.

In G. F. Chambers's *Handbook for Public Meetings* will be found a number of Cases allied to some of those given in this work. Committees of Societies who desire to understand their legal position and responsibilities under circumstances of difficulty will do well to consult that volume.

BEQUESTS.

1804. [1]
A.-G. v. *Stepney.* Bequest of residue of personal estate for the use of certain Schools, as long as they should continue, and for the purchase of new Bibles and other religious books, pamphlets, and tracts, at the discretion of the Trustees, the books to be kept in a house devised for the purpose—Devise of the house held void; but the personal bequest as to the Schools and as to the Books sustained, in the latter case as a general charitable purpose of promoting Christian knowledge; and it was directed that regard should be had to the Charity indicated. (10 Vesey, 22.)

1871. [2]
Attree v. *Hawe.* " Charitable Uses Act, 1735-6 "—Railway debenture stock created under the provisions of the "Companies Clauses Act, 1863," 26 & 27 Vict. 118, is not an interest in land within § 3 of the former Act—Such stock may therefore be given for charitable purposes—*Chandler* v. *Howell* over-ruled. (47 L. J., Ch., 863; L. R., 9 Ch. D., 337; 43 J. P., 124.)

1836. [3]
Baker v. *Sutton.* A bequest of the residue of personal estate for such Religious and Charitable Institutions and purposes within the Kingdom, as in the opinion of testator's Trustees should be deemed fit and proper is a good charitable bequest, and is not void for uncertainty. (5 L. J., Ch., 264; 1 Keen, 224.)

1791. [4]
Browne v. *Yeall.* Gift by will of money to be "applied in the purchasing of such books as . . . may have a tendency to promote the interests of virtue and religion, and the happiness of mankind "—Bequest held void as being too indefinite, and next-of-kin entitled to take the money. (7 Vesey, 50, n. 76; see also 10 Vesey, 27.)

1894. [5]
Canterbury, Mayor v. *Wyburn.* "Mortmain and Charitable Uses Act, 1888," 51 & 52 Vict. 42, 4 (1)—A domiciled Victorian by will directed his trustees to pay to a Corporation in England a sum of money to be applied in the purchase of land in England for the erection of a free Library and Reading Room—Held that the English Statute Law restricting gifts of land to charitable uses does not affect a will subject to the Law of Victoria, and that Testator's bequest was not invalidated by the English Act of 1888. (64 L. J., P. C., 36; 71 L. T., 554.)

1860. [6]
Carne v. *Long.* Penzance Public Library, established and maintained by subscription—A Rule that the property in the books, etc., should be vested in the officers as Trustees for the subscribers—A Rule that the Institution was not to be broken up as long as 10 members remained—Devise of freehold property to the Trustees for the time being to hold to them and their successors for ever, for the use and support of the said Library, held void, as tending to a perpetuity, though the Institution was held not to be a Charity within the meaning of the Statute of Mortmain. (29 L. J., Ch., 503; 2 De G. F. & J., 75; 2 L. T., 552.)

1872. [7]
Chamberlayne v. *Brockett.* A testatrix bequeathed all her residuary personal estate to be applied in building alms-houses *when land should be given for the purpose*—Bequest held good. (42 L. J., Ch., 368; L. R., 8 Ch. App. 206; 28 L. T., 248.)

1871. - [8]
Chester v. *Chester.* Charitable Institutions, of which one was empowered by Statute to hold, purchase, or receive lands not exceeding 2 acres, and to invest funds on mortgage, the security for which, after foreclosure, was not to be held for more than 2 years, and the other was empowered to acquire money secured on mortgage, with a proviso in the latter case that no grant should be valid which would be void under the " Charitable Uses Act, 1735-6 "—Held, nevertheless, that bequests to these Charities of debts secured to the testator's estate by equitable mortgage of leaseholds were void. (L. R., 12 Eq., 444.)

PART V.—DIGEST OF CASES. 289

1852. [9]
Clancy, Re. Gift of stock "for the establishment of a Charity School" held void—*Per* Romilly, M.R.:—"Any bequest tending to bring fresh land into Mortmain is void"—To "establish" an Institution points to a permanent establishment, and this implies the procuring of land for the purpose—The test is whether the proper mode of executing the Trust would be to buy land and build the School, which cannot be made permanent without it. (16 Bea. 295.)

1877. [10]
Cox, In re; Cox v. *Davie.* "Charitable Uses Act, 1735-6"—Bequest to a Municipal Corporation of a sum of money for the erection of a Dispensary, and of another sum for its endowment, held void—*Per* Bacon, V.-C.:—"To take it out of the Statute of Mortmain the gift must be to build upon land which is indicated, or there must be a prohibition as to laying out the money devoted to that purpose" [*quære*, the purpose of building] "to any other"—In other words, it must, in such a case, be distinctly provided that no part of the money is to be expended in the purchase of land. [Many kindred cases will be found alluded to in the Reports of this case.] 47 L. J., Ch. 72; L. R., 7 Ch. D. 204; 37 L. T. 457.)

1859. [11]
Darke, In the Goods of. Legacy to a Corporation wherewith to build and endow a Church—When the Executor named in a will is a Corporation Aggregate, Administration with the will annexed will be granted to its Syndic, *i.e.* to a person specially appointed by the Corporation for that purpose—The Clerk having been appointed Syndic, thereupon he was appointed Administrator. (29 L. J., P. 71; 1 S. & T. 516; 2 L. T. 24.)

1858. [12]
Denton v. *Manners.* A bequest of pure personalty to an Association called the Tithe Redemption Trust, which bequest indicated the Association as one "for buying impropriate Tithes and re-vesting them in the Church of England," and contained a direction for applying the personal estate "to the above-mentioned charitable purpose," held void under the "Charitable Uses Act, 1735-6," notwithstanding the 6 & 7 Vict. 37, 25, and the 13 & 14 Vict. 94, 23, on the ground that an illegal object for a bequest was thereby expressly indicated—*Quære*, Whether the Society has other and legal objects for a bequest? (27 L. J., Ch. 623; 2 De G. & J. 675; 31 L. T. (o. s.) 308.)

1855. [13]
Dunn v. *Bownas.* For a bequest to build a charitable Institution to be valid, the testator must indicate as the site some specific land already in Mortmain, and to which his gift is intended to apply—Otherwise the gift becomes void under the "Charitable Uses Act, 1735-6"—[*Sed quære; see Philpott* v. *St. George's Hospital.*] (1 K. & J. 596.)

1855. [14]
Edwards v. *Hall.* A gift of personal estate to be employed in the endowment of existing Institutions is not void, as being a gift of personal estate to be laid out in the purchase of land—*Per* Lord Cranworth, C.: —"The word 'endow' means giving a benefit to some existing thing; it supposes something to exist, either at the time when the gift is made or when the endowment is to take place; it has no reference at all to building or purchasing"—A bequest of a fund for building a charitable Institution, not expressing that it is to be erected on land already in Mortmain, or not otherwise expressly excluding the necessity of acquiring land for the purpose of carrying out the Trust, naturally im-

U

plies a power to purchase a site, and is therefore void under the "Charitable Uses Act, 1735-6"—If a testator indicates 2 objects to be selected at the discretion of his executors, the one lawful and the other unlawful, the Court will support the former. (25 L. J., Ch. 82; 6 De G. M. & G. 74; 26 L. T. (o. s.) 170.)

1854. [15]
Faversham, Mayor v. *Ryder.* A bequest of stock, to be applied "for the benefit and ornament" of a town, is not void under the Statute of Mortmain—A "benefit" may be a thing not at all connected with land, and an "ornament" to a town does not necessarily involve the bringing of lands into Mortmain. (23 L. J., Ch. 905; 5 De G. M. & G. 350; 18 Bea. 318.)

1879. [16]
Fearn's Will, In re. Bequest to "Society for the Propagation of the Gospel among the Jews"—No such Society, but two Societies named as follows:—(1) "London Society for Promoting Christianity among the Jews;" (2) "British Society for the Propagation of the Gospel among the Jews"—Held, that in view of the doubt as to which Society was designated, parol evidence might be admitted to show that testator had been an annual subscriber to No. 1, and meant her legacy for that Society. (W. N. 1879, p. 8; *Times*, Jan. 18, 1879.)

1834. [17]
Giblett v. *Hobson.* A bequest "towards" building almshouses to the said Institution" is, *primâ facie*, a bequest for buying land and building upon it, and consequently void under the Statute of Mortmain—But extrinsic evidence may be admitted to enable the Court to determine whether the testator contemplated building upon land already in Mortmain, or to be acquired by other means than the application of the legacy—Held in the particular case that the extrinsic evidence so admitted was insufficient to support the bequest. (4 L. J., Ch. 41; 3 Mylne & K. 517.)

1862. [18]
Graham v. *Paternoster.* Bequest to British and Foreign Bible Society, &c. —A testator directed his Trustees to invest his personal estate upon "real securities," with full power "to change the securities or funds," and he bequeathed a part to Charity—Held that the discretion as to the mode of investment rendered the Charitable gift valid. (31 L. J., Ch. 444; 31 Bea. 30; 10 W. R. 209.)

1872. [19]
Green v. *Britten.* Devise of house to a "Sailors' Home"—Devise void— Where a devise of premises is void under the Statute of Mortmain, a charitable legacy to be employed on the premises devised likewise is void, and cannot be applied *cy près*. (42 L. J., Ch. 187; 27 L. T. 811.)

1858. [20]
Hartshorne v. *Nicholson.* Gift of an annual sum to "establish" a school held valid—Such a school might be established by hiring a room, without involving any purchase of land; and the gift is not rendered void because one of the modes in which the testator's purpose could be carried out would be by the purchase of land. (27 L. J., Ch. 810; 26 Bea. 58.)

1864. [21]
Hawkins, In re. A legacy for the enlargement of an existing Church, surrounded by its own Churchyard, is good, as it does not involve the

PART V.—DIGEST OF CASES. 291

necessity of bringing additional land into Mortmain. (34 L. J., Ch. 80; 33 Bea. 570.)

1870. [22]
Hawkins v. Allen. Mortmain—Acquisition of land—Money given to a surgeon by cheque for the "erection, establishment, and maintenance of a hospital"—Declaration of Trust by a deed not disclosed to donor, but executed within his lifetime—Death of donor within a month after the gift—Held that the object of the gift did not exclude the acquisition of land, and that the gift was therefore invalid under the "Charitable Uses Act, 1735-6." (40 L. J., Ch. 23; L. R., 10 Eq. 246; 23 L. T. 451.)

1864. [23]
Hill v. Jones. A bequest to "establish" an Institution need not in all cases imply the purchase of land; a house might be hired for the purpose of the bequest—Bequest of £2000 for a new school held good. (23 L. T. (o. s.) 253; 2 W. R. 657.)

1876. [24]
Holdsworth v. Davenport. A Debenture of a Water Company in the form in the "Waterworks Clauses Act, 1845," Sched. C., by which the undertaking, including the Town Rates, was charged with the repayment of the advance, held not to be an interest in land within the "Mortmain Act," and therefore it might be bequeathed for charitable purposes. (46 L. J., Ch. 20; L. R., 3 Ch. D. 185; 35 L. T. 319.)

1853. [25]
Incorporated Church Building Society v. Barlow. Bequest for general purposes to a Society not empowered to purchase land—Held that, as the Society was not empowered as aforesaid, a bequest of pure personalty to such Society is not within the "Mortmain Act," and is therefore valid. (3 De G. M. & G. 120.)

1855. [26]
Incorporated Church Building Society v. Coles. Houses duly devised by a testator to Trustees upon trust to sell them and invest the proceeds, and pay the dividends to his widow for her life; and at her death to pay over the principal to the Society—Held that such a gift was not within the scope of the "Church Building Act, 1803," 43 Geo. III., 108, and could not be sustained either in its entirety, or as a gift of the proceeds of the sale to the extent of £500, but was void under the "Charitable Uses Act, 1735-6"—The first-named Act was passed to authorise limited dispositions of land by Deed or Will in favour of the charitable uses specified, but the intent of the Legislature was that the gift should be of specific lands for one or other of the specific purposes indicated in the Act, and therefore a gift of the proceeds of land is not within the protection of the Act, but is obnoxious to the provisions of the "Charitable Uses Act" named. (24 L. J., Ch. 713; 5 De G. M. & G. 324.)

1870. [27]
Lewis v. Allenby. Mortmain—"Charitable Uses Act, 1735-6"—Discretion of Trustees—Bequest of residuary personal estate (which included impure personalty), to Trustees to divide among such Charities in England as they in their sole discretion should think proper, held equivalent, as to the impure personalty, to a gift to Charities exempt from the Act, and therefore valid—If executors are empowered by will to employ two methods, one of which is lawful and the other unlawful, the lawful method is to be pursued, and the direction takes effect. (L. R., 10 Eq. 668; 18 W. R. 1127.)

u 2

1877. [28]
Luckraft v. *Pridham.* Local Poor Law Act—The " Mortmain Act " has a general application, and Guardians of the Poor are incapable of taking officially the benefit of a gift by will of land. (46 L. J., Ch. 744; L. R., 6 Ch. D. 205; 37 L. T. 204.)

1870. [29]
Maguire's Trusts, In re. Will—Charity *cy près*—Testatrix made several bequests to Charitable Institutions, and amongst others to the "Church Pastoral Aid Society" in England, and to the " Church Pastoral Aid Society " in Ireland—There was no such Society as the " Church Pastoral Aid Society " in Ireland, but the "Spiritual Aid Society " was founded for similar objects, and with rules almost identical with those of the " C. P. A. S." in England, and was the only such Society— Held that the bequest might be paid to the " S. A. S." in Ireland. (39 L. J., Ch. 710; L. R., 9 Eq. 632.)

1837. [30]
Mather v. *Scott.* Bequest of residue of personal estate to executors with a request that they would entreat a Lord of the Manor to grant a site for the erection of buildings to be appropriated to a charitable purpose; but the language of the will did not preclude the purchase of land if the executors thought proper—Held that, as the bequest did not clearly exclude a purchase of land, it was void under the Statute of Mortmain, as an inducement to draw lands into Mortmain. [See observations of Cranworth, C., in *Philpott* v. *St. George's Hospital.*] (6 L. J., Ch. 300; 2 Keen, 172; 5 Sim. 651.)

1878. [31]
Peake v. *Drinkwater.* Bequest of capital and income of a trust estate (subject to a life interest therein to testator's widow, and to the payment of certain legacies) " to the Trustees for the time being of the Tunstall Athenæum and Mechanics' Institute, to be applied by them towards the building fund in connection therewith "—Bequest held void as for a Charity under the "Mortmain Act," and also as tending to create a perpetuity—County Court Judge's decision affirmed on the second ground, there being nothing to show that the money should be disposed of during the lives of the then members, or within 21 years afterwards. (*Times*, May 11 and Dec. 5, 1878; [*Dutton, Re*] 43 J. P. 6.)

1857. [32]
Philpott v. *St. George's Hospital.* Where a will offers an inducement to other persons to bring fresh lands into Mortmain, but expressly prohibits any part of bequest therein being expended in the purchase of land, the gift will not be invalid by reason of the "Charitable Uses Act, 1735-6." (27 L. J., Ch. 70; 6 H. L. C. 338; 30 L. T. (o. s.), 15.)

1871. [33]
Pratt v. *Harvey.* To be valid, a charitable bequest for building must refer to an existing site already in Mortmain, or expressly exclude the application of the money to the purchase of land. (L. R., 12 Eq. 544; 25 L. T. 200.)

1881. [34]
Royal Society of London, and Thompson, In re. Society licensed to purchase and hold lands in Mortmain—On sale of a part, the purchaser objected that the property came within the "Charitable Trusts Acts, 1853 and 1855," and that the consent of the Charity Commissioners was requisite—Held that the case was within the exemptions of § 62 of the former Act, which were not interfered with by § 29 of the latter Act,

PART V.—DIGEST OF CASES. 293

and that therefore the consent of the Charity Commissioners to the sale was not required. (50 L. J., Ch. 344; L. R., 17 Ch. D. 407; 44 L. T. 274.)

1857. [35]
Salusbury v. *Denton.* A bequest " for the foundation of a charitable endowment" does not, *primâ facie*, authorise building operations, and is not necessarily void as being within the "Charitable Uses Act, 1735–6." (26 L. J., Ch. 851; 3 Kay & J. 529.)

1872. [36]
Sinnett v. *Herbert.* A gift for the *endowment* of a future Church is not necessarily void under the "Mortmain Act"—Where pure and impure personalty is given to Trustees to erect or endow a Church, they are entitled under 43 Geo. III., 108, to £500 out of the impure personalty in addition to the whole of the personalty—Where there is an option to erect *or* endow a Church, the Trustees are at liberty to apply the whole of the gift to endowment purposes, and so the gift would not be within the "Mortmain Act"—*Quœre*, Whether the Court will, for an indefinite time, hold a fund which has been given for a particular charitable purpose, where there is no reasonable prospect of carrying it into execution; and whether the doctrine of *cy près* applies in such a case? (41 L. J., Ch. 388; L. R., 7 Ch. App. 232; 26 L. T. 7.)

1826. [37]
Society for the Propagation of the Gospel v. *Att.-General.* A fund given to a Corporation for specified Charitable purposes ordered to be paid to the Corporation without the settlement of a scheme. (3 Russell, 142.)

1864. [38]
Tatham v. *Drummond.* Bequest to Society for Prevention of Cruelty to Animals of funded property, to be applied, according to the judgment of the Committee, towards the establishment of slaughter-houses remote from densely-populated districts—Society not incorporated, and without licence to hold land in Mortmain—Gift held void, as being within the "Charitable Uses Act, 1735–6"—When the testator's intention has been ascertained according to the ordinary rules of construction, inquiry will then be made whether any part of that intention is contrary to the Statute: no different mode of administration or of interpretation will be adopted for the purpose of escaping the operation of the Statute. (34 L. J., Ch. 1; 5 N. R. 24; 4 De G. J. and S. 484; 11 L. T. 324.)

1860. [39]
Thomson v. *Shakespear.* Bequest of £2500 to testator's Trustees and executors, to be laid out, with the concurrence of persons described in the will as the "Trustees of Shakespear's House," in forming a Museum thereat, *and for such other purposes as the Trustees of the will should think fit for the purpose of giving effect to testator's wishes*—Rent-charge given for support of a custodian—The house had been purchased by voluntary subscription, and testator had, by deed, vested money in Trustees to keep the house from decay—Held that the legacy could not be supported as a Charity or as a Trust for want of certainty as to the persons to be benefited (which doubt arose from the addition of the words in italics)—Custodian's charge void by the Statute of Mortmain. (29 L. J., Ch. 276; 1 De G. F. & J. 399; 2 L. T. 479.)

1857. [40]
University of London v. *Yarrow.* A bequest to a Corporation for founding and maintaining an Institution in London or Dublin for curing the maladies of animals useful to Man, held a good charitable bequest, and

not within the "Mortmain Act" on the ground of necessarily involving the acquisition of land in England, for the land might be acquired in Ireland—Trustees had an option of establishing a Charity in either of 2 ways, one valid, the other invalid—Fund ordered to be paid without any undertaking as to the mode in which they would apply it, and without any direction of the Court—They must act at their own peril if they acted wrongly. (26 L. J., Ch. 430; 1 De G. & J. 72; 24 Bea. 472.)

1822. [41]
Wellbeloved v. *Jones*. The Attorney-General is a necessary party to suits for Charitable funds, except where a legacy is given to an officer of an established Institution as part of its general funds—Where a legacy is given for permanent charitable purposes to persons having no corporate character, the Court will not, without a reference to the Master, allow the fund to be paid over to those persons, even where they are intrusted by the testator with the management of the fund. (1 L. J. (o. s.) 11; 1 Sim. & St. 40.)

1865. [42]
Wickham v. *Bath* (*Marquis of*). "Charitable Uses Act, 1735-6"—Conveyance of houses and lands, the rents to be expended in works of water supply, street improvement, and the formation of play-grounds—A grant of lands for charitable purposes does not comply with the provisions of the Statute unless the grantor grants, *bonâ fide*, all the interest he has in the property to be conveyed, whether from rents to be received, or from actual possession at the time of the grant—The conveyance to a Charity of lands subject to a lease must include the interest of the lessor in the rents reserved, as well as his interest in the reversion—Conveyance executed in presence of a witness who signed the attestation clause, and of 2 other persons who joined in the Deed, but did not sign the attestation clause, held not to be a compliance with the Statute. (35 L. J., Ch. 5; L. R., 1 Eq. 17; 13 L. T. 313.)

CLUBS AND COMMITTEES.
1889. [43]
Bristol Athenæum, In re. An unregistered literary society not established for gain cannot be wound up under § 199 of the "Companies Act, 1862," which applies only to Trading Associations—The property of such a Society, on its dissolution, ought to be given to some kindred Institution in accordance with the "Literary and Scientific Institutions Act, 1854," § 30—A society of this character is not within the proviso in § 30, which excepts Institutions established by the "Contributions of Shareholders in the nature of a Joint Stock Company," although some of its members may be shareholders. (59 L. J., Ch. 116; L. R., 43 Ch. D., 236; 61 L. T. 795.)

1831. [44]
Burls v. *Smith*. The subscribers who attend the managing Committee of a Hospital are liable to the creditors of the Hospital—The proper question for the jury is whether a defendant has so acted as to induce a plaintiff to believe that he might look to the defendant and the other members of the Committee for payment of goods supplied by him to them. (5 Moore & P. 735; 7 Bing. 705.)

1883. [45]
Cates v. *Pemberton*. Guarantee by members of a Club to Proprietor—Guarantee held enforceable against those who had put down their names for definite sums for the amounts severally specified. (*Times*, March 21, 1883.)

1883. [46]
Chamberlain v. *Boyd.* To speak disparaging words of a candidate seeking admission to a Club, whereby he loses his election, is too remote a damage to be actionable *per sc.* (52 L. J., Q. B. 277; L. R., 11 Q. B. D. 407; 48 L. T. 328; 47 J. P. 372.)

1857. [47]
Cockerell v. *Aucompte.* Coal Club—Liability of members—Liability of Secretary—Rule that Secretary should receive subscriptions and pay them to Treasurer, who should pay coal merchants on order of Secretary and Chairman—Secretary on requisition of members to apply for tenders and agree with merchant—Secretary ordered coals, but, owing to his default, the funds were insufficient to pay—Held that the Secretary was a mere servant of the general body, and that, as the Club never parted with the control of its funds, but only gave the Secretary authority to order the coals, the contract was made on the credit of the Club, and the members were liable. (26 L. J., C. P. 194; 2 C. B. (N. S.) 440; 2 F. & F. 448, n.; 5 W. R. 633.)

1871. [48]
Cocks v. *Manners.* *Per* Wickens, V.-C. :—"A voluntary association of women for the purpose of working out their own salvation by religious exercises and self-denial seems to me to have none of the requisites of a charitable institution, whether the word 'charitable' is used in its popular or in its legal sense." (40 L. J., Ch. 640; L. R., 12 Eq. 574 ; 24 L. T. 871.)

1881. [49]
Dawkins v. *Antrobus.* "Travellers' Club," London—After plaintiff was elected a member, Rule passed empowering a meeting to expel a member—Plaintiff expelled under this rule—Held that as during the four years the new Rule had been in force plaintiff had taken no steps to challenge it, it must be deemed binding on him by acquiescence—Publication by plaintiff of pamphlet libelling another member—Held that if the members at large deemed the publication of such a pamphlet to be "injurious to the character and interests of the Club," the Court would not interfere with their discretion. (L. R., 17 Ch. D. 615; 44 L. T. 557.)

1818. [50]
Delauney v. *Strickland.* "General Service Club," London—Where goods are ordered by one member of a Club for the benefit of all, every member who either concurs in the order or subsequently assents to it is liable, although the member who ordered the goods is made the debtor in the plaintiff's books, and the bill is sent to him, unless it clearly appears that the plaintiff meant to give credit to that member only. (2 Stark. 416.)

1878. [51]
Fisher v. *Keane.* "Army and Navy Club," London—Member expelled by a House Committee casually meeting for other business, and not specially summoned—Ground of expulsion, that plaintiff was drunk—Plaintiff not heard in his defence—Rules with proviso that no question of expulsion should be determined unless the Committee had been specially summoned, and two-thirds concurred—Injunction granted, with costs, to restrain the Committee from treating the member as expelled—*Per* Jessel, M.R. :—"The Committee of a Club were bound to act, in the words of Lord Hatherley, 'according to ordinary principles of justice,' and could not expel a member without fair and adequate notice being given to him to meet the accusation made against him." (49 L. J., Ch. 10; L. R., 11 Ch. D. 353; 41 L. T. 335.)

1836. [52]
Flemyng v. *Hector.* " Westminster Reform Club "—Club with Rules similar to the Rules of most London Clubs—Held that the members, as such, were not liable to tradesmen for debts incurred by the Committee on behalf of the Club; for the Committee had no authority to pledge the personal credit of the members—No liability for a member nominated on the Committee, but who had never accepted his nomination, nor acted. (6 L. J., Ex. 43; 2 M. & W. 172; 2 Gale, 180.)

1881. [53]
Foster v. *Harrison.* Plaintiff, a member of a Working Men's Club, expelled by the Committee because, being also a publican, he had caused beer to be bought at the Club by a stranger, and had then given evidence against the Club in a prosecution instituted for the alleged breach of the Excise Laws—Expulsion determined on by Committee without plaintiff being heard—Injunction granted to prevent the expulsion being enforced, the Court holding that a member could only be expelled for an infraction of the Rules, and that no such infraction had been shown. (*Times*, Dec. 10, 1881.)

1879. [54]
Froomberg v. *Balding.* Sailors' Home, Whitechapel—Beer sold without a licence—Proceedings against the Manager for breach of the " Licensing Act, 1872," § 3—Held that the alleged offence was not proved—*Semble,* that for such an Institution no licence is necessary. (*Times,* March 29, 1879.)

1882. [55]
Graff v. *Evans.* " Licensing Act, 1872," § 3—A member of a Club obtained *quâ* member some beer and spirits from the Club—Held that the transaction was not a sale by retail within the Statute. (51 L. J., M. C. 25; L. R., 8 Q. B. D. 373; 46 L. T. 347; 46 J. P. 262.)

1887. [56]
Harrison v. *Abergavenny* (*Marquis of*). Betting at cards—Warning notice put up by Committee—Abusive letter of complaint written by plaintiff —Further correspondence—Plaintiff expelled from the Club in due form —Held that he had no redress against the Committee. (3 *Times* L. R. 653.)

1867. [57]
Hopkinson v. *Exeter* (*Marquis of*). " Conservative Club, London "—No reference in Rules to political opinions beyond what was implied in the name of the Club—Rule authorising the expulsion of a member on a vote of two-thirds of the members present at a meeting specially called, in case any circumstance should occur likely to endanger the welfare and good order of the Club, to consider the question—Member expelled for having voted " Liberal " whilst professing to be a member of a Conservative Institution—Held that, as in the judgment of the Court the meeting was fairly called, and the decision arrived at *bonâ fide* and not through caprice, the decision of the meeting was final, and the Court had no jurisdiction to interfere. (37 L. J., Ch. 173; L. R., 5 Eq. 63; 17 L. T. 368.)

1844. [58]
Innes v. *Wylie.* Any Society may make Rules for the admission and expulsion of members, and members must conform to those Rules— Where there is no property in which all members have a joint interest, and where there is no Rule as to expulsion, a majority may by Resolution expel a member; but before that is done notice must be given him to

PART V.—DIGEST OF CASES. 297

answer any charge made against him, and an opportunity of making a defence afforded—Expulsion of member without notice to him, and without his being afforded an opportunity of defence, held invalid. (1 C. & K. 257.)

1898. [59]
Jones, In re; *Clegg* v. *Ellison*. "Literary and Scientific Institutions Act, 1854," § 30—Application asking that the defendants, being the trustees and committee of management of a body known as the "Sheffield Botanical and Horticultural Society," might be ordered to sell the Society's property and distribute the proceeds, in accordance with resolutions of the members duly passed—Application opposed by the Attorney-General on the grounds that the above Statute applied, and that the property ought not to be sold and divided, but should be given to some other institution of a like character—Held that the Society was within the exception laid down by the above-mentioned § 30 of the Act of 1854, and that the distribution of its property might legally be carried out as proposed by the members. (67 L. J., Ch., 504; L. R., 2 Ch., 83; 14 *Times* L. R., 412.)

1879. [60]
Labouchere v. *Wharncliffe (Earl of)*. Motion to expel a member carried without full inquiry; without notice to him of a definite complaint; without adequate notice to the other members; without a sufficient majority—Held that the member was entitled to an injunction against being debarred the use of the Club. (L. R., 13 Ch. D. 346; 41 L. T. 638.)

1882. [61]
Lambert v. *Addison*. Letters written by a member of a Club disparaging the Committee, and *vivâ voce* remarks to the same effect—Held to justify the Committee in calling upon the member to resign his membership. (46 L. T. 20.)

1862. [62]
Luckombe v. *Ashton*. Action maintained against medical officers of a Dispensary, who were members of the Committee, for drugs supplied on the order of others of its medical officers, with the knowledge of the defendants—The Jury were directed that defendants would be personally liable unless they clearly informed the plaintiffs that they were to look for payment only to the funds of the Institution. (2 F. & F. 705.)

1875. [63]
Lyttelton v. *Blackburne Proprietary Club*. On a member writing to the Committee an insulting letter they expelled him—Held that as the Committee had exercised their power *bonâ fide* and not capriciously plaintiff had no remedy. (45 L. J., Ch. 219; 33 L. T. 641.)

1876. [64]
Minnitt v. *Talbot de Malahide (Lord)*. Money raised for improvement of Club-house by authority of Committee—Personal liability of members —Lien on property of Club—Held that members liable might apply for sale of Club property in order to recoup themselves. (1 Ir. Ch. D. 143.)

1853. [65]
Mountcashel (Earl of) v. *Barber*. "Colonial Society" Club—Liability of member of Committee—Resolution by general meeting of Club, at which B., who was a member of Committee, was not present, directing and authorising Committee to raise a loan—Subsequent meeting of

Committee attended by B., and the question discussed—General meeting on the same day, at which the Resolution was confirmed—At a subsequent meeting of Committee (in B.'s absence) the loan was arranged, and the proceeds transferred to the Club account—Cheques were afterwards signed by B. drawn on the Bank at which the proceeds of the loan had been placed—B. held liable to contribution—Held also that the proceedings at the meetings which B. did not attend were admissible in evidence against him. (23 L. J., C. P. 43; 14 C. B. 53; 2 C. L. R. 60; 22 L. T. (o. s.) 134.)

1887. [66]
New City Constitutional Club, In re. "Companies Act, 1862," §§ 87, 163 —Club in arrears of rent when ordered to be wound up—New company formed—That also ordered to be wound up—Consideration of the right of the Landlord in regard to the furniture, and generally. (56 L. J., Ch., 332; L. R., 34 Ch. D. 646; 56 L. T. 792.)

1886. [67]
Newman v. Jones. Sale by Steward of intoxicating liquors in a Club to non-member—Conviction of members of committee held bad, they not being, under the circumstances, responsible for the wrong-doing of the Steward. (56 L. J., M. C. 113; L. R., 17 Q. B. D. 132; 50 J. P. 373.)

1887. [68]
New University Club, In re. "Customs and Inland Revenue Act, 1885" (48 & 49 Vict. 51)—The entrance fees and subscriptions of a social Club are not "funds voluntarily contributed to any body corporate or unincorporate" within § 11 (6), and the Club is therefore not exempt from paying Duty. (56 L. J., Q. B. 462; L. R., 18 Q. B. D. 720; 56 L. T. 909.)

1885. [69]
Parr v. Bradbury. A member of a Club who has duly retired may yet be liable to contribute to the payment of debts incurred whilst he was a member, he having knowledge of the existence of those debts, and of the Rules under which the debts were incurred. (1 Times L. R., 525.)

1826. [70]
Raggett v. Bishop. The "master" [*i.e.* proprietor] of a Club-house may properly sue members for arrears of subscription—If by a Rule every member is to be taken as continuing to be such unless he give previous notice of retirement, he is liable to be sued for arrears unless he can prove having given such notice. (2 C. & P. 343.)

1827. [71]
Raggett v. Musgrove. Club Rules neither posted up nor copies sent to members—If the Rules of a Club be contained in a book kept by the "master" [old equivalent to "proprietor"], but accessible to members, every member must be taken to be acquainted with them. (2 C. & P. 556.)

1844. [72]
Richardson v. Hastings. Club of 100 members insolvent and dissolved— Special subscription to assist in paying the debts—In the case of an insolvent partnership not formally dissolved, a Bill may be filed by one or more on behalf of the rest against the Governing Body to have the assets collected and applied towards payment of the debts, without seeking to ascertain the rights and liabilities of the parties as between themselves—Consideration of the rights of members of Clubs against one another, and against the members who belong to the Governing Body. (13 L. J., Ch. 142; 7 Bea. 123.)

PART V.—DIGEST OF CASES. 299

1870. [73]
Richardson-Gardner v. *Fremantle.* "Junior Carlton Club"—Great provocation to member—Where a Committee expels a member because they *bona fide* think his conduct has been injurious to the interests of the Club the Court has no jurisdiction to interfere. (24 L. T. 81; 19 W. R. 256.)

1879. [74]
Riley v. *Read.* "Working Men's Reform Club," Over Darwen, never having been furnished as a dwelling-house, or been slept in at night, held not assessable for Inhabited House Duty, although one floor was used during the daytime by an Auctioneer for business purposes. (48 L. J., Ex. 487; L. R. 4 Ex. D. 100; 40 L. T. 398; 43 J. P. 480.)

1898. [75]
Russell Institution, In re; Figgins v. *Baghino.* "Literary and Scientific Institutions Act, 1854," § 30—An institution known as the "Russell Institution" closed, its library and property sold, and £1600 left for ultimate disposal—Held that the Institution had been lawfully wound-up, and that the proprietors were entitled to the above sum of money *pro ratâ* according to the shares which they held at the time of the winding-up, and that the above-mentioned § 30 was not applicable. (67 L. J., Ch., 411; L. R., 2 Ch., 72; 14 *Times* L. R., 406.)

1889. [76]
Seaton v. *Gould.* Plaintiff, a member of the "Junior Army and Navy Club," was accused in a newspaper of being a part proprietor of a gambling club—On his failing to proceed against the newspaper, so as to vindicate his character, the Committee of the "Junior Army and Navy Club" expelled him—Held that if they thought fit to do so they were entitled to do so, and that no case had been made out for the interference of the Court. (5 *Times* L. R., 309.)

1880. [77]
Skipton v. *Rowley.* Member of "Hanover Square Club" expelled for alleged cheating at cards—On the facts becoming known to the Committee of the "Naval and Military Club" they called a special meeting, and he was also expelled from that Club—Meeting "specially summoned" in accordance with the Rules, but name of inculpated member not mentioned in the notice—Omission of name held immaterial—Rule empowering Committee to consider the "conduct" of a Member—Held that under the Rule the Committee were entitled to expel the plaintiff if they thought fit to do so. (*Times*, April 14, 1880.)

1887. [78]
Steele v. *Gourley.* "Empire Club"—Action by a butcher against 2 members of the Club Committee who had been active in the management—Judgment for plaintiff upheld, there being evidence that the defendants had acquiesced in orders given by the Steward, though the mere fact that they were members of the Club and of the Committee would not have been enough to make them liable. (W. N. 1887, p. 147.)

1887. [79]
Steele v. *Stevens.* Action by a butcher against the Solicitor of the "Empire Club" for meat supplied—Held that no right of action existed, the letter sued upon not being in the nature of a personal contract, and the credit given having been given to the Committee who had already been held liable in a previous action. (*Times*, May 26, 1887.)

1852. [80]
St. James's Club, In re. Clubs were not Partnerships or Associations within the meaning of the provisions of the "Joint Stock Companies

Winding-up Acts, 1848 and 1849 "—*Per* Lord St. Leonards, C.:—
"The Law . . . is now settled that no member of a Club is liable to a creditor, except so far as he has assented to the contract in respect of which such liability has arisen." [*Semble*, that the Law herein has not been altered by the "Companies Acts, 1862, 1867, and 1877."] (2 De G. M. & G. 383; 16 Jur. 1075; see Lindley, *Law of Partnership*, 4th Ed., pp. 57, 1229, 1231.)

1841. [81]
Todd v. *Emly.* "Alliance Club," London—Goods ordered by the House Steward, who had authority given to him by the Committee—Defendants members of the Committee, but they had not interfered in ordering the goods personally, nor were they shown to have been present when authority to make the purchase was given—Held that the question for the Jury was, not whether the defendants by their known course of dealing had held themselves out as liable, but whether they had individually authorised, or were privy to, the ordering of the goods. (10 L. J., Ex. 262; 8 M. & W. 505.)

1789. [82]
Wiltzie v. *Adamson.* Action by Tavern-keeper—Defendant member of a Club held at plaintiff's house—Book kept, open to inspection, in which plaintiff's servants entered things ordered by members—Entries in Book made up daily by plaintiff's servants—Book admitted as evidence of the delivery of the articles, though it was not proved that the servants who made the entry were dead, nor was their absence accounted for: only their handwriting proved—The daily account treated as a bill delivered and admitted by defendant. (1 Phill. & Arn., Evid. 10th Ed. 339; Taylor on Evidence, 7th Ed. 681.)

1861. [83]
Wood v. *Finch.* Member and Director of a Coal Club, formed on the principle of buying coals wholesale for *cash* out of *paid* subscriptions, held not liable for coals ordered on *credit* by the Secretary, there being no proof of authority to Secretary to pledge the credit of the Club. (2 F. & F. 447.)

RATING OF SOCIETIES CLAIMING EXEMPTION UNDER THE ACT 6 & 7 VICT. c. 36, AND OTHER ACTS.

1849. [84]
Birmingham New Library, In re; Birmingham Overseers, Ex parte. Literary Society held exempt—The remedy for an improper assessment is by appeal: if there is no appeal, the Rate cannot be resisted—Annual subscriptions are " voluntary contributions " within 6 & 7 Vict. 36, 1, if they commence of the party's own choice, and are so continued and may be withdrawn at pleasure, *i.e.* without subjecting the party to any legal liability or forfeiture except that of being deprived of the benefit of the Society. (18 L. J., M. C. 89; [*Reg.* v. *Birmingham JJ.*] 3 New Sess. Cas. 445; [*Birmingham Overseers* v. *Shaw*] 10 Q. B. 868.)

1851. [85]
Clarendon (Earl of) v. *St. James's, Westminster, Rector, &c.* Held that the "London Library" complied with all the requisites to obtain exemption, save that it sub-let a portion of its premises to another scientific body, and therefore its occupation failed to be "exclusive"—Where, on appeal to Quarter Sessions under 6 & 7 Vict. 36, a case is stated for the opinion of a Superior Court under 12 & 13 Vict. 45,

PART V.—DIGEST OF CASES. 301

11, costs are taxed as between party and party. (20 L. J., M. C. 213; 10 C. B. 806; 17 L. T. o.s.) 75.)

1897. [86]
Inland Revenue v. *Magistrates of Dundee.* "Income Tax Act, 1842," § 61, Rule 6—In the buildings of the Dundee Free Library accommodation was given to the books belonging to the Dundee Subscription Library, and the expenses attending their safe-keeping and circulation among the subscribers were defrayed out of the revenues of the Free Library— In consideration of the accommodation and services so given, each book, after being in circulation for a year, became the property of the Free Library—Held that the buildings in question did not fall within the exemption in the Statute, inasmuch as they were not used "solely" for the purposes of the Free Library. (24 Court of Sess. Cas., 4th Ser., 930.)

1854. [87]
Linnæan Society of London v. *St. Anne, Westminster, Churchwardens.* Under-letting—Society held exempt, on the ground that the premises let were no part of the rated premises in respect of which exemption was sought—An annual subscription may be "voluntary" though secured by an obligation for its payment so long as the subscriber continues to be a member—Apartments occupied by its officers for the purposes of the Society are within the exemption, even though such occupation is taken into account in fixing their salaries. (23 L. J., M.C. 148; 3 E. & B. 793; [*Reg.* v. *Linnæan Society*] 2 C. L. R. 761; 23 L. T. (o.s.) 186.)

1860. [88]
Liverpool Library v. *Liverpool, Mayor.* Institution held exempt, though the shares were valuable, and were transferable and transmissible, and though the members might at any time wind up and divide the property. (29 L. J., M. C. 221; 5 H. & N. 526; 2 L. T. 325.)

1890. [89]
London Library v. *Carter.* The "London Library" held liable to Inhabited House Duty on the ground that it does not come within any of the exemptions specified in the "Customs and Inland Revenue Act, 1878," § 13 (2.) (62 L. T. 466; 38 W. R. 478.)

1845. [90]
Purchas v. *Holy Sepulchre (Cambridge) Churchwardens.* "Cambridge Philosophical Society" held not exempt, on the ground that, though originally of a scientific character, it had become a Society which mainly spent its funds in buying newspapers. (24 L. J., M. C. 9; 4 E. & B. 156.)

1849. [91]
Purvis v. *Traill.* Scientific Society holding rooms which were occasionally let for general public meetings, lectures, concerts, etc., held rateable as not being a Society "exclusively" scientific, etc. (18 L. J., M. C. 57; 3 Ex. 344; 3 New Sess. Cas. 459.)

1858. [92]
Reg. v. *Bradford Library and Literary Society.* Society for literary purposes, the obligation to subscribe to which was voluntarily incurred, held exempt, though its privileges were confined to subscribers. (28 L. J., M. C. 73; 32 L. T. (o. s.) 105; [*Bradford Library* v. *Bradford Overseers*] 1 E. & E. 88.)

1851. [93]
Reg. v. *Brandt.* "Manchester Concert Hall Society" held to be primarily a mere Music Club formed for the gratification of its members, and therefore not exempt—The occasional grant of the hall for a concert, whereof the proceeds were given to a Charity, would not of itself invalidate the claim to exemption. (20 L. J., M. C. 110; 16 Q. B. 462; 16 L. T. (o.s.) 437.)

1851. [94]
Reg. v. *Gaskill.* Library and News-rooms held not exempt, as not being "exclusively" devoted, etc., but rather carried on for the private convenience and benefit of the subscribers. (21 L. J., M. C. 29; 16 Q. B. 472; 18 L. T. (o. s.) 72.)

1846. [95]
Reg. v. *Jones.* "Religious Tract Society" held not exempt—A Society is not exempt unless it has amongst its laws an express prohibition against dividend, etc.—It is not sufficient that there never has been a dividend, and that the making of such would be hostile to the aims of the Society—A Society for Religious purposes is not "literary." (15 L. J., M. C. 129; 8 Q. B. 719; 2 New Sess. Cas. 382.)

1851. [96]
Reg. v. *Manchester Overseers.* "Royal Manchester Institution" held exempt, although parts of the premises were sub-let to tenants who were themselves rated—Dividend, etc., expressly prohibited—The Rules declared that its purposes were the promotion of Literature, Science, and the Arts—Works of art were exhibited and allowed to be sold, deducting a commission; and admission fees charged to strangers, but such receipts did not cover the expenses of the Exhibitions—A power to use the premises for imparting knowledge consistent with the general purposes of the Institution did not invalidate the claim—A provision that on dissolution the property should be divided among the members held no answer to the claim, the provision not appearing by the case to be a pretext for accumulation. (20 L. J., M. C. 113; 16 Q. B. 449; 16 L. T. (o. s.) 435.)

1851. [97]
Reg. v. *Ogden.* The "Manchester Athenæum" consisted of shareholders and subscribers, the former of whom were allowed 5 per cent. interest on money advanced by them, and the building was used as a news-room and library, and for lectures and soirées, and devoted part of its funds for the purposes of a Chess Club and a Gymnastic Club—Held to be for the "pecuniary benefit" of its founders, and therefore not exempt. (18 L. T. (o. s.) 74.)

1848. [98]
Reg. v. *Phillips.* News-rooms owned by proprietors and let to a Society—Society held not exempt—A Certificate of exemption is not conclusive proof of the right thereto: it is only a condition precedent to exemption, and is not conclusive, even though the time limited for appeal against it may have expired. (17 L. J., M. C. 83; 8 Q. B. 745; 3 New Sess. Cas. 134; 10 L. T. (o. s.) 520.)

1846. [99]
Reg. v. *Pocock.* Premises of the "British and Foreign School Society" held not exempt, instruction in teaching being no branch of Science, or Literature, or Fine Arts. (15 L. J., M. C. 132; 8 Q. B. 729.)

PART V.—DIGEST OF CASES. 303

1857. [100]
Reg. v. *Royal Medical and Chirurgical Society.* Society would have been exempt if it had exclusively occupied for its own purposes the whole of its premises. (30 L. T. (o. s.) 133; 21 J. P. 789.)

1850. [101]
Reg. v. *Stacy.* 6 & 7 Vict. 36.—Certificate of exemption annulled by the Sessions—*Mandamus*, not *Certiorari*, the proper remedy for aggrieved Society. (19 L. J., M. C. 177; 14 Q. B. 789; 14 J. P. 415.)

1852. [102]
Reg. v. *St. Martin's-in-the-Fields, Churchwardens.* "United Service Institution," founded to advance "Professional Art," held not exempt. (21 L. J., M. C. 531; [*Reg.* v. *Cockburn*] 16 Q. B. 480; 18 L. T. (o. s.) 302.)

1854. [103]
Reg. v. *Zoological Society of London.* Scientific purposes—Society's property held not exempt on the ground that the Society's premises were not occupied solely for the purposes of Science, and that the contributions were not "voluntary," inasmuch as the members received a benefit not wholly scientific in return for their payments. (23 L. J., M. C. 65; 3 E. & B. 807; 2 C. L. R. 766; 23 L. T. (o. s.) 171.)

1898. [104]
Royal College of Music v. *St. Margaret and St. John.* The buildings of the Royal College of Music, being held exclusively for advancing the art of music, for providing musical instruction, and generally for the cultivation of music, held exempt under the Statute. (L. R., 1 Q. B., 809; 62 J. P., 357.

1898. [105]
Royal College of Surgeons, In re. "Customs and Inland Revenue Act, 1885 "—Exemptions—Institutions for promotion of "Education . . . Science"—Institution as a whole held liable but the Museum and house of Conservator of the Museum exempt. (14 *Times* L. R., 378.)

1854. [106]
Russell Institution, Governors of v. *St. Giles's-in-the-Fields, etc., Vestry.* Institution, including a general News and Reference Room, held not exempt. (23 L. J., M. C. 65; 3 E. & B. 416; 2 C. L. R. 755; [*Reg.* v. *Russell I.*] 22 L. T. (o. s.) 237.)

1896. [107]
Savoy, Overseers v. *Art Union of London.* 6 & 7 Vict. 36, 1.—A Society of which the membership is confined to annual subscribers, and the funds raised entirely by subscriptions, and which distributes among its members works of Art at least equal in value to the amounts subscribed, but does not make any "dividend, gift, division or bonus in money," although a Society "instituted for the purposes of the Fine Arts exclusively," is not a Society "supported wholly or in part by annual voluntary contributions," and is therefore not entitled to exemption under the above Act—The word "voluntary" in the section means "gratuitous," and does not apply to a case in which an advantage is obtained in return for the money paid. (65 L. J., M. C. 161; L. R., A. C., 296; 74 L. T. 497; 60 J. P. 660.)

1855. [108]
Scott v. *St. Martin's-in-the-Fields, Churchwardens.* Held that the "Work-

ing Men's Educational Union" was not exempt, for, being by its constitution designed to "effect the general elevation of the physical, intellectual, moral, and religious condition of the working classes," and engaging on this programme by means of lectures and discussions, political and social, its objects were different from those of Science, Literature or the Fine Arts. (25 L. J., M. C. 42; 5 E. & B. 558; [*Reg.* v. *St. Martin's*] 26 L. T. (o. s.) 121.)

1892. [109]
Sulley v. *Royal College of Surgeons of Edinburgh.* "Income Tax Act, 1842."—Hall, Library and Museum held not exempt in respect that the College was not a Literary or Scientific Institution, but an Institution whose main objects were professional. (19 Court of Sess. Cas., 4th Ser., 751; W. N., 1896, p. 98.)

APPENDIX TO BOOK II.

A PRACTICAL POINT IN CLUB MANAGEMENT.

BY THE VERY REV. F. PIGOU, DEAN OF BRISTOL.

"Is it not true that Clubs profess to have no conscience? The aggregate, co-operative principle has destroyed all sense of individual responsibility. It is not simply shaken off; it has never been felt. There is a practical isolation from all charitable and religious efforts on the plausible, but, I venture to suggest, flimsy, ground, that the income of a Club does not admit of disposal to objects extraneous to itself. . . . .
"The position taken up by Clubs in this matter is practically indefensible. Why should a large society of men agree to live in a particular part of London, and complacently acquiesce in ignoring the claim that the very fact of their presence palpably and fairly establishes? Are the rules which forbid subscription to parochial charities in the name and on behalf of a Club really like the laws of the Medes and Persians? Is it so that no pressure can be brought to bear upon Standing Committees of Clubs by members who are of different and more healthy opinion? or, haply, may it not be that Secretaries and Committees only want the support and countenance of members to do what conscience and every sense of obligation to a neighbourhood tells them is right and reasonable? And as regards the great world outside Club walls, of poverty, and privation and distress, might we not use the *argumentum ad hominem?* Is it creditable, to put it on the lowest grounds, is it calculated to raise the upper in the estimation of the lower classes, that there should be such centres of luxury, one of whose laws or by-laws is, 'We recognise as a body no parish and no charities'? Could not facilities be afforded in every Club for the voluntary subscriptions of individual members? Is it too much to ask that those opportunities should be placed in the *salons* of the Club, nay, through-

out them, in the form of boxes, and books kept for the entry of names, and care taken that these were always placed where they could readily be found, and where they would not fail to be seen ? Is there not, in the majority of Clubs, as a consequence of this irresponsibility, a disregard of, and indifference to, the spiritual interests of those employed in their service ? The reply to this may be, ' Not more so than in many private establishments.' Is this, therefore, a reply ? Servants of Clubs have souls to be saved, as they have whom they serve. Is it creditable to any large body of men, holding some veneration for religion, that they should be practically indifferent to the spiritual well-being of their fellow-creatures ? Is it wild and utterly unreasonable to expect that every reasonable facility should be afforded servants in Clubs for attending a place of worship, that rules or by-laws should be framed which shall at least show that a Committee is not oblivious of the spiritual interests of those employed, many of whom, now isolated from home, once enjoyed free access to all means of grace ? Is it pre-eminently ridiculous—only what a clergyman would conceive—that a Secretary, at an early and convenient hour, should gather together as many as possible of the household for a few still moments of prayer ? Facilities were accorded to me for visiting one or two of the Clubs, and for gathering together a few servants for a short Bible class, and, rare as these opportunities were, they were so prized, so gratefully embraced, that I would fain hope I might encourage any here, who may be in authority, to moot the subject and give the suggestion effect. . . . .

" If, instead of a holy observance of God's holy day, a Club must be a place of resort on Sunday, supremely dull, flat, and insipid as compared with week-day stir and life, is it an impertinence or liberty to suggest that, for the sake of appearances, for very decorum and decency sake, a stumbling-block be not put in the way of the working-classes, for whose observance of the Sabbath we are always legislating, and whose liberty many would restrict, that members of Clubs should not be seen by every passer-by leisurely reading their papers during the hours sometimes of Divine Service, and thus openly desecrating God's holy day ? Surely, whatever our own opinions or habits may be, we do owe something to others."—(*Sermon on Club Life*, preached at St. James's, Piccadilly, 1873, pp. 167-172 (S. P. C. K.).)

FORMS OF BEQUESTS TO LITERARY OR SCIENTIFIC INSTITUTIONS

I.—MONEY.

I give the sum of £   to the   [Society] [duty free], to be paid exclusively out of such part of my personal estate as I can lawfully charge with payment of legacies to charitable uses; and I desire that the same be paid to the [Secretary] for the time being of the said [Society], whose receipt shall be a good discharge for the same.

II.—BOOKS AND WORKS OF ART, ETC.

I give my [specified books, works of art, philosophical instruments, etc.,] to the [Society], and I direct the legacy duty (if any) on the value thereof to be paid exclusively out of such part of my personal estate as I could lawfully charge with payment of legacies to charitable uses, and I desire that the objects of my said specific bequests shall be handed over to the [Secretary] for the time being of the said [Society], whose receipt shall be a good discharge for the same.

NOTE.—By the "Charitable Uses Act, 1735-6," 9 Geo. II. 36, 1, "no manors, lands, tenements, rents, advowsons, or other hereditaments, corporeal or incorporeal, whatsoever, nor any sum or sums of money, goods, chattels, stocks in the publick funds, securities for money, or any other personal estate whatsoever," to be laid out or disposed of in the purchase or mortgage of lands, etc., can be given by will to any charitable institution, unless such gift be made by deed, indented, sealed, and delivered in the presence of two witnesses, twelve calendar months at least next before the death of the donor. Every such deed must be enrolled in Chancery, within six months next after the execution thereof, to take effect in possession absolutely and immediately from the making thereof, and no such deed will be valid, if it contains any power of revocation, reservation, trust, condition, limitation, clause or agreement whatsoever, for the benefit of the donor, or of any person claiming under him.

GENERAL INDEX.

₊ *Entries marked (*) refer to Book II.*

Accountability of officers 75, 103
Accounts and Audit under Public Libraries Acts 55, 56, 93, 94, 110, 146, 171
  ,,   Order of Local Government Board 57
Actions by or against library committee 41, 117
Adjustment of interests on termination of agreement 52, 151
Admission to libraries &c. 35, 37, 96, 118, 137, 141
  ,,   gymnasium 126
  ,,   museum 125
Adoption of Museums and Gymnasiums Act, 1891 124
  ,,   Public Libraries Acts . . . .
  ,,   in Cities, boroughs and urban districts . 11, 12, 159
  ,,   Ireland 26-28, 96, 174
  ,,   London and Metropolis 20-25, 144-151
  ,,   Rural parishes 13, 19, 162
  ,,   Scotland 25, 26, 109, 118, 173
Advertisement of adoption of Library Act 161, 173, 174
*Advertisement of application for registration by Board of Trade . . 215
Agreement for combination of library districts . 12, 52, 54, 136, 142, 151, 176
Annexation of parish to adjoining library district 136
*Application to Board of Trade for license 196, 215
Appointment of collector of voting-papers 154
*Appointment of trustees 254, 255
Art galleries 35, 37, 95, 137, 142
Art schools 35, 36, 37, 51, 53, 94, 105, 137, 142
*Articles of association limited company 199, 200
Authority, urban. *See* Urban authority

Ballot Act, 1872, to apply to poll of voters 13, 167, 175
Ballot paper, form of 17
  ,,   poll of electors in a rural parish 13-19, 162, 167
Begging in libraries 186
Behaviour, disorderly 180
Bequests, Digest of Cases 287
  ,,   form of 307
Betting in libraries 180
Board: definition 8, 108
*Board of Trade licence to company 193, 196, 270
* ,,   advertisement of application for licence . . . 215
Borough, adoption of Library Act 11, 12, 159
  ,,   rates under Libraries Acts 50, 144
  ,,   accounts and audit under Libraries Acts . . . 55, 146, 171
Borrowing by a parish council. 164

GENERAL INDEX. 309

Borrowing of money, provisions of Companies Clauses Act, 1845 . . 71
,, ,, Public Health Act, 1875 . 99, 145, 165
,, ,, Museums and Gymnasiums Act . . 127
Borrowing powers under Library Acts . . . 43-45, 99, 103, 112, 145, 165
Borrower's ticket, form 65, 66
Buildings. *See* Land &c.
Burgh : definition 7, 107
Burgh general assessment : definition 8, 108
Burghs : accounts 55
,, adoption of Public Libraries Act 25, 173
,, rates under Public Libraries Act 53
*By-laws : precedents 231
* ,, power to make 265
,, for regulations of libraries &c. (Scotland) . . 40, 41, 115-117
,, ,, ,, form of 61
,, ,, museums and gymnasiums 126

Cases, Digest of 181, 287
Catalogues 36
Certificate exempting from rates 191, 251
Charitable Uses Acts 194, 275, 284, 285
*Charitable Trustees Incorporation Act, 1872 271
*Charity Commissioners : appointment of trustees 194
,, Commissioners 52, 140, 142, 178
,, Land : power to grant for purposes of Library Acts 47, 49, 139, 177
,, Library 52, 142
*Charter of Incorporation (Institute of Engineers) 225
Chief magistrate : definition 8, 103
Clerk : ,, ... 9, 93
Closing of libraries 180
,, museums and gymnasiums 127
*Club : memorandum and articles of association 217
*Clubs : rules and regulations 231, 305
*Clubs and Committees : Digest of Cases 294
Collection of library Rate : Cost of 131
Collector of voting-paper : appointment 156
Combination of Metropolitan districts and parishes 149, 150
,, urban districts 12, 161
,, ,, in Ireland 28, 176
,, parishes 24, 136, 142
Commissioners (Library). *See* Library Commissioners
Commissioners Clauses Act, 1847 . . . . . 42, 45, 86-92, 112
Commissioners of Sewers 147
Commissioners in neighbouring parishes 24, 25, 136, 142
Committee (Joint) in combined urban districts 12, 161
,, ,, in rural parishes 31, 170
,, in rural parish 14, 30, 166, 169
,, (Ireland) 34, 95, 103
,, (Library) 29, 33, 141
,, (Scotland) 8, 33, 36, 40, 108, 113-115
Companies Act, 1867 . . . . 193, 270
Companies Clauses Consolidation Act, 1845 . . . . 45, 71-84, 103
Common Council : definition 5, 152
County Council : consent to borrowing 44, 164, 165
,, Loan to parish council 165
County district : definition 7

Damages : Recovery of 77
Damaging works of art &c. 97, 269

GENERAL INDEX.

Declaration of result of poll 18, 156
Default by urban authority in Ireland to carry Library Acts into execution 177
Definitions (interpretation of terms) 5-10, 21, 105, 106, 107, 111, 129, 151, 152, 153, 179
Demand note for rates 50, 52, 164
*Devise of land (Mortmain Acts) 284
Digest of Cases (libraries &c.) 182
*Digest of Cases 287
Digest of Statutes (libraries &c.) 5
*Digest of Statutes 189
Disorderly behaviour 180
*Dissolution of institutions 267
District authority: definition 21, 153
District council: appointment of committees 169
  ,, accounts and audit 171
  ,, definition 6
District (library) ,, ... 5 (2), 130
 ,, (urban) ,, ... 5, 6, 152
 ,, ,, ,, library authority 6, 133
Districts, combination of (Ireland) 28, 176
 ,, in Metropolis (Schedule B) 149

EDINBURGH Public Library Assessment Act, 1887 . . . 8, 180
Education Department: Parliamentary grant 37, 113
England and Wales: Public Libraries Acts:
 ,, ,, accounts and audit 55
 ,, ,, acquisition of lands &c. 46
 ,, ,, borrowing powers 43
 ,, ,, governing bodies: constitution of . . 29-33
 ,, ,, ,, proceedings of . . 39
 ,, ,, how brought into operation . . . 11-25
 ,, ,, interpretation of terms 5
 ,, ,, rates 50
 ,, ,, what may be supplied 35
*Enrolment of assurances under Mortmain Act 277
Estimate of expenses under Library Acts 56, 117
Evidence of by-laws 117
Exchange of lands &c. 111
Exemption from income tax 139
 ,, ,, legacy duty 190, 250
 ,, ,, Mortmain Acts 195, 278
 ,, ,, rates 190, 250
 ,, digest of cases 300
Expenses of determining as to adoption of Act . . . 109, 143, 164
 ,, museum and gymnasium 127
 ,, library authorities . . . 28, 50-54, 93, 110, 143, 164, 179

FEMALE householders 109
Financial provisions: Library Act 143
Financial year: definition 5, 152
Fines for detention of books 141
Form of advertisement of resolution adopting Library Acts . . 161
 ,, announcing result of poll 156
 ,, application for permission to borrow books . . . 68, 69
 ,, appointment of collector of voting-papers . . . 156
* ,, articles of association 199, 203
* ,, articles &c. for club 217
* ,, rules 231, 242
* ,, articles &c. for parochial institute 216

GENERAL INDEX. 311

Form of ballot paper 17
" bequest 307
" bond (Companies Clauses Act) 84
" borrower's tickets 65, 66
" declaration of result of poll 18
" grant of land to trustees 262
" intimation as to poll of voters 121
" label for borrowed books 67
" memorandum of association of limited company . . . 197, 200
" mortgage deed (Companies Clauses Act) 83
" notice calling meeting of parochial electors 14
"   "   to members of urban district council as to adoption . . 161
"   "   of poll of electors 16
"   "   public meeting as to adoption of Act (Scotland) . . 124
" regulations for a public library and museum 60
" report of result of poll 157
" requisition to take a poll of voters 133
" resolution adopting Libraries Act 15, 160
" resolution altering the limitation of the rate 160
* " Royal Charter of Incorporation 225
* " rules for institute or reading-room 236
" transfer of mortgage or bond (Companies Clauses Act) . . 84
" voting-paper 23, 122, 158

GAMBLING in libraries 180
*Gifts &c. of land 192, 257
*Governing bodies' powers &c. 193
Grant from Education Department 37, 113
"   " Science and Art Department 143, 178
" of charity land 177
* " land 262
Gymnasiums and Museums Act, 1891 124–129

HOUSEHOLDER: definition 7, 8, 9, 93, 108

INCOME TAX—liability of libraries &c. 139
*Incorporation, Charter of (Institute of Engineers) 225
*Incorporation of trustees 271
Injuries to Property Act, Malicious 97, 187
*Injury to works of art 269
Inspection of accounts of library authorities . . . 94, 110, 146, 171
*Institute under Companies Act 216
Interpretation of Terms Act, 1889 (*See* Definitions) 7
Ireland—Public Libraries Acts:
" accounts and audit 56
" acquisition of lands &c. 48
" borrowing powers 45
" governing bodies—constitution of 34
" governing bodies—proceedings of 42
" how brought into operation 26
" interpretation of terms 9
" rates and expenses 53, 178
" what may be supplied 37

JOINT commissioners of library districts 136
Joint committee in rural parishes 31, 170
"   " urban districts 12, 161

LAND, &c., acquisition of 46–49, 94, 95, 111, 137, 138, 163

GENERAL INDEX.

Land &c., application of, for museums and gymnasiums	128
*Land, gift &c. of	192, 257, 275, 284, 285
Lands Clauses Acts	46, 47, 48, 85, 95, 96, 99, 111, 138, 163
Language (offensive) in libraries	180
*Legacies: exemption from duty	190, 250
Legal proceedings: provisions of Commissioners Clauses Act	87
Lending library	35, 36, 137
Letting of building &c. by library authority	46, 49, 138, 178
Library authority: definition	6, 20, 29-34
,, ,, in Ireland	34, 94, 174
,, ,, London parishes and Metropolis	32, 147-151, 167
,, ,, rural parishes	29-32, 133, 163, 165, 166
,, ,, Scotland	33
,, ,, urban districts	29, 133
Library commissioners	29, 30, 32, 133, 134, 167, 176
,, ,, order as to accounts	57
,, ,, (Ireland)	34
,, ,, meetings and proceedings	39, 135
,, ,, regulations	32
Library district: definition	6, 130
,, rate (Scotland): definition	8, 108
Libraries and museums: definition	8, 108, 137
Libraries Offences Act, 1898	180
*License of Board of Trade	196, 270
* ,, ,, advertisement of application	215
Limitation of rates under Libraries Acts	51, 53, 94, 104, 110, 130, 160, 164, 166, 179
,, ,, ,, not to apply to London	147
*Limited liability company	193, 196
Literary and Scientific Institutions Act, 1843	139, *190
* ,, ,, ,, cases	300
* ,, ,, ,, 1854	257
* ,, ,, Institutions	189-307
* ,, ,, ,, Transfer of	283
*Literary or scientific society	200
*Literary society, exemption from rates	250
Local Acts	152, 180
*Local authority, transfer of schools of art &c.	283
* ,, grant &c. of land	284
Local Government Act, 1894	162-172
Local Government Board	10, 34, 43, 44, 57, 138, 150, 166, 171, 177, 179
London—adoption of Public Libraries Act	19, 32
,, authorised transfer of powers of Library Commissioners	167
,, City of—A library district	20, 147
Lord Lieutenant of Ireland	56
MAGISTRATES and Council: definition	7, 108
,, ,, adoption of Act	25, 173
,, ,, library authority	33, 173
Malicious Injuries to Property Act	97, 187, 269
Management of libraries &c.	95, 140
Manchester Improvement Act, 1871	180
Masculine gender, words in	109
Mayor: definition	9, 93
*Members: offences &c.	266-268
*Memorandum of Association: Limited Company	197, 200
Meeting, Public, as to adoption of Libraries Act	109, 122
Meetings of Library Commissioners	39, 135

GENERAL INDEX. 313

Meetings of Library Committee (Scotland) 40, 114
Metropolitan districts: adoption of Libraries Act . . . 20, 32, 147
„ „ authorised transfer of powers 166
„ parish 21, 150
„ districts, combination of 21, 148
Metropolis—Expenses of library authority 21, 148
*Mortgage &c. 193
Mortgage deed, Form of 83, 101
Mortgages, provisions of Commissioners Clauses Act . . . 89, 112
Mortgages of rates for library &c. 43-45, 101, 103, 112
*Mortmain and Charitable Uses Acts 194, 275, 284, 285
Mortmain, Licence in 47
Municipal register: definition 8, 108
Museums 35, 124-129, 178
Museums and Gymnasiums Act, 1891 124-129
Museums and libraries: definition 8, 108, 137
Music, Schools of 37, 103

NEIGHBOURING parishes 24, 136, 142
Notice to members of urban district council as to adoption . . . 161
Notices of poll of electors 16
„ „ publication of 18

*OFFENCES by members 266
Offences in Libraries Act, 1898 180
Officers and servants 35
„ „ accountability 75, 95, 102, 127, 141
Official documents 57
Order of Local Government Board as to accounts 57
Overseers and chairman of parish meeting 166
Overseers: definition 5, 152
Oxford Public Library 52, 151

PARISH: adjoining library district 24, 136
„ adoption of Public Libraries Acts . . . 13, 109, 162, 167
„ Council: library authority in rural parish . 6, 13, 29, 39, 133, 163
„ „ accounts and audit 57, 171
„ „ borrowing by 43, 164
„ „ rates to be levied 50, 51, 164
„ definition 6, 7, 107
„ library authority 6, 133, 163, 168
„ library district 6, 130, 162
„ meeting 13, 14, 30, 39, 51, 162, 165
„ rates under Public Libraries Acts 50, 51, 144
Parishes: appointment of committees 169, 170
„ combination of 21, 24, 136, 142
„ in Metropolis (Schedule "A") 150
Parliamentary grant to library authority . . 51, 53, 105, 113, 143, 178
Parochial elector: definition 6, 162
* „ Institute under Companies Act 216
* „ Libraries Act, 1708 . . . . 190, 246
Penalties and forfeitures 41, 77, 103, 117
Poll by means of voting-papers: regulations . 22, 104, 109, 118, 153, 158
Poll of voters in Ireland 27, 104, 175
„ „ London and Metropolis . . . 20-24, 131, 153-158
„ „ rural parish 13, 15, 162, 167
Polling agent 18

314 GENERAL INDEX.

Polling station 16
*Precedents of by-laws and regulations 231
,, forms &c. *See* Forms
* ,, formal documents 196
'Prescribed': definition 10
Presiding officer: definition 21, 153
Proceedings of Library Commissioners 39, 135
,, parish council or parish meeting 39
Public Health Act, 1875: clauses as to borrowing . . 43, 44, 99, 145, 165
,, by-laws 127
,, land &c. 163
Public Libraries Act, 1884 . . . . 105, 106
,, ,, ,, 1892 130–159
,, ,, definitions 5–7, 78
,, ,, Acts Amendment Act, 1877 104
,, ,, (Amendment) Act, 1893 . . . . . . 159, 161
,, ,, (Ireland) Act, 1855 92
,, ,, Act (Ireland) Amendment, 1877 103
,, ,, ,, 1894 174–179
,, ,, Consolidation (Scotland) Act, 1887 107–124
,, ,, (Scotland) Act, 1894 . . . . 172, 173
Public meeting as to adoption of Libraries Act 109, 122
Public Works Loans Act, 1875 . . . . 43, 145
,, ,, Loan Commissioners 43, 45, 145, 177

QUESTOINS authorised to be put to voters 18, 157

RATEABLE value: definition 6
Ratepayer: definition 9, 105
Ratepayers' opinions when ascertained by voting-papers 104
Rates, exemption from 190, 250
* ,, ,, Digest of Cases 300
Rates, limitation of. *See* Limitation of rates
,, in City of London 20, 147
,, in Metropolitan districts and parishes 21, 148
Rates under the Public Libraries Acts . . 50, 93, 110, 130, 143, 164
Rating of libraries and museums 139
*Reading-room rules 236
Recovery of damages and penalties 77, 103, 117
Register of mortgages 101
*Registrar of Friendly Societies: certificate exempting from rates . 191, 251
Regulations as to borrowing by a library authority 100
,, for libraries &c. 35–38
,, ,, form of 60, 95, 140
,, ,, museums and gymnasiums 126
,, ,, ascertaining opinions of voters in library district . 153, 167
Remaining in library after closing hour 180
Requisition for poll of voters 13, 14, 19, 27, 109
,, ,, form 133, 175
Resolution adopting Libraries Acts 11, 160, 173, 174
,, ,, Museums and Gymnasiums Act, 1891 . . . 125
Restrictions on expenditure of parish council 164
Result of poll: form of report 157
Returning Officer at poll of electors 16
Rotation of Library Commissioners 135
Rules as to poll of voters in a rural parish 167
,, to be made by Local Government Board under Public Libraries (Ireland) Act, 1894 179

GENERAL INDEX. 315

Rules of Local Government Board as to poll 15
* ,, and regulations for club 231, 242
* ,, ,, ,, institute or reading-room 236
Rural district council : definition 6
,, parish. *See* Parish

SALE or exchange of lands by library authority 46, 48, 95, 138
,, of museum or gymnasium 128
Schools for art 35, 36, 37, 51, 53, 94, 105, 137, 142, 178
,, . music 37, 103
,, science . . . 35, 36, 37, 51, 53, 94, 105, 137, 142, 178
* ,, Science and Art Act, 1891 283
Science and Art Department—Parliamentary grant . . 51, 53, 143, 178
Scientific and literary institutions 139, *189, *307
* ,, ,, ,, transfer to local authorities . . 283
* ,, ,, ,, exemption from rates 250
* ,, ,, Society 200
Scotland : accounts and audit 55
,, acquisition of lands &c. 47
,, adoption of Public Libraries Act 25, 173
,, borrowing powers 44
,, governing bodies, constitution of 33
,, governing bodies, proceedings of 40
,, how brought into operation 25
,, interpretation of terms 7
,, Public Libraries Acts 107, 172
,, rates 53
,, what may be supplied 36
Sheffield Corporation Act, 1890 180
Sinking fund to repay loan 44, 100, 112
*Specific Legacies Exemption Act, 1799 . . . . . . 190, 250
Statutes (Digest of) 5, 189*
Stealing in libraries 186
*Succession Duty Act, 1853 257

TAX (Property), liability of libraries &c. 139
Termination of agreements (adjustment) . . . 52, 151, 179, 179
Terms, Interpretation of (Public Libraries Acts) 5–10
*Titles of Religious Congregations Act, 1850 . . . . . 191, 253
Town commissioners : definition 9, 34, 93, 94
Town : definition 9, 92
Town fund : definition 9, 93
Town rate : ,, ... 9, 93
*Transfer to local authorities of science and art schools . . . 283
,, of mortgages 101
,, ,, powers in urban districts and London—provisions of Local
,, Government Act, 1894 . . . . . . 167, 168
,, ,, property, debts and liabilities 172
Treasury Commissioners—consent to loan 103
,, Her Majesty's—approval required to appropriation of land &c. . 94
*Trust deeds 191, 253, 257, 271
*Trustees, appointment of 191, 194, 255, 262
* ,, incorporation of 271
* ,, powers of 264
* ,, registration by Charity Commissioners 194
*Trusts for church institute or reading-room 236

URBAN authority: definition 5, 10, 29, 152
„ „ Ireland 26, 174, 179
„ authorities (Ireland), combination of 177, 179
„ district : definition 5, 6, 10, 152, 179
„ districts, accounts under Libraries Acts 55
„ „ adoption of Libraries Acts 11, 133, 159
„ „ appointment of committees 169
„ „ combination of, under Libraries Acts . . 12, 136, 161
„ „ Ireland 26, 177, 179
„ „ rates under Libraries Acts 50, 143
„ „ transfer of powers 167

VACANCIES in library committee (Scotland) 33, 114
*Vesting of land in trustees 264
„ property 140, 166
Vestry : definition 6, 43, 151, 163
„ in rural parish, powers transferred to parish meeting . . 163, 166
„ to sanction borrowing by Library Commissioners . . . 43, 145
„ „ rates by Library Commissioners 50, 144
Vestries of neighbouring parishes, combination 136
Voter, definition 5, 10, 152, 179
Votes, counting of 18
Voting-papers 19, 22, 153
„ form of 23, 104, 118, 158

*WORKMEN'S club 242

INDEX OF NAMES OF CASES.

⁎ *The names in Italic are alternative names of Cases which are otherwise indexed.*

BOOK I.
PUBLIC LIBRARIES AND MUSEUMS.

Andrews v. Bristol	. . .	1
A.-G. v. Croydon .	. . .	2
A.-G. v. G. E. R. .	. . .	3
A.-G. v. Sunderland	. . .	4
Greig v. Edinburgh	. . .	5
Harrison v. Southampton	. .	6
Holborn v. Bull .	. . .	7
Liverpool Corporation, *In Re*, Brown, *Ex parte*	. . .	8
Manchester v. McAdam	.	9
Nottingham Corporation v. Abbott	. . . .	10
Reg. v. Blenkinsop	. . .	11
Reg. v. Morris	. . . .	12
Reg. v. Portsmouth	. . .	13
Reg. v. St. Matthew, Bethnal G. .		14
Reg. v. Wimbledon L. B. .	.	15
Smee v. Smee and Brighton	.	16

BOOK II.
LITERARY AND SCIENTIFIC INSTITUTIONS.

A.-G. v. Stepney .	. . .	1
Attree v. Hawe .	. . .	2
Baker v. Sutton .	. . .	3
Birmingham Library, *In Re*	.	84
Birmingham O. v. Shaw	.	84
Bradford Lib. v. Bradford .	.	92
Bristol Athenæum, *In Re* .	.	43
Brown v. Yeall .	. . .	4
Burls v. Smith .	. . .	44
Canterbury v. Wyburn	. .	5
Carne v. Long .	. . .	6
Cates v. Pemberton	. . .	45
Chamberlain v. Boyd .	. .	46
Chamberlayne v. Brockett .	.	7
Chandler v. Howell, cited in	.	2
Chester v. Chester	. . .	8
Clancy, *Re* .	. . . .	9
Clarendon v. St. James's, W.	.	85
Cockerell v. Aucompte	. .	47
Cocks v. Manners	. . .	48
Cox, *In Re* .	. . . .	10
Darke, in the goods of	. .	11
Dawkins v. Antrobus .	. .	49
Delauney v. Strickland	. .	50
Denton v. Manners	. . .	12
Dunn v. Bownas .	. . .	13
Dutton, In Re .	. . .	31
Edwards v. Hall .	. . .	14
Faversham v. Ryder	. . .	15

Fearns, In Re	16
Fisher v. Keane	51
Flemyng v. Hector	52
Foster v. Harrison	53
Froomberg v. Balding	54
Giblett v. Hobson	17
Graff v. Evans	55
Graham v. Paternoster	18
Green v. Britten	19
Harrison v. Abergavenny	56
Hartshorne v. Nicholson	20
Hawkins, In Re	21
Hawkins v. Allen	22
Hill v. Jones	23
Holdsworth v. Davenport	24
Hopkinson v. Exeter	57
Incorp. Ch. Bldg. S. v. Barlow	25
Incorp. Ch. Bldg. S. v. Coles	26
Inland Revenue v. Dundee	86
Innes v. Wylie	58
Jones, In Re	59
Labouchere v. Wharncliffe	60
Lambert v. Addison	61
Lewis v. Allenby	27
Linnean Soc. v. St. Anne's, W.	87
Liverpool Lib. v. Liverpool	88
London Library v. Carter	89
Luckombe v. Ashton	62
Luckraft v. Pridham	28
Lyttelton v. Blackburne	63
Maguire's Trusts, In Re	29
Mather v. Scott	30
Minnett v. Talbot de Malahide	64
Mountcashel v. Barber	65
New City Const. Club, In Re	66
New Univ. Club, In Re	68
Newman v. Jones	67
Parr v. Bradbury	69
Peake v. Drinkwater	31
Philpott v. St.George's, 32: cited in	30
Pratt v. Harvey	33
Purchas v. Holy Sepul., Cam.	90
Purvis v. Traill	91

Ruggett v. Bishop	70
Ruggett v. Musgrave	71
Reg. v. Birmingham JJ.	84
Reg. v. Bradford Library	92
Reg. v. Brandt	93
Reg. v. Cockburn	102
Reg. v. Gaskill	94
Reg v. Jones	95
Reg. v. Linnean Society	87
Reg. v. Manchester Overseers	96
Reg. v. Ogden	97
Reg. v. Phillips	98
Reg. v. Pocock	99
Reg. v. Royal Medical Society	100
Reg. v. Russell Institution	106
Reg. v. Stacy	101
Reg. v. St. Martin's-in-F.	102
Reg. v. Zoological Society	103
Richardson v. Hastings	72
Richardson-Gardner v. Fremantle	73
Riley v. Read	74
Roy. Coll. Music v. St. Margaret and St. John	104
Roy. Coll. Surg., In Re	105
Roy. Soc. and Thompson, In Re	34
Russell Inst., In Re	75
Russell Inst. v. St. Giles	106
Salusbury v. Denton	35
Savoy Overseers v. Art Union of London	107
Scott v. St. Martin's	108
Seaton v. Gould	76
Sinnett v. Herbert	36
Skipton v. Rowley	77
Soc. Prop. Gosp. v. A.-G.	37
Steele v. Gourley	78
Steele v. Stevens	79
St. James's Club, In Re	80
Sulley v. Roy. Coll. Surg. Edin.	109
Tatham v. Drummond	38
Thomson v. Shakespear	39
Todd v. Emly	81
Univ. London v. Yarrow	40
Wellbeloved v. Jones	41
Wickham v. Bath	42
Wiltzie v. Adamson	82
Wood v. Finch	83

INDEX OF SUBJECTS OF CASES.

BOOK I.

PUBLIC LIBRARIES AND MUSEUMS.

Act of Parliament, powers under	3	Offences against "Libraries Acts"	7, 10
Bequest for public purposes.	6, 16	"Penny Rate," Meaning of the term	8
Corporation, land vested in.	4	Poll as to adoption of the "Libraries Acts"	5, 12, 14
Crown property, rating of	5	Powers of a corporation	4
Land, purchase of, for public purposes	6		
Liability to rates and taxes.	1, 9	Quo Warranto	12
Limited library rate	8		
Mandamus.	11, 13	University property, rating of	5
Meeting to adopt "Libraries Acts"	12–13	Voting-papers, formalities as to	2, 12

BOOK II.

LITERARY AND SCIENTIFIC INSTITUTIONS.

Administration of wills	11	CLUBS AND COMMITTEES	43–83
Almshouses	7, 17	Powers of members of	71, 72, 80
Annuity, gift of	20	Corporation, Bequests to	10, 11, 15, 37
Attorney-General, functions of	41	Cy près, doctrine of	19, 29
BEQUESTS	1–42	Debenture of water company	24
Bible Society, Bequest to	18	Debenture Stock of Railway	2
Bibles, Bequest for purchase of	1	Devise of house, void	1, 5, 19
Books, Bequest for purchase of	1, 4	Discretion of executors and trustees	3, 14
Building operations, Bequests for	7		
Charitable Institution, what is not	48	Endowments of Institution	10, 14, 35
Church, Legacy to	21, 36	Executors under a Will, discretionary powers of	30
Church Building Society, Bequest to	25, 26	Expulsion of members of clubs	49, 51, 56–61, 73, 76, 77
Church Pastoral-Aid Society, Bequest to	29		

Guarantees in respect of clubs . 45
Hiring of house to effectuate a
  Bequest 23
Hospitals 10,
                  22, 33
Houses, devise of void . 1, 6, 19

Land, purchase or acquisition of 7, 9,
  10, 13, 14, 17, 20, 21, 22, 23, 25,
                  32, 33, 35, 38, 40
Leasehold property, conveyance
  of 42
Legacy for museum . . . 39
Legacy to a corporation . 11, 19
Liability of club committees 44, 52,
                  62, 65, 72, 78, 81
Library, Bequest to . . . 6

Mortgage property . . . 8
Mortmain 8-10, 12-15, 17, 19, 21, 22,
          24-28, 30-36, 38-40, 42

Museum, Bequest for . . 35
Railway Debenture Stock . . 2
RATING OF SOCIETIES UNDER 6 & 7
  VICT. c. 36 . . . 84-109
Religious Institutions and Socie-
  ties 3, 12, 16, 18, 25, 26, 29, 38, 39

School, Bequests to . . 9, 20
Servants of clubs 47, 67, 78, 81, 82
Society for Prevention of Cruelty
  to Animals 38
Statutory powers, Institutions
  with special 8

Tithe Redemption Trust, Bequest
  to 12
Trustees under a Will, discretionary powers of . . 3, 40

Women, Voluntary Association of 48

www.ingramcontent.com/pod-product-compliance
Lightning Source LLC
Chambersburg PA
CBHW021209230426
43667CB00006B/622